CONTEMPORARY PUBLIC ADMINISTRATION

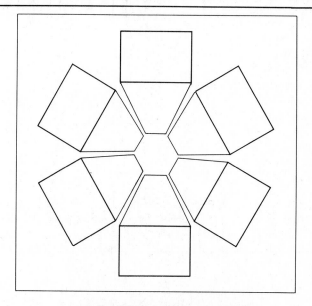

DENNIS PALUMBO

Arizona State University

STEVEN MAYNARD-MOODY

University of Kansas

Longman

New York & London

Contemporary Public Administration

Longman, 95 Church Street, White Plains, N.Y. 10601

Associated companies:
Longman Group Ltd., London
Longman Cheshire Pty., Melbourne
Longman Paul Pty., Auckland
Copp Clark Pitman, Toronto

Chapter 12 originally published in *Implementation and the Policy Process: Opening up the Black Box,* Dennis Palumbo and Donald Calista, eds. (Greenwood Press, Westport, CT, 1990), pp. 3–18. Copyright © 1990 by the Policy Studies Organization. Reprinted with permission of Greenwood Press, an imprint of Greenwood Publishing Group, Inc.

Senior editor: David J. Estrin
Development editor: Virginia L. Blanford
Production editor: Janice Baillie
Cover design: David Levy
Text art: Art Directions
Production supervisor: Anne Armeny

Library of Congress Cataloging in Publication Data
Palumbo, Dennis James
    Contemporary public administration / by Dennis J. Palumbo and
Steven W. Maynard-Moody.
      p. cm.
    Includes bibliographical references (p.) and index.
    ISBN 0-8013-0033-9
    1. Public administration. I. Maynard-Moody, Steven W. II. Title.
JF1351.P25 1991
350–dc20   90–6191
                                           CIP

ABCDEFGHIJ–HA–99 98 97 96 95 94 93 92 91 90

Contents

Chapter 12:   Program Implementation   **302**

Chapter 13:   Federalism and Public Administration   **323**

Preface

When most people think about government, they think of elected officials. It is an article of faith that we live in a democracy because we elect those who run our government. Nightly news programs and daily headlines broadcast the views of and conflicts among legislators, governors, and presidents. The attentive public knows these officials who live in the spotlight but not the public administrators who make governing possible; it generally gives them little thought unless it is to criticize "government bureaucrats."

But political speeches, press releases by senators and other Congress members, hearings, executive orders, bills, amendments, and other visible policy actions are only abstractions until they are translated into government actions. Moreover, such visible actions are only one moment in the continuous policy making and refining process. After the laws are passed or the executive order given, policies must then be tailored to fit local and specific situations and needs. Adjusting policies to fit local circumstances forces many administrators to find innovative solutions rather than merely to carry out mandates. These administrative innovations often become the basis for new legislation or changes in existing laws and regulations.

Public administrators are the translators, tailors, and tinkerers of government. If the elected officials are visible to the public, public administrators are the anonymous specialists listed in the closing credits. Without their knowledge, diligence, and creativity, government would be ineffective and inefficient; it would remain an amateur production.

The anonymity of much public administration raises fears that government policies are made by people who are not accountable to citizens. Many—especially those prone to lumping all administrators into a conspiracy of experts—fear that these so-called faceless bureaucrats subvert the intentions of elected officials. Administration is seen as a danger that requires constant vigilance. Abuse of power is a central concern in modern states and particularly in the United States where public confidence in government reached an all-time low as the 1990s began. But this problem is not solely administrative even though elected politicians often try to make administrators the scapegoat.

Others see administrators as mere cogs in the machinery of government. Most public administrators eschew public controversy and stay out of the public's view. Much of their work is quiet, small scale, and specialized. However, administrators live in a world of friction between abstract principles and actual practice. They must continually find a way to do what is right as well as what is realistic. Whether in the negative sense of subverting the intention of policy or the positive sense of making policy work for individuals, administration is policy making. And whether close to the centers of power as cabinet secretaries and agency heads or at the street level in local agencies, public administrators are policy makers.

DESIGN OF THE BOOK

This book is built on that premise: *Administrators are policy makers,* not just the faithful (or unfaithful) servants of elected officials. Part 1 explores this observation and traces the history of administrative thought and action. Administration also involves acting through organizations, and the chapters in Part 2 examine the organizational context of public administration. Chapter 2 describes theories of public bureaucracy, Chapter 3 examines several enduring issues in organization theory, and Chapter 4 looks at the behavior of individuals and groups within organizations.

Much of the policy-making activities of public administration is found in the details of government, and Part 3 examines these parts of what we call micro-administration. Chapter 5 explores the various roles played by public administrators and the conflicts among these roles. Chapter 6 focuses directly on decision making and leadership. Chapters 7 and 8 examine personnel and budgeting, two areas where the small-scale policy-making role of public administrators is most apparent.

Part 4 broadens the scope to macro-administration. In Chapters 9 and 10, the administrative role in policy making and the accountability problems administrative policy making creates are examined in detail. Two areas in which public administrators have strong influence over government decisions and actions are in evaluating and implementing public policy, the major topics of Chapters 11 and 12. The complex set of intergovernmental relations called *federalism* concludes the book in Chapter 13.

Each chapter (except for the first) ends with a case study. Although no individual case can contain all the issues discussed in each chapter, we wrote these case studies both as extended examples of the issues raised in each chapter and as a way of surfacing dilemmas and controversies. We intend that these case studies provide a basis for discussion and encourage students and teachers to develop other cases that illustrate the principles discussed in the text. Testing ideas against observations is a most telling and sensitive intellectual tool.

This book is intended for upper-division undergraduate as well as master's level courses in public administration. Our experience has taught us not to underestimate either the desire to learn or the understanding of students. We worked hard to express complex ideas with clarity and to draw the reader into what we consider fascinating issues and questions. We did not, however, try to simplify these nor did we assume that students are unwilling to stretch their curiosity and intellects. We hope that this book is both engaging and challenging. Although considerable literature is reviewed and the traditional subjects of public administration are described and dissected, we have also tried to develop and sustain our own line of argument. This book is therefore both an introduction to public administration and a statement about what we see as the direction of the field.

ACKNOWLEDGMENTS

The book was a collaborative effort. As a starting point, each author drafted individual sections (those who know us can probably guess which ones). We then thoroughly criticized each other's work, adding and revising until each chapter became a shared product. More important, this book is part of an intellectual collaboration that began a decade ago and has grown both in depth and pleasure despite job changes and the difficulty of collaborating via telephone.

We have had considerable help in producing this book. David Estrin, our editor, knew when to push and when to let us alone, when to criticize and when to flatter. He kept us going. Virginia Blanford, our development editor, commented on the entire manuscript and helped us find a coherent path in our many meanderings. She made painful revisions as painless as possible. Our copy editor, Patterson Lamb, corrected many of the little mistakes that authors are prone to commit. Janice Baillie, our production editor, pulled the project together.

Writing, like administration, is the sum of many small decisions and we greatly appreciate all the help we received.

We have learned a great deal from our reviewers. Jameson Doig, John Nalbandian, and Elaine Sharp critiqued individual chapters, adding greatly to their strength and coherence. Patricia K. Freeman, Charles McClintock, and Mark Huddleston reviewed much of the manuscript, generously providing scores of comments that were both detailed and general, gentle and harsh, that guided revisions.

A slightly different version of Chapter 12 was originally published in *Implementation and the Policy Process: Opening up the Black Box,* Dennis Palumbo and Donald Calista, editors, Greenwood Press, CT, 1990. We are grateful to Greenwood Press and to the authors for use of the material in this book.

We conclude this book with a greater appreciation for both the intellectual depth and the excitement of the field of public administration. If in some small measure we can communicate this to you, our reader, then we will have succeeded.

PART ONE

Public Administration: Its Nature and Context

CHAPTER 1

Introduction: What Is Public Administration?

In 1990, some 16.5 million people in the United States were public administrators. The jobs they held ranged from accountant to zoologist, and included (among many others) art specialist, biologist, cartographer, dental officer, food technologist, geneticist, nurse, petroleum engineer, sociologist, teacher, and welding engineer. The label *public administrator* can be applied to individuals as diverse as Hyman Rickover, the father of the nuclear submarine; former New York City public works commissioner Robert Moses, who was responsible for the building of New York's network of bridges and tunnels; and J. Edgar Hoover, director of the Federal Bureau of Investigation for more than thirty years.

The faceless federal bureaucrat, so often criticized by politicians looking for an issue or a scapegoat, may be stereotypical but is hardly typical. For one thing, the vast majority of public administrators work not for the federal government but for state and local governments (see Table 1.1). For another, public administrators are a diverse lot who do many different tasks.

Public administration is not confined to what public employees do. Millions of people working for private agencies, both profit and nonprofit, also administer or implement public policy; they contract with or receive grants or insurance reimbursements from government agencies. Physicians take care of Medicare or Medicaid patients; bankers decide about federally guaranteed loans for students or farmers; social workers and psychologists work for or are consulted by social service agencies; halfway house employees look after offenders sentenced to community corrections programs, recovering drug addicts, and semi-independent individuals with a variety of disabilities. Although not directly employed by government agencies, such individuals are indirectly paid by government agencies—and therefore by taxpayers—and since they administer public programs, they can be called *public administrators*.

This book is for and about all public administrators—not just supervisors, managers, agency heads, or federal executives, and not just public employees. Our

TABLE 1.1. Federal, State and Local Paid Government Employees, 1960–1986 (Thousands)

	1960	1970	1975	1977	1978	1979	1980	1981	1982	1983	1984	1985	1986
Total	8,808	13,028	14,973	15,459	15,628	15,971	16,213	15,968	15,841	16,034	16,436	16,690	16,933
Federal	2,421	2,881	2,890	2,848	2,885	2,869	2,898	2,865	2,848	2,875	2,942	3,021	3,019
State & Local	6,387	10,147	12,084	12,611	12,743	13,102	13,315	13,103	12,993	13,160	13,493	13,669	13,914
Percent	72.5	77.9	80.7	81.6	81.5	82.0	82.1	82.1	82.0	82.1	82.1	81.9	82.2
State	1,527	2,755	3,271	3,491	3,539	3,699	3,753	3,726	3,744	3,816	3,898	3,984	4,068
Local	4,860	7,392	8,813	9,120	9,204	9,403	9,562	9,377	9,249	9,344	9,595	9,685	9,846

(Source: U.S. Department of Commerce, Bureau of the Census. *Statistical Abstract of the U.S.*, 106th ed., 1986, p. 244; 109th ed., 1989, p. 293.)

approach is not managerial. We believe in the importance of all levels of public administration and, more important, we believe that administrators at all levels *make* as well as *implement* public policy.

The traditional focus in the study of public administration—and in public administration texts—has been on management concerns that are primarily internal to an organization. The emphasis has been on matters such as staffing, leadership, hiring, firing, and morale, and on budgeting, personnel, and managerial skills. Although we find management principles useful for the study of public administration, we believe that the *act* of administration is an art or a craft—that personalities, friendships, and politics are as important in successful administration as scientific principles. Our attempt, therefore, is to cover all the main topics of public administration, and to add to that coverage and broader developments concerning public policy making that pervade the current literature in public administration.

Traditionally public administrators have needed the ability to develop plans, to build or alter organizational structures, to track the progress of their organizations, to develop a system of compensation that captures the interest of those needed to carry out policy, to cultivate individual relationships, and to call and conduct meetings. More recently, analysts have suggested the need for other kinds of skills: the ability to analyze the substance of problems, to map out the political context, and to deal with interest groups, the legislature, the press, and private agencies. Our emphasis in this text will be on all these skills—on both *management* and *policy making*—in the belief that *both* these functions are carried out at all levels of administration. This book is built upon a simple premise: administration is—and therefore needs to be understood as—policy making.

In order to see more clearly where we have come, we need to look back briefly at the history of public administration in the United States.

THE HISTORY OF PUBLIC ADMINISTRATION

Early Years: 1789–1880

For the first forty years of this country's history as an independent nation—roughly from the adoption of the United States Constitution through the presidency of Andrew Jackson—public administration was conducted by partisan elites. The federal government began small. Three federal departments—state, treasury, and war—were created after the adoption of the Constitution in 1789; the attorney general's office and the post office were created later that same year. The Department of the Navy was established in 1798.

In 1800, the State Department consisted of the secretary of state, a chief clerk, seven ordinary clerks, and a messenger boy. The entire federal government in 1800 employed only 3,000 people, most of them drawn from the landed gentry or the professions of law, medicine, or the clergy and most of them (95 percent) were employed outside the nation's capital (Mosher 1982a, 61). The War of 1812 brought reforms to the Departments of War and Navy, but no major administrative initiative. By 1821, the federal government had little more than doubled to 6,914 employees. (See Table 1.2.)

After Andrew Jackson's election to the presidency in 1828, the federal bureaucracy remained small but its character changed significantly. The only new department created between 1828 and the Civil War was the Interior; the states retained primary jurisdiction for protecting health and safety, building roads and canals, and regulating banks, commerce, and insurance. But those functions the federal government did administer fell increasingly into the hands of average citizens; the landed gentry lost its grip on government. President Jackson believed that most public employment was "so plain and simple" that it did not require elite background and education. Moreover, to Jackson, more was gained by breaking up the inheritance of offices than was lost in expertise (see Chapter 7).

Unfortunately, the Jackson administration also encouraged the creation of the *spoils system,* under which elected officials freely replaced office holders with their own appointees; connections and cronyism replaced social standing as a prerequisite for public office. New administrations began by replacing up to 90 percent of all federal employees. This kind of turnover is only partially moderated today: Over a million of the federal government's 2.9 million employees departed in 1980 when the Republican Reagan administration replaced the Democratic Carter administration.[1]

Under the spoils system, political party loyalty, rather than wealth, education, or social status, became the main criterion for giving out government jobs. Sales of offices, graft, and kickbacks to the party coffers became the order of the day. This practice contributed to the growth in power of political parties, and the system was favored by many in Congress because they could name the people who would take jobs in their own states and districts. Political parties now had access to rewards for their supporters, and they used these rewards to create powerful political machines.

Reform: 1880 to World War II

The abuses of the spoils system led directly to the first wave of reform in public administration. Reformers, led by members of the Progressive party, added the notions of control and efficiency to the lexicon of government administration. In this new model, the principal responsibility of public administrators was to implement faithfully policy directives sent from above. The major responsibility of subordinates was obedience to superiors (Seidman 1979; Warwick 1975).

TABLE 1.2. Paid Civilian Employees of the Federal Government, 1816-1959

Year	Number of Employees	Year	Number of Employees	Year	Number of Employees	Year	Number of Employees
1816	4,837	1871	37,020	1918	854,500	1940	1,042,420
1821	6,914	1881	100,020	1921	561,142	1945	3,816,310
1831	11,491	1891	157,442	1929	579,559	1946	2,696,529
1841	18,038	1901	239,476	1931	609,746	1950	1,960,208
1851	26,274	1911	395,905	1934	698,649	1953	2,558,416
1861	36,672	1915	395,429	1938	882,226	1959	2,382,807

See Table 1.1 for the number of federal employees for 1960-1986. (Source: U.S. Department of Commerce, Bureau of the Census. *Historical Statistics of the U.S. Colonial Times to 1970* (Part 2), September, 1975, pp. 1102-1103.)

When a frustrated federal office seeker assassinated President James Garfield in 1883, Congress moved quickly to find a system for equitably distributing such jobs. The Pendelton Act of 1883 created the Civil Service System and initiated the merit principle; examination rather than party loyalty became the means of determining who would be hired.

At the heart of the reform movement was the notion that politics and administration could and should be separated—a belief called the politics-administration dichotomy. Based on corporate management theory, the new model included expert managers whose function was to carry out policies formulated by elected or appointed officials. An example is the city manager system, developed at about the same time for local government, in which a professional with expertise in operations and management is responsible to an elected city council. Frank Goodnow (1900), an early scholar of public administration, published the first textbook in the field in 1900 in which he wrote that the duty of the bureaucracy is to administer, impartially and nonpoliticallly, the policies enacted by elected officials.

At about the same time the reform movement started, the federal bureaucracy began to grow. It reached 100,000 employees in 1881 and 200,000 by 1901, of whom over 50 percent were covered by the merit system. This growth was a result of several factors. First, a number of groups sought representation in the bureaucracy: In response to pressure from various segments of the population, the Bureau of Education in the Department of the Interior was established in 1869, and the Departments of Labor (1888), Agriculture (1889), and Commerce (1903) were subsequently created. Second, growth was spurred by the addition of new responsibilities at the federal level in response to the burgeoning industrial age. Reformers succeeded in passing the Sherman Anti-Trust Act (1890), in establishing government agencies to regulate corporate monopolies, and in establishing the Interstate Commerce Commission (1887) to regulate railroads. Responsibilities that had rested with the states were gradually absorbed by the federal government. Wars had the biggest impact on growth, however. The number of federal government employees more than doubled during World War I and then tripled during World War II (see Table 1.2).

The dichotomy between politics and administration emphasized by the reform movement continued to be the accepted wisdom of public administration theory throughout the first half of the twentieth century. Leonard White's (1926) influential *Introduction to Public Administration* not only was rooted in this division but also advocated the notion that a *science of administration* existed. This science was based on a set of enduring principles—or laws—that could be learned and employed to create good government in any setting. These principles were value free and politically neutral; the emphasis was on economy and efficiency in government—popular notions with the growing middle class that supported the reforms.

A little more than a decade later, Luther Gulick and Lyndall Urwick published *Papers on the Science of Administration* (1937) in which they defined the principles of administration that are embodied in the term POSDCORB (*p*lanning, *o*rganizing, *s*taffing, *d*irecting, *c*oordinating, *r*eporting, and *b*udgeting), which generations of public administration students have memorized. Managers were taught to (1) *plan* their tasks carefully; (2) *organize* their agencies on the basis of closely related purposes, grouping like activities in a single unit; (3) *staff* their agency so that responsibility and authority are equated; (4) ensure proper *direction* through unity of command; (5) *coordinate* tasks and offices while limiting the span of control of supervisors; (6) ensure good communications and *reporting*; and (7) *budget* on scientific and objective bases.

The reform principles—emphasis on expertise, merit hiring, and promotion, and a clear line between administration and politics—gave public administration an independence from the rest of government that it had not had before. Senators, representatives, city councils, mayors, and other elected officials, less expert about the increasingly complex thicket of government responsibilities, could not challenge administrators on details and technicalities. The president, still able to replace the highest officials of the executive branch, could no longer control the other layers of the bureaucracy. The size and expertise of the bureaucracy conspired to limit top-down control.

The management theory that supported these general principles of administration and the politics-administration dichotomy began to erode in the 1930s. The general principles of administration were based on the theory—or belief—that work and organizations could be designed and managed to optimize efficiency, a view called scientific management. In a series of management efficiency studies done at an industrial plant outside Chicago, researchers inadvertently discovered that complex human social needs were central to effective management (Roethlisberger and Dickson 1939). Thus, the human side was found to be as important in management as proper organizing or span of control, and human motive, behavior, and meaning cannot be reduced to simple scientific axioms.

In 1946 one of the most influential books about public administration was published. Originally written as a political science doctoral dissertation at the University of Chicago, Herbert Simon's (1946) *Administrative Behavior* criticized the principles of management. Simon argued that these "rules" were no more than proverbs, because for each principle one could find a contrary one. For example, one principle suggests that a manager should delegate responsibility; another says that the span of control should be limited to a few subordinates. How can a manager delegate many responsibilities and yet maintain a narrow span of control? Simon's behavioral approach emphasized the importance of communications. The key to effective management, according to Simon, is ensuring that subordinates have the appropriate information on which to base their decisions (Simon 1946).

Administrative practice was dramatically altering the shape of government at the same time that these intellectual changes were occurring. The Great Depression and the victory of Franklin Roosevelt's New Deal led to the creation of numerous agencies in an attempt to solve the nation's debilitating economic problems. In 1933, the Farm Credit Administration was reorganized to help farmers; the Federal Deposit Insurance Corporation was created to help banks and ensure depositors that their savings were safe; the Tennessee Valley Authority was created in an attempt to revitalize the economy of that depressed region; and the Civilian Conservation Corps was organized to help conserve eroding soil. The Works Progress Administration was created in 1935 to provide jobs for individuals building roads, dams, schools, and parks. Even actors, artists, and writers were employed by the federal government to help pull the nation out of the Depression.

Finally, the Social Security Act was passed in 1935 in an attempt to guarantee security and protection against the vagaries of the economy for older Americans. Too many old people in the 1930s lived in poverty, their savings drained by sickness or bank failures. The Social Security Act promised hope for their "golden years." Altogether, over 140 agencies were created, touching every aspect of economic life.

With all of this governmental activity, the federal bureaucracy grew 45 percent adding 272,580 employees between 1931 and 1938. An even more significant jump in the number of employees occurred during World War II; from 1940 to 1945 the federal bureaucracy expanded to 3,816,310 employees, mostly defense related—a size it has not since duplicated. In 1945, 2,634,575 federal employees worked in defense-related jobs. The number of defense jobs had dropped to 753,149 by 1950, and the size of the federal bureaucracy had shrunk to 1,960,208. The advent of the Korean War in 1950 led to an expansion of defense employees again and the federal bureaucracy grew to a little over 2.5 million employees in 1953, where it remained until the early 1960s. By 1970 the bureaucracy had reached about 3 million employees, a consequence of the Vietnam War, and it has been relatively stable since then. Thus in the 1930s, 1940s, and 1950s, the exponential growth in the size of government raised doubts about the ability of top leaders to control administration according to traditional management principles at a time when the theory behind those principles was questioned. It was time for new ideas.

World War II to the Present

The federal bureaucracy has comprised a relatively small percentage of total government employees since 1960, and it has decreased relative to state and local governments since then (see Table 1.1). The greatest increase in government since 1960 has been at state and local levels; local government employees make up about 58 percent of all government employees, and most of these are in education and law enforcement.

World War II stimulated new intellectual developments in administrative theory and practice. Operations research and other quantitative management techniques, which had their origins in the war effort, were subsequently applied to business decisions and then to the public sector. The basic tenets of these developments was that many public as well as private resource allocation decisions could be made on the basis of statistical analysis. Instead of making budget decisions on the basis of politics, program goals were to be specified and the most efficient means of attaining them identified. President Lyndon Johnson was so enamored of these ideas that he mandated that such management systems be used in all federal agencies.

This attempt to rationalize all government decisions proved impractical, and a number of new intellectual developments occurred in the 1970s that began to change the nature of public administration in yet another way. One of the more significant of these developments was the research on the implementation of public programs. Another was the growing recognition that human organizations, both public and private, are complex social institutions that exist within a larger social environment and that they develop patterns of beliefs and social behavior independent of stated goals or mandates. Public organizations are no longer seen as machines, and public administrators are no longer seen as engineers who tinker with and control their organizations for maximum efficiency.

IMPLEMENTATION AND PUBLIC ADMINISTRATION

Prior to the 1970s, most scholars assumed that once a law was passed or an executive order given, policy making was completed. Administration or putting these laws and orders to work was merely a matter of carrying out decisions. In the early 1970s a number of scholars discovered the "implementation gap"—the belief that many well-intended social programs failed to achieve their objectives because they were not properly implemented. Early implementation studies took the top-down view, suggesting that the goals and perspectives of those at the top of an organization are the only legitimate ones, and deviations from them are implementation failures. In order to avoid implementation failures, the top-down approach recommends that we have fewer and clearer goals (Mazmanian and Sabatier 1983). This position has been criticized as "denying and renouncing the very existence of politics" (Winter 1983, 2).

Later implementation scholars began to argue that changes in programs as they are implemented are natural and often constructive. These researchers built support for a bottom-up approach, which encourages those charged with implementing policy to find effective ways of realizing policy objectives in diverse local settings. For example, Johnson and O'Conner (1979) found that social workers in the Pennsylvania Department of Welfare who did not follow the directives of those at the top did not consequently produce implementation failures; rather they often were more likely to want to serve their clients' needs than those workers who rigidly followed the directives. Johnson and O'Conner (1979, 195) concluded that "clients' needs come first, and field personnel in a bureaucracy have important policy insights that central management lacks."

Called "backward mapping" by Richard Elmore (1979), this view suggests that workers at the street level are more familiar with the problems encountered in program implementation, and their role in policy making must be recognized. Of course, field-level personnel can be wrong: simply accepting the descriptive reality that those at the point of delivery are most knowledgeable about implementation and turning it into a prescription for action can be dangerous (Linder and Peters 1987). We would not want racist police officers, for example, to make policy about the appropriate amount of force to use in handling minorities (Hogwood and Peters 1983). But the bottom-up view has substantial validity and it has changed the way we think about public administration because it violates traditional management concepts and the politics-administration dichotomy.

Evolutionary Implementation and Adaptation

Implementation studies have also suggested that in most—if not all—cases, we need to adapt or change publicly administered programs *during* implementation so that they fit local circumstances. Thus a program will never be identical in all locations in which it is implemented (Palumbo and Hyer 1985). This view runs counter to the classical model, in which the obligation of administrators is to carry out faithfully the goals of the elected "policy makers," not to make or change policy themselves since they are not elected and therefore not accountable to the people. The classical model thus accepts the separation of politics and administration, but the reality is that administrators do make policy and cannot be prevented from doing so. More important, agencies that are flexible are more likely to be successful.

Contemporary management theory "encourage[s] habits of flexibility, of continuous learning, and of acceptance of change as normal and as opportunity" (Brassier 1985, 26; see also Drucker 1985; Majone and Wildavsky 1984). Several studies have found that self-correcting or adaptive organizations are more successful in implementing programs. For example, Orfield (1975) found that in order to make desegregation work, teachers have to adapt their teaching methods to accommodate to their new students. Lowry (1985, 297) found that adaptation was necessary in the implementation of federal policy pertaining to managing the nation's shorelines and concluded that

> many of the most challenging . . . issues . . . involve policy problems that are only partially understood or require the achievement of multiple-objectives . . . for which acceptable intervention strategies have not been identified. Such issues challenge implementation theory and planning practice to identify and create conditions in which adaptation, experimentation, and collaboration can flourish as appropriate implementation strategies.

Micro- and Macro-Administration

Perhaps the most significant contribution of implementation research to our understanding of public administration is the distinction between micro- and macro-administration. In addition to relying on general principles of management, classical public administration focused almost exclusively on micro-administration, or on the factors that are *internal* to an organization. Its concern was mainly with how to get people in an organization to work toward achievement of the objectives that managers at the top of the organization deemed appropriate.

Macro-administration, on the other hand, focuses on the relationships *between* the organization and the multiplicity of agencies and groups with which an organization must work in order to get its programs implemented. The first macro-administration research focused mainly on the federal system (Pressman and Wildavsky 1984; Van Meter and Van Horn 1975) and showed that program delay is "a function of the number of decision points, the number of participants at each point, and the intensity of their preferences" (Pressman and Wildavsky 1984, 118). Such conditions are not confined to federal administration. Most policy is implemented through numerous actors and decision points, a trend accelerated by the push for privatization in the Reagan administration. Salamon (1981) calls this a shift to third-party government. Currently the *majority* of government programs are being implemented by third party agencies such as special districts, banks, hospitals, corporations, states, and cities: "Instead of a hierarchical relationship between the federal government and its agencies," Salamon (1981, 160) writes, "what frequently exists in practice is a far more complex bargaining relationship in which the federal agency often has the weaker hand."

Interorganizational administration, or macro-administration, increased the number of organizations and the consequent need for coordination; much less reliance can be put on mandates, or top-down leadership. According to political scientists O'Toole and Montjoy (1984, 492), "Even specific mandates are, in principle, less amenable to monitoring and enforcement in the interorganizational setting. Recalcitrant agencies are generally less visible to mandating authorities where many actors are involved; and other agencies, which may depend upon their actions, have few mechanisms for enforcement."

In the more complex macro-administration context, political skills are required for effective administration. Getting agencies that have diverse and sometimes competing interests to work together requires entrepreneurial ability (Palumbo, Musheno, and Maynard-Moody 1986). Entrepreneurs can generate support for programs and get people to agree on common goals. For example, implementing community corrections programs at the state level requires the coordinated action of prosecutors, judges, sheriffs, probation officers, counselors, halfway house directors and staff, county commissioners, psychologists, community corrections administrators, the state department of corrections, and private, nonprofit agencies that often have religious affiliations. More than traditional management skills are required to persuade these people and their agencies to cooperate in implementing programs.

The political skills required to convince various groups to coordinate and work toward common goals are not unlike those needed to manage internal organizational politics. Contemporary organization theory stresses the importance of interorganizational relations and the interpersonal and intergroup negotiating and bargaining generally called "organizational politics." Although politics is often viewed as a grubby activity practiced by ward bosses, logrolling legislators, lobbyists, and the like, ignoring organizational politics makes administration appear falsely "scientific, rational and Boy Scoutish" (Yates 1985, 4). According to classical management theory, organizations are *supposed* to be rational and objective, but conflict and politics exist in all organizations, public and private. Managing that conflict is a large part of public administration: It requires a proper understanding of the relative power position of individuals and units in an organization (Yates 1985, 73), abandoning the simplistic notion that what top decision makers decree, lower-level implementors sheepishly follow, and recognizing the importance of the politics of administration.

POLICY MAKING VERSUS MANAGING PROGRAMS

The men and women who perform the general management function in the public sector are not usually thought of as *policy makers*. That label is generally reserved for the movers and shakers in elected legislative or executive roles such as president, governor, or mayor. But in selecting goals and making (and then bending) rules for their department or agency, the managers of public agencies interpret very broad and often contradictory mandates. One of the leading casebooks in public administration begins with the assertion: "In designing their detailed organizational arrangement, particularly in the allocation of personnel and in budgeting, [managers] shape what policy will be'' (Bower and Christenson 1978, 1). This certainly is true of top-level administrators such as budget officers. For example, budget analyst Michael March (1984, 20), who worked in the Bureau of the Budget (BOB)[2] from 1946 to 1966, writes, ''I anonymously played a key role for nearly 20 years from my BOB position in shaping Executive Branch philosophy and policy in veterans' programs.'' By virtue of his position as a BOB analyst, March had unusual ability to influence and even initiate changes in policy. For example, policy making with regard to veterans' benefits was ''a tidy, three-cornered game: the veterans organizations developed the policies, the House Committee on Veterans Affairs got them enacted into laws, and the VA cooperatively administered the resultant benefits'' (March 1984, 30). Federal administration often takes place in the context of such triangles; interest groups, congressional committees, and federal agencies are the principal groups involved in making and administering policy in many areas. These triumvirates have been called *subgovernments* or *iron triangles* by researchers (Heclo 1978).

Another way that administrators make policy is by delaying programs with which they do not agree. For example, in February 1987, a federal judge cited the Equal Opportunity Commission of the Reagan administration for ''slothful delay'' regarding enforcement of a rule to require employers to continue pension contributions for workers who stay on the job until age 70. He ordered the commission to rescind a 1979 interpretative bulletin that ''contrary to law, supports the refusal of employers to make pension contributions for employee service that occurs after the 'normal' retirement age'' (''Slothful Agency'' 1987, A16). The judge described how the agency essentially made policy for seven years by piling ''delay upon delay.'' According to the story, ''It scuttled rules that would have corrected the erroneous interpretation, and that would have helped save at least some $450 million lost by older Americans every year'' (quoted in ''Slothful Agency'' 1987, A16).

On the same day that this judge was chiding the Equal Opportunity Commission, the Nuclear Regulatory Commission adopted a new rule that eased emergency planning standards for nuclear power plants, and which cleared the way for two East Coast nuclear plants to begin operation. The governors of New York and Massachusetts opposed the ruling, arguing that there was no way to guarantee the safe exodus of residents in case of a major accident, and representatives and senators from the same states argued that if the rule changes were adopted, Congress would try to override them with legislation.

The same kind of policy making is undertaken by a wide variety of administrative organizations, including (1) cabinet departments, (2) agencies outside departments such as the National Security Council, (3) independent regulatory boards and commissions such as the Federal Trade Commission or Nuclear Regulatory Commission, (4) independent administrative boards such as the Federal Home Loan Bank Board, and (5) federal corporations such as the Tennessee Valley Authority.

Most scholars now recognize that administrators make public policy as well as manage programs (Nakamura and Smallwood 1980; Ripley and Franklin 1984; Taylor 1984). Equally important, although not as often recognized, is the policy-making role of the people lower down in the hierarchy, especially those Michael Lipsky (1980) calls street-level bureaucrats. These individuals, who have direct contact with citizens, really *are* the government as far as many citizens are concerned. They include teachers, social welfare workers, drivers' license examiners, police officers, judges, unemployment office workers, and the like. They have an inherent and irreducible amount of discretion in doing their jobs and, in using that discretion, they make policy. No matter what the person at the top does—the president, governor, mayor, city manager, or agency head—lower-level administrators perform millions of tasks that in essence make policy. When providing services they must select policies for action and interpret often vague and conflicting policies and rules. Their actions and inaction give flesh to the laws, orders, and rules made by those higher up, and by filling out the interstices of the policies, they are in fact creating policy (Heclo 1977).

The dilemma this creates for public administration in a democracy is that since administrators are not elected, they are accountable to citizens only through elected representatives,[3] but placing too many checks on administrators through the traditional hierarchical controls may turn out to be dysfunctional (Knott and Miller 1986). The paradox is this: "If democratic institutions are to work, government must not only be checked from doing what is not wanted but also must be competent as an administering organization to do what is wanted" (Heclo 1977, 5).

The Nature of Public Policy

Part of the difficulty in describing how administrators make policy is that the term *public policy* is itself ambiguous. If, as is commonly thought, public policy is synonymous with law, then public administrators are not policy makers. But policy is not the same as law, court decisions, or even administrative rules and regulations. Rather, public policy is all of these and more. A leading policy analyst describes policy as an "existential phenomenon . . . much too complex and dynamic to be fully caught in concepts, models, and themes" (Dror 1983, x). Some scholars see public policy as the intentions of what officials would like to accomplish (Marcus 1980). For example, President Reagan from the beginning of his first term in 1980 wanted to limit the use of abortions. His policy intentions were quite clear, but he did not succeed in getting this goal accepted completely because many other agencies, institutions, and people are involved in making policy.

Policy is never "set in concrete." It is constantly changing and highly subjective. It is how people interpret various actions—a rationalization of actions taken—rather than some objective characteristic of these actions (Palumbo 1987). Public policy expert Laurence Lynn, Jr. (1987, 30) writes, "Authoritative decision makers act first then rationalize the completed action and its consequences." They may start with goals and objectives in mind, but there is no public policy until governmental actions produce consequences that are perceived by various publics. According to Lynn (1987, 30), "Public policy can be said to comprise the meanings or interpretations ascribed by various affected politics to identifiable sequences of governmental actions based on the perceived or anticipated consequence of these actions." The goals of the Education of All Handicapped Children Act of 1975 (PL 94-142) was to provide free, appropriate education in a regular classroom for all handicapped children. In fact, a number of compromises had to be made because of lack of resources. The end result was quite different. In some cases, only a select few were served; in others, only inexpensive services were provided; and in most cases, parents were not fully involved in decision making because such involvement is time consuming and costly. Thus, some saw the legislation as a step in the right direction while others saw it as a less-than-earnest attempt to help the handicapped.

Like beauty, public policy is somewhat in the eye of the beholder. Actual change in governmental actions is not always necessary for a policy maker to claim success; often "the creation of a favorable impression is enough" (Lynn 1987, 38). Some people are better at this than others. President Reagan and his administrative officials claimed that they did not have a policy of promoting discrimination against blacks and women, for example, and yet his administration tried to remove the Internal Revenue Service (IRS) ruling that denied tax-exempt status to schools practicing racial discrimination (in the Bob Jones University case in 1983) and tried to get the U.S. Supreme Court to rule that racial or gender preferences in hiring and promotion—affirmative action—were unconstitutional. The Reagan administration's public interpretation of its own policy regarding discrimination was quite different from others' perceptions of these same actions—and from the facts themselves.

The Stages of Policy Making

Several developments in policy studies during the 1980s help us conceptualize how administrators make policy. One is the classification of policy making as a *process* that involves several stages and the other is the clarification of the role of lower-level administrators in policy making.

As we have already suggested, administrators do not just implement policy as was once believed; they are involved in each stage. These stages typically include (1) agenda setting or problem definition and legitimation, (2) policy formulation, (3) implementation, (4) evaluation, and (5) termination.

Agenda setting is determining which issues will receive priority treatment for government action and therefore will be placed on the public agenda. The public agenda is always crowded with issues left over from previous policy debates—issues that once were acted upon but which have been brought up again by the opposition, or new items.

Problems are defined during agenda setting. (Some scholars consider problem definition a separate stage [Dery 1984], but we include it in agenda setting.) How a problem is defined is very important because the definition determines the direction that policy will take. For example, defining abortion as a health rather than a moral or a privacy-or-choice issue has a large impact on what solution is deemed best. As a health problem, abortion accessibility centers on questions of fetal deformity and threats to maternal life or health. As a moral problem, abortion questions include those of privacy, incest, rape, and when life begins. As a privacy-or-choice issue, abortion debate centers on individual rights of women to control their own bodies. Defining the issue, then, sets the terms of the debate.

Issues will not be acted upon if they do not get onto the agenda. There are several ways items can be placed on this agenda (Cobb and Elder 1983; Kingdom 1984; Palumbo 1987). Administrators play a large role in placing issues as well as in defining the problems once they are on the agenda (O'Toole 1989). Administrators often bring up a problem by contacting legislators about it, working with interest groups, and helping define the problem before legislative committees during hearings.

Policy formulation is the stage at which alternative means of handling problems are considered and a particular alternative or set of alternatives is selected and legitimized through legislation. Although administrators do not make laws, they have a large impact on defining the alternatives and in influencing the alternative that is finally selected. Moreover, by adopting administrative rules and regulations they operationalize or give concrete meaning to what often are vague and broad statutes. They thus play a crucial role during the formulation stage.

Implementation is the stage in which policies are turned into programs and carried out—in other words, the stage during which administration, as traditionally defined, occurs. Public administrators are the principal implementors, of course, but they certainly are not the only ones. As noted above, legislators, interest groups, and a host of private agencies (both profit and nonprofit) are involved during implementation, and politics continues unabated during this stage. Because administrators are the key actors, they play a more visible role in policy making during implementation than they do during any other stage. Some scholars claim that policy is in fact fashioned mostly during implementation and thus, administrators are the major policy makers (Meier 1979; Palumbo 1988; Ripley and Franklin 1984).

Evaluation is the stage in which programs are assessed as to how well they have been implemented and what kind of impact they have had. Evaluation is typically done formally by government agencies such as the Program Evaluation Division of the General Accounting Office, by the departments themselves, by outside consultants or research firms, or by university-based researchers. Program evaluation is a large enterprise in the United States with its own professional association, the American Evaluation Association. Administrators have a large impact on evaluations because it is the agencies themselves that have the data on which evaluations are based, and they play a key role in defining the parameters of evaluations.

Termination of programs occurs rarely (Kaufman 1976, 1985). It most often occurs when new administrations come to power; for example, the Reagan administration terminated several alternative energy programs such as those involving synfuels and solar energy credits. Programs may also be terminated if they are deemed failures through program evaluation, although the more likely reason for termination is political opposition (de Leon 1983).

Involvement of Administrators.   Administrators are involved in policy making at each of its stages. Administrators often bring up issues that become part of the agenda, sometimes as a result of problems encountered during the implementation of a program or because of pressures brought by interest groups that are a part of the iron triangles we described above. Administrators become involved in formulating public policy through their testimony before legislative committees. Their expertise is relied upon in designing policies because they are the ones who have the technical competence to make recommendations regarding alternatives for achieving policy goals. For example, in the food stamp program several administrators from the U.S. Department of Agriculture decided that recipients would have to pay for their stamps. This restricted the number and kinds of people who received the stamps and had a major effect on the policy (Berry 1984).

Implementing public policy is, of course, an area in which administrators play the major role. They operationalize goals and in so doing sometimes substitute goals in a process known as "goal displacement" (Bardach 1977). They issue rules and regulations that determine what policy will be.

Of course, administrators are not the only implementors of policy. As we noted above, many programs are implemented by third parties under contract with government. The role of administrators in these cases is to set the conditions of the contract and monitor its implementation.

Legislators and interest groups also are involved in implementation. Legislators often contact agency officials directly to ensure that their states and districts are receiving the benefits of specific programs. Interest groups continue applying their pressure during implementation to see that their interests are protected. In other words, the politics that take place during the agenda-setting and formulation stages do not suddenly stop when a program is being implemented; they simply shift to a different and more administrative arena (Knott and Miller 1986).

Finally, administrators play a vital role during evaluation of programs. Programs may be evaluated informally or formally by the agencies themselves, by congressional staff, the Congressional Budget Office, the General Accounting Office, and outside agencies. In all of these cases, only the agency that runs the program has the data required for an evaluation. An evaluation obviously cannot succeed without agency cooperation.

Thus administrators are involved in policy making at all stages of the policy cycle. They are policy makers as well as program managers. And it is not just the top-level administrators who are involved; middle- and street-level administrators also play an essential role.

SUMMARY

There are more than 16 million public administrators in the United States. They are a remarkably varied group encompassing a number of professions, most of whom are local employees. In addition, numerous private agencies are involved in implementing programs. This book focuses on public administrators at all levels, as well as on the policy-making and management aspects of administration.

Public administration during the first half-century of our nation's history was very limited, involving only a few functions. A major shift occurred in the Jacksonian period when federal employment was used for political patronage. The abuses of the spoils system led directly to reform around 1883, when the Civil Service System was created by the Pendelton Act. The central tenet of reform was the belief that administration should be separated from politics and run on the merit system. The size of the federal bureaucracy also began to grow in the 1880s, reaching 200,000 by 1901 as the federal government took on a number of new responsibilities.

Reform principles dominated public administration during the first half of the twentieth century. Emphasis on expertise, merit hiring and promotion, and the separation of politics from administration were dominant forces, but in the 1930s the human relations and behavioral sides of administrative behavior were "discovered." At the same time these intellectual changes were occurring, the federal government expanded during the 1930s in an attempt to alleviate the debilitating social and economic problems of the Depression. The size and scope of the government expanded yet again during World War II.

Following World War II the major intellectual developments involved the application of operations research and program planning and budgeting systems to public administration. The attempt to apply such methods to all public administration decisions failed. New development in the 1970s, particularly implementation research, changed public administration in yet another way. This research emphasized the role of middle- and lower-level administrators in making policy and emphasized an adaptive or evolutionary approach to program administration. Implementation research also stressed the importance of interorganizational relationships in administering programs—a process called macro-administration.

The role of public administrators in policy making became apparent and the various ways that administrators make policy were identified, including the crucial role of street-level administrators. Public policy is an ambiguous term because policy is not a concrete factor that can be identified as any single document or decision. It is instead the way people interpret the actions of government.

The process of policy making consists of a number of stages. The principal ones are agenda setting, formulation, implementation, evaluation, and termination. Administrators play a role in each one of these stages, not just during implementation as was assumed under classical administrative theory. Thus, it is not possible to separate politics and administration. Any contemporary account of public administration must take into account the policy-making as well as management role of administrators, which is what this book does.

NOTES

1. Such turnover is less frequent when administrations of the same political party succeed each other, as when President Bush took office in 1989.
2. Now called the Office of Management and Budget or OMB.
3. This is the traditional view of administrative accountability. Maynard-Moody (1989) argues, however, that many public administrators, especially street-level bureaucrats, are directly accountable to citizens as clients or consumers of services and that this accountability confers legitimacy similar to that given elected officials who are accountable to citizens as voters.

PART TWO

The Organizational Context of Public Administration

CHAPTER 2

Public Bureaucracy: Problems and Prospects

Many issues in public administration are abstract. Public administrators spend long hours over nuances in policy papers, legislative testimony, and administrative rules. Budget recommendations, reorganizations, merit evaluations, employment statistics, safe levels of radon gas, and other confusing and complex questions fill the workdays of countless public employees.

At the same time, public administrators face issues that are painfully concrete. Should Sam, a difficult ten-year-old, be returned to his neglectful family or be moved to yet another foster home? Is a Vietnam veteran's health problem the result of exposure to Agent Orange? Should the fire department hire a qualified woman over a slightly more qualified man? Should the eligibility rules be stretched to allow a refugee family a place in public housing?

This daily confrontation between the abstract issues of governing and the concrete needs of individuals requires public administrators to shape public policy. The confrontation and the policies that result are the essence of public policy making within the administrative state and are fundamental to both the theory and practice of public administration. As we discussed in Chapter 1, the public administrator is not a passive implementor of the elected official's vision. The first step in understanding how governmental actions emerge out of the conflict between abstract principles and specific situations is to recognize the importance of organization theory. The organizational setting defines, to a large extent, the manner in which this conflict is resolved in each specific case. Defining the aspects of the organizational context that shape administrative policy making is the goal of this and the next three chapters.

CROSS-CUTTING ISSUES

Before we turn to specific topics in organization theory, three general issues need attention. These overlapping issues present social and political dilemmas to public administrators; they are not problems waiting to be solved but rather enduring concerns that require constant attention. These issues create the fundamental tensions within public administration. In varying degrees of salience, they are present every working day in the career of a public administrator.

Public Servant versus Independent Actor

The first dilemma public administrators face concerns the purpose of the public organizations within which they work. On one hand public organizations—such as federal agencies, police departments, and schools—are, however indirectly, the servants of the general public. The secretary of defense reports to the president. Through several intermediate steps, the police officer is accountable to an elected sheriff or mayor. Similarly, the public school teacher is ultimately responsible to an elected school board. Elected officials, in turn, are directly accountable to the general public (or at least to those who vote). These and all other public organizations are legitimate only to the extent that they serve the public interest.

On the other hand, public organizations, like all organizations, are independent social settings. They are places in which people work, interact, and build careers. Public administrators develop routines and procedures based on their own individual and organizational needs. Programs, such as Head Start or the Space Shuttle, are established with certain policy or service goals, but once established, all programs become organized work settings shaped by their histories, habits, and employees. Few public policies can be realized without establishing an organizational context, but once established, the organization takes on a life of its own. The public interest as articulated by elected officials and the interests and routines of the organizations implementing policies exist in constant tension.

Accountability versus Discretion

The fact that public organizations are simultaneously servants of the public interest and independent social settings is the basis for the second dilemma of public administration. Basic ideals of representative democracy demand that public organizations be accountable to elected officials. The chain of legitimacy links the policeman on the beat and the civil servant behind the desk to supervisors. These supervisors are accountable to elected officials, and they, in turn, are accountable to the electorate. The public at large is distrustful of public officials who stray from legislated mandates. At times the accountability is more direct as individuals and interest groups demand direct participation in the decisions of public agencies.

The chains of accountability, however, are often long and tangled. The link between the public and public administration is often more tenuous and philosophical than real. Most of the activities of public administrators take place in the shadows of public attention, and public administrators are granted much de facto discretion by this inattention (Maynard-Moody 1989a).

Moreover, the very nature of the work of many public officials requires that they have the discretion to make individual judgments. No set of laws, rules, or procedures can eliminate the variability of individual problems, circumstances, or needs. Public administrators are often forced to use their discretion to balance the general policy mandates with specific needs, cases, and situations. The individual discretion to overlook problems and bend the rules often overwhelms efforts of elected officials to hold public agencies accountable. Discretion exercised by unelected government officials is a central characteristic of the modern state (Handler 1986).

Need for Stability and Change

The third dilemma troubles all organizations, public and private. This dilemma is the need for both stability and change. Organizations are always in flux. Employees enter and leave, bringing and taking their skills, perspectives, and ideas. Moreover, public organizations are buffeted by frequent and periodic changes brought on by elections. The election of new presidents, governors, or mayors is followed by the replacement of many top managers in public organizations. Career civil servants stay on after changes at the top, but reorganizations and reassignments may drastically affect their responsibilities and influence. In addition, changes in legislative bodies following elections often signal adjustments in the budgets and importance of programs, while new laws have profound effects on public organizations' structure and activities.

While public and private organizations constantly adjust to internal and external changes, all organizations resist change. Organizational change is often painful and destructive (Biggart 1977). Profound personal losses and disruptions accompany seemingly innocuous changes in policy, procedures, and position. For example, the introduction of a new computerized accounting system may reduce the bookkeeper's job to mindless data entry. Moreover, organizations develop standardized procedures and routines that structure their activities and choices and resist change. A classic example occurred during the Cuban missile crisis of John Kennedy's presidency (Allison 1971). To stop Soviet ships while giving Soviet leaders time to reconsider their placement of nuclear weapons in Cuba, Kennedy ordered the Navy to place their blockade closer to Cuba than called for in standard naval procedures. Nevertheless, the blockade was placed not where the commander in chief ordered but where the rule book indicated. Routine proved more powerful than the president.

Thus, despite the need for new ideas, new approaches, new procedures, and new types of employees, stability needs usually dominate organizations (Hannan and Freeman 1984). The forces of stability are, perhaps, even stronger in public organizations. These institutions are generally insulated from survival concerns by legal mandates. Few declare bankruptcy; many endure despite doubts about their efficiency and effectiveness.

THE MEANING OF *PUBLIC*

Thus far we have repeatedly referred to public and private organizations as if they can be meaningfully distinguished (for a review of research see Perry and Rainey 1988). The terms *public* and *private* convey very different connotations to the general public. Public organizations are commonly pictured as large mazes that employ bureaucrats to create red tape; private organizations, on the other hand, are run by hard-nosed managers who worry about profit and consumers. Public organizations are wasteful; private organizations are efficient. Although these perceptions do not withstand careful scrutiny, the distinction between public and private organizations has troubled scholars for years and warrants examination.

Historical Roots

The profession of public administration was born in a period that, not unlike the 1980s, lionized the successful businessman. In the late nineteenth century, government appeared most squalid at a time when business seemed most productive. Jacksonian democracy of the early 1800s gave way to the buying and selling of government jobs. At the same time, the Industrial Revolution brought new wealth to the successful entrepreneur and a higher standard of living to the working public.

Successful business was seen as the model for the proper management of government. These views were captured by a political science professor who would later become president. In 1887, Woodrow Wilson emphasized in a paper, "The Study of Administration," the importance of proper management to the running of government. He stressed the distinction between politics and administration, a distinction that has shaped the intellectual history of the profession. To Wilson, "The field of [public] administration is a field of business. It is removed from the hurry and strife of politics" (p. 202).

The desire that government administrative agencies should be managed in a "business-like" manner was the central slogan of government reformers in the early twentieth century. Public employment should be based on skills and training, not used as rewards for political supporters. Public programs should be designed to produce goods and services efficiently, not used as bargaining chips in political deals. Decisions should be based on careful planning, not self-interest. An example is the city management form of government that was developed during this period. It gives considerable managerial autonomy to the unelected and professionally trained city manager while restricting elected mayors and city councils to broad policy directives and public ceremonies. The mayor cuts the ribbon, but the city manager decides where to build and how to finance the new industrial park.

The Generic School

This view of public administration provides the historical roots to the *generic school*. In this school of thought, the science of administration is devoted to the general principles underlying the study and management of *all* organizations. The generic school stresses the similarities of government and business organizations. Where differences exist, they do not alter the fundamental principles of management. In this view, the primary focus of management is efficiency or the best use of resources to achieve legitimate ends.

The clearest statement of the generic school was Luther Gulick and Lyndall Urwick's edited book *Papers on the Science of Administration* (1937). Their view of business and government management is summarized by the term POSDCORB. Management of all organizations involves *P*lanning the activities and establishing goals; *O*rganizing work activities; *S*taffing and training; *D*irecting or decision making; *Co*ordinating to assure that the various work activities come together; *R*eporting the status of work and problems to both supervisors and subordinates; and *B*udgeting or assuring that work activities correspond to fiscal planning, accounting, and control.

The Uniqueness School

The view that administration is the same in government and business organizations has, however, been strongly challenged as obscuring important distinctions. The alternative view, the *uniqueness school,* stresses the differences between public and private organizations. This school of thought raises doubts about whether observations and techniques based on private organizations have any value when applied to public organizations. Wallace Sayre summarized the alternative view with the aphorism that government and business are "alike in all unimportant aspects" (quoted in Allison 1982).

Critics of the generic school argue that public organizations are more dependent on government allocations, more constrained by law, more exposed to political influences, and more difficult to evaluate than business organizations (Rainey, Backoff, and Levine 1976; Rainey 1989). Focusing on only one difference, the funding of public organizations by government allocations rather than by the sale of a product, a service, or stock, radically changes the view of their management. It is more important to convince elected officials than customers or stockholders of the value of an organization's services. These differences suggest caution in applying business management techniques to government agencies. As Donald Warwick (1975, 204) warned, "It is not enough to pack a briefcase with concepts and measures developed in other settings, unload them in a public agency and expect them to encompass all other worthwhile reality to which they are exposed."

Barry Bozeman (1987) recently examined this controversy from the opposite direction. Rather than advocating that public organizations should become more business-like, he argues the position stated in his title: *All Organizations Are Public.* In Bozeman's view all organizations require legitimacy to come into existence and endure. There are two fundamental sources of legitimacy: economic and political authority. Economic authority, in a capitalist economy, is based on ownership and property rights. In representative democracies, political authority is based on the state's legitimate use of force through laws and policies determined by elected officials.

Bozeman argues that *publicness* is determined by the extent to which political authority affects the behavior and processes of the organization. In other words, a manufacturing firm such as General Dynamics with a large proportion of its sales based on government contracts (in this case 99 percent) is public even if it is privately owned. Such organizations exist because of government and are as subject to the ups and downs of political processes, such as the budget allocations for defense, as any governmental agency. One could reasonably consider General Dynamics a subsidiary of the Department of Defense and not an independent corporation. Similarly, a public authority, such as a turnpike authority, that sells a service and keeps the profits shares many characteristics of a private business.

We follow Bozeman's lead and take a middle ground in the generic versus uniqueness debate. There are certain functions and activities that all organizations perform, such as hiring and firing personnel, motivating their workers, budgeting, planning, and evaluating their output. On the other hand, we acknowledge the important distinctions between public and private organizations but argue that they are a matter of degree. The differences are not absolute; moreover, trends are toward blurring rather than sharpening the differences. Some believe that private agencies should consider the social consequences of their activities. For example, companies that pollute the environment should either be charged a fee for this or regulated to prevent it. So many different types of public and private organizations exist that exceptions can be found to any rule. Public organizations include organizations as different as the U.S. Department of State and a neighborhood community action council. Private organizations include firms as different as General Motors and a local restaurant. Given these differences, a thoughtful observer or administrator must always pay attention to the specific context. Nevertheless, we retain the distinction between business and government administration but cautiously apply ideas and observations from all types of organizations to problems in public administration.

DEFINING BUREAUCRACY

Structure

A particular form of administration that has grown in importance and prevalence in the twentieth century is the *bureaucracy*. Most of our work lives are spent in bureaucratic organizations; most of the products and services that affect our nonwork lives are provided by bureaucracies.

Bureaucracies are more maligned than understood. In the study of public administration, the concept of bureaucracy is important on three levels. First, a large number of governmental as well as private organizations are bureaucracies. The concept has descriptive importance. Second, the concept of bureaucracy is important in understanding the role of public organizations in our representative democracy. Third, many social critics see bureaucracy as a major contributor to the alienation of contemporary life. We need to understand the concept better before applying it to larger social issues. We begin with a definition of bureaucracy and then elaborate on each element.

Bureaucracies are generally defined as organizations that (1) are large (generally more than 100 employees); (2) are hierarchical in structure, with each employee accountable to the top executive through a chain of command; (3) provide each employee with a clearly defined role and area of responsibility; (4) base their actions and decisions on impersonal rules; and (5) hire and promote employees based on skills and training related to their specific jobs. The term *bureaucracy* is not, then, restricted to public or governmental organizations. Most large businesses are bureaucracies. We also need to note that other structural forms exist (such as voluntary and communal organizations), and that bureaucracies themselves come in several variants (Rothschild-Whitt 1979), But, typically, bureaucracies share these five characteristics.

A fundamental tenet of organization theory and of social science in general is that the structure of a setting has a major influence on the pattern of choices and actions within it. You can see this on a variety of levels. Students who complain about being treated like a number at a large university or of the intrusiveness of a small college acknowledge the effects of institutional size on social interactions. The worker who laments that his friend has "changed, is now like any other boss" after a promotion testifies to the importance of hierarchy. The characteristics of bureaucracy discussed below are not merely abstract principles but forces that shape our lives.

Size.   Organizational size is commonly measured in terms of numbers of employees. Several alternative measures have been explored, but these measures—budget size or net worth, for example—are closely associated with the number of employees (Kimberly 1976). Moreover, changes in number of employees are closely associated with changes in organizational structure.

Most organizations begin small. An entrepreneur and a few employees introduce a new product, or a community activist and a few supporters advocate a new social program. If the product sells or the program is funded, the organization is likely to grow. During these early stages all those involved are likely to have hands-on working knowledge of all aspects of the operation. Right after college, I (the second author of this text) directed a small preschool. When the bus driver was sick, I drove the bus. When I was out, the cook answered the telephone. The preschool had elements of bureaucracy; we all had different jobs, and a short chain of command linked aides and teachers to me, the director. But most decisions were collaborative and everyone knew what everyone else was doing.

When organizations grow they change. Although the research cannot clearly distinguish small from large, at some point in an organization's growth the looseness and flexibility characteristic of small organizations, like the preschool, become a major problem. With more employees, group decision making breaks down. Greater size requires a higher degree of structure. Face-to-face contacts cannot solve all problems, and as the number of employees increases, problems of coordination and fair treatment surface. The boss can no longer oversee everyone's work, and the problems of supervision and accountability demand attention. In short, with greater size, bureaucracy is born.

The question of size is compounded by two other elements: *geographic dispersion* and *complexity*. Organizations that exist in a single location and produce only one product or service may need minimal structure. More complex organizations located in many geographic locations and producing a variety of products or services require more coordination. For example, a single but large organization responsible for trash collection in a major city may have a simpler organizational form than a relatively small organization, such as the Center for Disease Control, that provides a wide range of services across the nation. Although patterns vary, increases in the number of employees generally are accompanied by increases in organizational complexity and require a greater amount of structure and rules. The most common structure of moderate-to-large organizations is hierarchy.

Hierarchy.   Hierarchy is a central element of bureaucracy; it is so prevalent that it is almost synonymous with organization. Herbert Simon (1981) extends this observation and suggests that hierarchy is a fundamental characteristic of all complex systems. In simplest terms, a hierarchy is a division into ordered components. An outline of this book divided into chapters, headings, and subheadings is a hierarchy. When the term is applied to social systems it takes on the added meaning of defining *authority* and *rank*. Within the family hierarchy, the parents are the ultimate authority, with the oldest child bossing the youngest who in turn dominates the family dog.

The hierarchy of a typical bureaucracy has a single position at the top. The organization is then divided into major sections and further subdivided into programs. The programs may include several subprograms. Except for those at the top and bottom of the hierarchy, individuals both supervise those ranked below them and are supervised by those above. In addition to the internal hierarchy, many public organizations exist within a hierarchy of organizations with the leaders of one organization responsible to top executives in other organizations. The secretary of state, the chief executive in charge of a massive, international bureaucracy, reports to the president.

The number of individuals under a supervisor is called the *span of control*. Narrow spans of control provide more direct supervision but necessitate additional layers of middle management. Wide spans of control reduce the number of management layers as well as the extent of direct supervision. As shown in Figure 2.1, two layers of middle management are required in a small organization of fifteen people if the span of control is restricted to two. If the span of control is increased to four, as in Figure 2.2, only one layer of management separates the top from the bottom in a larger organization of twenty-one. The narrow span will increase the level of direct supervision—supervisors need worry about only a few individuals—but can create communications and control problems. You can imagine the layers of hierarchy in an organization of 500 employees with a narrow span of control.

Organizational hierarchies also confer status. Offices, desks, as well as salaries get larger as you move up the organizational chart. Although many innovative businesses are shedding overt signs of status—the boss loses reserved parking privileges and eats in the cafeteria—the legitimacy of status differences is a basic assumption of bureaucratic life. These status differences are based on the fundamental authority of who has the right and responsibility to hire, promote, fire, and evaluate other workers (Dornbusch and Scott 1975). In bureaucracies these rights are reserved for supervisors, the supervisor's supervisor, and on up the hierarchy.

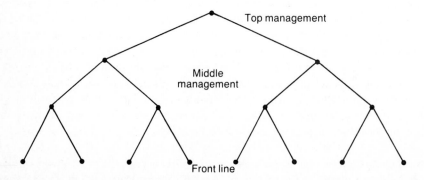

Figure 2.1. Narrow Span of Control

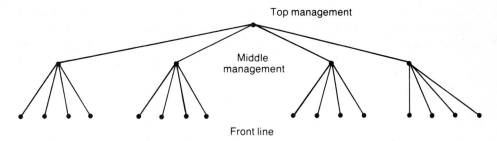

Figure 2.2. Wide Span of Control

Although those at the top often lament their inability to command bureaucracies, we should not underestimate the power of position. Supervisors have considerable influence over the careers of those further down the hierarchy. Even tenured civil servants strongly feel the influence of position power: A displeased boss may lack the authority to fire them but possesses the authority to reassign them to trivial work—to, as the bureaucrats call it, "send them to Siberia."

Specialization.   In a bureaucracy, hierarchy confers both obligation and independence. Although ultimate responsibility resides at the top of hierarchical organizations, hierarchy isolates specific areas of responsibility. When organizations grow to the point that a few individuals can no longer do everything, jobs and responsibility must be delegated. A fundamental purpose of hierarchy is, therefore, the *division of labor.* Individuals are granted areas, however small, of independent responsibility, and this delegation creates specialization.

Specialization is the breaking down of tasks and responsibility into small, discrete components and is based on two sources of expertise: experience and education. When individuals work exclusively on specific tasks or policy areas, they develop skills, routines, and insights that far exceed those of the generalist. The skilled butcher works with a speed that would cost most of us our fingers.

Other specializations are achieved through education or training. Epidemiologists, policy analysts, highway engineers, computer programmers, and many others learn specialities during study in universities or other outside organizations. They bring their specializations to the organizations. Most often such specialists belong to professional organizations that reinforce their status as experts and encourage continuing education so they will keep up with advances in their subfield. These two sources of specialization, experience and education, are complementary. Prior education often leads to repeated experience, as with the heart surgeon who has completed hundreds of coronary bypass operations.

Specialization is, therefore, both a result and a cause of *expertise,* and expertise is a source of power and authority independent of position in the hierarchy. For example, the director of the family violence program within a large state department of social services will wield considerable autonomy over his or her bailiwick. Family violence may be one of hundreds of programs, and top administrators may have only general understanding of this program. In addition, with years of work in the subfield a specialist is likely to build relationships with key actors including outsiders such as citizen groups and legislators. Those at the top, while retaining formal authority, often defer to the specialized expert further down the chain of command. Many top decision makers feel they do little more than ratify the decisions already made by those they supposedly direct (Weiss 1980).

Rule-Based Decisions.   Specialization and division of labor require coordination. Top-level officials want assurance that those in the middle and at the bottom follow—or at least partially conform to—their orders and expectations, and people working in one part of a large organization must rely on the work of others. Bureaucracies achieve predictability and coordination largely through rules. Some of these rules define how tasks are accomplished (these are called *standard operating procedures*), who qualifies for a service, and who in the organization is responsible for decisions and actions. Some rules are broad allowing discretion while others are narrow prescriptions permitting little discretion. Some administrative rules have the effect of and are treated as laws.

A major task of many public bureaucracies is to translate laws and executive orders into rules to guide programs. This rule making is a major decision process in government and often requires public administrators to take general legal mandates and define rules that are both responsive and practical. For example, the Americans with Disabilities Act will, if passed, require all businesses of more than fifteen employees to provide the disabled with "reasonable accommodations" as long as these provisions do not bring "undue hardship" on the business (DeParle 1989). How these terms are defined in bureaucractic rules will determine in large measure the impact of this legislation. Whether restrictive or discretionary, legalistic or informal, bureaucracies base decisions and actions on rules: "There ought to be a rule" is a basic bureaucratic principle that guides all aspects of organizational life.

Merit Hiring and Evaluation.   The fourth major principle of bureaucracy is hiring and job evaluation based on skills and merit. Max Weber (1946), the turn-of-the-century German scholar who most fully developed the concept of bureaucracy, was primarily interested in changes in authority relationships. The emergence of bureaucratic organizations marked a shift in sources of influence. Charismatic leaders and those whose authority is based solely on family position gave way to those with specific skills and legally authorized positions. In addition, hiring and promotion shifted from reliance solely on contacts and family connections to educational background and performance. The shift to credentials and performance—the ingredients of merit evaluation—resulted from specialization. If work is rationally divided into subtasks, then organizational effectiveness depends to a good measure on the ability of individuals to contribute their speciality.

The contemporary evidence of this aspect of bureaucracy is abundant. Many levels of employment, especially public employment, require specific and specialized education. For those in which advanced degrees are not a prerequisite—the post office or fire department, for example—entrance examinations are given with hiring based on score rank. Once hired, performance is supposed to be measured by objective criteria, not determined by a supervisor's whim. However, we should stress that this is the ideal. In actuality these elements of objectivity have not eliminated the importance of personal contacts, subjective judgments, nor prejudice from employment. Bureaucracy does, however, temper these personal aspects of organizations.

Variations of the Form

Too often bureaucracy is considered to have only one form of organization. In reality, the pyramid with a single top executive, many steps, and a defined chain of command is but one of several types of bureaucracy. Although the elements of bureaucracy are found in most complex organizations, the elements combine into various forms. Two alternative forms of bureacracy that are common among public organizations are the *professional bureaucracy* and the *adhocracy*.

Professional Bureaucracies.   Many of the activities of government organizations cannot easily be reduced to routine or programmable operations. Providing services, such as education, counseling, or policing, requires making judgments about specific situations. Although such work is guided by rules and procedures, organizations such as schools, mental health clinics, and police departments cannot be run like assembly lines. They require flexible guidelines tempered by professional judgment. Professionals are individuals trained to work in complex and ambiguous situations. They gain their expertise through training and education rather than through apprenticeship. Their educational backgrounds establish procedures and criteria for discerning problems and designing solutions; their work requires both the discretion and the autonomy to make judgments. (See Chapter 5.)

Bureaucracies that depend on a large number of professionals are usually less hierarchical. They tend to have fewer supervisors, and the supervisors are likely to spend most of their time coordinating rather than controlling activities. A university (which can be either public or private) is an example. Even in a large public university, only a few layers of administration separate the newly hired professor and the president. In addition, professional bureaucracies grant much autonomy to their workers.

Adhocracies.   Organizations that are responsible for producing innovative solutions often form adhocracies. The term *adhocracy* was coined by Alvin Toffler (1970) in *Future Shock* as the harbinger of future social structure. Like professional bureaucracies, adhocracies employ a large number of experts. The structure of the adhocracy, however, is more ephemeral, more complex, and less coordinated—more ad hoc. In a professional bureaucracy, different professions are often assigned to different divisions. In a health department, the division of child health may be headed by a doctor and staffed with nurses whereas the division of water quality employs engineers. These two professions may rarely interact.

In an adhocracy, individuals from different professions and different parts of the organization form teams to work on specific problems. In effect, an adhocracy takes the informal structure of most organizations, the interdepartmental and interpersonal connections, as the basic structure. Adhocracies tend to have many more connections between individuals and units than the traditional chain of command in most bureaucracies. Moreover, these connections are more fluid or loosely coupled (Weick 1976). At times teams may work together closely and in isolation from the rest of the organization. At other times, teams may meet irregularly to pull together ideas and concerns from across the organization. These teams may be of long or short duration.

Adhocracies can form within more traditional bureaucracies or can characterize the entire structure. For example, the health department discussed above may form an interdisciplinary team of doctors, engineers, and policy analysts to deal with a toxic waste dump. When the project ends, team members revert to their roles in the hierarchy. Other organizations, especially research organizations such as the National Aeronautics and Space Administration (NASA), may rely almost entirely on project-oriented teams. The advantage of these teams is that they bring a variety of perspectives and skills to bear on the problem.

A common element of adhocracies is the *matrix form*. In the traditional bureaucracy each individual has one boss. This centralizing assumption often defeats collaborative efforts. For example, if members of the toxic waste team are responsible only to their program directors in the established hierarchy, then team members will likely bring their program agendas and biases into team activities. Typically such teams dissolve into turf conflicts. In a true matrix form, the members of the team have at least two supervisors, the team leader and their traditional supervisor. The team leader evaluates members' performance in proportion to the time spent on the project. Typically, group members may serve on several teams, thus multiplying the network of relationships and competing demands. (See Figure 2.3.)

The professional bureaucracy and the adhocracy, two alternatives to the form of the traditional, hierarchical bureaucracy, illustrate an important element of contemporary organization theory: No single organizational form is appropriate for all situations. An organization concerned with producing standardized services, such as testing for drivers' licenses, should not have the same form as a research institute.[1] The nature of the work, or what organization theorists call *technology*, is closely associated with the structure of the organization. Traditional bureaucracies are well suited for routine work, adhocracies for innovation. The basic observation that the size, nature of the work, type of employee, and amount of change in the environment indicate different organizational forms is called *contingency theory* (Lawrence and Lorsch 1967; Galbraith 1973). No one has uncovered a universal formula that indicates *what* form suits *what* set of factors, but the basic observation is valid: No single organizational form fits all circumstances.

THE PROBLEMS OF BUREAUCRACY

An irony of bureaucracy is that its strengths are its weaknesses; its greatest assets are the sources of its greatest problems. Several of these problems of bureaucracy are

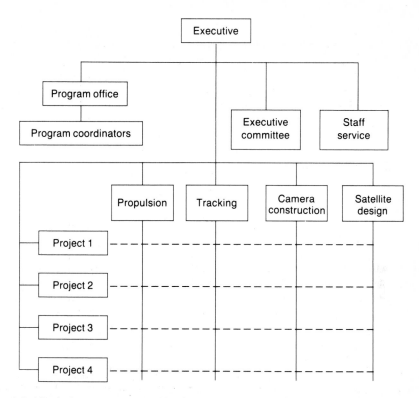

Figure 2.3. Matrix Structure in the NASA Weather Satellite Program, by Alan C. Filley
SOURCE: Mintzberg, Henry. *The Structuring of Organizations,* © 1979, p. 174. Reprinted by permission of Prentice-Hall, Inc., Englewood Cliffs, New Jersey.

discussed in this section. We will focus on problems associated with the structure and power of bureaucracies.

Structure

Overcomplexity.   Bureaucracy has become synonymous with labyrinthine organization. Rather than maintaining clear lines of authority, bureaucracies grow into Rube Goldberg contraptions in which simple acts or decisions require endless intervening steps. And, as with most complex devices, large bureaucracies become prone to breakdowns. If plans require approval from several bureaus, each with an interest in part of the problem, little gets accomplished. The top priority of one office may be far down the list of another. The key person in one office is on vacation while personnel in the other department see the new policy as a threat to their turf. Top managers become insulated from the central issues by layers of subordinates. Too often decision making in bureaucracies resembles the childhood game of "telephone," a good idea becomes garbled as it moves up, down, and around the hierarchy. Bureaucracies become overcomplex.

Segmentalism. The complexity of bureaucracies also produces segmentalism. Rosabeth Kanter (1983) studied numerous organizations to identify the factors that encourage and inhibit creative ideas. She found that organizations tend to break apart into self-contained, inward-looking subparts or segments. Seeing only part of a problem or process is a predictable result of specialization and division of labor. This pulling apart, or *loose coupling,* can be a source of innovation as individual subunits produce new ideas to solve their problems (Weick 1976). Segmentalism sets in when there is little effective coordination between the parts. Kanter found that without coordination many organizational innovations are lost for lack of interest in the organization as a whole.

Fragmentation.   Specialization also fragments work. When jobs are broken down into smaller and smaller tasks, they lose their connection to the whole and require less skill. The most extreme examples are found on assembly lines where complex tasks, such as building a car, are reduced to the single actions of workers repetitiously tightening the same bolt. No wonder robots are better at building cars than people.

Although extremes of specialization are rare in public organizations, the fragmentation of jobs is common. In most large social service agencies, one unit helps the new client apply for service, a different one provides drug counseling, while still another works with family problems. Most clients have problems that spill across bureaucratic divisions, yet many feel as though they are rolling down an assembly line (Prottas 1979). Other clients find bureaucracies unresponsive because their requests are met with the ubiquitous "I'm sorry, that is not my area, you need to see. . . ."

Thus, like other aspects of bureaucracy, specialization has advantages and disadvantages. Without specialization and expertise, the quality of public goods and services declines. Most of us would prefer that our roads were built by specialist engineers rather than by generalist administrators. But specialization can reduce the quality of products and services by treating complex problems as if they were the sum of little problems. Moreover, fragmentation can reduce the intrinsic meaning of work. Repeating the same task builds skills but also increases monotony. Completing one little job over and over trivializes work. Reducing the variety and complexity of jobs can also reduce self-motivation and, therefore, overall productivity. (See Chapter 7.)

Red Tape.   The bureaucratic preference for formal rules creates an additional problem: red tape. "Too much red tape" is a catchall complaint about public organizations. Red tape, originally a red ribbon used to bind British government documents, refers to numerous, needless, and irrelevant rules and requirements. Drug companies complain that the federal government takes years to approve new treatments, a poignant problem for those dying from acquired immune deficiency syndrome (AIDS). The disabled complain about the lengthy forms they must fill out to qualify for benefits. Of course, as Herbert Kaufman (1977, 4) reminds us, "One person's 'red tape' may be another's treasured safeguard." A developer may malign the restrictive zoning requirements preferred by neighborhood groups.

Kaufman also examines the reasons for red tape. As with other problems, red tape is the negative side of several positive features of bureaucracy. In analyzing the causes of the proliferation of bureaucratic rules, Kaufman isolates pressures for equal treatment and due process. Treating similar cases in a similar manner forces bureaucrats to develop clear, if unduly complex, guidelines. And providing opportunities for due process and appeal requires documentation and may add months to the process. Complexity and delays are the essence of red tape, but would we prefer a government without such rules? Most of us find standing in line annoying but prefer lines to allowing those with greatest clout the privilege of butting in.

Power

Bureaucracies concentrate power in large organizations and in the hands of a few organizational leaders (Perrow 1979). Weber described and admired the power of bureaucracies, but he also recognized their danger, especially for democratic societies. Two samples from his work show his ambivalence. His admiration and fear of the power of bureaucracy is directly relevant to a contemporary American government that must increasingly rely on authoritarian administration to sustain our democratic institutions. Weber (1946) wrote in admiration:

> The decisive reason for the advance of bureaucratic organization has always been its purely technical superiority over any other form of organization. The fully developed bureaucratic mechanism compares with other organizations exactly as does the machine with the non-mechanical modes of production. (p. 214)

A few pages later, admiration turns to concern:

> Under normal conditions, the power position of a fully developed bureaucracy is always over towering. The 'political' master finds himself in the position of the 'dilettante' who stands opposite the 'expert,' facing the trained official who stands within the management of administration. (p. 232)

Although Weber and others worried about the overwhelming power of bureaucracies, Kanter (1979) expressed the opposite concern. She observed that large, complex organizations tend to dissipate rather than concentrate power. She found power-*less*ness more common and more damaging than the abuse of power. Too many individuals lack the connections, resources, and autonomy to accomplish meaningful work. Managers may have the power to reward and punish—what Kanter calls *oppressive power*—but many lack the power to get anything accomplished. They lack *productive power*. Kanter, however, does not deny that bureaucracies are potentially powerful social organizations and that their power can serve both positive and negative ends.

The Case of Adolf Eichmann.   The inherent dangers in the power of bureaucracy are perhaps best and most disturbingly captured by Hannah Arendt (1976) in *Eichmann in Jerusalem: A Report on the Banality of Evil.* Arendt, a political philosopher who reported on the Nazi war crimes trial in Jerusalem, draws a stark picture of Adolf Eichmann. Eichmann was a high-level bureaucrat in Hitler's Germany. As a transportation expert with an interest in Jewish affairs, he rose to a position of authority over the efficient transfer of Jews and other minorities from all over Europe to their deaths in various extermination factories. Yet Eichmann showed little personal involvement. Arendt (1976, 287) wrote: "Except for an extraordinary diligence in looking out for his personal advancement, he had no motive at all."

Eichmann, the German bureaucrat, was the darkest realization of the fears voiced by Weber, the scholar of German bureaucracy. Eichmann claimed innocence; he was following orders. He was a skilled organizer faced with the exceedingly difficult task of relocating a large segment of the population, a task inconceivable without bureaucratic efficiency. He was a transportation expert who neither helped make nor questioned the overall policy of extermination. His job, transportation, was only one piece of a larger system, and he focused merely on his narrow area of responsibilities. As Arendt concludes,

> Of course it is important to the political and social sciences that the essence of totalitarian government, and perhaps the nature of every bureaucracy, is to make functionaries and mere cogs in the administration machinery out of men, and then to dehumanize them. No one can debate long and profitably on the rule of Nobody, which is what the political form known as bureaucracy truly is. (p. 289)

The story of Eichmann highlights the great danger bureaucracy poses for democratic forms of government. The scale of the evil of the Holocaust depended on a high level of mindless efficiency: One man can kill many, but only bureaucracy can exterminate 6 million. In much smaller ways, hierarchy and expertise pose direct threats to core democratic values, because the implementation of public policies that affect our daily lives are delegated to unknown and faceless bureaucrats—the "Rule by Nobody"—not elected officials. When the important policy questions are highly technical—nuclear weapons, laser-beam defense systems, genetic engineering, controlling the money supply, and many others—is there any room for public participation? When advanced degrees and years of experience are required even to understand the questions, technical expertise replaces public involvement. And without public participation will not bureaucratic organizations dominate elected officials, just as Weber feared? (See Chapter 10 for a discussion of administrative accountability.)

THE CASE FOR BUREAUCRACY

The common problems of bureaucracy and the fears of bureaucratic power present two negative but conflicting images of public organizations. Bureaucrats are simultaneously seen as incompetent bunglers awash in red tape and powerful and secretive usurpers of public authority. In *The Case for Bureaucracy,* Charles Goodsell (1985) challenges both perceptions. Goodsell acknowledges that incompetence mars the performance of public organizations but insists that government has no monopoly on incompetence. In his view, the major performance problems in public organizations result from unrealistic expectations rather than incompetence. The public demands and elected officials are quick to promise solutions to all sorts of social ills, from pollution to poverty. These most difficult problems are then assigned to public organizations, and when our ability to solve these problems often falls short, public administrators are held responsible (see also Wilson 1967).

The image of public administrators as powerful and unaccountable actors is similarly exaggerated. Goodsell examines three major actors in government: elected officials, special interest groups, and public administrators. Elected officials are clearly the most accountable to the public; if they lose favor, they lose office. Elected officials, however, often lack the expertise and knowledge to deal with many social issues. Special interest groups are well informed about their narrow areas, but like defense lawyers, they use their expertise to argue on behalf of their clients. Special interest groups are not accountable to the general public; they deliberately serve narrow interests and often withhold information when it weakens their case.

In contrast to elected officials and special interests, public administrators are both expert and accountable. Goodsell (1985, 138) writes:

> Public bureaucracies, by contrast [to legislators and private interest groups], possess technical expertise *and* formal legal authority at the same time. This is a unique combination in terms of both efficaciousness and providing ties to a larger order. Without it, the society would be even less equitable and the polity more adrift.

In addition, the bleak picture of bureaucracy drawn by Weber and the conflict between bureaucracy, democracy, and humanistic values described by Arendt are blunted by the last three decades of research on organizations. Bureaucracy is no longer seen as a sociological bulldozer. Within even the most rigid hierarchies, informal organizations grow and flourish. Patterns of influence and communication overflow chains of command. Bureaucracies are now seen as rich social settings in which interpersonal needs, motives, and interactions shape much of organizational life.

Moreover, organizations are guided by norms and ideology as well as by formal goals and structure. These aspects of modern organizations are essential in both understanding organizations and protecting society from the potential abuses of bureaucracy. George Fredrickson and David Hart (1985) contrast the Danish and German civil service during the Nazi occupation. At the time Eichmann was acting as a mindless cog in the government machinery, Danish bureaucrats were bending the rules and resisting orders to transport their Jewish population. Their strong belief in the role of public administration in protecting the rights of all citizens superseded the bureaucratic pressure for compliance with rules, laws, and orders. Rather than merely machines of production or oppression, organizations are now viewed as living, organic social systems.

OPEN SYSTEMS THEORY

Organizations are more than the sum of their parts. Knowing an organization's size, structure, and specialization is only a beginning for understanding how that organization actually works. Structural descriptions often leave out the essential, dynamic elements of organizations that result from their being living, natural social organisms: individual needs, group processes, and informal relationships. Describing how the various parts of organizations interact, and how organizations respond to the world around them, is the focus of a growing body of organizational theory called *open systems theory.*[2] Open systems theory broadens the context of organization study by suggesting that to understand organizations one must examine their inputs, throughputs, and outputs. *Inputs* are the material, human, and social resources that organizations require. *Outputs* are the products or services of the organizations. *Throughputs* are the organizational processes that transform the inputs into outputs, however indirectly. Open systems theory describes the *subsystems* that exist within most organizations and explores the processes of *coordination* and *maintenance* by which organizations attend to their own existence.

Subsystems

System theory identifies five common subsystems within most complex organizations. Although specific organizations may have unique designs, the basic building blocks are almost invariably similar. These subsystems contain clusters of specializations. Different scholars identify the subsystems differently, but general agreement exists on the various functions performed by each subsystem. Henry Mintzberg's (1979) five basic organizational parts, which we will use as a model here, closely correspond to those identified by Talcott Parsons (1960) and Daniel Katz and Robert Kahn (1978).[3] More important, Mintzberg's five subsystems correspond to the hierarchical levels of most bureaucracies.

At the bottom of most organizations is the *operating core,* or production subsystem, that performs the basic work of the organization. (See Figure 2.4.) Individuals in this subsystem, whether assembly-line workers, teachers, lab technicians, or whatever, are responsible for the output of product or services which the organization must deliver. The operating core must secure the necessary resources and change inputs— whether raw materials or clients—into outputs.[4] The direct supervision of frontline staff and the distribution of products and services are also operating core responsibilities.

At the top of the hierarchy sits the *strategic apex,* which contains top executives—such as department secretaries, agency directors, county administrators, sheriffs, and their assistants. Those in the strategic apex must wear metaphorical bifocals. They must focus on the details of running the organization so that it meets or approximates its mission, but they must also assure that the organization serves the needs of the external actors who influence the organization. Myopic preoccupation with everyday details may obscure the need to adapt to changes in the external environment. High-level public administrators must be aware not only of how their organizations are functioning day to day, but also of the changing needs and priorities of elected officials, other agencies with whom theirs interacts, and public interest groups. They must both manage present operations and discern and articulate necessary changes.

Middle-line managers connect the strategic apex with the operating core by communicating directions down and problems up the hierarchy. They are the primary agents of coordination, as we shall see in the following section. When mutual adjustment is called for, middle-line managers must negotiate informal collaborations; they must also provide direct supervision to those within their span of control and assure that products and processes meet standardized requirements. Much of the manager's work is evaluative and control oriented. Middle-level managers must also resolve, or at least address, the many conflicts that arise in most organizations within individual

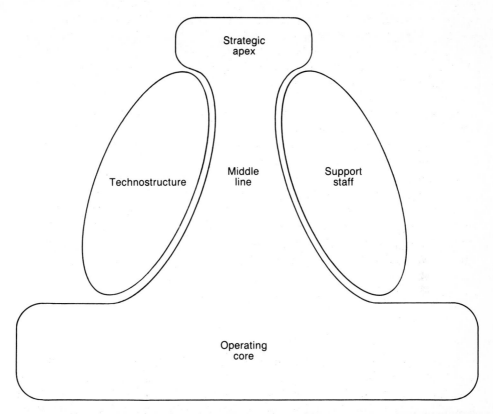

Figure 2.4. Five Basic Parts of Organizations
SOURCE: Mintzberg, Henry. *The Structuring of Organizations,* © 1979, p. 20. Reprinted by permission of Prentice-Hall, Inc., Englewood Cliffs, New Jersey.

units and between hierarchical levels and subsystems. Middle-line managers spend considerable time in meetings, on the phone, and relating to other people.

Mintzberg identifies two other components in organizations that exist throughout all other levels of hierarchy: the technostructure and the support staff. The *technostructure* is primarily responsible for facilitating standardization; work analysts redesigning jobs, accountants checking results, and teachers training personnel in new skills are all part of the technostructure. The *support staff* includes such diverse operations as legal counsel, public relations, product research, and day care. These functions do not directly contribute to providing products or services, nor do they involve coordinating work, yet they are essential to the maintenance of the organization. The violation of laws, bad marketing, outdated products, or employees worried about their children can all lead to reduced organizational functioning.

All five subsystems in most organizations are involved in both coordination and maintenance functions—the two areas identified by open systems theory as vital to organizational health.

Coordination

In our earlier discussion of bureaucracy, we stressed the importance of specialization and division of labor. Systems theory elaborates on this point in two ways: by identifying subsystems and by focusing on the importance of coordination. Mintzberg (1979, 3) identifies three main means of coordination and argues that "these should be considered the most basic elements of structure, the glue that holds organizations together." Most organizations rely in varying degrees on all three.

Mutual adjustment is simply the informal give-and-take of people working together. Modifying a report to accommodate individuals' responses, changing a rule to deal with an exception, adjusting work habits to respond to others' needs: These are all examples of mutual adjustment. What appears to be the simplest form of coordination is often, however, the most difficult and important. Mutual adjustment cannot be reduced to clear rules. It requires attention to the interpersonal and informal side of work, and successful mutual adjustment requires developing and then constantly maintaining relationships. It also often requires considerable and apparently unproductive socializing including informal negotiations and compromise—and lots of informal banter.

Direct supervision is more straightforward than mutual adjustment. Coordination is relatively easy to achieve when one individual is clearly responsible for the work of others, and workers are clearly responsible for following orders. Obviously, extreme reliance on direct supervision can reduce workers to mindless, obedient servants and deprive the organization of their ideas and observations. Most organizations rely on some form of direct supervision, but the top-down coordination is tempered by efforts to engage lower-level workers in the decision-making process. Including lower-level workers is especially important in organizations—like most public organizations—in which the work of such employees requires considerable discretion (Maynard-Moody, Musheno, and Palumbo 1990).

Standardization is the third form of coordination that most organizations employ. Standardization typically involves designing the components of a product or service so that they work with or complement other components; coordination is built into the design. In manufacturing a computer, for example, the worker installing disk drives does not need to customize each machine with whoever is designing the boards of chips; the part interaction was worked out by the designers. Standardization may also refer to end products as well as processes. A government agency awarding a contract for a road, for instance, may specify the requirements that the road must meet but will allow the individual contractor to figure out how to achieve that result.

In public agencies, standardization may refer to the practice of hiring individuals with specific skills or knowledge, or with a particular professional accreditation. Trained social workers, city planners, or medical researchers—to name only a few—may work in vastly different settings, but they apply standardized skills to complex, sometimes unique, problems.

Maintenance

Organizations must not only attend to the coordination of their production efforts but must also maintain themselves as healthy systems in order to adapt and ultimately to survive. Maintenance needs come in a variety of forms. The most obvious is the maintenance of the physical plant: The police department must keep patrol cars in working order; the census bureau needs up-to-date computers. Short-term improvements in efficiency or cost-effectiveness achieved by postponing expensive maintenance will inevitably result in eventual organizational harm or collapse.

A more subtle but no less important maintenance need involves the interpersonal or social side of work. What on the surface may appear to be laziness, gossip, or other non-work-related activities may actually be essential social actions that make demanding or boring work possible. A central insight of open systems theory is that ignoring the human, or social, dimension of work can prove just as destructive as letting a patrol car's brakes wear out. A one-dimensional search of efficiency, for extracting the maximum out of every worker, may in fact cause human breakdown and, finally, poor performance. Production demands must always be balanced with maintenance needs. The social needs of organizations are treated in detail in Chapter 4.

Open Systems: Controlling the Environment

In addition to its emphasis on subsystems, coordination, and maintenance, open systems theory helps us understand the importance of organizational relationships with the external environment. Organizations cannot exist in isolation. All organizations must acquire resources (including raw materials, supplies, and employees), find markets for their products and services, and meet a variety of other external needs. Public organizations often relate to their environment in ways that differ significantly from those of private organizations.

A critical resource for public organizations, for instance, is *legitimacy* (Bozeman 1987). Most business organizations define themselves by the products or services they sell; a restaurant, even if licensed by the government, would close if enough people did not buy dinner there. For most public organizations, however, the right to exist and to provide products or services depends on the conferral of a legitimate right to do so by another actor or set of actors. Police hand out speeding tickets; nursing home inspectors cite violations; social service agencies approve adoptions; city planners permit zoning variances; the National Institutes of Health awards grants: All these activities are possible only because each organization has received legitimacy from, most commonly, elected officials.

Another fundamental resource for all organizations is capital. Manufacturers must sell cars to acquire income to continue manufacturing cars. When income decreases, the natural tendency is to try to increase sales. This relationship between inputs and outputs is more ambiguous in public organizations. Most public organizations receive their operating capital from budget allocations set by elected bodies: legislatures, school boards, city councils. Such allocations may be only partially or indirectly based on the quality and quantity of the services provided. Many public organizations exist on fixed or even declining budgets, and rather than trying to increase demand for their services in order to increase income, as private organizations might do, they direct their energies into controlling or even reducing these demands. A preschool for disabled children, for example, may work wonders with ten children, adequately serve twenty-five, and only warehouse forty. If their budget is fixed, the incentive may well be to avoid finding new clients.

An organization's interaction with the environment is a major impetus for change. Shifts in the availability of resources, in the demand for products or services, or in the competition may require adaptation (see Chapter 3). What we need to stress at this point is simply that an organization's relationship with its environment is a major source of uncertainty. Organizational leaders cannot be certain that present circumstances will hold; the unanticipated occurs and requires response.

Two aspects of the environment contribute to this uncertainty. First, compared to internal operations, the environment is less controllable. Managers can determine much of what goes on within their organizations. They cannot, however, force other organizations to follow their policies and conform to their strategic plans. Despite the massive amounts of time and energy that organizations often spend on trying to manage their relationships with other organizations, with the producers of their requisite resources, and with the users of their products or services, their ability to control those relationships is necessarily limited. Second, environmental change is unpredictable. Most public organizations develop long-range plans based on forecasts of future demands for their services. Public schools, for example, continually project school-age populations. But changes in the environment can discredit the most carefully constructed forecasts. Funding and building prisons takes years of planning, but minor changes in parole rules can invalidate predictions overnight.

Open systems theory focuses on both internal and external factors in the functioning of organizations. Its premises and hypotheses can enable us all to gain a better understanding of how organizations—particularly public organizations—work.

SUMMARY

In our administrative state, the confrontation between abstract principles and specific cases and situations largely shapes policy making. This confrontation occurs primarily within the context of public organizations. Chapter 2 begins our examination of public organizations. First, three fundamental dilemmas facing public administrators are described. Public administrators are torn by the demands of serving the public and their self-interest, the requirements for accountability and discretion, and the need for stability and change.

Second, the definition and implications of the term *public* are examined. Public or government organizations share many characteristics with private or business organizations. Early in the history of the field of public administration, scholars emphasized the similarities and encouraged public administrators to emulate business management. More recently, the differences between public and private organizations are underscored, with one scholar noting that many business organizations depend on political authority for legitimacy.

Whether in business or government organizations, a dominant form of administration is bureaucracy, a third major topic. Bureaucracies are generally defined as organizations that (1) are large; (2) are hierarchical in structure, with each employee accountable to the top executive through a chain of command; (3) provide each employee with a clearly defined role and area of responsibility; (4) base their decisions on impersonal rules; and (5) hire and promote employees based on skills and training related to their specific jobs. Although these elements of bureaucracy are found in most complex organizations, the elements combine into various forms. Two alternative forms of bureaucracy that are common among public organizations are the *professional bureaucracy* and the *adhocracy*.

The characteristics of bureaucracy create structural problems and abuses of power. Large bureaucracies often become overcomplex with simple acts and decisions requiring endless intervening steps and delays. Complex organizations tend to break apart into semi-autonomous segments which in the absence of effective coordination can stifle collaboration and innovation. When taken to extremes, division of labor can fragment jobs to add further to coordination problems. Often the need for standard procedures creates so many rules that decisions and actions become tangled in red tape.

Bureaucracies also concentrate much power into a few large organizations and organizational leaders. The ability of bureaucracies to command the efforts of so many individuals and to develop and apply expertise to problems challenges the authority of democratic institutions over policy. The dangers of bureaucracy were epitomized by the case of Adolf Eichmann. Bureaucracy has promise as well as problems and, rather than efficient machines of production oppression, organizations are now viewed as living, organic social systems.

Open systems theory builds on the definition of bureaucracy. This broad theoretical perspective emphasizes inputs, throughput, and outputs and the coordination and maintenance of these organizational activities. Organizational activities tend to cluster into subsystems and depend on relationships to the external environment. The environment creates uncertainty for organizations because external pressures and changes are more difficult to control and are often unpredictable.

CASE STUDY: THE NATIONAL SECURITY COUNCIL

In November 1986 the presidency of Ronald Reagan seemed to run aground. Twin discoveries shook the administration: The United States, in contradiction to stated policy forbidding all dealings with terrorists, had secretly sold military equipment to Iran to free American hostages held by Iran-backed terrorists. Profits from the arms sales were then used covertly to support rebels in Nicaragua, the Contras, backed by the United States. These major policy contradictions were conceived and implemented by the National Security Council (NSC) staff. We will focus on what might appear the least dramatic but most fundamental aspect of this crisis: how the structure of government alters policy.

The Tower Commission was assembled by President Reagan to review the structure and working of the NSC in light of the Iran-Contra policy failure. The commission was directed to conduct "a comprehensive study of the future role and procedures of the National Security Council (NSC) staff in the development, coordination, oversight, and conduct of foreign and national security policy." The central question for study was whether the NSC should be more formally structured, made more bureaucratic, to avoid similar policy fiascoes. To understand the role of the NSC, the history and structure of its principal policy rival, the State Department, must also be reviewed. (In addition, the NSC competes with the Central Intelligence Agency (CIA) and Department of Defense for a voice in foreign policy. We choose to contrast it with the State Department for reasons of simplicity.)

The Department of State is nearly as old as the nation; it was established in 1789, shortly after the ratification of the U.S. Constitution. Two centuries later, the State Department is a large, international bureaucracy with a reputation for avoiding policy risks. The secretary of state and several of the department's top-level officials are appointed by the president but must be approved by the U.S. Senate. State department officials are continually called to Capitol Hill to testify before Congress, and most activities of State are carefully monitored. The State Department is a huge, complex, multinational bureaucracy; presidents pushing new ideas in foreign policy often find the department a barrier to policy change. It suffers from many of the problems of bureaucracy discussed earlier in this chapter.

In contrast, the National Security Council (NSC) and its staff is barely an organization. Established in 1947 to assist the president, the NSC has only four statutory members: the president, vice-president, and the secretaries of the State Department and the Defense Department. The NSC is a highly personal instrument of the president; he shapes its form and responsibilities to suit his management style and policy preferences. It is designed to coordinate policy discussion dealing with national security matters. Often these discussions center on crises, such as the taking of American hostages by terrorists. At other times, the president uses the NSC to initiate new policy directions. For example, when President Nixon negotiated the opening of China he sent his national security adviser, not the secretary of state. As the Tower Commission (Tower et al. 1987, 7) states: "The National Security Council deals with issues that are difficult, complex, and often secret. Decisions are often required in hours rather than weeks. Advice must be given under great stress and with imperfect information." Clearly, the slow deliberate process of a massive bureaucracy like that of the State Department is ill suited to the policy problem requiring fast and innovative action.

The national security adviser, a position created by President Eisenhower, is the principal executive officer of the NSC and has become the personal adviser to the president on national security. Except for brief lapses, most national security advisers have had direct personal access to the president; they often meet several times a day. Especially as compared to the State Department, the NSC staff tends to be "lean and responsive." John Kennedy and Lyndon Johnson kept the staff to fewer than twenty. Richard Nixon allowed the staff to grow to fifty, and Jimmy Carter reduced it to thirty-five.

During the Nixon and Carter years the national security advisers and the secretaries of state were in constant battle over the control and direction of foreign policy. Ronald Reagan at first downgraded the role of the NSC. He established numerous interagency work groups (senior interagency groups [SIGs] and interagency groups [IGs]) to coordinate policy. These matrix forms, however, fell into functional disuse as traditional departments at the State Department and the NSC staff asserted their traditional roles.

Although the facts are not absolutely clear, the Iran-Contra affair was apparently initiated and implemented by the NSC with minimal or no oversight or direction and against the expressed views of the secretaries of the State and Defense Departments. The policies were managed by a marine lieutenant colonel, Oliver North, assigned to the NSC staff. Contacts inside a hostile Iranian government were secured, weapons were transferred from Israeli stocks, Swiss bank accounts were opened, shadowy middle men paid, secret trips taken, and off-the-record deals made—all without the detailed knowledge and approval of the president, the secretary of state, or Congress. Aspects of these initiatives were against stated policy; some were of questionable legality.

The NSC stepped beyond its traditional role of providing advice and assumed operational responsibility for implementing these policy initiatives. Moreover, the national security adviser, Vice-Admiral John Poindexter, deliberately chose not to ask approval of or even to inform the president. The venture was considered too risky for general discussion and standard operating procedures. The policy initiative was innovative—North described the use of Iranian money to finance Nicaraguan rebels as a "neat idea"—but was implemented with little formal control or record keeping. By cutting the strings of accountability, these initiatives wandered far from policy intents and became a major crisis for President Reagan.

Discussion Questions
1. What are the organizational structures of the State Department and the NSC?
2. Should the structure of the NSC be changed to increase accountability?
3. What are the positive and negative implications of increasing the level of bureaucratic control over the NSC?
4. What is the proper organizational design for the NSC?

NOTES

1. We should also emphasize here that we are discussing ideal types. In reality, most organizations are a mixture of these forms. These differences are more a matter of degree than kind.
2. Open systems theory represents a broad and diverse body of theory. Major works include those of Thompson (1967), Katz and Kahn (1978), and Scott (1981).
3. Parson's (1960, 52) systems are production, supportive, maintenance, adaptive, and managerial. Katz and Kahn's (1978, 84) are production, maintenance of work structure, production-supportive, institutional, adaptive, and managerial.
4. The language of systems theory, which equates clients in a service organization with raw material in a factory, creates conceptual problems for many public organizations (Maynard-Moody 1982). Too often clients are "processed" rather than helped (Prottas 1979).

CHAPTER 3

Enduring Issues in Public Organization Theory

Theories of bureaucracy and open systems broadly define the structural forces that shape public organizations. In this chapter we narrow the focus and examine three enduring issues or problems in understanding public organizations: organizational effectiveness, change, and culture. These issues suggest the dynamic tensions within public organizations and several intellectual challenges in the field of public administration.

ORGANIZATIONAL EFFECTIVENESS

Questions and concerns about organizational effectiveness are fundamental to understanding contemporary work organizations, public and private. Work organizations presumably exist for a reason: Manufacturing firms make certain products; human service organizations address defined community needs. This logic extends to the various parts of organizations as well: The personnel office is expected to deal with affirmative action and staff benefits; accounting keeps track of the books.

The assumption that organizations and their subsystems are purposeful is so fundamental that few question its validity or importance. Thus, at first glance, organizational effectiveness is a simple matter of comparing results with intentions. Did the organization or program achieve its stated objectives? If yes, it is effective; if no, it is not.

Like many simplifications, measuring effectiveness by comparing results to intentions provides only limited insight into public organizations. Organizational studies over the past thirty years have raised serious doubts about this one-dimensional definition of effectiveness, and these doubts have spurred new insights into the nature of organizations (Maynard-Moody and McClintock 1987). The new insights fall into three broad categories: redefining organizational goals and purposiveness; recognizing the many dimensions of organizational effectiveness; and underscoring the political nature of all evaluations of programs and services.

Organizational Goals and Purposiveness

It is difficult to think about organizations without discussing organizational goals. The characteristics of bureaucracy described in Chapter 2 imply that organizations are purposeful or goal directed. Hierarchy, specialization, and merit-based personnel—major ingredients of bureaucracy—all assume purpose. It makes little sense to divide up work, provide specialized training, or carefully evaluate someone's efforts if you have no idea of what you want.

Theories of bureaucracy view organizations as instruments or devices for goal attainment (Georgiou 1973). They are social machines that combine the efforts of many individuals to create planned products and services. Viewing government organizations as goal attainment devices has deep intellectual roots in classical public administration theory. When in 1887 Woodrow Wilson stressed that government agencies must become more business-like, he urged public administrators to emulate the efficiency and purposiveness of business.

Moreover, employees act as if organizations are purposeful. Program directors request funding based on promises of future accomplishment, top executives rally support by appeals to their organizations' mission, and staff recognize the limits of their responsibilities based on program goals. When lobbying state legislators or rich alumni, university presidents stress educational goals, not that their school is a great place for faculty to work. The city planner does not stop on the way to work to hand out a speeding ticket. Drug counselors, when they recognize their clients' need for help in getting a job, refer them to an employment agency. All of these actions are based on the assumption that certain organizations pursue specific goals and not others.

Tenets of the Goal Attainment Model.   The goal attainment view of organizations has several tenets. First, organizations are founded and maintained to do something. They do not exist because of happenstance but for a reason. Goals, therefore, are the fundamental source of legitimacy; they are the organization's *raison d'être.*

Second, referring to goals allows one to define the overall mission of the organization or its parts. Organizations, in this view, have general, overarching goals and smaller subgoals. In effective organizations, the subgoals are related to the overall goals; they form a hierarchy that guides the coordination of individual effort. Goals represent either incremental steps in a longer process (orbiting the earth was a step toward landing on the moon) or components in a complex process (the successful design of landing gears and space suits also contributed to the lunar landing).

Third, knowing an organization's or a program's goals provides a starting place for understanding organizational processes. In the goal attainment view, goals constrain organizational activities. Knowing an organization's goals does not tell you exactly what occurs in the organization. Goals rarely determine, in the absolute sense, organizational behavior. Nevertheless, goals constrain organizational behavior by limiting the variety of acceptable choices and actions. In this way, goals provide guides for action for organization members.

Fourth, as implied above, the goal attainment model of organizations provides a conceptually simple definition of organizational effectiveness. Effectiveness is defined as the extent to which the organization achieves its goals. Answering effectiveness questions may prove difficult. It is often hard, at times impossible, to define clearly goals and measures of goal achievement. But the underlying logic of this approach is simple and clear: organizational effectiveness equals goal achievement. Most evaluations of the various products, processes, and services provided by public organizations are based on this assumption.

The goal achievement approach to organizational effectiveness often leads to additional questions about *efficiency*. If an organization or program does meet its stated objectives, then administrators question whether the success was cost effective, or justified the cost per unit of output—for instance, the cost per pupil in school, or the cost per miles of street paved. Efficiency questions examine the resources needed to provide products or services. A second, more complicated dimension is the question: Are the benefits worth the costs?[1] A job training program that took unemployed, unskilled workers, provided technical education, and found them high-paying jobs would be considered extremely *effective*. If it cost $100,000 for each client, however, it would not be considered *efficient*. The goal is achieved but at too great a cost; it is effective but not efficient.

James Thompson (1967) provides a useful guide or typology for describing the difficulty of evaluating organizational effectiveness by measuring goal achievement. He suggests that two types of information are important: the extent of agreement about the value of the goals and the degree of certainty in how to achieve the goals. Table 3.1 suggests how these two factors alter the possibility of measuring effectiveness by goal achievement. In Cell I, everyone agrees that the goals are important; everyone is relatively certain that knowledge on how the achieve the goals exists. If you know what you want and how to get it, the primary question is one of efficiency or cost-effectiveness. A good example is preventing a well-understood disease such as polio. No one doubts the value of polio prevention, and several good vaccines exist. The effectiveness question centers on what approach reduces the risk for the least cost.

If either goals or means are uncertain, evaluations of program effectiveness must answer additional vexing questions about the appropriate ends and means before the issue of efficiency is examined. For example, few would argue against the goal of reducing the number of homeless living on our city streets, but many do argue

**TABLE 3.1. Uncertainty about Means and Goals and the Evaluation
of Organizational Effectiveness**

Agreement of Goals	Understanding of Means	
	Certain	Uncertain
Certain	I	II
Uncertain	III	IV

(Adapted from Thompson 1967, 87)

about the best way to solve this problem (Cell II); we share a goal but do not agree on the means. Well-understood means but controversial goals present different problems. For example, no one doubts our technical ability to perform abortions, but many argue about the value of abortions (Cell III). In other cases, controversy surrounds both goals and means (Cell IV). For example, many citizens question the use of taxes to support local businesses, and many economists doubt that such incentives spur growth. When either goals or means are uncertain, evaluating goal achievement is more difficult; when both are uncertain, such evaluations become a practical impossibility.

Criticisms of the Goal Attainment Model

Both practical and conceptual problems with the goal model have led observers to question the underlying assumption that organizations are purposeful. The goal model has been the target of three fundamental criticisms—criticisms so strident that several scholars doubt that organizations have goals at all.

Organizations Contain Numerous Goals.   First, critics dispute the view that organizations have single, overriding goals. Large, complex organizations may have broadly defined realms of responsibility or niches, but these niches cannot be easily defined. The State Department is primarily concerned with foreign affairs, but foreign policy often overlaps with domestic economic concerns and defense policy. The police department is charged with fighting crime but also may become deeply involved in public education and helping children cross streets.

These broad niches are defined, in part, by *official goals*—the goals stated in speeches, program descriptions, legislative testimony, and public pronouncements. Official goals often reflect public relations needs and wishful thinking and are only tenuously related to actual activities and choices. *Operative goals* are more realistic. Operative goals are the short-term intentions of programs within a large organization. These goals are linked to specific choices and actions. The official goals of reducing drunk driving may encompass the operative goal of increased arrests.

Within these broadly defined niches and official statements of purpose, complex organizations pursue a multitude of different goals. Critics argue that in contrast to the assumption of the goal attainment model, these various goals rarely add up to overall purpose. Thus, most organizations move in many directions at once. They lack the efficiency and consensus that the goal attainment model implies. Even when there is a sense of direction, organizations move in a disjointed and incremental manner.

Karl Weick (1977, 211–215) compared organizational movement to an octopus: Organizations meander with one leg going this way and another going in another direction. In the process of making small incremental steps, an organization may discover that the preset policy goal is unrealistic or even undesirable. Using this new information they take a slightly different tack and deviate from plans. This meandering raises doubts about relying on goals as criteria for performance. If organizations take small incremental steps and discover new information along the way, effective organizations may, by necessity, deviate from plans (Simon 1981). Holding organizations and programs strictly accountable to out-of-date goals confuses rigidity and blind persistence with effectiveness.

Goal Conflict.   The second criticism grows out of the first. Not only do most organizations have many different goals, but these goals often conflict. Investing effort to pursue one goal often detracts from efforts to pursue another. Goal conflict arises from many sources. Goal conflict occurs between individuals and the organization: Medical doctors worried about contracting AIDS may put their own personal safety over the service goals of their hospital, and some may refuse to treat infected patients. Goal conflict often arises between departments: One department charged with ensuring public health may engage in a constant battle with another in the same agency charged with reducing the costs of health care. Such interdepartmental goal conflicts often emerge during budget battles.

Goal conflicts also arise across levels within organizations: What is paramount to top administrators may be irrelevant to lower-level staff. A common complaint of direct service providers in social service agencies is the endless paperwork. They find all the forms time consuming and irrelevant to their own work with clients. The information gathered may be essential, however, to their supervisors and to planning department personnel who use the records to monitor caseloads and project future needs.

Goals Are Not Related to Behavior.   The first two criticisms of the goal attainment model—organizations contain many and often conflicting goals—do not challenge the importance of goals. They do, however, indicate that the picture of organizations is more complex and fractured than the assumptions of goal attainment theory suggest. The third criticism raises more fundamental doubts about the usefulness of goals in understanding organizations. Numerous organization scholars suggest that the relationship between organizational goals and individual behavior is weak and, in many cases, meaningless. In their view, identifying an organization's goals provides little, if any, information about the organization.

This startling view grew out of research on individuals, particularly that of Daryl Bem (1974) and Philip Zimbardo (1969). A considerable body of psychological research suggests that people rarely develop goals prior to taking action; that when actions do not lead to goal achievement, people tend to invent new goals rather than discontinue their actions (for a review of cognitive dissonance see Wicklund and Brehm 1976); and that when actions are taken without preset goals, people invent explanations (Nisbett and Wilson 1977). These observations suggest that many actions that appear goal directed and highly rational are not. Instead the reasons come *after* the choices, a process called *retrospective rationality* (Weick 1979, 194).

These observations of individuals were reinforced by studies of organizations. After carefully observing top-level managers at work, Henry Mintzberg (1973) found that they rarely engage in goal-directed planning and reflection. Rather, managers react to crises, problems, phone calls, chance encounters, and opportunities. Some of their actions may be purposeful but only in the short term. William McKelvey (1982, 115) suggested that organizations are at best myopically purposeful; they are short sighted, not future oriented. Strategies or general organizational goals emerge out of this crisis-oriented, short-term decision making. Like the individual rationalizations discussed by psychologists, organizations discover their plans by looking back over what they have done.

Charles Perrow (1978) suggests another way that goals are unrelated to behavior. In his view, goals are a mask. Organizations require legitimacy, and in our rational, bureaucratic society, legitimacy is based on statements of purpose. He concludes that the real purpose of most public organizations is to regulate behavior (see also Piven and Cloward 1971), not achieve stated goals, and that measuring effectiveness by assessing goal achievement adds to the delusion.

> But the important point for organization theory is that it is on the basis of the regulatory functions that organizations are judged, not their announced service goals. Wardens are not fired for not rehabilitating prisoners; psychiatric administrators or therapists for not curing the insane; welfare administrators for not getting people to work or mending broken homes or raising their allotments. The criteria [sic] is more likely to be "how many people do you regulate at what cost per person." (p. 109)

To Perrow, goals are the trappings of rational faith worn proudly yet concealing the power struggles and pursuit of self-interest that motivate actual organizational behavior. Planning and goals are, for the most part, an illusion.

Thus, in exploring the limits of the seemingly obvious statement that effective organizations achieve their stated goals, a more complete and realistic picture of organizations emerges. Rather than efficient machines for goal achievement, complex organizations are disjointed, and while they may be purposeful in the short term, their plans do not determine their results.

The multiplicity of organization goals also highlights the ever-present conflict between individuals and units, and across levels in organizations. Organizations are turbulent political arenas. And organizations are places in which individuals and groups act and then try to make sense out of their actions. Rejecting as simplistic the view that effective organizations achieve prespecified goals does not, however, mean that organizational effectiveness is not an important issue. It does mean that models of organizational effectiveness must encompass more than goal attainment.

Organizational Effectiveness Is Multidimensional

Although the simple equation that organizational effectiveness equals achievement of official goals has been discredited, the importance of achieving goals or other predetermined outcome criteria has not been entirely rejected. Organization theorists have turned to examining a wide variety of effectiveness criteria in which the goal achievement approach is one of several dimensions. After reviewing the proliferation of measures of organizational effectiveness, John Campbell (1977) identified thirty conceptually distinct criteria, ranging from profit to job satisfaction and including such apparently conflicting indicators as organizational growth and stability. The numerous effectiveness criteria do fall into several categories.

Outcomes.   The first is the traditional measurement of performance based on outcomes, including goal achievement. Effectiveness criteria within this category vary with the specific type of organization. Minimum competency scores for schools or the number holding jobs after employment training measure effectiveness based on results. Linking results to performance is often difficult, however. Was the increase in competency scores caused by changes in the curriculum or the closing of the private school? Did training or the opening of a new manufacturing plant reduce unemployment? In addition, emphasis on outcomes usually focuses on quantitative measures and stresses narrow factors. When effective schools are measured by scores on standardized tests, other less-quantifiable goals of education are ignored. Despite the conceptual problems with measuring outcomes, the goal achievement model remains an important element in both the theory and measurement of organizational effectiveness.

Adaptation. Questions about the effective achievement of results naturally lead to questions about the organization itself. According to open systems theory, healthy organizations must import resources and adapt to changes in the environment. Organizational effectiveness is the "ability of an organization, in either relative or absolute terms, to exploit its environment in the acquisition of scarce and valued resources" (Yuchtman and Seashore 1967, 898).

In open systems theory, organizational survival, not success in achieving goals, becomes the ultimate criterion of effectiveness. The systems view portrays organizations as living organisms that compete for resources in a changing and dangerous environment. They are not machines designed with a specific purpose. Therefore, flexibility and adaptability, not rigid adherence to goals, are considered essential characteristics of effectiveness. Goals are important to the extent that they contribute to survival needs; most organizations must produce products or services to acquire needed resources.

Clearly an organization that declares bankruptcy or loses government funding because its products or services are inadequate cannot be considered effective. But effective organizations can close down, and many marginal ones endure. The March of Dimes came close to organizational death in the early 1950s. Its primary mission was the treatment and prevention of polio, a disease that was nearly eliminated by medical advances made possible, in part, by the March of Dimes. Its own success threatened its existence, but the March of Dimes survived by adapting—by shifting its focus to other diseases and disabilities.

System Health. The systems view also directs attention to a third dimension of effectiveness. According to open systems theory, organizations must balance production goals with maintenance needs. Organizations that devote all their energy to producing results achieve short-term success but risk long-term collapse. Although the costs of neglecting maintenance is most obvious with equipment—putting off the repair of schools may require costly renovations—the needs of individuals are of greater importance. The biggest investment of most public organizations is in their human resources. Most services are delivered on a person-to-person basis, and most government agencies depend on the commitment and skills of a large work force.

Yet, the human resources of many public organizations are depleted. "Burnout" is epidemic in service organizations, as social workers, teachers, doctors, and others in the helping professions become drained by the emotional demands of their jobs (Cherniss 1980; Jones 1981). Bad working conditions and inadequate pay and benefits provide limited rewards for difficult jobs. And, perhaps most important, the constant public criticism of public employees devalues the intrinsic worth of public sector jobs (see Chapter 7). Attention to human resources is central to effective organizations.

Early research into the human side of organizational effectiveness focused on shaping individual behavior in "organizationally useful directions" (Kahn 1958, 74) and on eliciting commitment and enthusiasm for management goals (Bowers and Seashore 1966). In this view, an effective organization reduces absenteeism and encourages employees to work diligently, creatively, and with others and to contribute to the overall functioning of the organization. Procedures for increasing conformity, commitment, and effort are the cornerstones of contemporary behavioral management theory (Scott and Hart 1979).

More recently attention has shifted to improving the nature of the work itself. Making work more interesting and less monotonous encourages greater involvement. Whether by pay and benefits, improved group processes, or redesign of the work, this approach stresses the importance of the quality of work experience as a key ingredient to organizational effectiveness. Unfortunately, the relationship between these characteristics of individual performance, job satisfaction, and organizational effectiveness remains tenuous (Argyris 1968).

In sum, in contemporary organization theory, organizational effectiveness is a complex, multidimensional problem. As Kirchoff (1977, 437) summarized, "Trying to view organizational effectiveness as a single dimension is much like trying to visualize a cube without depth perception—the result is distortion." Kim Cameron's (1978) study of the effectiveness of several universities incorporates this more complex view. He examined and categorized over 100 measures of organizational effectiveness for nine universities. These included objective student performance scores and the observations of students, faculty, and administrators.

Cameron's findings highlight an important characteristic of effectiveness; it involves tradeoffs among multiple criteria. None of the universities performed consistently well or poorly on all criteria. Universities that stressed student career development scored lower on student academic development. Similarly, universities that stressed faculty satisfaction were less successful in acquiring resources. Each university produced what Cameron called a *distinctive effectiveness profile;* each had its own pattern of performance that reflected its distinctive characteristics.

In later research, Kim Cameron and David Whetten (1981) added a further complication: The effectiveness profiles not only vary among organizations, but the patterns of emphasis on different effectiveness criteria change during the life history of individual organizations. Young, entrepreneurial organizations, for example, stress productivity and adaptability, while established bureaucracies emphasize stability and predictability.

Effectiveness for Whom?

These various dimensions of effectiveness leave out an important question: For whom is the organization effective? Effectiveness criteria always represent someone's values, and any complex organization contains groups that systematically differ in how they define effectiveness. For example, the social worker who considers close contact with clients important will resist caseload increases demanded by the supervisor, who sees effectiveness in terms of costs per client.

Power struggles, bargaining, and conflict over whose definition of effectiveness will dominate organization decision making are common. W. Richard Scott (1977) takes the extreme position that judging organizational effectiveness is nothing more than an exercise in self-interest. We need not go as far as Scott to accept that emphasizing certain dimensions of effectiveness over others has a dramatic effect on the nature of an organization. Identifying the winners and losers in the choices of criteria is an important element in a full understanding of organizational effectiveness. The profiles identified by Cameron are not innate characteristics; they result from decisions to stress certain criteria.

Competing Values Theory.   The conflicts that result in distinctive effectiveness profiles are best captured by the *competing values* theory of organizational effectiveness. Robert Quinn and John Rohrbaugh (1983) suggest that the different models of organizational effectiveness encompass different values which represent positive or desirable characteristics but are in constant tension. For example, few question the value of efficiency, but a single-minded stress on efficiency may exact major losses in staff morale and cohesion. Similarly, emphasizing accountability and control reduces innovation and adaptability. This model suggests that organizational effectiveness is a complex act of balancing competing values—a task further complicated by the facts that different groups in and around organizations are more invested in certain values, and that the importance of different values changes over time (see also Quinn 1988).

Current thinking about organizational effectiveness is well summarized by Richard Hall (1987, 288–296):

1. Organizations face multiple and conflicting environmental constraints . . .
2. Organizations have multiple and conflicting goals . . .
3. Organizations have multiple and conflicting external and internal constituents . . . [and]
4. All organizations have multiple and conflicting time frames.

Hall's repetition of the words "multiple and conflicting" emphasizes the abandonment of the one-dimensional view that organizational effectiveness is the achievement of official goals.[2] This multiple and conflicting view of effectiveness greatly complicates the life of public and private administrators. Like scholars, they must abandon a singular preoccupation with results and must recognize the costs of stressing only one criterion or satisfying one constituency. Administration is a complex balancing act; it is "camping on seesaws" (Hedberg, Nystrom, and Starbuck 1976).

Acknowledging the ever-present conflicts over effectiveness criteria raises another fundamental question: Is organizational effectiveness the ultimate criterion for managerial decisions? Our most deep-seated assumption about modern work organizations, both public and private, is that they exist to accomplish things. Organizations are no longer seen as simple goal achievement devices, but they are still primarily viewed as settings for getting things done. This assumption makes effectiveness, however defined, the ultimate criterion for understanding and managing organizations. Companies introduce fitness or day-care programs not because they are good in themselves but because they improve employee commitment which, in turn, is expected to increase effectiveness.

A growing number of organizational scholars question the centrality of effectiveness. In simplest terms, this alternative view suggests that organizations are primarily social settings that give structure and meaning to the lives of their members. Organizations are only secondarily centers of production. This issue will be addressed in detail in the section of this chapter examining organizational culture. What is important here is to raise the question: Does the great emphasis of scholars and managers on effectiveness, no matter how defined, obscure a great deal about organizations? Karl Weick (1979, 264) ends his book on organization theory with a statement that directly challenges the stress on effectiveness:

> Organizations keep people busy, occasionally entertain them, give them a variety of experiences, keep them off the streets, provide pretexts for storytelling, and allow socializing. They haven't anything else to give.

ORGANIZATIONAL CHANGE

Descriptions of structure capture organizations as in a still photograph, but organizations exist through time. Understanding how they change and, conversely, how they resist change is important. Rapid change infects most aspects of modern life. In 1980 a handful of research organizations relied on microcomputers; in 1990 organizations without them are rare. The computer revolution is but one example of the changes that buffet organizations. New organizations are created while others die. New demands for products and services require adding new divisions. Government regulations outlaw old practices, while removing regulations requires new skills. For government organizations each legislative session brings new demands and different budget priorities.

At times organizational changes are destructive. For example, the U.S. State Department retains scars from the McCarthy investigations of the early 1950s (Warwick 1975). Searching for communist sympathizers, the investigations ruined careers and shattered the foreign service's commitment to independent and forceful reporting. At other times, innovations bring new life to organizations. New ideas, approaches, and employees rejuvenate organizations.

Nevertheless, organizations resist and blunt efforts to change structure, practices, and policies. Formal organizations add predictability to the social world. Employees confidently anticipate a workday, knowing what to expect and what is expected. They know when to arrive, where to go, what to do, and how to behave. Such patterns and routines are necessary to healthy organizations, but they tend to calcify and limit an organization's capacity for change and adaptation. For example, a regulatory organization may be unable to prevent abuse in nursing homes because of the simple rule that every home must be visited once a year. Reducing the number of visits to homes with excellent records of care could permit greater scrutiny of those with records of abuse. But such a minor adjustment to practice may never be considered.

Visits are made annually because they have always been made annually. These routines are called *standard operating procedures* and they often can result in an organization's applying an inappropriate solution in a specific situation. Graham Allison (1971) describes how naval standard operating procedures confounded President Kennedy's efforts to respond to Russian missiles in Cuba.

Thus, organizations are pulled by the opposing forces of change and stability. In the following section, we examine the sources and consequences of organizational change, beginning with James March's analysis of how routine processes produce organizational change. The section then reviews three major schools of thought on organizational change: the strategic management, environmental selection, and life cycle views.

Routine Processes and Organizational Change

Most discussions of organizational change focus on dramatic events, such as a new law establishing a new program. James March (1981) suggests a different view: Organizational changes most commonly result from routine practices and everyday events.

> Most change in organizations results neither from extraordinary organizational processes or forces, nor from uncommon imagination, persistence or skill, but from relatively stable, routine processes that relate organizations to their environment. (p. 564)

March suggests that any theory of organizational change is a theory of "ordinary action," of everyday behavior. This view is paradoxical, since change connotes a break from the routine. March identifies six routine aspects of organizational life that encourage change:

Rule Following.   Following rules or established procedures is a major source of stability and predictability in organizations. Nevertheless, following rules requires the matching of rules and actions to specific events or problems. When the rule fits, the status quo is reinforced. Often, however, the match of the rule to the situation is imperfect. Following rules highlights their limits and leads to changes or refinements in established procedures. A social worker faced with a client with a severe speech problem may force administrators to change the rules defining who is handicapped and therefore eligible for assistance.

Problem Solving.   The underlying process of change involves choosing among alternatives and inventing novel solutions when none seem to work. Most problem-solving efforts follow established procedures or processes, but the ordinary process of working through the details of problem solving can lead to new ideas or approaches. Most organizational innovations are novel solutions to nagging problems.

Learning.   Without learning, which accompanies both rule following and problem solving, all changes are ephemeral. This third routine process is at times the result of trial and error and at times the result of careful study. Learning occurs by watching others or in formal training and education.

Conflict.   Organizational conflict is often considered negative and destructive. Nevertheless, the clash of differing perspectives and interests is an essential source of change. People with different perspectives see problems or issues differently, and these differences often correspond to different roles (see Chapter 5). The interaction of enduring conflicts keeps the organization churning and encourages change. At times, conflicts over policies and practices are temporarily resolved giving one view dominance. Often conflicts are never completely resolved, and the losing parties seek opportunities to push anew for their interpretation of events and preferred solutions.

Contagion.   Organizations also follow fads. An organization installs a computerized management system or experiments with a new approach to providing services. Others copy the innovation, and the change spreads like contagion, March's fifth routine process.

Regeneration.   And finally organizations change through regeneration. New employees are hired bringing a different mix of skills and predispositions. Programs for the disabled will change as counselors trained to encourage independent living replace those accustomed to sheltered workshops. Even equipment replacement can require organizational adjustments. Replacing a large computer with micros often encourages a shift from centralized to decentralized control.

The change processes described by James March do not preclude nor depend on careful planning. He sees organizational change as the result of the interplay of planned or purposeful activity and the creative response to happenstance. As we will shortly discuss, some views of organizational change stress planning while others stress chance. March (1981) emphasizes the importance of small, routine processes in sustaining organizational change. He concludes that,

> within some broad constraints, the adaptiveness of an organization can be managed. Typically, it is not possible to lead an organization in any arbitrary direction that might be desired, but it is possible to influence the course of events by managing the process of change, and particularly by stimulating or inhibiting predictable complications and anomalous dynamics. (p. 575)

Strategic Change

March emphasizes the importance of routine, ordinary processes as sources of organizational change, but he does not deny the possibility of large-scale, planned change. Planned or strategic change has traditionally been an important element in the theory and management of business organizations (Chandler 1962). Strategic change involves the conscious, deliberate effort to examine the organization and its environment (Bryson 1989). Strategic planners carefully chart trends in the demand for products or services, technological innovations that either improve or make obsolete current products or services, and problems and strengths of the organization and its competitors. This analysis is the foundation for judgments about the future, about what the organization should do to adjust to the changes that surround it. These strategic plans are primarily the concern of top managers and planning or forecasting departments. In many business firms strategic plans are often kept secret from other organizations and lower-level employees. Workers in a textile mill may learn of a long-anticipated plant closing only after receiving their two-week layoff notice.

Strategic management addresses the fundamental question: What should this organization be doing? It also broadens the time frame, asking, What should this organization be doing *in the future?* Strategic management involves monitoring and comparing two types of information: information about the organization's current resources, competencies, and problems; and information about future changes in the organization's environment. A management information system that channels information about organizational functioning up to top decision makers is one of the strategic manager's essential tools. And, finally, strategic management requires examining three broad categories of choices: (1) strategic options, (2) structural options, and (3) performance options (Child 1972).

Strategic Options.   Strategic options are the fundamental choices about the nature of the organization and its general purpose. Although most government organizations have relatively fixed overall missions—a police department cannot sell off its street surveillance division because of poor cost-effectiveness—public organizations do make choices about the scope and nature of their services. In addition, two public agencies may compete for different services. A health department may compete with a social service agency over the responsibility to inspect nursing homes. Whoever captures the nursing homes inspection market can expect a large and consistent budget allocation.

In his study of changes in the tobacco industry after the first surgeon general's report linking smoking with disease, Robert Miles (1982) described three major strategic options applicable to many organizations.

Domain defense involves keeping competitors and other threats from challenging the organization's core operations. Public school principals who denounce massive spending for highways are probably not against new roads; they are simply defending against threats to their own budgets. Domain defense also involves threats to an organization's legitimacy. Organizational leaders are very sensitive to questions about the value of their services or products. The tobacco industry reacted to the surgeon general's report by asserting that it has not been proven that cigarette smoking causes lung cancer and other diseases, only that there is a correlation between these and other factors, such as air pollution and heredity.

Domain offense involves entering new domains of products or services and requires growth or expansion. For example, federal funding for new programs, such as community development block grants, encouraged numerous local governments to set up neighborhood improvement programs. Universities sensing growing student interest in marketable skills invest more heavily in business schools and computer science departments.

The most successful domain offense strategies involve expansion in areas of established strengths. A liberal arts college will be less able to take advantage of increased federal funding for technology research, such as supercomputers, than will a major research university. The matching of opportunities to organizations is an essential element in strategy formation.

Domain creation is the most difficult strategic option and requires developing new areas of services of products. In business firms, domain creation usually follows major technical advances. The invention of the photocopier and microcomputer created entire new industries. Examples of domain creation in public organizations are rare, but one example is public preschool education. Legislation during Lyndon Johnson's presidency provided funding for preschools for underprivileged children. This policy innovation created a domain for programs like Head Start which spread throughout the country.

Structural Options.   The second major area for strategic planning involves rearranging the internal organizational structure and processes. Reorganizations are common in public organizations and receive a special focus at the end of this section. Structural adjustment involves rearranging the organizational chart, the scope of responsibilities, and the flow of resources. The process of tinkering and at times overhauling the structural framework of an organization preoccupies public and private managers.

These reorganizations are strategic when designed to assure that organizational functioning matches the strategic plans. Structural adjustment is important in implementing strategic plans. For example, a hospital that forecasts a reduction in the demand for inpatient treatment may develop a strategy of increasing outpatient care. The success of this strategy may depend, in part, on rearranging the management structure of the hospital to give greater importance and more resources to community programs. They may be moved out of the basement and into the new wing. The director of community services may need a place on the management team. In other words, the structure of the organization must correspond to the strategic plan.

Performance Options.   The third major planned option involves adjustments of performance expectations and evaluations. Implementing new plans requires changes in both employee behavior and the mix in types of employees. The most effective way to alter current employee behavior is to change the criteria by which they are evaluated. A university attempting to build its reputation on research stresses publication over teaching in promotion decisions. Although not everyone conforms to performance criteria, changing criteria leads over time to general shifts in behavior.

Over a longer time period, strategic plans often require hiring a different type of employee. Employees are a primary resource of public organizations, and altering the relative mix of types of employees is an essential means of implementing plans. Hiring economists rather than lawyers or computer operators rather than social workers will profoundly alter the nature of an organization. Robert Scott (1967) studied the history of sheltered workshops for the blind. When the workshops were established in the early part of the twentieth century, they emphasized service goals. During this period, the programs were often run by social workers. During the 1930s and 1940s, changes in government policy required the workshops to become more self-sufficient. Business managers replaced social workers as directors. A change in strategy required a shift in managerial skills.

Public Agencies and Strategic Change.   Legal mandates and civil service constraints limit a public organization's choice of domain and freedom to alter structure and to hire, fire, and promote workers. Nevertheless, strategic choice or planned change play an important role in public organizations. Barton Weschler and Robert Backoff (1986) examined four state agencies and found evidence of a variety of strategic orientations. A large established agency carefully defended its domain against intruders. A different agency, the Department of Mental Retardation and Developmental Disabilities, responded to the general move away from institutional care by restructuring its services and entering new community-based service domains. These actions illustrate the importance of strategic change. Had this department retained its emphasis on institutional care, its funding and legitimacy would have declined. Other agencies would have expanded or been created to fill the need for community services. Strategic change proved essential.

Most of the literature on strategic change emphasizes the importance of top-level decision makers. They are the ones who supposedly glean information about the organization and changes in the environment. Top leaders devise and implement strategies. While top-level decision makers have an important role in strategic change, Henry Mintzberg and Alexandra McHugh's (1985) research indicates that lower-level organizational actors have an important role as well. Mintzberg suggests that there is always a gap between intended and realized strategies—between the strategies worked out by the top decision makers and the strategies carried out by those farther down in the organization.

As our previous discussion of goals suggested, strategies are not devised and then implemented without alteration. In the process of implementation, *deliberate strategies* are mixed with *emergent strategies*. Emergent strategies are smaller scale decisions based on specific problems. They are the answer to the questions of how do I solve this problem, deal with this client, evaluate this employee, and so on. Emergent or grass-roots strategies result from the work of lower-level employees. *Realized strategies,* then, are the mix of deliberate, top-down and emergent, bottom-up choices. As Mintzberg and McHugh (1985, 196) conclude,

> No organization can function with strategies that are always and purely emergent, that would amount to a complete abdication of will and leadership, not to mention conscious thought. But none can likewise function with strategies that are always and purely deliberate, that would amount to an unwillingness to learn, a blindness to whatever is unexpected.

Chance and Environmental Selection

Scholars sharing the *natural selection* or *population ecology* views have a radically different theory of organizational change (Hannan and Freeman 1977; Aldrich 1979). They acknowledge that planned change is possible but consider it unlikely. These scholars suggest that except during an organization's early turbulent years, the forces of stability, such as the characteristics of bureaucracy discussed in Chapter 2, overwhelm the pressures for change. Rigidity and resistance to change are more prevalent in large, complex organizations than are flexibility and adaptability. Most of the time predictability and stability are desired and therefore rewarded organizational characteristics (Hannan and Freeman 1984). In this view, individual organizations that accomplish strategic changes that go beyond cosmetic adjustments to structure and processes are the exception, not the rule.

Instead, change occurs in the mix of different types within the population of organizations. This view makes strong parallels to biological evolution (Aldrich 1979). The physical makeup of individual organisms does not change to accommodate to different or changed environments. Evolution does not depend on strategic planning. Those organisms that are better suited produce more offspring, while those that are less fit are reduced in numbers. Thus, the species evolves or changes, not the individual.

The population of organizations changes in a similar pattern. While individual organizations, at least firmly established ones, are unlikely to change significantly their structure, activities, and orientations, organizations that are no longer well suited to current circumstances will, according to this view, die off or decline in numbers. An example is the diners that populated the nation's roadsides in the 1950s. Many diners served good, local food, but despite myths about truckstops, the quality was unpredictable. As more and more people traveled farther from home, consistency became more important than local color. Now, only forty years later, international chains of fast-food restaurants serve the same hamburger around the world. Predictability, not local flavor, predominates, and a diner was recently installed as a relic at the Smithsonian Museum in Washington, D.C.

Another example is the Health Maintenance Organization (HMO). Thirty years ago, most people relied on a family doctor for routine care and on hospitals for emergencies and major health care problems. Today health care relies more on technology than bedside manner, insurance policies and not individuals pay the bills, and patients with major health problems fly to major medical centers to get the most advanced care. Local hospitals and individual family doctors as a form of service delivery are greatly threatened by these changes in the health care environment. HMOs and other group practices can, on the other hand, take advantage of these changes. Organization scholars taking the natural selection point of view would underscore that changes in the environment, not insightful management, brought about these changes.[3] The best strategic plan may not slow the decline of a local hospital while an HMO may flourish with little foresight.

Herbert Kaufman (1985) recently summarized this view of organizational change in *Time, Chance, and Organization*. Kaufman makes the following arguments.

Organizations both form and dissolve. Although it seems rather obvious that organizations are created and disband, this assumption is not as simple as it seems. After the 1917 Russian Revolution, the despised secret police of the Tsar was disbanded, but the new Soviet secret police, first the Chekka and now the KGB, use the same building and essentially the same methods. Is this an example of a new or merely renamed organization? On the other hand, some organizations, such as the British Office of the Exchequer, are centuries old and have changed significantly in form and function while retaining the same name. It is, however, reasonable to say that people do form an organization when they establish and maintain an identity, boundary, processes, and relationships; similarly, organizations die when these features are no longer maintained.

Organizations protect their identity, boundaries, processes, and relationships through growth. Large organizations develop the resources and command the attention of the public and are, thereby, protected from external threats. Many thousands of businesses fold each year. Large organizations have the resources to endure temporary losses. Moreover, when large corporations, such as Lockheed or Chrysler, have financial problems, government help may ensure their survival. But growth creates problems as well. With growth comes greater organization complexity and the need for highly predictable processes. Complexity and predictability reduce flexibility and the organization's ability to respond to rapid changes in the environment.

The environment of organizations is in constant flux. The environment of public organizations is difficult to describe because that environment is both immense and complex. The environment can logically include everything—political and natural entities as well as other organizations. Political turmoil in the Middle East can cause oil prices to rise, and people waiting in gas lines are less likely to support efforts of the Environmental Protection Agency to protect the wilderness from oil drilling. The most important aspect of the environment for organizations consists of other organizations with which they have direct cooperative or competitive relationships (Wamsley and Zald 1973). For public organizations, clients' organizations, legislative bodies, funding agencies, interest groups, and competing agencies are the most important elements in the environment. (See Chapter 9 for a further discussion of this aspect of administration.)

Organizational environments also differ in levels of resources and rate of change. Numerous typologies have been tried to describe the effects of different environments on organizational adaptation. Dess and Beard (1984) suggest three variables: munificence, dynamism, and complexity.

Munificence is the relative richness of resources. For public organizations, changes in the membership of legislatures can radically change the resources available. The environment also varies in the rate and predictability of change, which is the second characteristic: *dynamism. Complexity* refers to the number and concentration of different types of organizations within the same environment. For example, the organizational environment for preschool programs includes many different types of organizations—co-ops, Montessori schools, religious schools, and small in-house baby sitting—competing for the same children. The organizational environment for primary education is less complex since standardized public schools have a near monopoly in most communities.

Survival pressures on organizations, then, vary with different characteristics of the environment. Rapidly changing environments providing limited resources and populated with various competing organizations will have more organizational births and deaths. Predictable environments with few competitors encourage organizational longevity. A well-managed preschool providing creative and responsive programs is less likely to endure than a poorly run, unresponsive public school; they operate in different environments.

The environmental perspective suggests that managers can do little, if anything, to guide their organizations. Chance, not strategy, determines success. Alan Meyer's (1982) research suggests that the environmental and strategic management views are not as conflicting as they appear. He observed the effects of an unanticipated doctors' strike on several hospitals. Even though several of the managers identified problems with the way the hospitals operated, the hospitals, like most organizations, resisted change. Established procedures and routines blunted efforts to reform.

The strike was, in Meyer's term, an *environmental jolt* that forced the organizations to break with the routine. The temporary disruption threatened the survival of the hospitals but also offered opportunities for the more strategic-minded administrators to implement long-considered reforms. Ironically, the hospitals that entered the strike with the greatest financial resources merely expended their reserves and returned to old routines after the strike. They were poorer but otherwise unchanged. Other hospitals used the strike as an opportunity to cut back on declining programs and introduce changes that were more adaptive to the general trends in the hospital environment. Strategy was successful when it encouraged the opportunistic use of unanticipated events.

Organizational Life Cycles

A final perspective on organizational change suggests that organizations go through predictable changes over their life histories. The environmental perspective corresponds to biological evolution: Change occurs by adaptation and differential survival in a threatening environment. The life-cycle approach is based on the analogy to the predictable stages of individual development and change during one's life span (Kimberly and Miles 1981).

Like individuals, most organizations begin small with lots of energy. The largest multinational corporations of today had their starts, with few exceptions, as small businesses founded by an entrepreneur or inventor. Henry Ford, Thomas Edison, and Stephen Jobs are all part of organizational folk history. Although less dramatic, public organizations often begin as small, community organizations. Even the Department of Defense began with a few generals advising the president. These early years are marked by great energy; workers at all levels devote time and commitment well beyond expectations. This is the period of greatest danger, and a large proportion of new organizations do not survive their founders. This phenomenon is called *the liability of newness* (Stinchcombe 1965).

If an organization is successful, it grows beyond the founders' abilities to control every action, or it lives past the founders' tenure. The organization then enters a productive middle age. Increased size and complexity require greater structure and routine. The organization loses some of its vigor and capacity for rapid change, but it gains considerable predictability. At this point, the organization typically becomes more bureaucratic.

As the process of growth with the accompanying complexity and bureaucracy continues, an organization may lose its ability to respond to changes in the environment. A large university with many departments will find it more difficult to adjust to demands for a new curriculum than will a smaller, newer college. These predictable forces of stagnation are the basis for the environmentalists' doubts about the impact of strategic management. Therefore, older organizations may eventually enter into dotage, decline, and eventual death. At other times, shifts in the environment of organizations may greatly reduce the resources available to groups of organizations, forcing even the adaptable into decline (Hambrick and D'Aveni 1989).

In the 1980s, many public organizations faced dramatic resource erosion. In many cases, funds did not keep pace with costs. In others, budgets were actually cut. In a few, programs were ended. The bankruptcy of New York City, taxpayer revolts, and the election of fiscal conservatives threatened scores of public organizations. Charles H. Levine (1978) writes that managing decline presents novel and extremely difficult problems for managers.

During periods of growth, organizations enjoy at least the promise of new resources. New resources give administrators freedom. Without expanding resources, hard choices are required: To fund new programs, old ones must be trimmed; many legitimate demands for services must be ignored. And, given the political context of public management decisions, cutback decisions must often give greater weight to powerful and vocal citizen or special interest groups. Cutting welfare is easier than cutting loans to college students. Therefore, decline widens social cleavages and threatens general social consensus.

We can learn much by recognizing the predictable process of life-cycle change in organizations, but we must be careful not to carry this, or any other, analogy too far. Despite the promise of exercise enthusiasts, human aging is irreversible (although it can be slowed down). Even if the number of successful organizational rebirths are rare, organizations can change and start anew. Moreover, the life span of organizations is not fixed; many endure for centuries (e.g., the Catholic church). Finally, we must not equate either survival or longevity with effectiveness. As we discussed previously, organizational effectiveness cannot be separated from value judgments. We may marvel at the longevity of an abusive insane asylum and bemoan the closing of a caring group home. Organization theory may help us understand their differential survival rate. But labeling endurance *effective* is misleading.

ORGANIZATIONAL CULTURE OR MEANING SYSTEMS

The term *organization* usually brings to mind tangible dimensions: an office building, an organizational chart, specific individuals and groups, products or services. Previous discussions of structure, effectiveness, change, and conflict focused on these aspects. There are, however, other, less tangible dimensions to organizations. Organizations are cultural and meaning systems as well as places for work. Feelings and emotions as well as purpose are important to work life (Van Maanen and Kunda 1989).

The "where do you work?" question that quickly follows most introductions hints at the importance of organizations in providing meaning to our lives. The despair of the unemployed goes deeper than financial worries; many feel lost, without significance. Where you work, what you do, your profession or rank, and other dimensions of work life give focus to much of contemporary life. Andrew Pettigrew (1979, 574) directs our attention to this dimension of organizational life: "In the pursuit of our everyday tasks and objectives, it is all too easy to forget the less rational and instrumental, the more expressive social tissue around us that gives those tasks meaning."

Viewing work organizations as cultural or meaning systems changes our understanding of modern social organization. Contemporary social thought generally accepts the view that modern life is characterized by a sharp distinction between work and play, the rational and emotional, and the everyday or mundane and the sacred or esthetic. At the turn of the century, Emile Durkheim (1915), a French sociologist, suggested that in so-called primitive, nonindustrialized societies the everyday aspects of life, such as getting and preparing food, were imbued with sacred or mystical explanations and meaning. In his view and that of most social thinkers who followed, the compartmentalization of modern life relegated the richly symbolic aspects of life to religious and artistic realms. The work world was reserved for the practical side of life.

This view has begun to change (Stull, Maynard-Moody, and Mitchell 1988). Contemporary organization theorists describe organizations as held together by shared meaning as well as common purpose. Management best sellers, such as *In Search of Excellence* (Peters and Waterman 1982), as well as scholarly journals (for example, see Jelinck, Smricich, and Hirsch 1983) stress the importance of organizational culture. These works have examined the influence of culture on structure, effectiveness, and change in organizations. Founders and entrepreneurs emerge as mythic heroes. Bureaucrats and executives act as tribal leaders: They tell stories, repeat myths, and stage rites and ceremonials. In this view, contemporary work organizations, public and private, are not only places of production; they are also sites rich with symbols. The symbolic and cultural dimensions of organizations are increasingly viewed as essential to understanding individual organizations and their role in society.

Defining Organizational Culture

The concept of culture, however, is difficult to define. One reason is that the term has meaning on a wide variety of levels. Culture is used to distinguish groups with different religious, historical, and national experiences. Despite similar work and procedures, police departments in Japan, Germany, and India differ greatly. When comparing organizations in different nations, these cultural differences are extremely important. For example, offering a small gift to a policeman may be considered corruption in one nation and a sign of respect in another.

At another level, individual organizations are properly viewed as "minisocieties" (Morgan 1986, 121) with their own histories, beliefs, and norms. As illustrated in the case presented in Chapter 2, the norms of the State Department for caution and the National Security Council for bold action distinguished the two organizations. An individual being transferred from one to the other would likely experience the kind of culture shock felt when one moves to a foreign country.

Further narrowing our focus, large complex organizations include numerous subgroups, each with their own subcultures. Edgar Schein (1985) writes that culture formation is best understood at this narrow group or subcultural level. Focusing on small groups allows us to see how cultures form and endure. At this level, you can observe how culture is linked to the actions and beliefs of specific individuals. Organizations differ widely on the number and variety of different subcultures (Van Maanen and Barley 1983). We may properly speak of an organizational culture when there is only one or one clearly dominant subculture. In other instances it is more useful to think of organizations as multicultural.

Viewed from the group perspective, organizational cultures are a set of shared assumptions about the nature of problems and solutions that face a group. William Renner, the vice-chairman of the Aluminum Company of America, offers an excellent definition of organizational culture:

> Culture is the shared values and behavior that knit a community together. It's the rules of the game; the unseen meaning between the lines in the rulebook that assures unity. (quoted in Kilmann 1984, 92)

This set of shared but often unspoken assumptions that make up a culture or subculture are rarely deliberately examined. In fact, the members of any culture may not recognize the assumptions that guide their actions.

If organizational culture develops without deliberate guidance, how does culture form? In Schein's (1985) view, group or organizational culture forms in response to "(1) survival in and adaptation to the external environment and (2) integration of its internal processes to ensure the capacity to continue to survive and adapt" (p. 51). A galvanizing crisis or persistent problem forces a group to respond. The group's shared assumptions grow out of this joint problem solving. They develop approaches and ways of thinking about problems and questions that appear to work, and these assumptions are handed down to new group members. Thus, with time these assumptions determine how problems are perceived and what solutions are considered. Group cultures coalesce as specific approaches to problems pass from one generation to another. Like learning a difficult sport, culture forms through conscious effort but quickly becomes ingrained.

For example, police on the streets are constantly faced with difficult and subjective judgments in distinguishing dangerous from harmless offenders. Their lives may depend on such accurate snap judgments. Their police academy training and the rule book will offer specific advice, but young recruits are also "shown the ropes" by experienced officers who teach the street wisdom of the police culture. These informal rules include lessons on how to act as well as cues to distinguish danger. These cultural rules may differ significantly from the official rules and may include many unspoken and negative assumptions, such as norms that encourage police officers to harass blacks in a white neighborhood. Even negative norms commonly serve some purpose for those within the subculture. These norms often endure across many generations of group members and prove exceedingly difficult to change.

The intergenerational character of organizational culture is extremely important. The topic of socialization will be examined in the next chapter, but we should stress here that the passing of cultural assumptions from one generation of employees to another is an important ingredient in the predictability and stability of organizations. A research team led by the second author examined the rise, long dominance, and eventual fall of a particular subculture within a public bureaucracy (Maynard-Moody, Stull, and Mitchell 1986). The values and mode of action of a charismatic founder became part of the character of the organization. These cultural assumptions guided the organization for over eighty years through a turbulent century—the years between 1900 and 1985 span radical changes in the role of government—and numerous changes in personnel. The persistence of subcultural assumptions provides not only relatively fixed interpretations and explanations of organizational actions, "but also norms and values that proclaim to system members the rightness of certain beliefs and practices over others" (Trice and Beyer 1984, 654).

Cultural Artifacts

The evidence of culture is found in many aspects of organizational life. Office *gossip* and *stories* often contain important messages regarding proper behavior. Many organizational stories retell events behind conflicts and leading up to promotions or firing. The story told a newcomer about the time a politically active outsider was promoted over a diligent insider communicates more information about personnel practices than the official handbook.

Harrison Trice and Janice Beyer (1984) identify the expressive side of many organizational acts. For example, hiring a consultant to run a retreat for top management is a "rite of renewal." The office Christmas party serves important social functions as a "rite of integration." These *rites* are often condemned as wastes of time—accountants tally the lost work hours—but cultural acts express important values to organizational members. They are the glue that holds groups and organizations together.

Recognizing the importance of organizational culture has implications for understanding organizational change. Although cultures and subcultures do adapt to changing environments, they are generally a conservative force in organizations. Cultural assumptions can blind organizational members to important and novel dimensions of issues or problems. People rarely recognize and examine the assumptions that underlie their actions, according to Chris Argyris (1980). Conscious efforts to change cultural assumptions are difficult to implement; these assumptions are both hidden and ingrained. And when successful, challenges to assumptions can prove destructive. Denying cultural assumptions can split the social atom, releasing destructive forces that may greatly damage the organization.

REORGANIZATION: ORGANIZATION THEORY IN PRACTICE

The various dimensions of organization theory presented in this chapter are evident in one of the more common events in public organizations, the periodic reorganization. As we mentioned in the section on structural options, reorganizations are frequent and significant. Like a car that is running well, the inner working of an organization receives little routine attention when it is functioning smoothly. Making sure that adequate resources are available and that products and services are provided preoccupies public managers. But when the car breaks down, attention shifts to its inner workings. Reorganizations are the organizational equivalent of a trip to the repair shop.

In public organizations, reorganizations are common at all levels of government. Most organizations are in a state of constant flux. Individual departments and agencies at the federal, state, and local levels are continually reshuffled. Programs expand or contract, informal patterns of relationships develop, and new functions evolve. This low level of continual change leads to a widening gap between the formal and actual organizational structure: The formal structure becomes a wardrobe that no longer fits.

Although reorganizations are highly varied—some involve minor adjustments to individual departments, others the creation of entire new organizations—they share common traits. *First, they are based on the assumption that changing the formal structure will improve organizational performance.* Reorganizations testify to the serious consideration given the organizational chart. They express the fundamental belief that altering reporting relationships and functional responsibilities can lead to improved effectiveness.

Reorganizations may involve breaking large departments into several smaller ones to clarify programs and create more manageable spans of control. Then, several years later, the next reorganization may consolidate programs back into larger units to trim bureaucratic sprawl and augment accountability. Regardless of the ebb and flow of structure, reorganizations are evidence of the managerial belief that structural arrangements matter. Improved organizational effectiveness is the rationale for changes, and the espoused model of effectiveness applied to most reorganizations is the simple goal model. Reorganizations tend to sever informal ties and clarify formal responsibilities even at some cost in flexibility and freedom.

Second, in public organizations, reorganizations are periodic. They occur in relatively set patterns usually following elections. Elected and appointed officials inaugurate their terms by trying to gain control over the organizations responsible to them. Reorganizations are exercises in organizational power. They are opportunities for those with formal authority to reshape, however temporarily, the inner workings of the organizations. As Donald Warwick (1975) found in his study of the reorganization of the State Department, once the reorganization process is over, those lower down in the organization begin to reassert their preferences. The evolution of the structure of an organization has a life of its own, but formal reorganizations underscore the power of those at the tops of hierarchies.

Third, reorganizations are highly symbolic events. Decades of research into the effects of reorganization have failed consistently to document objective improvements in effectiveness or efficiency. But as the second author (Maynard-Moody, Stull and Mitchell 1986) found, reorganizations are rich cultural events that communicate the status of groups and the informal structure. Reorganizations are dramas with similarities to other organizational rites and ceremonials (Stull, Maynard-Moody and Mitchell 1988). Rearranging the organizational chart and promoting some individuals while overlooking others communicates to organization members and key constituents the status of certain programs and values. For example, President Carter reorganized the Department of Health, Education, and Welfare, creating a new Department of Education. This change did not dramatically alter education policy, but it did communicate the importance of education issues and education constituencies to his administration. Ronald Reagan promised, a promise unfulfilled, to eliminate the new department to underscore his disdain for bureaucracy.

Thus reorganizations are like most organizational events: They are complex and must be understood at a number of different levels. Questions about organizational structure, effectiveness, change, and cultures are tightly bound up in single events. For the scholar or the public administrator, organizational events are more complex than our theories or analyses.

SUMMARY

This chapter examined organizational effectiveness, change, and culture. Organizational effectiveness proves more complex than merely achieving stated goals. Rather than efficient machines for goal achievement, complex organizations are disjointed, and while they may be purposeful in the short term, their plans do not determine their results. Contemporary organization theory sees organizational effectiveness as a complex, multidimensional problem that takes into account both organizational adaptations and system health. In addition, organizational effectiveness always reflects competing values.

Organizations are also pulled between change and stability needs. James March suggests that most organizational changes result from routine processes rather than grand designs. Strategic planning or the continual monitoring and comparing of information about organizational capacities and environmental threats and opportunities is, according to some scholars, an important source of change. Top managers in public and private organizations spend considerable effort in guiding their organizations. The effectiveness of planned change is challenged, however, by scholars sharing the natural selection or population ecology perspective. This theory of change suggests that individual organizations rarely change but the relative mix of types of organizations in the population does change as old forms diminish and new ones, that are more suited to a changed environment, flourish. The observation that organizations develop through a series of life-cycle stages was also discussed.

This chapter also describes organizations as cultural and meaning systems as well as places of work. Contemporary organization theorists describe organizations as held together by shared meaning as well as common purpose. The concept of organizational culture is difficult to define, in part because culture exists on a variety of levels, from large global units—Western culture, for example—to the work group. In general, culture refers to shared and taken-for-granted assumptions that are passed from one generation to another. The cultural perspective suggests that many organizational events, from Christmas parties to reorganizations, are highly symbolic events that are important for what they communicate to organizational members rather than what they accomplish.

CASE STUDY: THE REORGANIZATION OF THE KANSAS DEPARTMENT OF HEALTH AND ENVIRONMENT

In 1983, Barbara Sabol was appointed secretary of the Kansas Department of Health and Environment (KDHE).[4] Early in her tenure, she initiated a reorganization that generated two years of turmoil. On the surface, the reorganization attempted to change this large, complex agency to improve effectiveness. Structural alterations are important strategic options in public organizations, but the efforts to change also revealed a conflict of cultures. Although reorganizations—sometimes trimming, other times elaborating the organizational structure—were common throughout KDHE's 100-year history, the 1983 reorganization was unique. Previous reorganizations involved minor adjustments to structure as the department grew or took on new tasks, but reorganizations prior to 1983 left the same group in control of the agency. From 1904 to 1983, the department was dominated by a subculture with roots back to the department's founder.

Although not the health department's first secretary, Dr. S. J. Crumbine was the founder of the modern department. Secretary from 1904 to 1923, Crumbine's primary legacy was an organizational philosophy and approach to solving the state's public health problems. Crumbine's highly visible public health pamphlets repeated such slogans as "Dare to do it different." To fight cholera, he armed troops of Boy Scouts with fly swatters ("Are you a swatter or a quitter?") and had the sidewalks of the capital paved with bricks admonishing "Don't spit on the sidewalk." (One can only imagine what this rather wild man with an extravagant waxed mustache would have tried in the era of AIDS: free condoms at the Fourth of July parade?) A true muckraker, he published lists of companies that sold adulterated and spoiled food and examined drugs and remedies in his labs, often at his own expense. He fought railroads, meat packers, farmers, politicians, and anyone who stood in the way of his public health campaigns. During this formative stage in the organization's life history, organizational norms were established that stressed freedom from political interference, the innate power of science, and a commitment to do whatever was needed without regard for the political consequences.

In 1974 a major structural reorganization occurred: The department became a cabinet-level agency within the executive branch of state government. Prior to 1974, an appointed board of health insulated the department from direct political influence; earlier the department reported to this board, not the governor and state legislature. Initially this profound change in organizational structure was hardly felt within the agency. This was, in part, because the first secretary of the reorganized department was a long-term employee with strong allegiance to the organization's traditional values. But this structural change exposed the department to an increasingly turbulent political environment.

Over the next decade, growing concern about environmental pollution and the regulation of nursing homes brought the department into conflict with legislators and interest groups. In 1983, the governor appointed a secretary who, for the first time in the department's history, was an outsider to both the agency and its dominant subculture. Secretary Barbara Sabol had held top-level positions in state and federal bureaucracies and placed a high priority on relations with elected officials. Within months of taking office, the new secretary ordered a major reorganization.

This reorganization altered the organizational chart: Two offices that existed previously as support services became divisions headed by political appointees, and eighteen bureaus were reduced to eight. This reduction, except in one case, was based on consolidating bureaus under new bureau managers. Nevertheless, nearly all of the original eighteen bureaus remained as intact programs with a new layer of middle management added to the department's hierarchy.

The 1983 reorganization, like most, was presented as a strategic plan for organizational change. It promised to increase efficiency and improve responsiveness to elected officials and citizens. The reorganization was described as necessary to bring the department more in line with the policy goals of the governor. The terms *efficiency* and *responsiveness* are often used to justify administrative reorganizations—who can argue with these values?—but they just as often obscure the conflicts and resistance to change common in most organizations.

The reorganization opened up all management positions, and position descriptions were rewritten to emphasize managerial, not technical, skills. Individuals who had held key administrative positions, some for many years, were encouraged to reapply but none were guaranteed their old jobs. In the end, three of the four division directors were new or very recent employees. The bureau manager positions were filled with a mixture of insiders and outsiders, but no one who was strongly identified with previous administrations retained a position of authority. Many of the old guard, who were later referred to as "the malcontents," were given jobs with little formal authority. Thus, under the guise of impersonal alterations of the organizational chart and promotions solely based on qualifications, a coup was staged. This coup was politically bloody. The old guard fought hard to retain their positions of influence. They leaked to the press distorted accounts, rallied sympathetic interest groups among the regulated industries, and courted legislators. They lost no opportunity to make life hard for the new leaders.

Although those working in KDHE generally agreed on the events that transpired during the reorganization, their interpretations of the meanings of these events and actions differed markedly. The interpretations of events clustered into two identifiable groups: the Crumbine subculture who were guardians of the established values and beliefs and the Sabol subculture who represented change. These groups were not defined by status within the organization; both included a range from top management to clerk-typists. What distinguished the groups was their assumptions about the organization, its work, and core values.

Especially instructive were the two groups' views of the reasons for the reorganization. Proponents of KDHE's reorganization argued for "maximum accountability to the [secretary] as the representative of the people." Opponents decried the interference of "political hacks" over "technically qualified personnel." The incoming Sabol subculture saw KDHE as a stale, overly bureaucratic organization run by people promoted beyond their capability and concerned only with defending their organizational turf. The outgoing Crumbine subculture saw the reorganization as a ruse. They complained that highly skilled, committed employees were replaced by "pure bureaucrats" and saw the structural changes as adding needless layers of middle management. Each denounced the other as bureaucratic; each attached different meaning to the epithet.

In addition, members of the two subcultures differed in their interpretations of the reasons for and meanings of the new hiring process. Both groups recognized the emphasis of administrative over technical skills, but the Sabol subculture pointed to the value of trained administrators in management jobs while the Crumbine subculture lamented the downgrading of experience and expertise. The incoming subculture viewed responsiveness to elected officials as a central value and defined sound policy in terms of legislative intent. To the old guard, relations with politicians were a necessary evil. For them good policies meant the technically correct response to the situation regardless of the political consequences; technically correct policies were, in their view, responsive to the long-term interests of citizens.

The new leaders had different views of management efficiency as well. Budgets and standard operating procedures became sacrosanct, and all internal communication strictly adhered to the "chain of command." This view differed sharply from the Crumbine subculture who boasted of using money for important, but not budgeted, projects. Working relationships and communication lines were informal; they took pride in the lack of formal procedures within the agency. For the Crumbine subculture cutting red tape and bypassing the chain of command defined efficiency. In reorganizations, as with all organizational changes, finding that different groups attach different meanings to the same concepts underscores the importance of examining the cultural dimension of organizations.

Discussion Questions

1. Evaluate this reorganization from each of the major definitions of organizational effectiveness. What do we learn from each perspective? What important points does each theory leave out?
2. In what ways did this reorganization result from strategic planning? From chance events?

3. What does the longevity of the Kansas Department of Health and Environment tell us about organizational change?
4. Chart the various life stages of the Kansas Department of Health and Environment.
5. What does the 1983 reorganization reveal about organizational culture?

NOTES

1. Cost-effectiveness analysis computes the costs per unit of output, whereas cost-benefit analysis attempts to assign a dollar value to each unit of output so that a cost-benefit ratio can be computed. If the ratio is greater than one, the program is said to be cost-beneficial. For example, if the benefits for a job-training program are valued at $1 million and the costs of the training are $500,000, the benefit-cost ratio is $1,000,000/$500,000 or 2. See Chapter 11 for a more complete discussion.
2. A parallel development in program evaluation is called "stakeholder" evaluation; in this form of evaluation a number of different stakeholders' views are recognized as being the appropriate basis for evaluation even if their views are not all the same and are in conflict. See Chapter 11 for a discussion of this.
3. Of course, there was a mixture of insightful management and government policy as well as changes in the environment that led to the development of HMOs. Thus, any theory about organizational change that stresses one factor is likely to be only partially correct.
4. The case description is based on Maynard-Moody and Stull (1987).

CHAPTER 4

Organizational Behavior

Discussions of bureaucracy, effectiveness, change, and culture leave little room for the individual. They portray the impersonal side of organizations, the forces that shape individuals. But organizations, especially public organizations, are crowded with individuals. Visit a state or federal office building and you will see that public organizations are alive with individual effort, conversation, and movement. They are settings for deeply personal experiences. Work is a place where we earn our living but also where we learn about ourselves, develop friendships, and contribute to the community.

This chapter narrows our focus to the individual within public organizations. We examine first the complex mix of motives and needs that individuals bring to organizations. Next, we examine how we learn about ourselves through social interaction, the tension between self-interest and cooperation, and the dual nature of commitment. We will then turn our attention to small groups. Most work depends on ensemble, not solo, effort. Groups are a source of conflict as well as creativity, and this aspect of organizations will also be examined.

INDIVIDUAL NEEDS
AND ORGANIZATIONAL REWARDS

The relationship between individuals and organizations is an exchange but not a simple, or one-dimensional, exchange. Individuals bring diverse needs to organizations, and organizations require diverse responses from employees. At a minimum, organizations require individuals to join and remain. Organizations spend considerable time and effort attracting, selecting, and hiring new employees. Hiring decisions are often the most crucial; skilled, energetic employees are scarce resources. Once an employee is hired, organizations need to minimize worker absence and turnover. Employees avoiding work or looking for a new job create coordination problems and major organizational costs.

Hiring and keeping employees is, however, only the beginning. Organizations require dependable performance. They need individuals who will consistently act as expected, and they need employees who will meet or exceed performance standards. Most public organizations rely on evaluation and reward systems to sustain consistent and encourage exceptional performance.

One irony of performance appraisal is that if all workers strictly fulfilled their job descriptions, organizations would suffer. This is a tactic used by workers engaged in a work slowdown; by obeying, but not exceeding, written job requirements, employees can retard the flow of work so that not much gets done. To function well, organizations require innovative and spontaneous behavior that exceeds specific role requirements. One such behavior is cooperation. As will be discussed below, group work is fundamental to most organizational activities. Without cooperation groups become arenas for conflict, not collaboration. This cooperation must also extend beyond groups. Organizations need individuals to develop good working relations among groups. Collaboration must extend across the organization.

In addition, organizations require creativity. Few organizational activities can be reduced to unchanging formulas. Unless individuals are encouraged to invent novel solutions to problems, organizational performance is reduced. Creative response is important in even the most routine work. Barbara Garson (1979, 234) writes of a woman, responsible for checking insurance forms, who discovered an obvious error in an insurance policy. The simple act of going beyond her job description could have saved the organization an embarrassing mistake, but this constructive response was discouraged.

> I was just about to show it to Gloria [the supervisor] when I figured, "Wait a minute! I'm not supposed to read these forms. I'm just supposed to check one column against another. And they do check, so it couldn't be counted as my error. . . If they're gonna give me a robot's job to do, I'm gonna do it like a robot! Anyway it just lowers my production record to get up and point out someone else's error."

Theories of Individual Needs and Motivation

To attract and keep people and to encourage dependable and innovative performance, organizations must take into account individual needs and motivation. This is no simple matter; human motivation is complex. Even the immediate pleasure of eating ice cream is complicated by the long-term worry about calories. Individuals are often torn by conflicting motives, different time frames, and different expectations.

Work organizations are settings in which individuals address their most fundamental needs. Food, shelter, health care, and future security are bought with money earned through work. Like a potential drought for the subsistence farmer, the threat of losing your job is deeply troubling. But individuals also strive to belong and to contribute to social groups. Activities gain value and meaning when they contribute to others. As we stressed in Chapter 2, organizations are social settings, not just production devices. In addition, organizations are settings in which we strive to fulfill our highest aspirations.

Fulfilling individual needs in organizations requires interaction and interdependence. The organization must provide an opportunity to satisfy these needs. Fulfilling needs requires that the organization make various rewards available to individuals. Since these rewards are generally provided and distributed by management, managerial assumptions about individual motives directly affect the manner in which individual needs are met or thwarted. Before we look at the kinds of rewards organizations offer individuals, we will review several fundamental theories about human motives.

Maslow's Hierarchy.   Abraham Maslow (1954) developed one of the most widely known theories of human motivation. His theory of motivation has two main components: recognition of five different categories of needs; and recognition that these needs exist in a hierarchy, in which the needs at the top will not be strongly felt until the lower order needs are adequately satisfied (see Figure 4.1). The needs categories are the bases of motivation; when needs are inadequately met, individuals strive to satisfy them.

At the bottom of the hierarchy are *physiological needs* for food, shelter, and reproduction. Putting myths of starving artists aside, most of us would do almost anything to satisfy our absolutely basic needs. Even though few of us are likely to starve or become homeless, fear that a loss of job or income will leave basic needs unsatisfied is a strong, if negative, motivator. Once basic needs are adequately satisfied, needs for *safety and security* become important. We want reassurance that our basic needs will be met in the future, after retirement or despite disability. So much depends on continued work and continued income that job security is a strong motivator.

When physical and security needs are adequately met, then, Maslow points out, most of us begin to demonstrate a need for *affiliation;* developing meaningful interpersonal relationships becomes important. Belonging to social groups—families,

              I. Self-actualization

          II. Esteem and recognition

       III. Social and affiliation

     IV. Safety and security

   V. Physiological or basic

Figure 4.1. Maslow's Hierarchy of Needs
SOURCE: Eddy, William. *Public Organization Behavior and Development.* Cambridge, MA: Winthrop, 1981, p. 45.

neighborhoods, and work groups—is, according to Maslow, a fundamental human need. Social interaction is a necessity, not a diversion from more important activities. The "loner" cut off from social ties is not only an anomaly but also often a highly disturbed person.

Needs for *esteem* or recognition and *self-actualization* top the hierarchy. Once accepted in groups, people generally strive to distinguish themselves through achievement, and once adequate recognition is received, they turn to more personal needs for creative self-expression. Although self-expression is usually associated with the arts, Maslow argues that self-actualization is possible and important in all walks of life.

Exceptions to Maslow's hierarchy are common. The workaholic who pursues recognition without regard for costs to relationships is satisfying higher-order needs while starving lower-order needs. Maslow's ideas nonetheless have strongly influenced studies of organizations. Clayton Alderfer (1972) reduced Maslow's five needs to three (existence, relatedness, and growth) while partially conforming Maslow's observation that the need for interpersonal relations and personal growth strongly motivates organization behavior. David McClelland (1961) identified three basic needs—those for achievement, power, and affiliation—and suggested that, rather than a hierarchy of needs, individuals have basic orientations that stress one set over another: Some people stress achievement while others are driven to achieve power.

Herzberg's Two Factors.   Frederick Herzberg's (1966) research linked ideas about different needs to different characteristics of work. He examined eight job factors, roughly corresponding to Maslow's five needs, that contribute to motivation. Herzberg found that the first four—working conditions, salary and benefits, supervision, and fellow workers—were frequently sources of negative motivation—what he called dissatisfiers—but were rarely sources of positive motivation. Poor working conditions could discourage performance, but great working conditions did little to augment performance. The other factors—recognition, advancement, responsibility, and job challenge—motivated above-average performance. These characteristics of the work itself brought out higher levels of performance.

We should note that workers can be simultaneously satisfied and dissatisfied with work. Opportunities for creative freedom may be a source of deep satisfaction but still not erase the negative motivation caused by crowded offices or inadequate health insurance. Moreover, dissatisfaction is not necessarily bad. Karl Weick (1977, 220) observed that "effective organizations are grouchy"; a lack of complaints may mean that the organizational actors have given up hope of improvement. The central issue, then, is not necessarily the amount of dissatisfaction but the issues that are the source of the complaint. Maslow (1971, 242–3) argued that

> complaining that the rose gardens in the park are not sufficiently cared for is, in itself, a wonderful thing because it indicates the height of life at which the complainers are living. To complain about rose gardens means that your belly is full, that you have a good roof over your head, . . . that the police and fire departments work well . . . and many other preconditions are already satisfied.

These ideas about human motivation share common threads. Needs may or may not exist in a hierarchy and individuals may or may not have basic orientations, but clearly an individual's relationship to work is complex. Once our most basic survival needs are satisfied, most adults strive to balance material, social, and self-actualization needs through their work. The rewards of work extend well beyond the paycheck.

ORGANIZATIONAL REWARDS AND MOTIVATION

Organizations provide three forms of rewards. *External rewards,* such as pay, promotions, and recognition, are the most obvious. Generally, external rewards are given or withheld on the basis of a supervisor's judgment about performance. *Intrinsic rewards* result from the work itself—from the feelings of accomplishment, creativity, or impact that accompany meaningful work. A special education teacher may take deep satisfaction from his or her work despite poor working conditions and modest pay. The *social rewards* of work include friendships, conversation, and acceptance. They can enliven dull, repetitive work and build higher levels of commitment among workers. Intrinsic and social rewards result from the individual's personal experience with work and are not directly given or withheld by supervisors, but supervisors can shape the setting that either fosters or inhibits these rewards. We will look more closely at these three classes of rewards in the sections that follow.

External Rewards

Rewarding performance is the most common way that organizations encourage constructive actions, while withholding rewards may be the organizational response to actions judged less than constructive. Individuals can be fired, demoted, or given less responsible work if supervisors feel that their work is poor, of course, but in general, layoffs and demotions result from larger organizational failures or problems that have little to do with individual performance. (In 1987, for example, some 200 Chicago teachers were laid off. They layoffs were made for budgetary reasons and were based solely on seniority—last hired, first fired.)

Individual performance is more likely to be acknowledged by rewards (for good performance) and the withholding of awards (for performance judged less good). After an individual is hired and becomes reasonably secure in his or her job, the organization will typically reward performance with recognition, status, and pay. Acknowledgment of a job well done, particularly public acknowledgment, provides the esteem and recognition that Maslow identifies as an important motivator. Such esteem can also be conveyed by overt recognition of status. In *Blind Ambition* (1976), for instance, Watergate conspirator and eventual whistle-blower John Dean recounts how his successes in the illegal maneuverings of Watergate were rewarded by a move from a cramped office in the Executive Office Building to a large space in the White House. The symbols of success that came his way—the office, an official parking space, invitations to White House dinners, praise from the president himself—were intoxicating. The most common external reward, however, is pay.

The Paradox of Pay.   Money is the common denominator of contemporary society, the symbol of value. And most of us earn most of our money working in organizations. Paychecks purchase the means to satisfy our physical needs, and health coverage and retirement plans address our security needs. Pay also confers status. Displays of consumer goods or expensive leisure activities advertise our material success. (For a historical study of the social meaning of money see Zelizer [1989].)

Moreover, decisions about raises are most frequently made by supervisors in response to relative performance. Pay, therefore, connotes organizational value judgments about worth. These value judgments are then transformed into material success, which communicates status and achievement to others. Pay is a powerful motivator.

Pay is not, however, a simple motivator. The first question about pay is "How much is enough?" When individuals are given raises that they consider too small in relation to their efforts or accomplishments, the raises not only lose value as rewards, but may actually reinforce the feeling that the organization is indifferent. Conversely, receiving a raise greater than what a worker thinks he or she deserves breaks the connection between the reward and individual action. A reward must be perceived as appropriate in order to motivate. This observation is the central insight of expectancy theory.

Expectancy Theory.   Expectancy theory suggests that performance is affected by perceptions about three dimensions of rewards. The first is *perceived reward attractiveness.* The individual must consider the reward rewarding. For example, earning a plaque at an annual banquet may be considered a great honor to some and a joke to others. A $500 bonus after a year of sixty-hour work weeks may appear more insulting than rewarding. Small pay differences may, however, be perceived as rewarding. An essential element of how we perceive a reward is what the reward signals about our worth or performance. Trivial dollar difference can communicate considerable symbolic difference, and symbols alter perceptions.

But the perceived value of the reward is not enough to alter performance. The reward must be *perceived as linked to performance,* and the performance must be *perceived as linked to effort.* Workers must reasonably expect that improved performance will lead to rewards and that their own effort will enhance performance. For example, cost of living raises given without regard to performance may be welcome but are not likely to motivate improved effort. The perception that rewards are arbitrary or based on favoritism, not performance, also breaks the perceived linkage between performance and reward. Similarly, if individuals doubt that increasing their effort will improve performance then there is little incentive to try harder. This situation is most common in groups in which the extra efforts of a few are blunted by the minimal efforts of others.

Performance Problems.   Expectancy theory highlights motivation problems for public organizations. Especially in recent years when many government programs have been limited or cut back, the rewards available to public employees have ranged from stingy to nonexistent. If underachievers receive no raise, average achievers a 1 percent raise, and overachievers a 2 percent raise, there is little incentive to put in the extra effort. Unless the symbolic values of these slight differences remain important, consistently small increments challenge the perception that high performance is rewarded.

Moreover, in many public sector jobs the connection between greater personal effort and actual performance differences is unclear. What difference will one more arrest make in the crime rate? Will spending overtime on job training lower the unemployment rate?

Social Comparison Process.   Expectancy theory stresses individual perceptions and expectations. To understand further the relationship between individual motivation and performance, we need to probe the sources of these perceptions. One important source is the process of *social comparison,* which suggests that there is no absolute value attached to certain rewards or performances but that their value results from comparing one's own performance and rewards with those of a *referent group.*

The theory of social comparison was first articulated by Leon Festinger in 1954. Festinger argues that we develop views of our opinions, abilities, and worth based on how we compare to others. The choice of a specific reference group for comparison is, therefore, extremely important in developing these perceptions. A researcher may consider herself the most productive in her laboratory, but if her reference group includes internationally renowned scientists, she may consider her achievements inadequate. In the same way, her salary may be high relative to others in her lab but still be a source of dissatisfaction if below those of colleagues in other labs. For example, Samuel Stouffer (1949) found that soldiers with college degrees were much more dissatisfied with their rate of promotion than were those without degrees even though the degreed soldiers were promoted at a higher rate.

Most people are reasonable in their selection of referent groups; they choose groups that represent similar skills and socially accepted salary differences. A city manager's responsibilities may greatly exceed those of many corporate leaders. Most city managers, however, realize that corporations pay more than government and compare their salaries and achievements to those of other city managers. Nurses compare their salaries to the salaries of social workers or occupational therapists, not to surgeons.

The choice of referent groups is usually reasonable, but it is generally beyond the control of the organization. Civil engineers working for the federal government may compare their salaries with civil engineers working outside government, and relatively low government salaries may result in high turnover or diminished performance despite a careful and fair internal performance appraisal system.

External Rewards and Alienation.   External rewards are basic to the relationship of the individual and the modern work organization. Individuals exchange their time, energy, and creativity for specific organizational rewards. This exchange is formal; it is the basis of the employee contract. Moreover, as stressed above, external rewards—pay, status, and recognition—are highly motivational. They address three of the five needs identified by Maslow: physiological, security, and recognition needs. But reducing work to the exchange of effort for external reward is also a major source of employee disaffection.

The preoccupation with external rewards creates two closely related problems. First, external rewards have little impact on social and self-actualization needs. To the extent that these are important, external rewards are limited motivators. Second, stressing external rewards alters the relationship between the individual and the organization.

External rewards are based on rational-economic assumptions about individuals. In this view, individuals follow the path of least effort to the greatest return; they are primarily motivated out of self-interest. In economic terms, individuals strive to maximize their self-interest. Stressing external rewards reduces the relationship between employees and employers to a market exchange that places them on opposite sides of the bargaining table.

Rational-economic assumptions are powerful because they are at least partially correct. Individuals *are* motivated by self-interest. Nevertheless, these assumptions color relations with employees when they dominate management thinking. If you treat people as if they are primarily selfish—as if they are out to get the most pay for the least effort—then people are likely to respond selfishly. Assumptions become self-fulfilling prophesies. Edgar Schein (1980) has identified four managerial assumptions that derive from the rational-economic view of human motivation, the first two of which are listed below:

a. Employees are primarily motivated by economic incentives and will do whatever affords them the greatest economic gain.
b. Since economic incentives are under the control of the organization, the employee is essentially a passive agent to be manipulated, motivated, and controlled by the organization. (p. 53)

These assumptions have two negative consequences for individuals in organizations. First, they reduce work to a commodity. The worn-down salesman in Arthur Miller's play *Death of a Salesman* (1949, 82), who loses his job after years of work, complains, "You can't eat the orange and throw away the peel—a man is not a piece of fruit." As with any other commodity, the organization owes no further obligation when the employee is used up. Such obligation is not part of the deal of work for pay.

Second, rational-economic assumptions force managers to spend considerable time and ingenuity monitoring and controlling workers. For the worker, it is rational to be lazy, to try to get by with the least effort. Unpunished laziness increases the individual's net gain. The diligent worker is the fool for producing more for the same reward. Therefore, managers must constantly look over workers' shoulders to assure efficient effort. Conversations, unplanned breaks, even trips to the bathroom become, in this view, opportunities for avoiding work.

Rational-economic assumptions create adversaries out of managers and workers. Reducing work to a commodity and assuming that employees must be constantly watched are sources of alienation. Work loses meaning when it is merely bought and sold and when individuals are not personally responsible for decisions and actions.

This alienation, in turn, reduces motivation to the minimum needed to sustain external rewards.

Intrinsic Rewards

Work is more meaningful when individuals are rewarded by the work itself. Accomplishment, self-expression, and personal impact are intrinsically rewarding, Maslow argued. The intrinsic rewards of some jobs are more obvious than others. Artists, writers, and scientists all do work that demands creativity. Top decision makers and professionals can easily see the impact of their actions. The intrinsic rewards of more routine, less responsible jobs are not so dramatic but may be no less important.

The nature of the work or tasks affects the opportunity for intrinsic rewards. Jobs with greater variety, responsibility, and challenge are inherently more rewarding. As we discussed in Chapter 2, division of labor and specialization create repetitive work. Bureaucratic efficiency is achieved, in part, by dividing complex tasks into simple components assigned to individuals who by training or experience become specialists. But complex tasks are inherently more interesting. If we are assigned the task of evaluating nursing homes, we will no doubt find it more interesting to attend legislative hearings, review relevant legal and policy literature, visit nursing homes, draft policy guidelines, and present ideas at a state conference than to do any one of these tasks week after week. Repetition and specialization build expertise, but routine can generate lack of interest and boredom.

Personal responsibility also enhances the value of work. Merely implementing someone else's decisions—doing as you are told—reduces involvement in work. Without personal responsibility for shaping the job and the results, workers derive little satisfaction from successfully completing a job. The architect, not the construction worker, is given an award for the innovative building. Personal responsibility is enhanced when those charged with carrying out decisions have the discretion and authority to adjust or modify actions based on their own judgments. By increasing personal responsibility, individuals can take greater pride in work and personally feel the rewards of success. For example, in their research on the implementation of community corrections, Maynard-Moody, Musheno, and Palumbo (1990) found that those agencies that allowed their street-level workers to participate in making decisions were more successful in achieving a number of different goals than were the agencies that did not empower workers at this level.

Work that challenges individuals is also more intrinsically rewarding than easy jobs that confer little sense of accomplishment. Even routine tasks such as putting a ball through a hoop can be intrinsically rewarding when challenging. Impossible jobs, however, except to the driven few, are a source of frustration. Solving puzzles, overcoming difficulties, and devising innovative solutions are intrinsically rewarding activities that fulfill self-actualization needs.

Intrinsic rewards are powerful incentives for above-average performance. They encourage individuals to push beyond role requirements and to provide organizations much needed innovative and creative energy. Supervisors, however, cannot directly manipulate intrinsic rewards in the same way that they give or withhold external rewards. Intrinsic rewards involve a personal relationship of individuals to their work.

Nevertheless, organizations can increase or decrease the availability of intrinsic rewards through the design of work and the nature of supervision. Routine and unrewarding work assignments can be enlarged to create more variety. Participation and responsibility can extend throughout the organization. Minimizing routine while augmenting responsibility also increases the level of challenge.

In addition, managers can reward others with a greater opportunity for intrinsic rewards. Assignment to an interesting project, for instance, is a highly desired but scarce organizational resource. Often the greatest reward for constructive and creative performance is the opportunity to perform again. The computer designers in Tracy Kidder's *The Soul of the New Machine* (1981) called these opportunities "playing pinball": the prize for winning was playing again. Organizations are not only exchanges of work for pay but are also arenas of opportunities.

Concentrating on the intrinsic rewards of work changes the role of supervision. The assumption of self-interest underlying external rewards forces supervisors into the roles of tough bargainer and persistent monitor. When the performance of individuals is based on intrinsic motives, they require less supervision; they work hard even when not watched. They require opportunities, guidance, and collaboration rather than control. In fact, stressing control and close supervision—what is now called *micromanagement*—decreases intrinsic motivation by reducing personal responsibility.

That individuals are motivated by both external and intrinsic rewards can create a fundamental dilemma for managers. Stressing external rewards may discourage intrinsic motivation, but assuming that people will perform without accountability can prove disillusioning.

Social Rewards

External and intrinsic rewards focus on individuals and their relationship with either the organization or the work itself. But working in organizations is a social experience. As Maslow and many others argue, individuals have strong social or affiliational needs. Like neighborhoods, voluntary associations, and families, work organizations are settings for developing relationships.

The importance of social rewards goes well beyond the pleasures of social contact. Hall conversations, lunchtime poker games, and office romances enliven even the most routine work. One of the more telling descriptions of the way socializing flourishes in the least likely settings is Donald Roy's (1979) " 'Banana Time': Job Satisfaction and Informal Interaction." Roy begins, "My account [examines] how one group of machine operators kept from 'going nuts' in a situation of monotonous work activity" (p. 192). The case study describes the way a group of low-paid workers, trapped by twelve-hour days of mindless work, developed numerous small "festivals" to break up the day. These included irrepressible bursts of horseplay, in addition to scheduled breaks, which provided settings for unrestrained, often foolish, socializing and interrupted the mechanical monotony of factory work. This "leavening of the deadly boredom of individualized work routines with a concurrent flow of group festivities" (p. 205) may not have directly improved productivity, but it did enrich the workers' lives and may have reduced turnover. The social rewards made the job psychologically possible.

Roy's observations identify two important aspects of social rewards. First, social behavior is spontaneous in work settings. Socializing can be channeled and inhibited by supervisors but rarely eliminated. Second, nonwork socializing may have important effects on work activities.

This second observation has provoked considerable interest among organization researchers. As we discussed in Chapter 1, some early findings on the value of social rewards were discovered by chance in the 1920s when a research team studied the effects of the length of workdays, number of rest periods, and improved lighting on the performance of work teams assembling telephone equipment at Western Electric Company's Hawthorne (Illinois) plant (for a summary see Schein 1980, 56–60). As the researchers predicted, each change brought performance improvements. But to their confusion and surprise, the performance gains continued when the workers returned to their original working conditions.

Further study suggested that the performance gains were caused by unanticipated side effects of the work environment changes, among which were a variety of social rewards. Participation in the experiment conferred a feeling of importance. In addition, the workers had been allowed to develop their own pace and division of work, and this freedom fostered constructive social relationships. As Edgar Schein (1980, 57) summarized, the Hawthorne studies led to a new hypothesis about work: "that motivation to work, productivity, and quality of work are all related to the nature of *social* relations among workers and between workers and their supervisors." This finding subsequently became known as the *human relations* view of administration.

Self-Interest and Cooperation.   Social rewards are undeniably important, although researchers argue as to the degree. Individuals have social and affiliational needs in addition to the more personal needs for security and interesting work, and fulfilling or thwarting these needs affects organizations. Self-interest may prove neither a reliable nor an organizationally productive guide to individual behavior. Self-interest when not restrained by group or community interests can prove highly destructive. Under many circumstances, the apparent pursuit of self-interest may not reflect collective interest—or even, finally, an accurate assessment of self-interest.

This paradox—that individuals apparently pursuing their own interests may in fact damage their own interests—is best captured in Garrett Hardin's (1968) "The Tragedy of the Commons," a parable in which several shepherds share common grazing land. It is in the self-interest of each shepherd to increase his flock, but the unchecked pursuit of self-interest inexorably leads to the overgrazing of the common land and the eventual financial ruin of all the shepherds. Only when collaboration is established and self-interest tempered by group consideration do all shepherds benefit.

The lesson of the "Tragedy of the Commons" was recently reinforced in Robert Axelrod's (1986) *Evolution of Cooperation,* which demonstrates that when individuals engage in repeated contacts of uncertain duration, cooperation produces a more stable environment and more constructive results than does competition. Axelrod simulated cooperation on a computer and examined the spontaneous development and surprising durability of cooperation across enemy lines during

World War I. When forward movement was stalled with units facing each other across well-established trenches and despite pressure from officers to risk their lives, soldiers in both lines spontaneously developed unstated cooperative agreements to avoid killing each other. Shelling occurred at predictable times and for predictable lengths of time so the other side could take shelter. Latrines became illegal targets. Restraint of one side was reciprocated as a live-and-let-live group ethic developed. During combat and without direct communication, cooperation evolved naturally in the interests of both individuals and groups.

To recap, working in organizations is a social endeavor. The social context of work satisfies fundamental human needs for interpersonal interaction and affiliation. Although socializing activities often appear counterproductive, these interactions and social rewards are essential to organizational life. Cooperation and collaboration may prove more fundamental to organizational effectiveness than the individual pursuit of self-interest. Organizations are not machines; they are human social institutions.

Promotions: A Complex Reward

A promotion is one of the more common organizational rewards. Hierarchy makes organizational life a tournament: With each promotion, you move to the next, more competitive, round. As you move up the hierarchy there are fewer and fewer opportunities for advancement. At some point, individuals "top out"; they reach the pinnacles of their organizational careers. This competition and the eventual lack of advancement profoundly influence social relations within work organizations.

Promotions are complex blends of external, intrinsic, and social rewards. Higher pay, a better office, and public recognition accompany promotions. Smaller doses of external rewards may follow good performance, but promotions generally bring major increments. Promotions may also bring greater job security.

In many jobs, promotions also increase the opportunity for intrinsic rewards. Typically, work at the bottom of organizational hierarchies is more routine and constrained than is work higher up. Job variety, challenge, and responsibilities—key ingredients of intrinsic motivation—tend to increase as one rises through the organizational ranks. There are, of course, exceptions—a researcher promoted to manager may trade creative work for status and pay—but in general, promotions broaden responsibilities and reduce routine.

Promotions also affect social rewards. Promotions may involve leaving one social group and entering another. Work groups often form within levels in the hierarchy, and groups at one level are sometimes defined by the friction with those above and below them. Promotions may involve crossing social group boundaries—leaving the norms and expectations of one group and accepting the norms and expectations of another. If the individual has always aspired to membership in the new group, such a change may be highly rewarding. At other times, promotions can be socially confusing. New managers are often upset by the loss of friendships with their old colleagues. Becoming a boss makes you one of "them" and no longer one of "us."

Promotions alter social rewards in yet another way. Promotions are generally individual rewards and are, therefore, a source of competition. Even if group effort and genuine collaboration prove more productive, group success does not provide the evidence of individual achievement necessary for promotion. Rewarding individuals for group accomplishments—the organizational equivalent of the "most valuable player" award—sustains competition and may reduce the social rewards available at work. Individual competition diminishes social involvement.

The structure of the organization dramatically affects the availability and social impact of promotions. Organizations with tall, narrow hierarchies offer numerous and less competitive promotions. Conversely, flat hierarchies, such as those of schools, offer few opportunities for advancement. A public school with twenty teachers may have only one principal, and a school system with twenty schools may have only a handful of administrators. In such a system, most teachers are never promoted; they stay at the same rank their entire career. Proposals made in recent years to create new titles such as *master teacher,* and higher salaries to go with this, are attempts to motivate teachers in the hope that this will improve schools.

Many public organizations blend tall and flat hierarchies. They have a large number of lower-level management positions but very few upper-management positions. Early success is met with rapid promotion, and competition is less pronounced. But as the individual moves up, opportunities quickly vanish. The nursing profession as well as public school teaching is like this. In such organizations, frequent promotions can lead to career deadends. After ten years of promotion, change, and challenge, the fast tracker may face a career of stagnation, stability, and routine.

Hiring individuals from outside the organization to fill higher management positions also adds to the lack of upward mobility in organizations. The competition is expanded to include others outside the organization. In public organizations, the top administrator—for example a cabinet secretary—is often appointed by the governor or president. Most commonly these appointments come from outside the organization and the new executive brings in his or her coterie of assistants. The opportunities for career civil servants to rise to upper management are severely limited.

Promotions are also important for what they communicate. Many organizational rewards are private; salary raises are often kept secret and pleasure in work is a personal matter. Promotions, however, are public events and are carefully scrutinized by organizational members. We all ask what someone else's promotion means for our career. If the diligent conformist is promoted over the risk-taking innovator, we learn something about expectations. Or if outsiders are preferred over insiders, our own thinking about career plans may change; we may start scanning job ads. By observing who is promoted and who is passed by one may discover unwritten expectations for what behavior will be rewarded and what opportunities will be provided. These expectations form the psychological contract between the individual and the organization.

GROUPS IN ORGANIZATIONS

Most work in organizations depends on ensemble rather than solo effort. Committees, work groups, and meetings fill the days of most public administrators. As we discussed in Chapter 2, group effort can take several forms. Individuals often work collectively on a project, either simultaneously or consecutively. In developing a policy to clean up hazardous wastes, a group may brainstorm ideas, argue over responses, and coauthor a proposal; individuals may work on part of a problem but depend on others to continue where their work ends. Most organizational efforts are a mix of collaboration and interdependence.

Formal and Informal Groups

There are two basic types of groups in organizations: formal and informal. *Formal groups* are identified by organizational leaders. They include bureaus or departments assigned specific areas of responsibility, which may exist for years. Over time, the directors and members of these groups will change, yet this turnover rarely alters group functioning. The selection and socialization of group members are major sources of this stability.

Other formal groups include standing and temporary committees and task forces, which tend to cut across bureaucratic boundaries. Their membership is more heterogeneous than that of more institutionalized formal groups, and their functioning is more dependent on the interpersonal styles and skills that individuals bring to the group. With temporary groups, there is rarely time for the group to develop stable and enduring patterns of interaction. Regardless of the form, however, the central characteristics of formal groups are *overt organizational legitimacy* and *task orientation.*

Informal groups, on the other hand, are not created by management but evolve out of the rich social environment of organizations. Some informal groups are not directly work related; they form to amplify the social rewards of work and can include individuals from several bureaus and levels in the hierarchy. For example, the coffee klatch or lunch-hour joggers get together over shared interests, not work. Family problems or sports are more common topics of conversation than work problems. Nevertheless, these informal groups can have profound effects on work. Much bureaucratic work is highly routine, and the periods of socialization can greatly enrich the workday. Bureaucrats need their "banana time" as much as factory workers do.

Equally important, both formal and informal groups create opportunities for making contacts and building trust, which are in turn the basis for informal organizational *networks*. These networks create an alternative and more fluid organizational chart. The formal structure and chain of command in most organizations provides only the general structure. Except in the most rigid organizations, such as police departments, formal structure does not greatly constrain interactions. The informal network cuts across levels and divisions. A jog becomes an opportunity for off-the-record discussions of mutual problems; a neighbor proves to be a key contact in another department; a phone call to someone you used to work with adds a vital piece of information. Returning old favors, supporting friends, trading rumors, and so on can be as important to organizational functioning as formal assignments.

Networks are also the basis for *coalitions*. A coalition is an issue-specific, informal collaboration that centers on individual self-interest (Stevenson, Pearce, and Porter 1985). Groups have more clout in organizations than do individuals, especially individuals in the middle or bottom of hierarchies, so coalitions often form around specific interests. These interests may be purely self-centered (nurses may form a coalition to ensure that the new director of the outpatient program has a nursing degree) or they may represent policy preferences (a coalition of conservatives in the State Department may closely collaborate to defeat arms control agreements with the Soviet Union). Coalitions, like other informal groups, tend to form and dissolve as issues arise and are resolved. Membership and alliances are fluid.

Certain forms of coalitions do, however, endure over time. Such coalitions represent views and values that cut across specific policy conflicts. Enduring coalitions develop and, more important, pass on *subcultures* (Maynard-Moody, Stull, and Mitchell 1986; Van Maanen and Barley 1983). Organizational subcultures exist when a particular set of organization members identify themselves as a distinct group, share a set of commonly defined problems and routines, and base their actions on collective understandings and values. Subcultures are more ambiguous than coalitions but tend to last longer. Once subcultural assumptions are passed from one generation of members to another, direct interaction becomes less important in holding the group together.

Norms and Socialization

Both formal and informal groups are settings for collaboration, information sharing, and socializing, and behavior in groups follows both formal and informal rules. *Formal rules* may determine who is the leader, delineate individual responsibilities, and specify how decisions are reached. Groups that make decisions based on majority votes differ in form, interaction, and results from those that rely on either consensus or leader prerogative. Formal rules are often found in employee handbooks and are the topic of on-the-job training. They provide the broad context for more informal interaction.

Informal rules or group norms are more ambiguous but are no less binding. Informal rules are learned through attentive interaction with established members of the groups; they alter the way people dress, interact, address problems, and treat others. These informal rules of behavior often endure over long periods, are central to group culture, and are likely to serve important group and organizational functions. For example, the norm of teasing described in Roy's "Banana Time" enlivened a deadly routine. At one point during his observations, however, the teasing went beyond acceptable bounds and the group nearly dissolved.

Individuals sometimes form new groups, but more frequently they join established groups with entrenched norms. Joining occurs with both formal and informal groups. Hiring and promotion involves entry into new work relationships, and changes in formal status can bring changes in informal relations as well. Entry into a new group by an individual initiates an intense period of learning the formal expectations and norms, and discovering how to balance different and competing expectations. Entering a new group is like acting; it involves learning and practicing new roles. Learning new organizational roles is called *socialization*.

Socialization refers to a wide range of learning experiences that transmit established procedures and norms. It can occur in groups or individually and generally involves a mix of formal training and informal mentoring. Although this process continues throughout a career, socialization is most intense when one first enters an organization or group.

> The more experienced members must therefore find ways to insure that the newcomer does not disrupt the ongoing activity on the scene, embarrass or cast a disparaging light on others, or question too many of the established cultural solutions worked out previously. Put bluntly, new members must be taught to see the organizational world as do their more experienced colleagues if the traditions are to survive. (Van Maanen and Schein 1979, 221)

The impact of socialization on individuals varies widely. Groups and organizations need to hand down traditions and expectations, but if new members sheepishly conform to the habits and expectations of old members, socialization robs the group of an important source of change. Recall that James March identified new members as an important and predictable resource for change (see Chapter 3). If socialization requires absolute adherence to established norms, then new members become replacement parts, not opportunities for renewal. Conversely, inadequate socialization can disrupt established patterns and discard the wisdom of experience. Oversocialization that produces rigid conformists and undersocialization that discards traditions are both group failures and should be avoided.

Prior Socialization.   Groups and organizations do not, however, completely control socialization. Individuals are not infinitely malleable. Resistance to socialization pressures comes in part from prior socialization in families, schools, and other organizational affiliations. Prior socialization affects group participation in several ways: Experience in one group or setting may encourage certain beliefs and actions that orient members toward future group memberships. Prior socialization may set members on a path that leads to membership in certain groups. Once in a group, prior socialization may provide a backdrop for present experiences. Membership in the Sierra Club during college may guide a scientist to select a career in the Environmental Protection Agency. Her scientific training, another source of prior socialization, may lead her to evaluate pollution problems in purely technical terms. And her disregard of the political and economic impacts of pollution control may, in turn, preclude her entry into management or policy-making groups in which compromise is the norm. Finally, prolonged experience in EPA may weaken her insistence on purely scientific standards, as ongoing socialization alters her values.

Prior socialization is also an entrance requirement for many jobs. Medicine, law, academia, and other professions demand years of training before group membership is bestowed—training that involves teaching both the skills and the behaviors expected of professionals. Practitioners then enter their professions with pre-established norms of behavior and orientations to problem solving. These pre-established norms are often as important as the specific skills professionals bring to an organization.

Becoming a Policeman.   An excellent description of socialization is provided by John Van Maanen (1978) in "Observations on the Making of Policemen." Van

Maanen points out that police socialization does not start with a blank slate; individuals choose police work based on prior socialization. This is a complex choice, but one that is guided in part by a belief that police work is a public service. After passing a qualifying examination and other screening procedures, the new recruit enters the most formal phase of socialization, the police academy. In the academy the recruit endures long and tedious lectures on the rules and laws that guide police work.

More important than the formal lessons is the opportunity the police academy provides to learn the traditions and norms of police work. These are part of the oral history of the department. Van Maanen (1978, 297) observes:

> The novice's overwhelming eagerness to hear what police work is really like results in literally hours upon hours of war stories . . . told at the discretion of many instructors. . . . By observing and listening closely to police stories and styles, the individual is exposed to a partial organizational history which details certain personalities, past events, places, and implied relationships which the recruit is expected eventually to learn, and it is largely through war stories that the department's history is conveyed.

This informal socialization continues once the recruit is on the job. Novice patrolmen are guided through their first months by an experienced officer, their mentor. "By watching, listening, and mimicking" (Van Maanen 1978, 298), the novice learns how to handle the ambiguities of police work: how to deal with drunks, dangerous arrests, supervisors, and the criminal justice system. In this way, the wisdom, prejudices, and routines of one generation are carefully passed on to the next. Only after this initiation process does a recruit become a "cop," a trusted member of the group.

Few public sector jobs will involve the intense socialization of police work. Nevertheless, the selection based on prior experiences, a mix of formal training and informal learning, and passage from newcomer to group member are common to most jobs. As the skills, expectations, and traditions associated with a job are learned, identities and values also change. The process of socialization builds a bond between the individual and the group. Commitment to a group, its values, and its goals is necessary for collective action. As we begin to consider ourselves group members, we also identify others as outside the group. This identification is a major source of organizational conflict. These two concepts, commitment and conflict, are examined in the sections that follow.

Commitment

The commitment of individuals to groups and organizations is a necessary ingredient of collective performance. Commitment can be thought of as an extension of self-interest. When individuals become committed to a group they identify the group interest with their own interest. This identification may even require self-sacrifice or abandoning personal needs for group success.

Commitment is not automatic, unchanging, or absolute. Deliberate socialization, such as the formal and informal training of police recruits, builds an initial bond of commitment. This bond is modified—at times strengthened, at others diminished—during an organizational career. Commitment, like rewards, is an exchange; an individual's commitment to the organization must, with some degree of balance, be matched by the organization's commitment to the individual. An organization is unlikely to develop the same degree of loyalty for a temporary intern as for a career civil servant. Commitment is also rarely absolute. Most individuals have multiple commitments that vie for their attention. Commitment, therefore, ranges from indifference to total immersion. In general terms, commitment is a psychological bond between the individual and the group. This bond is demonstrated by (1) a strong belief in and acceptance of the group goals, (2) the willingness to exert considerable effort to achieve those goals, and (3) a desire to maintain group membership (Porter, Steers, Mowday, and Boulian 1974).

Commitment both builds and is the result of greater personal identification with the group or organization. It increases involvement with work; a committed individual will often diligently persevere with routine, tedious tasks if they are important to the group. A good example is a volunteer's fervent devotion to door-to-door canvassing in a political campaign. Commitment also strengthens loyalty. Committed individuals endure temporary setbacks—such as a year of no raises—yet retain their level of effort and involvement.

The Dangers of Commitment.   All of these aspects of commitment appear positive, especially to management. For individuals to place group interest over personal interest, sustain involvement in important if not intrinsically rewarding tasks, and have a sense of loyalty serves the organization. When carried to extremes, however, commitment can create individual and organizational problems. Overcommitment, like oversocialization (the two are related), involves the near-total submersion of the individual in the group or organization. The individual becomes "the organization man," a phrase William Foote Whyte chose for the title of his 1956 book. As Donna Randall (1987, 460) summarized,

> the organization man [is] a person who not only worked for the organization, but also belonged to it. Organization men believed in the group as the source of creativity and in belongingness as the ultimate need of the individual.

As Randall pointed out, this overwhelming need to belong is potentially hazardous for both individual and group. An organization or group that encourages—or does not actively discourage—complete loyalty diminishes the contribution of individuals. If everyone conforms, few leaders or innovators emerge. Creativity is a break with established norms and views and is suffocated by conformity. High levels of commitment may also increase organizational misconduct, since highly committed individuals may feel compelled to use any means, even illegal ones, to achieve desired ends. One humanly tragic aspect of the Watergate scandal, in addition to the fall from power of President Nixon, was the willingness of devoted, well-meaning individuals to abandon personal compunction to achieve group goals. "The climate within which the White House aides worked was one of total loyalty to the man at the top and a willingness to do anything to serve him" (Mullen 1976, 211).

Ironically, one antidote to overcommitment to work groups may be commitment to other groups. The problems cited above result in part from the singular identification of the individual with one group, in this case the work organization. Most individuals have multiple commitments. Commitment to family, profession, religion, and associations balance a singular preoccupation with work. These multiple commitments are often a source of stress, but this very stress reduces the unquestioning loyalty to any one affiliation. Barbara Romzek (1989) found that individuals with high work and nonwork commitments did not experience the problems of overcommitment anticipated by Randall.

Commitments to Ideas and Actions. Thus far we have discussed commitment to groups, but individuals can be equally committed to ideas and actions. Gerald Salancik (1977, 4) defined commitment as "the binding of individuals to behavioral acts." These acts include the loyalty and diligence that accompany group affiliation, but individuals can also become committed to certain courses of action that may counter group norms. For example, members of a department of corrections in a state agency may be committed to the notion that offenders can be rehabilitated even though the director and official department policy reject this idea.

Salancik (1977) suggests that commitment is increased by three factors: explicitness of actions; irreversibility of actions; and degree of perceived choice. If an action such as joining a group or making a decision is public and unambiguous it will increase commitment. If no one knows you joined a political party or undertook a diet, changing your mind is much easier. Similarly, if an action is difficult to reverse, commitment is increased. Explicitly identifying an action as a trial is a way of deliberately avoiding commitment. And finally, commitment is increased when an action is freely chosen. Forced actions, such as required membership in a group, reduces personal commitment. When supervisors demand compliance, they cannot expect commitment. The possibilities of multiple group affiliations and the commitment to ideas and actions as well as groups helps explain the presence of whistle-blowers (see Chapter 10).

Most organizations have strong norms regarding public and private dissent. Dissent is tolerated, even encouraged, as long as it is kept within the group. Loyal members owe the group honest, unguarded opinions of plans and decisions, but once the decision is made, group members are commonly expected to give it public support. The norm of expecting internal dissent but suppressing external dissent is referred to as being "a team player." Here the caricature of the "faceless bureaucrat" may have its roots. Team players show their identity—their individuality, their personal opinions—to the group, but when they relate to the public they obscure their individuality behind the group.

This pressure to hide differences and support group decisions creates numerous organizational failures. At times the pressure to conform becomes so great that no one brings up important doubts; at other times, groups persist with bad choices, thinking that more effort will turn things around.[1] Group pressure can encourage illegal activities ("everyone does it so it must be OK") or cover-ups (shredding or falsifying records, constructing SYA—"save your ass"—files). As long as those outside the group do not know about the errors or problems, then the group retains the illusion of success.

Whistle-blowers who go public with doubts or problems break this norm. Some, like "Deep Throat" of the Watergate scandal, anonymously leak the news to the press or an elected official. Others publicly announce their criticism. Ernest Fitzgerald was a middle-level accountant in the Defense Department who testified before Congress about cost overruns in the development of military aircraft. His dissent showed the complexities of commitment. Like other whistle-blowers, he put his commitment to the goals of the department and the public over his commitment to support "the team." To the public he was courageous; to the Defense Department he was a heretic, a deviant.

Fitzgerald, like other whistle-blowers, suffered retaliation. He lost his job; eventually reinstated, he has abandoned hope for future promotions. Organizations generally take strong retaliation against whistle-blowers, especially those with little public support (Parmerlee, Near, and Jessen 1982). The pressures to conform and threats of retaliation are real. Kermit Vandiver, an engineer for the B. F. Goodrich Company, described the pressures not to blow the whistle on a bad aircraft brake system. He was told to cover up and had to decide to comply or dissent.

"At forty-two . . . I had decided that the Goodrich Company would probably be my 'home' for the rest of my working life. The job paid well, it was pleasant and challenging, and the future looked reasonably bright. . . . If I refused to take part in the A7D fraud, I would have to either resign or be fired. The report would be written by someone anyway, but I would have the satisfaction of knowing I had no part in the matter. But bills aren't paid with personal satisfaction, nor house payments with ethical principles. I made my decision. The next morning, I telephoned Lawson and told him I was ready to begin the [false] quantification report" (quoted in Kanter and Stein 1979, 169–170).

Whistle-blowers must, at the risk of retaliation, balance their commitment to the public, to organizational goals, and to their work group. The rocket engineers who privately protested to their supervisor that the space shuttle was not safe to launch may forever regret not going public after watching the *Challenger* explode in space, killing all seven people aboard. Since conformity pressures are a natural part of groups and since external dissent is, at times, in the public interest, whistle-blowing in the public sector is now protected by law. The Civil Service Reform Act (PL 95-454, section 2301, 9) reads,

(9)   Employees should be protected against reprisal for the lawful disclosure of information which the employees reasonably believe evidences—
    (A) a violation of any law, rule or regulation, or
    (B) mismanagement, a gross waste of funds, an abuse of authority, or a substantial and specific danger to public health or safety.

Conflict

The formation of formal and informal groups within organizations generates both competition and conflict. At times this conflict is the natural consequence of intergroup rivalries for resources; two work groups may compete for the same project, or, when working on different projects, for resources such as personnel, equipment, and budget. In a hospital, the emergency room staff may push for the purchase of a helicopter ambulance in competition with the cancer units' advocacy of a computerized axial tomography (CAT) scanner (Roos and Hall 1980). Often informal coalitions form for the explicit purpose of influencing resource decisions (Pfeffer and Salancik 1978). Conflict is both a consequence and a cause of group identity, and conflict has both positive and negative effects on groups. These effects are quite predictable.

Competition changes groups (Schein 1980, 172–181). Groups themselves become more cohesive as individual differences are overcome by group loyalty. Competitive groups also become more goal directed, less playful, and more willing to follow autocratic leaders. The group demands more conformity and is less concerned with individual differences and needs.

Competition also changes the relationships between groups. Competition tends to define other groups as "the enemy." Groups may develop distorted views of each other while developing idealized and unrealistic perceptions of their own motives and skills. If forced to work with competing groups—for example, competitors serving on the same task force—members tend to see only the information that reinforces the positive image of their own group and the negative stereotype of others.

Winning and losing also have predictable consequences for groups. Winners tend to retain or increase their cohesiveness; they may, however, become complacent and less task oriented. Losers may actually learn more about themselves. At first, losers tend to deny or distort the reasons they lost. They look for someone or something to blame. Often, losing shatters group cohesion as individual differences and unresolved within-group conflicts come to the surface. This process can be a source of learning, however, if not carried to the extreme. Winners tend not to question their success. Winners—even chance winners—tend to attribute their success to their own actions, while losers tend to reevaluate and often become more task oriented.

COMMUNICATION

Organizational conflicts rarely come to blows. They are usually fought with words and actions expressed through words. Words also sustain cooperation and transmit norms. The communication process is, therefore, central to understanding organizations. When stripped of their formal structure and specific products and services, organizations are little more than intricate nets of communication tied together by shared understanding. As Daniel Katz and Robert Kahn (1978, 428) asserted,

> Communication—the exchange of information and the transformation of meaning—is the very essence of a social system or an organization. . . . Communication is thus a social process of the broadest relevance in the functioning of any group, organization or society.

Communication is, however, difficult to examine. It is a continuous process engaging an indefinite and changing number of actors; it includes words and deeds ("action speaks louder than words") as well as overt and implied meaning. Sometimes what is not said speaks louder than what is said: Withheld praise is as clear a statement of disappointment as criticism. Moreover, meaning has history and context, and perception depends on preconceived frameworks. We simply do not see or hear things that our minds have not led us to expect. Walter Lippmann, a journalist writing in the 1920s, captured this paradox:

> For the most part we do not first see, and then define, we define first and then see. In the great blooming, buzzing confusion of the outer world, we pick out what our culture has already defined for us, and we tend to perceive that which we have picked out in the form stereotyped for us by our culture. (quoted in Katz and Kahn 1978, 433)

Within these continuous exchanges and interpretations we can draw several distinctions that help us make sense of the communications process.

The Communications Process

Data and Information.   Data are raw, uninterpreted sensory responses or records. The word *data* on this page makes a neural imprint on your retina. A newborn child can see the shapes of the letters but they convey no meaning; they are sensation without information. *Information* is interpreted or organized data that communicate meaning. Information is refined data. A public manager bewildered by stacks of computer reports suffers from too much data and not enough information.

Sender and Receiver.   Although most communications involve a large number of actors, reduced to its simplest level communication involves two people: *sender* and *receiver*. The distinction between sender and receiver highlights the importance of both roles in shaping the information content of any communication. Take a simple monologue. The information contained in the speaker's statements is determined both by what is said and what is heard. Receiving information, hearing, is as active a mental process as sending or articulating. Even in its most basic form communication is an exchange or *double interact* (Weick 1979, 110–117). Change the monologue to a dialogue, place the conversation within a history of interaction, add an ever-changing set of senders and receivers and you begin to describe the complexity of communications in organizations. Little wonder organizations become "towers of babble."

Up, Down, and Across.   The way in which organizational messages are sent and received is shaped by the structure of the organization. Messages communicated from the top to the bottom differ from those coming up from the bottom or going laterally across the organization. Communications from superiors to subordinates tend to contain information about how or why to do a task, or about judgments of performance. Communications centering on instruction and evaluation reinforce the power and authority associated with hierarchical position.

Communications across organizations tend to break down boundaries between organizational subunits. Lateral communication often bypasses the established chain of command. Such communication is necessary when tasks involve more than one unit and when there is a need to secure peer support within the organization.

Information about performance, problems, and new policies dominate upward communications. The communication from subordinates to supervisors is extremely important to organizations. Most managers, especially top administrators, have only second- or thirdhand information about key organizational issues. The accuracy of this information gives subordinates considerable influence over the policy process. This is especially true for certain *gate-keepers* within organizations.

Gate-keepers are individuals who control the access and flow of information. One extreme example is communication to the president of the United States through his chief of staff. Even though the president is the top policy maker in the federal government, he cannot consider even a small fraction of the issues facing the country. His chief of staff typically decides what memos the president will read and with whom the president will talk. In this way, a subordinate shapes policy by determining what information the president considers. This process of making policy by limiting what is communicated upward occurs on a smaller scale throughout organizations and is a primary source of power for lower-level actors.

Communications are inevitably distorted as they move up and down the organization. "The members of a hierarchy do not, in fact, think of themselves as mere messenger boys, faithfully transmitting the reports of their superiors" (Tullock 1964, 139). Dennis Palumbo (1988, 99) notes that

> subordinates add to and subtract from the messages they receive. They decide what parts of policy directions affect their part of the hierarchy. They prepare orders and pass along to their subordinates only those parts of the directions they consider relevant. By the time the directive reaches the lower level, there are major differences among the versions received by the comparable bureaucrats in different parts of the organization.

Economist Gordon Tullock (1964) calculated how much change occurs in messages in the transmission process. He concluded that in a small organization of only forty people, individuals at the bottom spend only about 40 percent of their time doing things those at the top want. In this way, policy is made or changed by street-level administrators. (See Chapter 5 for a detailed discussion of the policy role of street-level bureaucrats.)

Upward influence is also determined by the form of the communications. The most common and most successful method of influencing superiors is the logically presented idea (Schilit and Locke 1982; Kipnis and Schmidt 1988). Articulating a reasonable argument, especially one backed up by facts and figures, is the most valued communication skill in modern bureaucracies. The importance bureaucracies place on rational decision making results in a paradox. Most organizations collect and examine more information than they can reasonably expect to use, yet few organizations make much use of the information they have (Feldman and March 1981). Bureaucratic organizations are information pack rats.

Formal and Informal.   Organizational communications include everything from legally binding policies to office gossip. Formal and informal communications take different forms, but both are part of the information environment. Memoranda, policy papers, and official bylaws follow certain clear rules of etiquette; some things, however important and understood by everyone, cannot be written in formal organizational documents. Formal communications become part of the official record; informal communications—gossip, off-the-record conversations, personal letters, and stories—are less constrained. Like the "war stories" repeated at the police academy, they communicate important organizational messages.

Both formal and informal organizational communications can be further divided into *argument* and *narration,* although these categories are neither exclusive nor exhaustive (Weick and Browning 1986; Maynard-Moody 1989b). Organizational communications commonly attempt to convince others of the correctness of certain positions. Such argumentation can take various forms; carefully crafted legal briefs, colorful graphics, and emotional appeals are all attempts to persuade. Organizational communications can also take the form of narration or story telling, which tells organizational members how to act and think. Gossip is an importance form of organizational narration. Karl Weick and Larry Browning (1986, 250) summarize the effects of gossip:

> In the context of narration, gossip emerges as a device to give order to experience. Gossip contributes to system maintenance because it communicates rules, values, and morals by dwelling on failures to satisfy them. Gossip is a way to diffuse traditions and history. Gossip maintains links among people during those periods when instrumental communication is not needed. It also functions as a means to gather bits and pieces of information into an information inventory which may be useful for problems no one can anticipate.

Open and Restricted.   The distinction between open and restricted communication has two elements: size and permeability. A network is more open if it includes large numbers of participants, but even a relatively small network may be open if individuals who want information are allowed access. Small, closed networks are the most restricted; large, permeable ones are the most open.

By definition, organizations require restricted or channeled communication. The concepts of structure defined in Chapter 2 limit communication. If every decision required the attention of every organizational member, or if every member had equal access to meetings, memos, or conversations, nothing would ever be accomplished. We all need to ignore a large percentage of the information available to us in order to concentrate on our tasks. Sherlock Holmes told Watson that having learned the earth was round, he would quickly forget that information. Unless knowledge was directly applicable in solving crimes, it only cluttered his brain. Completely open communication greatly reduces our ability to sort out information from data.

On the other hand, overly restrictive communication reduces innovation. Few innovations are novel ideas; most result from novel connections between existing ideas (Kanter 1983). A highly successful approach for working with nonviolent criminals grew out of the interaction between parole officers and drug counselors (Musheno, et al. 1989), and discussions between marketing experts and designers led to the development of a new computer (Kidder 1981). These novel connections are a major contribution of informal communications. Formal communications are more easily and routinely controlled and restricted.

Restrictive communication is also a source of distrust. Decisions, even reasonable decisions, reached in secret are likely to garner little support. Open communications, listening to alternative views and publicly examining options, broadens the support for decisions. Greater openness is especially important if individuals charged with carrying out the decisions can subvert the best plans through indifference. Good decisions reached by top administrators must be reasonable and engage the active support of those lower down the hierarchy who put the decision into action.

The need for openness extends beyond organizational boundaries. For public organizations, many decisions are strengthened by citizen participation. The processes of open discussion and public hearings often slow down and complicate deliberations, but allowing citizens to participate increases the likelihood that the eventual decisions receive public support, or, at least, avoid public protest.

Computers and Information Systems

In recent years, computerized information systems have supplemented the memo and policy paper as major forms of organizational communication. The most common computerized information system is the management information system (MIS). MISs are primarily computerized record systems that keep track of spare parts for the military, the number of clients for social workers, and so on. The better MISs are closely linked to accounts and budgets; they help keep track of resources and project costs.

A more unusual form of computerized information system is the decision support system (DSS). In general, a DSS simulates the human judgment process with the goal of reducing errors and increasing speed. A DSS for physicians would incorporate the steps to diagnosis; it could sequentially ask for symptoms, suggest a probable prognosis, and advise appropriate tests and treatment. (For a general discussion of computers in public administration see Bozeman and Bretschneider [1986].)

The introduction of computers has been hailed by some as the harbinger of the new "Information Age." Harlan Cleveland (1985) foresees the transformation of our society as information, especially scientific information, becomes a dominant resource. Current assumptions about power and hierarchy must change when discovering and communicating become more important to the economy than growing, extracting, and manufacturing. An information-based society or organization depends on knowledge sharing and innovation and therefore requires more participation, less structure, and more freedom, according to Cleveland.

Other observers are less optimistic about the trends. Initially at least, computers have served primarily to strengthen management control and to increase surveillance within organizations (Fischer 1990). The computer directly monitors the rate of productivity of the new information worker while keeping track of the performance of others. Moreover, most MISs merely augment the traditional content of organizational communications. Managers communicate their instructions downward via the computer network, which also collects data on the subordinates' performances to communicate back upward to managers. For example, most social workers must fill out computerized report forms after each client contact. This information is used to keep track of the amount of work they do and to catch errors. These systems augment control and accountability; they are not designed to enable frontline staff to make more thoughtful use of their discretion.

Moreover, such systems are susceptible to great distortions because of errors and bias in the data entered into the computer. The more any measure is used to evaluate performance, the greater is the likelihood that it will be subject to corruption (Campbell 1979, 85). If the client contact hours recorded in the MIS are used on performance appraisal, each social worker may well exaggerate each contact; a forty-minute interview will typically be recorded as taking an hour.

The introduction of computers into public organizations has not yet radically changed organizational communications. Computers have speeded up analysis and improved the graphics in reports, but they have not transformed organizations as much as they have fit into the existing organizational structure (Kraemer and King 1987, 494). James Beniger (1986, 435) concludes, "Microprocessing and computing technology, contrary to currently fashionable opinion, do not represent a new force only recently unleashed on an unprepared society but merely the most recent installment in the continuing development of the Control Revolution." The first "installment" of the Control Revolution was the development of bureaucracy.

A leading computer scientist, Joseph Weizenbaum (1976, 31–32), suggests that computers, like other new tools, initially reinforce the status quo but eventually will encourage change. Over the past fifty years, the U.S. government and public organizations have grown larger and more complex. Computers have allowed this trend to continue beyond limits that might otherwise have been imposed by an inability to communicate. Eventually, however, computers may encourage the decentralization predicted by Cleveland.

SUMMARY

From the broad discussion of organizational structure, effectiveness, change, and culture, this chapter narrows the focus to individuals within public organizations. Individuals bring to their work lives diverse needs and motives. These needs include basic physical and security needs and needs for affiliation, esteem, and self-actualization. How organizations meet or thwart these individual needs affects worker motivation. Herzberg found that poor working conditions, low pay, and contentious office relationships could reduce motivation, but that good working conditions, adequate pay, and office relationships were not enough to encourage above-average performance. Satisfying higher-order needs for recognition and job challenge encourages above-average performance. It is important to recall, however, that workers are often both satisfied and dissatisfied by different aspects of their work, and that dissatisfaction, in itself, is not necessarily a bad thing; it may be evidence of higher aspirations.

Organizations satisfy individual needs by providing external, intrinsic, and social rewards. External rewards such as pay, benefits, and status are the most obvious and most easily manipulated by supervisors. Expectancy theory indicates that for external rewards to prove motivating they must be perceived as rewarding by recipients who must also see a link between their own performance and the reward, between their effort and their performance. How workers perceive rewards is shaped by social comparison to a relevant referent group.

Intrinsic rewards are based on a sense of accomplishment, self-expression, and personal impact that derive from the work itself. Work that provides greater variety, responsibility, and challenge produces greater intrinsic rewards. Supervisors have less direct control over intrinsic rewards than external rewards, but they can make work more intrinsically rewarding by changing work assignments to increase variety and decrease routine and by increasing worker participation in decisions.

For most people, work is a social experience. Even in the most unlikely organizational settings, social relationships develop. Social rewards can make dull, routine work more fun and interesting. In addition, cooperative and collaborative working relationships within organizations can also increase productivity. Much of the non-work socializing that occurs in organizations develops the contacts, trust, and cooperation that make collaboration possible and motivating.

The importance of social rewards underscores an important feature of organizational life: Most work depends on group, not individual effort. Organizational groups are formal (deliberately created to work on tasks) or informal (spontaneously formed, often for nonwork activities). Once established, groups develop norms of behavior that are passed on to new members through socialization.

Groups and organizations depend on the commitment of their members. This psychological bond is based on the acceptance of group goals and the devotion to achieving the goals and maintaining group membership. While positive and necessary, commitment is dangerous if it becomes so extreme that individuals lose their identity to the group or are unable to challenge the group. Whistle-blowers are individuals who break with group norms prohibiting external dissent to expose organizational failures and cover-ups.

Dividing organizations into groups increases the opportunity for conflict. Intergroup competition increases within-group cohesion while increasing between-group conflict. Competing groups develop negative stereotypes of their opponents while developing unrealistic and idealized views of themselves. When intergroup competition leads to winners and losers, the winners tend to experience greater within-group cohesion; losing groups may break apart and suppressed intergroup conflicts may surface. Losing, however, is an opportunity for learning and change.

A primary individual behavior in organizations is communication. As Katz and Kahn (1978, 428) summarized, "Communication—the exchange of information and the transformation of meaning—is the essence of . . . an organization." Organizational communication is an exceedingly complex phenomenon. To make sense of organizational communication, organization members must be aware of its characteristics: the distinction between data and information, senders and receivers; the direction of communication—up, down, or lateral; the differences between communications that are formal or informal, open or restricted. Recently, more and more organizational communications are mediated by computers. Some scholars see the increased use of computers as opening up access to information and thereby increasing decentralization and reducing bureaucracy. Others see computers as increasing managerial control and fostering the continued growth of large bureaucracies. Although no one is sure of the direction in which the computer revolution is taking public organizations, computers are becoming the vehicle for many organizational communications.

CASE STUDY: THE CHALLENGER DISASTER

On January 28, 1986, the space shuttle *Challenger* exploded seventy-three seconds after launch, killing its crew of seven, including Christa McAuliffe, a school teacher. A horrified nation watched as news programs replayed pictures of the massive explosion and falling debris, but several rocket engineers watched with added torment. The night before, they had warned of an accident, yet acquiesced to a management decision to recommend launch. These events tell us much about behavior in organizations.

Designing and launching a space shuttle is an enormous and complex task, one that leaves little room for error and requires coordinating the activities of contractors and several National Aeronautics and Space Administration (NASA) research, launch, and recovery sites. Prior to the launch of the *Challenger,* the space shuttle program had proven a costly success. Missions were completed flawlessly, but delays kept the shuttle from becoming the reliable and cost-effective "space truck" its advocates had promised. The launch of the *Challenger* had followed the pattern of delays that had haunted the entire program. NASA managers felt growing pressure to increase the efficiency of the shuttle program; they needed to meet their flight schedule.

After several delays, the *Challenger* launch was scheduled for January 28. On the evening before, several rocket engineers, working for Morton Thiokol, Incorporated, in Utah, learned of the unusually cold, wet weather at the launch site, the Kennedy Space Center in Florida. Temperatures well below freezing were expected; much of the launch pad was encased in ice. By a teleconference, these engineers contacted the appropriate Level III flight readiness review committee at both the Marshall Space Center in Huntsville, Alabama, and the Kennedy Space Center. As shown in Figure 4.2, launch decisions follow a multilayered chain of command.

The Thiokol engineers were concerned that the O-rings that seal the joints between the segments of the booster rockets would not work in the cold conditions; they feared that the rings would become too hard to prevent "blow-by" or the escape of gas and perhaps flames from the side of the rocket. Past flights had raised sufficient doubts about these O-rings that they had been classified "criticality 1," meaning that their failure could cause a complete failure of the mission. For at least a year prior to the *Challenger* launch, Roger Boisjoly, a Thiokol engineer, had expressed fears about O-ring safety. He had repeatedly raised the specter of an on-launch explosion to force a reevaluation of the O-ring seal design. On January 31, 1985, a year before the explosion, Boisjoly wrote his superior,

It is my honest and very real fear that if we do not take immediate action to dedicate a team to solve the problem, with the final joint having the number one priority, then we stand in jeopardy of losing a flight along with all the launch pad facilities. (Presidential Commission of the Space Shuttle Challenger *Accident 1986, vol. IV, 692)*

The three-way teleconference between Utah, Alabama, and Florida began at approximately 8:45 P.M. (EST). The Thiokol engineers vehemently insisted that they could not

Readiness Reviews

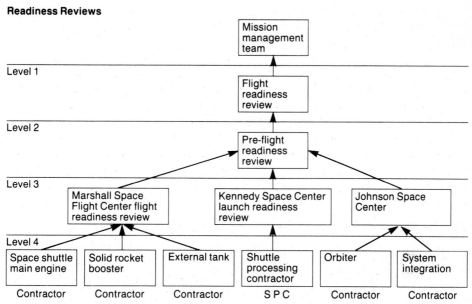

Level 1

Level 2

Level 3

Level 4

Readiness reviews for both the launch and the flight of a Shuttle mission are conducted at ascending levels that begin with contractors.

Figure 4.2. Decision Structure for Shuttle Launch
SOURCE: Presidential Commission of the Space Shuttle *Challenger* Accident 1986, vol. I, p. 83.

guarantee the safety of launches if the temperature of the booster rockets was less than 53 degrees Fahrenheit. Since temperatures below 20 degrees Fahrenheit were expected, Joe Kilminster, a Thiokol manager, recommended cancellation to Laurence Mulloy, a NASA manager. At this point George Hardy, a more senior NASA manager, expressed great disappointment with Thiokol's recommendation; two of those present said he used the word "appalled." Mulloy was reported to have asked, "My God, Thiokol, when do you want me to launch, next April?" Thiokol management interrupted the teleconference and asked for a five-minute internal "off-air caucus," one that took nearly an hour. After the caucus, Kilminster presented a revised recommendation to go ahead with the launch. Although the engineers did not agree, they did not restate their doubts. As Hardy recalls, "Mr. Reinartz [a NASA manager] asked if anyone in the loop had a different position or disagreed or something to that effect, with the Thiokol recommendation [to launch] as presented by Mr. Kilminster. There were no dissenting responses" (Presidential Commission of the Space Shuttle *Challenger* Accident 1986, vol. I, 100).

Roger Boisjoly recalls the off-air caucus at Thiokol in Utah and the decision to recommend launch,

After Arnie and I had our last say, Mr. Mason said we have to make a management decision. He turned to Bob Lund and asked him to take off his engineering hat and put on his management hat. From this point on, management formulated the points to base their decision on. There was never one comment in favor, as I have said, of launching by any engineer or other nonmanagement person in the room before or after the caucus. I was not even asked to participate in giving any input to the final decision charts. . . .

I must emphasize, I had my say, and I never [would] take [away] any management right to take the input of an engineer and then make a decision based upon that input, and I truly believe that. I have worked at a lot of companies, and that has been done from time to time, and I truly believe that, and so there was no point in me doing anything further than I had already attempted to do.

I did not see the final version of the chart until the next day. I just heard it read. I left the room feeling badly defeated, but I felt I really did all that I could to stop the launch.

I felt personally that management was under a lot of pressure to launch and that they made a very tough decision, but I didn't agree with it. (Presidential Commission of the Space Shuttle Challenger *Accident 1986, vol. I, 92–3)*

The doubts raised by Thiokol's engineers were never expressed to upper-level decision makers. The Level III managers felt they had resolved the issue—that the arguments were merely "professional in nature," not a serious question about the launch—and that the question need not be communicated to their superiors. Regarding the decision to launch the Presidential Commission investigating the accident concluded,

3. The Commission is troubled by what appears to be a propensity of management at Marshall [Space Center] to contain potentially serious problems and to attempt to resolve them internally rather than communicate them forward. This tendency is altogether at odds with the need for Marshall to function as a part of a system working toward successful flight missions, interfacing and communicating with the other parts of the system that work to the same end.

4. The Commission concluded that the Thiokol Management reversed its position and recommended the launch of 51-L [the Challenger*], at the urging of Marshall and contrary to the view of its engineers in order to accommodate a major customer. (Presidential Commission of the Space Shuttle* Challenger *Accident 1986, vol. I, 104)*

For the Thiokol engineers the space shuttle disaster did not end with the explosion. Although they chose not to voice their doubts about the safety of the cold-weather launch outside proper channels, they testified fully to the presidential panel investigating the accident. In preparing for his testimony, Boisjoly wrote in his notes, "I hope and pray that I have not risked my job and family security for being honest in my conviction, to stand up for what is right and honorable" (Presidential Commission of the Space Shuttle *Challenger* Accident 1986, vol. IV, 680). Those who presented critical testimony did, however, experience retaliation from Thiokol. None were fired, but several were reassigned to less important work; one was given a new title but the engineers he supervised were assigned to someone else. Chairman of the Presidential Commission, William Rogers, commented,

In this kind of an accident where people come before a Commission and tell the truth and that they are treated as he [Mr. McDonald] believes he has been treated, which obviously is in some way punishment or retaliation for his testimony, it is extremely serious, and the whole idea of the program is to have an openness and to have an honest exchange of views.

And in this case, Mr. McDonald and Mr. Boisjoly and others, Mr. Thompson and others, were right. If their warnings had been heeded that day and the flight had been delayed, there's no telling what would have happened. We might never have had the accident. And to have something happen to him that seems to be in the nature of punishment is shocking. (Presidential Commission of the Space Shuttle Challenger *Accident 1986, vol. V, 1595).*

Discussion Questions

1. Do you think that the Thiokol engineers who thought the launch was unsafe had an obligation to express their views to those at the top of NASA or the press?
2. What are the pressures that discouraged the Thiokol engineers from blowing the whistle to prevent the launch of *Challenger?*
3. Did the formal communications process provide the top decision makers with adequate information?
4. Do you think that it is ever possible to design a communication process that eliminates problems such as those found at NASA?
5. What sort of pressures are brought to bear to discourage public dissent?
6. How does the reward system discourage blowing the whistle?

NOTE

1. These common decision problems—called *groupthink* and the *trapped administrator syndrome*—are more closely examined in Chapter 6.

PART THREE

Micro-Administration— The Art and Science of Management

CHAPTER 5

Public Administration Roles

Large organizations employ many individuals clustered in groups. Individual personalities, quirks, and strengths shape organizations in profound ways. Charismatic leaders, caring supervisors, innovative program directors, and scores of street-level or frontline employees lend their individuality to the collective; they give an organization its character. We should never lose sight of this diversity, but too narrow a focus on individual differences and unique contributions may obscure the patterns of behavior across individuals.

As we suggested in Chapter 4, individuals take on a series of roles in organizations during socialization. Socialization restricts or channels, but does not eliminate, individual differences. Consistency of behavior despite persistent employee turnover is a primary asset of formal organizations. An organization that falls apart when individuals leave has not built an adequate structure of roles; roles provide the consistency that holds organizations together.

In this chapter we examine five role-types that are prevalent in public organizations: the political executive, the desktop administrator, the professional, the street-level bureaucrat, and the policy entrepreneur. This list is neither exhaustive nor exclusive, but these five overlapping roles exist across a wide range of public organizations and are characteristic of those organizations. Although analogous roles exist in private firms, political authority (see Chapter 2) gives each of these roles a distinctive public flavor. As will be discussed, a street-level bureaucrat may occupy the bottom of the organization hierarchy, but the role differs from that of a frontline worker in a business.

ROLE THEORY

Before we can understand these five role-types, we need to explore role theory more fully. A *role* is a predictable set of expectations and behaviors associated with an office or position. Social science borrowed the term from drama and retained important connotations for organizations from the original source. Like an actor assigned a part, cabinet secretaries, police officers, and policy analysts step into roles that are already largely defined. As Daniel Katz and Robert Kahn (1978, 187) wrote, "Human organizations attain stability in terms of patterned recurrences of such acts rather than in terms of the persons who perform them."   .

Just as actors appear to be different people when portraying different roles—the gentlest actor might portray a brutal murderer—individuals change as they take on and shed organizational roles. But an equally important aspect of roles is their adaptability. Individuals who take on roles often contribute something unique: They may turn a routine role into a virtuoso performance, or they may change the role for those that follow. Thus, the role concept encompasses both predictable actions and unique contributions.

Examining roles highlights another important aspect of human organizations. Organizations are contrived, not self-creating, systems. Although no single playwright creates organizational roles, these roles are continually invented and reinvented, often following changing social patterns. The role of secretary, for instance, used to mirror that of the traditional housewife, from serving coffee to tidying up. With significant changes in women's roles both at home and in the workplace, the secretarial role has become more professional (and not incidentally, attracts more men).

The role concept is useful at a variety of levels. For individual organizations, we can examine the specific roles associated with individual positions or offices and their relationship to other roles in the organization. From such an examination, we can draw conclusions that help us understand the organization more clearly. These immediate relations, or *role-sets,* are based on the bonds of work flow and authority relationships (Merton 1957). The role of supervision, for example, may be best understood in relationship to the role of the administrator in charge of the unit, those of the other supervisors, and of the positions supervised.

Beyond the individual organization, certain generalized roles characterize large numbers of positions in large numbers of organizations. We call these *role-types.* The department head of the Bureau of Toxic Wastes in the Environmental Protection Agency is a specific role, but that specific role shares many common traits with department heads in many public agencies. It is a role-type, one that we will define later as a desktop administrator. Because role-types are generalizations, each individual example may not perfectly match the characteristics, but the general characteristics do describe many of the roles.

Sources of Stress

Viewing organizations as a system of roles also helps identify an important source of stress. Individuals frequently don several roles, both within organizations and across work and nonwork roles. At work, the head of the planning office may assist the legislative liaison committee; a group leader in the first role, he is required to act as follower in the second. Assertive and respected at work, this same individual may become anxious in his role as a student in night school and nurturing when he is at home with the children.

These various roles are often a source of enrichment but can also produce overload. Role overload is more than just too much work; overwork is a different source of stress. *Role overload* exists when the demands of various roles overwhelm an individual's ability to balance expectations, when the demands of one role make it difficult to fulfill the demands of others. The lawyer who must cancel an appointment to care for a sick child or the professor who neglects his students to fulfill administrative obligations is experiencing role conflict. When these conflicting expectations reduce the role player's ability to perform, variety becomes stressful overload.

A second source of stress is *role ambiguity* or uncertainty about what the role player is supposed to do or how he or she is supposed to act. People vary in their ability to deal with ambiguity, but for most, uncertainty about expectations and responsibilities creates tension. Extreme uncertainty reduces job satisfaction. At times role ambiguity subjects people to arbitrary criticism since individuals often must discover expectations by trial and error. Many workers complain that they are never told what to do and yet are constantly criticized when they make mistakes.

Dominant Role-Types

Although public organizations contain many specific roles, the five role-types we mentioned at the outset (the political executive, desktop administrator, professional, street-level bureaucrat, and policy entrepreneur) are common. Not all public organizations contain all types, and the number of each type varies widely across agencies. The National Science Foundation has few street-level bureaucrats, whereas this role-type dominates police departments and schools. Except for the policy entrepreneur, these role-types generally correspond to the levels in an organization's hierarchy—political executives on top; desktop administrators and professionals in the middle; and street-level bureaucrats at the bottom.

Although these positions correspond to roles in private organizations—political executives are similar to chief executive officers in corporations—the role-types are particularly distinctive of government organizations. These five role-types also help explain organizational conflict: Boundaries between the different roles can easily become fracture lines that cleave public organizations. The distinctive characteristics of the different role-types and the sources of conflict among them are the subjects of the sections that follow.

THE POLITICAL EXECUTIVE

Political executives occupy the top, or in Mintzberg's (1979) term, the *strategic apex* of public organizations (see Chapter 2). The secretary of the Defense Department, director of the Office of Management and Budget, the head of the Arms Control and Disarmament Agency, the Colorado Secretary of Corrections, the city manager of Dallas, Texas, and the county administrator in Fairfax County, Virginia, are all political executives. In larger government agencies, political executives fill the top several layers of management. Although their jobs and responsibilities vary widely, political executives share three distinctive features or subroles: political aide, policy maker, and top administrator.

Elements in the Political Executive Role

Role of Political Aide.   Political executives are *political appointees.* Elected officials give them their jobs. The president and governors appoint their own cabinet secretaries who are in turn approved by legislators. Mayors and city councils select city managers. In most cases, politicians can also fire political executives, although most out-of-favor political executives resign and receive the standard regrets of political leaders. Some political executives—the chairman of the Federal Reserve, for example—are appointed for a fixed term; they can be impeached but not fired and have, therefore, a greater degree of independence.

To insulate political executives further from political interference, fixed terms that overlap with those of elected officials are set for some. For example, President Carter appointed Paul Volcker as chairman of the Federal Reserve, and his term extended into President Reagan's first term in office. Although at times unhappy with Volcker's economic policies, Reagan could not fire him. In fact, Volcker eventually became so respected among economic leaders that Reagan reappointed him. Similarly, Reagan's Federal Reserve chairman, Alan Greenspan, will serve well into the presidency of George Bush.

All political executives are, nonetheless, political appointees, and this changes their role. Their position, their tenure (except for the few with fixed terms), and their influence while in office derive from the authority of elected officials. They are advisers to elected officials. (A secretary is, literally, someone who can hold a secret, a confidante.) They may have responsibility for major decisions and massive organizations; the secretary of defense leads one of the largest organizations in the world. The ultimate authority, however, rests with the elected official.

Political appointees at the top of public organizations increase the responsiveness of public organizations to the public. Administrative agencies represent the more stable and enduring elements of American government; most outlast elected officials. The Department of Education was created by President Carter, slated for early death by President Reagan, but outlived both presidencies. The Department of State was founded in 1789. Democracy would mean little if elected officials did not have influence over these and all the other government agencies. Imagine the change in American government if the cabinet secretaries were all appointed to fixed, six-year terms of office. The president could no longer choose and dismiss the cabinet and would lose control over policy. Such a system would reduce the president to a figurehead.

The appointment of political executives is, therefore, the primary means of asserting political authority over administrative agencies. It also changes the type of person appointed; the party or group that wins the election most commonly appoints loyal supporters. Although the practice is less common in local government, presidents and governors frequently select personal advisers for executive positions. Occasionally these individuals have had many years of experience and have developed strong influence networks in the policy area of that agency; some have held elected office. Often, however, a political appointee has little expertise in the particular policy area. Many have had no experience at all in the agency they are appointed to head. Some, as outsiders, may actually have strongly criticized the agency. This contrasts sharply with the top executives in most businesses—Lee Iaccoca of Chrysler, for example—who have devoted their careers to that particular industry or firm.

Role of Policy Maker.   Political executives are also policy makers. Even the most diligent mayor, governor, or president can personally deal with only a small set of policy concerns; the more successful focus on only a small number. In policy areas that do not preoccupy top elected officials, political executives are, by default, the highest-level decision makers. The mayor, governor, or president may give final approval, but for many policies the political executive initiates, shapes, promotes, and then oversees policy changes. To the extent that they can mobilize their respective agencies, political executives can enlist considerable expertise, resources, and energy to bear on a policy problem. During Reagan's second term as president, his secretary of education, William Bennett, was continually in the public eye. Education reform was far down on the list of Reagan's priorities, yet Secretary Bennett independently and aggressively crusaded for reforms and policy changes for all levels of education. (Bennett was rewarded for his feistiness when President Bush appointed him "drug czar"—a position for which he had no visible credentials except precisely that feistiness.)

Even when a policy area is of immediate concern to elected officials, political executives retain considerable influence. Elected officials can do little more than point the general direction and scrutinize the final result. Departments and agencies, led by political executives, give form and substance to these broad directives. A president may be interested in tax reform, but it is the Treasury Department that comes up with the specific proposals.

Role of Top Administrator.   Political executives are also top-level administrators. They must cut through the red tape, resistance to change, and interorganizational and intraorganizational conflict to assure that the public is well served. They are responsible for large organizations or major programs within organizations. The budgets and size of major public organizations often exceed those of large corporations.

Although political executives play an important role in developing and promoting policy, they are also legally responsible for implementing policy. When Congress allocates money for AIDS research, the director of the National Institutes of Health is responsible for supporting socially productive research. He or she is answerable to Congress for progress. But, except in a few small agencies, success in implementing policy depends in large part on the efforts of hundreds of agency employees: the desktop administrators, professionals, and street-level bureaucrats discussed later in this chapter. These individuals often spend their careers working in specific department or policy arenas. Moreover, they have views about the correct approaches and solutions that may conflict with those of newly elected officials and political executives.

Political executives who fail to reach down and enlist the support and enthusiasm of their agency personnel will effect little change in policy. New political executives often see their first task as reorganizing their agency to make it more responsive to a new policy agenda. While this process is healthy and necessary for democratic control, it can also create considerable conflict between the short-term political executive and the permanent bureaucracy. When the conflict becomes extreme, the permanent bureaucracy can minimally comply, balk whenever possible, and enter a policy "hibernation" while waiting for a new appointment or new election.

Political executives must, therefore, walk a swaying tightrope. If they completely disregard the preferences, knowledge, and experience of their agencies, stalemate ensues. If, on the other hand, they uncritically adopt the views and routines of their agencies—referred to as "going native"—they may lose influence with elected officials. And without the support of elected officials, political executives cannot compete for the resources and shape policy decisions that are essential to agency vitality. If they cannot successfully balance these competing demands, their effectiveness as policy makers is hobbled. The relationship between elected official, political executive, and public organization is symbiotic. Maintaining this collaboration is the primary responsibility of the political executive; it is a difficult role (Mosher 1982a, 184).

The Time Factor

To add to their difficulties, political executives must accomplish this balancing act within a brief period of time. As we mentioned above, few political executives come to top administrative positions with experience in the agencies they are chosen to head. They must quickly learn how their agencies are structured and run, and they must acquire a knowledge of the history and beliefs that shape agency views. Disregarding established beliefs can quickly create conflict, as when Secretary James Watt tried to place economic development before the traditional emphasis on environmental protection at the Department of Interior during President Reagan's first term.

Moreover, the tenure of most political executives is short. With few exceptions, such as J. Edgar Hoover who lorded over the FBI for decades, those who survive the infighting and inherent conflicts are unlikely to retain their positions when elections change leaders. Few cabinet secretaries serve more than two or three years. Within this time, they must learn a difficult and complicated job and introduce whatever policy changes they hope to accomplish.

This short time horizon reduces the political executive's control over the agency. Presidents and governors who cannot run for another term of office are called *lame ducks;* they lose clout as their terms near the end. Political executives are often lame ducks the moment they take office. Career civil servants who disagree with the new director's policy direction need only wait for a rarely too-distant departure.

The City Manager, a Local Government Example

Political executives are present at all levels of government, wherever political appointees are in positions of substantial managerial responsibility. Cabinet secretaries and under secretaries are visible examples at the state and national levels, but political executives exist at the local level as well. City and county managers are the primary examples. Like cabinet secretaries, city managers are appointed by elected officials— mayors and city councils. They are responsible for the day-to-day operation and management of the various departments of local government. In larger cities, such as Dallas, Texas, city managers administer several large departments and million dollar budgets. In small towns, city managers often work with just one or two officials to make sure the streets are plowed, zoning rules are obeyed, and whatever it takes to run the government is accomplished.

The city management form of local government was devised to separate the administrative role of the manager from the policy role of the elected official. Although carrying out policy can theoretically be separated from making policy, in practice city managers, like all political executives, typically have considerable influence on policy. A city manager opposed to building a shelter for the homeless might overlook federal grant opportunities or strictly enforce zoning requirements. The same city manager may aggressively seek funds and overlook zoning violations of a favored project, such as a new industrial park. City managers, like other political executives, are advisers to elected officials, often downplaying their own contributions; they manage complicated organizations, and they shape the economic growth patterns and local services that directly affect citizens.

DESKTOP ADMINISTRATORS

Desktop administrators are career civil servants down the hierarchy a few steps from political executives. The term *desktop administrators* is not derisive; the work of career civil servants is difficult and important. The term simply emphasizes the internal focus of their work. In large public organizations, high-level civil servants are often in charge of large divisions or bureaus and supervise major government programs. At times these civil servants are asked to testify before Congress, state legislatures, or city commissions. A few develop constituencies in special interest groups and the public to rival those of politicians and political executives. But their primary domain—and for many, their exclusive domain—is the organization.

Desktop administrators are middle managers and closely fit the general description of a bureaucrat. Whether a social work supervisor or the director of a major government program, the desktop administrator spends days filled with memoranda and meetings. These individuals are primarily concerned with assuring that the policy directives of elected and appointed officials are effectively translated into the actions of service providers or the decisions of regulators. The governor and the secretary of aging may insist during a press conference that patient abuse in nursing homes will stop, but until the desktop administrators define abuse in objective language and assure inspector vigilance, such promises are only promises. Desktop administrators guide policy intentions into policy actions that actually change, for better or worse, people's lives.

In addition, desktop administrators are responsible for the efficient or cost-effective delivery of government services. They must not only effectively translate policies into actions but must do so with limited and, after a decade of progressively restricted government expenditures, generally declining resources. The governor may promise better care for the aged, but the desktop administrator must ascertain what *better care* means in practice and—and this is an important *and*—must find a way to deliver better care within severe budget constraints.

Many of the negative caricatures of bureaucrats result from the unresolvable dilemma of translating public preferences and political promises into government programs within the constraints of law and budget. Laurence Lynn (1981), in *Managing the Public's Business,* provides an excellent example. There is widespread public and political consensus that the federal government should financially assist poor people who are blind. But who is poor and who is blind? How these questions are answered dramatically alters the nature and costs of the program. Lenient definitions greatly increase costs by making more and more citizens eligible; narrow definitions lower costs but may exclude those needing services.

In addition, the programs must be designed to increase their just application. An ambiguous definition of blindness encourages unequal treatment; someone with the same poor vision may receive help from one agency but be denied help from another. The translation of social and political preferences into workable policies leads to detailed and complicated rules and programs—the federal definition of *blind* takes nearly 80 words. Complicated rules and programs lead, in turn, to complaints of too much red tape. The desktop administrator is torn between the promises and practicality of governing. If government programs and services work, even if they don't live up to our unrealistic expectations, it is largely due to the successful balancing act of desktop administrators.

Organizational Careers

Desktop administrators differ fundamentally from political executives in that most are career civil servants. After a relatively brief probation period, usually less than a year, most earn job tenure and, except in unusual and difficult circumstances, cannot be fired. Tenure insulates the civil service from direct political interference in the day-to-day working of government. Newly elected officials cannot fire all the appointees of their political rivals and replace them with loyal supporters, as happens under the politicized government system known as the *spoils system,* discussed in Chapter 7. At the higher levels of government, most officials have devoted their working lives to government service. The average tenure of high-level federal civil servants is seventeen to twenty-five years in the same agency or department. They have achieved their positions of authority by working their way slowly up the organizational hierarchy. Along the way, senior desktop administrators have gained considerable knowledge and experience in their policy specialities and the practical workings of government. This depth of experience is an essential asset of American government; without it all areas of life touched by government, from defense to trash removal, from prenatal to hospice care, would be diminished.

Job tenure also lengthens the career civil servant's time horizon. As mentioned, elected officials and political executives live in a short-term world. They need results before the next elections and are often attracted to quick fixes. An example is a cure for AIDS. With each new appropriation congressional leaders press for promises for an immediate medical breakthrough. The civil servants in the Department of Health and Human Services must adjust to this unrealistic expectation while supporting research that may take years to bear fruit.

The longer time horizon is also a conservative influence. Most desktop administrators know they will outlast their politically appointed directors. When they disagree with the policy direction or interpretation, the desktop administrators can clog the process with red tape. Active or passive resistance to the direction of elected and appointed officials does not mean that these administrators are free to pursue their own policy agendas, however. Resistance has career costs. Job tenure protects civil servants from losing their jobs, but it does not insure their influence and position. Desktop administrators who lose favor with political executives may be reassigned to less important jobs of equal rank. Their budgets may be slashed and their access to top decision makers cut off. As one desktop administrator painfully observed after reassignment, "[Political executives] can't take away your job because of civil service, but they can take away your work" (quoted in Stull, Maynard-Moody, and Mitchell 1988, 229).

Changes in formal or informal status within organizational hierarchies are especially significant for desktop administrators. Desktop administrators pursue organizational careers. With their long tenure, they tend to join near the bottom of their hierarchy and work their way up and define their success by their position and by the level of those with whom they interact. They perceive the organizational world according to the organizational chart; their world is composed of supervisors, equals, and inferiors based on position in the hierarchy. Much of their behavior within the organization is motivated by their competition with equals for influence with and favorable evaluations by superiors. The impact of hierarchy on motivation and behavior was discussed in the previous chapter, and that impact is strongest with desktop administrators. Anthony Downs (1967, 80) summarizes the organizational perspective of desktop administrators:

> The official is vitally concerned with those people in the organization with whom he interacts frequently. Most of them are in the same section of the bureau, and many report to the same superior. It is within this section that the official's struggle for promotion, power, prestige, and control are normally waged, and he is acutely aware of its hierarchical structure.

Political but Nonpartisan

Successful careers require skill in organizational politics and in building solid working relationships with elected and appointed officials. Nevertheless, the desktop administrator needs to avoid politics. In the federal government and most state and local governments career civil servants are in fact barred from direct involvement in political campaigns. (See the discussion of the Hatch Acts in Chapter 7.) This distance from partisan politics must also be maintained if desktop administrators want to retain influence after the reigning political party, or faction within the party, loses an election.

Desktop administrators must remain nonpolitical while working in organizations that serve political leaders. This presents them with a fundamental dilemma: Success with the current administration requires diligent and creative work in developing and implementing policies that may be strongly opposed by those who come to power a few years later. Strong association with the policies of the previous administration may limit influence in the current administration, but avoiding involvement with the priority issues of the current administration lessens influence, power, and, ultimately, advancement. The more successful desktop administrators can energetically support the policy agenda of the current political leaders while appearing to be above politics.

Motives

Like all others, desktop administrators are motivated by a range of personal goals, from the purely self-interested (money, power, prestige, convenience, and security) to the more socially or community minded. But desktop administrators are also motivated by loyalty to others within the organization—a mentor or a diligent staff member—and by pride in their own and their program's performance. These organizational motives are also mixed with societal goals. Many desktop administrators are deeply committed to ideals of public service and have devoted their careers to specific policies or programs.

Anthony Downs (1967) suggests a typology of different types of desktop administrators—or in Downs's term, *officials*—based on this different mix of motives. *Climbers* seek more power, income, and prestige and are less encumbered by loyalty, service, or specific policy. They often are attracted to whatever policy area is fashionable. With time and success they become conservers. *Conservers* are also preoccupied with power, income, and prestige, but they are motivated by convenience and security as well and are preoccupied with retaining rather than enlarging their status. Climbers and conservers focus on self-interest.

Zealots, advocates, and statesmen are more policy oriented. *Zealots* are loyal to specific and narrow policies or concepts. For example, many zealots opposed to abortion, affirmative action, and government spending became desktop administrators during President Reagan's two terms. *Advocates* are motivated more by general, broader policy concerns, such as protecting the environment or promoting public health. Zealots and advocates push their policy concerns forward with little regard for other policy concerns. Environmentalists or health educators are often deaf to arguments about the economic costs of providing clean air or eliminating tobacco subsidies. *Statesmen,* on the other hand, are concerned about the broader social trade-offs of most policies. They are, therefore, often less aggressive in pressing their views.

PROFESSIONALS

Professionals make up the third major role-type in public organizations. The original meaning of the term *profession* has important contemporary connotations. A profession was a ceremonial vow made when joining a religious community. This vow usually followed years of training and some certification that the acquired knowledge and appropriate norms of behavior justified an individual's initiation. Like traditional religious orders, professions still require years of specialized training and enforce norms of behavior, and professionals view their work as a calling and a service to others.

The number and importance of professionals is increasing in public organizations. Some organizations employ a handful—a small staff of lawyers advising the political executive—while others contain highly professional units, such as the city planning department. Some public organizations—hospitals and NASA are examples—are staffed primarily by professionals. As will be discussed, the extent of professionalization alters the nature of organizations.

Definition of Professionals

Certified Training.   Professionals receive specific training that ends with certification. The form of the training has evolved into a more or less standard form. A century ago lawyers and physicians learned their craft much as a carpenter did: They worked as apprentices to masters and learned by emulation and practice. Professional education now requires more in-class learning but retains a period of practice. The disciplinary or scientific base of practice is the core of most academic professional education: Physicians learn biology and anatomy while public administrators learn organization theory. The education of a professional goes beyond specialized knowledge, however. Professionals, like the police recruits described in Chapter 4, learn values and norms of behavior. For doctors these norms include confidentiality and for scientists the open criticism of findings. The nature of professional education is largely determined by professional standards.

Professional Standards.   Professional standards cover two related issues: work and behavior. Work standards are based on the skills and knowledge that undergird professional practice. For example, there are generally accepted standards on the structural requirements of a building or the proper method of performing a tonsillectomy. The standards for good teaching or effective clinical psychology are less precise but are nonetheless important. Professionals define problems, design solutions, and evaluate results based on criteria established by their peers and associations. These standards take precedent over specific organizational expectations: A hospital administrator trying to cut costs of operations cannot ask a surgeon to violate medical standards.

The second form of external standards involves professional ethics. Professionals not only apply specific skills to cases but they are expected to act in certain ways. Most ethical codes focus on the proper handling of the relationship between professional and client. Professionals are often in positions of authority and their work requires intimate knowledge of clients. For these reasons, norms of confidentiality and commitment to placing client interests above personal interests are central to most professional practice. Sexual relations between clients and psychologists are not surprising given the intimacy of therapy, but such behavior violates norms of professional relationships and can lead to censure of the professional.

One area of controversy in professional ethics is advocacy. Professionals usually define their practice in terms of service to their clients. At times, however, the welfare of the individual client depends on larger social problems. For example, the greatest health threat in the United States is poverty. Gerald Weissmann (1985) tells of treating a homeless woman for a rare disease. She received expensive, state-of-the art care in an expensive medical center, but when cured, the woman returned to the streets of New York to scrounge for food, shelter, and safety. Most physicians, like members of other helping professions, accept the responsibility of assuring that their clients receive the best possible care. Many argue that this responsibility should extend beyond the individual, that professionals should become advocates for groups of clients and principles. The American Civil Liberties Union (ACLU) is one such advocacy group. Members of this organization extend the lawyers' commitment to due process and legal rights beyond the individual case to all citizens.

Knowledge to Practice.   Learning the knowledge base and behavioral expectations of a profession is only the beginning; in most circumstances, professionals apply general knowledge to specific cases or problems. A doctor examining a patient, an architect designing a building, and a lawyer reviewing a case must bring their general understanding of medicine, structure, and law to the individual situation. The application of general knowledge to specific cases requires more than applying formulas or following recipes. Some cases present unique characteristics that test the limits of general knowledge. Others present such complex problems that several rules of practice may apply.

In other cases the problems are ambiguous and make diagnosis difficult. Diagnosis is, after all, a decision process in which a case is classified so that the professional knows what general rules apply. A lawyer drafting regulations covering surrogate motherhood must first decide to treat the problem as a contract, an adoption, or a divorce. If the legal agreement between the woman bearing the other couple's child is like any other purchase agreement, then the surrogate is obliged, like any other supplier, to fulfill the contract. Claims about emotional bonding have no relevance. But if the general rule is one of adoption, then the birth mother must agree to terminate her rights after the baby is born. If, however, the general rules of divorce hold, then some sharing of the newborn would be more appropriate.

The choice, therefore, of the appropriate set of general principles to apply to the specific case is central to professional practice. This process does not end with the initial diagnosis. Professionals must make judgments about the effects of their efforts. Donald Schön (1983) called this process the "conversation with the case." In the human service professions, this is a literal conversation with individuals and groups. In other fields such as engineering or architecture, the conversation is not literal. Architects, computer programmers, and other professionals working with things and not people nevertheless get a feel for good design based on their intimacy with specific cases. Whether with people or things, professional practice involves exploration, diagnosis, trials, and evaluation. Harland Cleveland (1985) referred to the process as "dynamic improvisation" to capture the skilled trial and reevaluation process at the heart of most professional practice.

Self-Regulation.   Professional training ends with some form of certification: an advanced degree and often a state license. Although a government agency may issue the license to practice, the professional association defines the nature of the training and certifies both the educational program and the individual performance. In addition, peer review committees—committees dominated by fellow members of the profession—examine practice and complaints. Professionals are self-regulating; they determine the nature of their own training, evaluate both programs and individuals, and judge and punish violations of professional norms and codes.

An important difference between professional and nonprofessional work lies, therefore, in who evaluates performance. Nonprofessionals are evaluated by their immediate supervisors. Most professionals now work in large organizations and therefore accept levels of bureaucratic control. Professionals resist, however, any constraint that intrudes on the exercise of their judgments and actions. Professionals typically assert their independence from supervisors. Quality control is established through peer, not administrative, review; panels of doctors, lawyers, social workers, and other professionals review the work of their colleagues. The argument for peer review is that only fellow professionals can judge the adequacy of the work; only they have the prerequisite expertise.

Self-regulation has flaws. Peers rarely censure peers unless the offense is egregious. Fellow professionals are sometimes more willing to overlook the mistakes of colleagues: Perhaps they made similar errors or lapses in judgment. Perhaps they are uncomfortable sanctioning a co-worker. Perhaps, their shared professional training has blinded them to the limits of their own professional standards. Lawyers claim that medical malpractice is often covered up by peer review. Whatever the reasons, the conflict over malpractice is a conflict over the right to control the work of the profession.

In this chapter, we define desktop administrators and professionals as separate role-types, yet the increased number of management professionals blurs this distinction. More and more top-level administrators in public organizations have master's degrees in business or public administration. Trained in management science, these professionals often have careers and allegiances that are more similar to those of other professions than to those of desktop administrators. Other administrators in public organizations are crossovers: lawyers, doctors, engineers, social workers, or college professors whose career paths take them away from direct service and into administration. Some are both administrators and practicing professionals. For example, Lewis Thomas was the director of the Memorial Sloan-Kettering Cancer Center while an active medical researcher. And, as we noted in Chapter 1, public administrators include biologists, cartographers, dentists, geneticists, nurses, petroleum engineers, school teachers, and so on, all of whom are professionals who are employed by government.

We need to emphasize that roles and role-types are separate from the individuals who enact them. The bureau director with a master's degree in public administration must balance the conflicting demands of enacting both the desktop administrator and professional roles. The roles remain distinct even when one individual enacts both.

Administrative versus Occupational Principle

The trend in many organizations, public and private, is to hire more and more professionals. This is the natural development of bureaucratic specialization and has been accelerated by the evolution from an industrial to a service- and knowledge-based economy. Donald Schön (1983, 326–327) writes,

> Increasingly, the lives of professionals in our society are bound up with the lives of formal bureaucratic organizations through which most work is done. . . . Max Weber, the prophet of bureaucracy, saw very clearly that bureaucracy would require and foster the professionalization of its members. . . . From the earliest intellectual awareness of the bureaucratic phenomenon, then, it has been clear that bureaucracy is bound up with technical expertise.

Professionals bring important benefits to organizations. Professional education—a tightly bound process of selection, socialization, and learning—produces individuals who behave predictably in uncertain and complex circumstances (Benveniste 1987, 3). Professionals require, often demand, less direct supervision. Moreover, professionals bring to their organization the specific skills required to complete each organization's mission. Learning on the job remains important, and many professional skills can be picked up with years of practice. Nevertheless, the extensive on-the-job training required to bring generalists up to the skill level of professionals is beyond the means of most organizations. Professional education also provides the foundation for continual self-directed learning that enables professionals to keep up with rapidly developing knowledge. Professionals are, therefore, a source of predictability and a resource for change. They are, however, often in conflict with their organizations and administration.

The conflict between professional and administrative roles is based on two principles described by Eliot Freidson (1973). The *administrative principle* emphasizes supervisory control. Supervisors decide what jobs should be done, how they should be performed, and who should perform them. The second principle, the *occupation principle,* contradicts the first. The occupation principle gives the individual doing the work control over problem definition and solving. Administrators may retain control over resources but do not have control over work activities. Professionals claim much control over their work because of their expertise; they know more than their administrative supervisors. Hospital organizations are good examples. Hospital administrators manage and allocate resources but have little direct influence over the practice of medicine. Rarely are the lines between administrative and professional control drawn as clearly as they are in hospitals. The push and pull between the administrative and occupational principles continually defines the competition between desktop administrators and professionals.

One area in which this competition is most visible is the right to evaluate work performance. As we discussed in Chapter 2, the right to evaluate work is the foundation of supervisory control. But can a supervisor, even one with a master's degree in administration, evaluate the work of a toxicologist, engineer, lawyer, or other professional? Desktop administrators may not be able to test blood, design a sewer system, or write a brief, but they insist on their ability to judge those that do. The professional counters that lay supervisors lack the technical expertise to evaluate his or her performance; that should be left to fellow professionals. As Friedson (1973, 33) concludes, "Control over work performance is of course the basic prize over which occupation and administration contend in a particular setting."

The Politics of Expertise.   The conflict between the administrative and occupation principles profoundly influences policy making and implementing in the United States. Political executives and desktop administrators, who are more concerned with top-down control, stress the importance of accountability: Professionals are neither elected or appointed and must be held accountable by those who were. But increasingly, professionals and other experts are major and often autonomous actors in policy making. Economists, scientists, and other specialists often define the terms and nature of policy (Lowi and Ginsberg 1976). In a technical society, elected and appointed officials often merely ratify the experts' decisions. Francis Rourke (1984, 134) observed,

> From the professional's perspective, the administrator is often looked upon as merely a bookkeeper, or that ultimate insult, a paper shuffler. The professional commonly regards administrative rules and procedures that are designed to promote organizational efficiency as stifling both energy and imagination.

Professionals strive for freedom from bureaucratic constraint, but democratic control requires accountability. This conflict remains a fundamental problem in contemporary public administration, a problem that demands innovative solutions. Guy Benveniste (1987) suggests that procedures for accountability must change in professional organizations. Successful professional organizations concurrently encourage professionals to pursue careers with recognition outside their organizations while attending to the needs of that particular organization. Management must find ways to foster discretion while retaining control over results. An important step in this direction is to share management responsibilities with professionals, to bring administrative work within the boundaries of professional discretion.

The Reflective Practitioner

As public organizations must change in response to increased reliance on professionals, the professions themselves are changing. Donald Schön (1983) foresees a shift from professional as expert to professional as reflective practitioner. Professionals as experts apply their specialized knowledge to solve problems or help clients. This specialized knowledge is based on, or as many would say "proven by," scientific research. Nonprofessionals are best served by following this expert advice rather than voicing their own, nonexpert, views.

Schön suggests a change in our thinking about professionals. This change does not involve abandoning knowledge and expertise but recognizing that the application of knowledge is a situation for learning and discovery. The reflective practitioner has views about his or her own uncertainty that are different from those of the expert. Experts see their own uncertainty about how to solve a problem or help a client as a professional failing. Reflective practitioners see uncertainty as an opportunity to work with the client or problem to achieve a new understanding. In this process, clients are viewed as partners who bring their understanding to the setting. This sharing breaks down the professional facade that often separates clients and professionals or the public from the expert. This change is not an end to professionalism but rather a redefinition of the role. Schön (1983, 344–345) concludes,

> So long as the conduct of society depends upon special knowledge and competence, there will be an essential place for the professions. . . . The idea of reflective practice . . . leads us to recognize that the scope of technical expertise is limited by situations of uncertainty, uniqueness, and conflict. When research-based theories are inapplicable, the professional cannot legitimately claim to be expert, but only to be especially well prepared to reflect-in-action.

STREET-LEVEL BUREAUCRATS

Street-level bureaucrats, the fourth role-type, form the base of most public organizations. In social work, policing, teaching, and other forms of direct service, street-level work is challenging and varied. However, some street-level bureaucrats share many of the negative traits of all those who work at the bottom of the organizational hierarchy. Although many street-level bureaucrats accomplish the primary work of the organization (see the discussion of the operating core in Chapter 2), they also are generally the lowest paid, have the shortest vacations, are the least valued, and are considered the most expendable (Kanter and Stein 1979, 176). They work in the worst conditions—in crowded, usually windowless offices or outdoors on the street—and some, such as police or fire officers, risk physical danger. In addition, street-level careers are often limited. Among those who desire organizational advancement, only a few rise to the lower rungs of management. A very few work their way up to middle or top management, and those who do most often must return to school to qualify for advancement. Most street-level bureaucrats face careers with little advancement.

Street-level bureaucrats who are at the bottom of the organizational hierarchy share this common plight with those at the bottom of private organizations. The street-level bureaucrat role differs fundamentally, however, from that of frontline employees in private organizations. In Kanter and Stein's (1979) view, the central characteristic of life at the bottom of private organizations is the extent to which the person is controlled by those higher up in the hierarchy. Street-level bureaucrats lack formal authority, and desktop administrators attempt to control their actions, but street-level bureaucrats nevertheless retain considerable autonomy. To understand this bureaucratic anomaly, the role-type needs further definition.

Characteristics of Street-Level Bureaucrats

The street-level bureaucrat role has three characteristics (Lipsky 1980), and it is important to stress that not all frontline staff in public organizations are street-level bureaucrats. Only those who meet all three characteristics fall into this role-type.

First, they are *frontline staff* at the bottom or near the bottom of public organizations. This characteristic is their common bond with those at the bottom of all organizations. The second and third elements are closely related and mark the distinctive characteristics of the role-type. These two additional characteristics add elements from the roles of professional and political executive to work at the bottom.

Second, like professionals, street-level bureaucrats *interact directly with clients or citizens* in the delivery of government or human services. Social workers, police officers, job and drug counselors, public health nurses, and public school teachers are examples of street-level bureaucrats. The political executive sets the agenda for expanded services to the disabled; the professional drafts rules defining who is disabled; desktop administrators assure that programs are within budget. But the street-level bureaucrat delivers the service to disabled individuals. This direct relationship with clients is similar to professional practice, but street-level bureaucrats rarely have the status and authority of professionals.

Third, street-level bureaucrats *exercise considerable discretion* over the delivery of government services. Unlike other frontline workers, street-level bureaucrats are not easily controlled by managers and are decision makers. They do not have the formal authority granted desktop administrators but exercise considerable authority over the delivery of services. Their authority does not come from rank, since they are at the bottom of the hierarchy, but rather from the discretionary nature of their work. The sources of this discretion are important aspects of this role-type.

Sources of Discretion.   Michael Lipsky (1980, ch. 2) identified several characteristics of street-level work that encourage the use of discretion. The situations and clients these workers face cannot be easily reduced to standard procedures or routines. Street-level bureaucrats deal with people and people are complex and unpredictable. Rules and procedures suggest the way a street-level worker should deal with a person being arrested or with an abusive parent. These are general guidelines only; rules cannot eliminate the variability of each case. The police officer or social worker must use judgment, and judgment requires discretion.

In addition, street-level work is based on a dilemma (Lipsky 1980, 16). Street-level workers should treat everyone fairly and impartially: Families enduring similar poverty should receive the same level of welfare benefit; drunk drivers in expensive cars should suffer the same punishment as those in junkers. Nevertheless, street-level bureaucrats need to treat individuals with compassion and flexibility. Individuals are not all the same; they require individual attention. A common complaint about public bureaucracies is that they treat everyone like a number; they ignore unique problems or circumstances. This dilemma cannot be solved by writing better rules or guidelines. Street-level bureaucrats are continually faced with judgment calls as they apply rules, procedures, and laws to unique situations.

Street-level bureaucrats also work in settings or situations that defy direct supervision. The police officer on the street, a social worker making a home visit, and an inspector visiting a nursing home make decisions away from their supervisors' scrutiny. Even when supervisors are physically nearby, much work with clients is done in private. Supervisors can, of course, evaluate work, but they cannot control the problems or issues that are left unnoticed or unrecorded. Most paperwork and computerized management information systems attempt to increase managerial control over street-level bureaucrats, who in turn become skilled in filling out forms to satisfy supervisors while maintaining their own autonomy.

Street-Level Bureaucrats as Policy Makers

The discretionary authority street-level bureaucrats enjoy gives them considerable control over the delivery of public policy. Street-level bureaucrats do not draft legislation, nor do political executives routinely ask them for advice on policy matters, but street-level bureaucrats change policy and sometimes functionally rewrite policy as they deliver it. Rather than rule-bound implementors of policies made by those higher up, street-level bureaucrats typically are the ultimate policy makers (Weatherley 1979). They determine the distribution and character of governmental sanctions and benefits.

But how can street-level bureaucrats, those with the least authority, make policy? First, they often decide what policies to implement. A police officer on the beat or an inspector visiting a day-care center may choose to ignore some infractions while strictly enforcing others. They may, in fact, need to ignore some violations to concentrate on others. When a patrol officer ignores a jaywalker to ticket a drunk driver, she is deciding which law is more important.

Other times the street-level bureaucrats' beliefs can affect their work with clients. For example, when doing research in a social services department in the rural Northeast, the second author discovered that many social workers would not tell poor clients that they qualified for a special heating supplement. The stories about welfare recipients turning their thermostats to 80 degrees violated local norms of frugality and the tradition of spending the autumn cutting firewood. The poor, in the eyes of these social workers, did not deserve the supplement and the workers effectively thwarted federal and state law and policy.

Street-level bureaucrats can also interpret policy to benefit clients. For example, children having trouble reading may be identified as "learning disabled" to qualify for a special class or program. Sometimes these labels are harmful and the treatment ineffective, but street-level bureaucrats, in this case teachers and school psychologists, can determine how a policy is delivered by deciding who qualifies.

Street-level bureaucrats shape policy by altering the manner in which it is delivered as well. Individuals contacting government agencies can be brusquely treated or warmly received. The success of a program to encourage the homeless to live in shelters depends in large part on how they are treated in the shelter. Humane treatment can, however, lead to service overload or too many clients for limited resources. Poor treatment of clients is an effective, if unfortunate, means of reducing demand for inadequately funded programs.

In addition, street-level bureaucrats are often forced to change policy while implementing it. The laws or policy may be ambiguous or vague, and street-level bureaucrats must make sense out of managerial gobbledygook. Laws and policies may also prove impractical. This situation is especially common when resources do not match ambitions: The mayor may announce a crackdown on drugs, but may not allocate additional money for law enforcement. The school board may require schools to offer special programs for the hearing impaired and then provide only one specialist for the entire district.

Whenever resources do not match the scope of the problem—the situation in nearly all areas of social policy—street-level bureaucrats must ration services. They are faced with an impossible situation: If everyone who qualified for a service received the service, the program would be uniformly bad and no one would benefit. If only a small portion of those eligible are served, however, the program could make a difference in those particular lives. How should the street-level bureaucrats choose? Should they take the neediest—who are often the least responsive to intervention—or should they take those most likely to be helped?

This dilemma tears apart most social programs. For example, community corrections programs in most states exclude violent criminals. The fear is that placing violent criminals in halfway houses threatens the community; one rape and the program is closed down. These states take nonviolent criminals and provide counseling, job training, and close supervision to guide their transition from prison to the community. On the other hand, the violent criminal, who has probably served more time and is less likely to find work and acceptance, is released without the added assistance of help from a halfway house.

In sum, street-level bureaucrats have a major influence on policy as delivered to citizens. Street-level bureaucrats deal with policy on a level different from that on which political executives operate. For them policy is not a grand scheme or abstract principle but a constant set of small-scale choices in how to deal with specific individuals in specific settings. These small steps can add up to major policies, however. As Michael Lipsky (1980, xii) summarizes,

I argue that the decisions of street-level bureaucrats, the routines they establish, and the devices they invent to cope with uncertainties and work pressures, effectively *become* the public policies they carry out. I argue that public policy is not best understood as made in legislatures or top-floor suites of high-ranking administrators, because in important ways it is actually made in the crowded offices and daily encounters of street-level workers.

Relations with Clients

As this discussion indicates, working with clients is central to the street-level bureaucrat role and deserves special attention. Clients of government services often have no choice of services: If you are arrested for drunk driving you have no choice about dealing with the police. If the judge sentences you to an alcohol treatment program you have little choice about attending. In other instances, participation is voluntary but government holds a monopoly on the service: If you qualify and choose to apply for food stamps, the state department of social services is the only source. You can't shop around for the best deal or the best treatment. In other services—adoption, education, and health care—choice depends on income. Some private hospitals refuse even the emergency treatment of patients without private insurance. The poor have little or no choice and are often at the mercy of street-level bureaucrats for life's necessities: food, shelter, and medical care.

The dependence of clients on street-level bureaucrats creates conflict. In most public organizations, street-level bureaucrats have little to gain by satisfying dependent and powerless clients. Given limited resources, public organizations want fewer, not more, clients. This is an important difference between public and private organizations. A business that attracts more clients or customers earns more profit; in public organizations, however, most resources are allocated by elected officials and attracting more clients means that fixed budgets must be stretched further.

In addition, poor people, law breakers, substance abusers, the sick, and the aged are often difficult and unpleasant; some are threatening. They are real people, not policy abstractions, and street-level bureaucrats must find ways to satisfy them while preserving their own safety and sense of accomplishment. One way they accomplish this is to give a few clients special attention while treating others perfunctorily. Lipsky (1980) writes:

> In short, street-level bureaucrats develop conceptions of their jobs, and of clients, that reduce the strain between capabilities and goals, thereby making their jobs psychologically easier to manage. (p. 141) . . . The street-level bureaucrat salvages *for a portion of the clientele* a conception of his or her performance consistent with ideal conceptions of the job. (p. 151)

POLICY ENTREPRENEURS

The last role-type, the policy entrepreneur, is generally considered to be the charismatic person at the top (Lewis 1980). However, entrepreneurs can exist at all levels of an organization. Although we will focus on those working in public agencies, policy entrepreneurs can hold elected office or remain formally outside government. This role is less tied to organizational position than are other roles; it is, however, affected by position. Policy entrepreneurs who are also political executives act out their roles in a manner different from that of policy entrepreneurs who are middle managers, technical specialists, or direct service providers.

At first glance the term *policy entrepreneur* makes little sense: Entrepreneurs belong in business, not in government bureaucracies. In business, entrepreneurs start new businesses and their personal fortunes depend on the success or failure of this venture. The common stereotype tells us that public bureaucrats stifle rather than reward taking risks. This, of course, is *not* true (Nalbandian and Maynard-Moody 1989). But there are dilemmas confronted by public administrators that private sector entrepreneurs do not face. On one hand, the emphasis on accountability and predictability that strengthens the control of high-level elected and appointed officials discourages new ideas; desktop administrators and street-level bureaucrats are supposed to implement, not change, policy. On the other hand, our complex political system of dispersed and balanced powers places great obstacles in the path of new policies. Even presidents have difficulty pushing through their favored policy initiatives. Herbert Kaufman (1963, 113) observed:

> A political system characterized by numerous decision centers . . . facilitates deadlock, delay, and obstruction. As long as every proposal and every innovation must run a gauntlet, the system is loaded against change. With so many participants possessing a veto, it encourages obstruction.

Fortunately, the fragmentation that complicates innovation also creates opportunities for new and creative programs. The conflicts and overlaps in authority between different branches and levels of government create cracks and niches in which innovation occurs (see Chapter 13 on federalism). Despite the forces that discourage change, policy innovation is common at all levels of government. Some innovations are changes in procedures, such as a computerized register for tracking stolen goods. Others are new programs to deal with enduring social problems, such as hospices for the dying. Less common are major national policy initiatives, such as Medicare or income tax reform. The cards are stacked against all such changes, and each requires policy entrepreneurs to make the unlikely happen.

Characteristics of Policy Entrepreneurs

A few policy entrepreneurs are famous: Franklin D. Roosevelt, J. Edgar Hoover, Henry Kissinger. Innovators in high office are the most visible (see Lewis, 1980, and Doig and Hargrove, 1987, for case studies), but obscure entrepreneurs in middle- or low-level positions or working far from the nation's capital share the traits of the more famous. Theodore Marmor and Phillip Fellman (1986) suggest that policy entrepreneurs have two important characteristics. They are strongly committed to specific programs. Policy entrepreneurs are focused often to the point of narrow-mindedness. Commitment, however, is not enough; policy entrepreneurs are also strong managers. More than zealots, they are also skilled in gathering support and guiding an idea into reality. Policy entrepreneurs often remain in a single policy area for much of their career. Unlike generalist managers who migrate from agency to agency, entrepreneurs develop the expertise and networks to implement innovation successfully.

As advocates and managers, the policy entrepreneurs take on three roles or functions (King and Roberts 1987). The first role is *conceptual leader*. As discussed in the section on organizational change in Chapter 3, these new ideas often come from mundane problem solving rather than inspiration, but policy entrepreneurs generate new ideas. The second role is *strategist*. Successful policy entrepreneurs must find resources and devise plans to put ideas into place. Innovation without implementation is the greatest failure of entrepreneurs. Third, a policy entrepreneur is a *political activist*. This entrepreneur must put his or her strategy to work within the political arena. This feat requires compromise and timing, two skills rare among zealots. Skillful policy entrepreneurs must often wait for opportunities, what John Kingdon (1984, ch. 8) called "policy windows," to push their ideas forward.

Policy entrepreneurs are the movers and shakers of government (Palumbo, Musheno, and Maynard-Moody 1986). They must go beyond the narrow rules and limits of government. They can, therefore, produce considerable harm as well as benefit. In the 1930s, President Roosevelt pushed through several unconstitutional programs to pull the nation out of economic depression. Frustrated by the constraints of shared powers, he then unsuccessfully tried to reverse the Supreme Court's rejection of these policies by adding new, more sympathetic members to the highest court. More recently, Colonel Oliver North and others bent the laws to avoid congressional oversight to fulfill their zealous commitment to support the anticommunist rebellion in Central America.

Although policy entrepreneurs often bend rules and at times lead policy astray, additional procedures and constraints on innovation may only damage governance. As Tower, Muskie, and Skowcroft (1987, 4) concluded after their critical evaluation of the National Security Council's involvement in selling arms to terrorist Iran to support anticommunist rebels: "It is not possible to make a system immune from error without paralyzing its capacity to act." Policy entrepreneurs take risks and push limits, and are necessary for a dynamic government. Policy entrepreneurs are the source of what is best and worst in public policy and administration.

SUMMARY

This chapter examined five prominent public administration role-types: the political executive, desktop administrator, professional, street-level bureaucrat, and policy entrepreneur. Roles are defined by a predictable set of expectations and behaviors associated with an office or position. Roles are a source of organizational consistency; when individuals take on roles they conform to the behavioral demands and expectations associated with that role. This conformity is not absolute, and role theory allows room for individual differences. Nonetheless, enduring roles highlight the patterns of behavior that help us understand organizations.

Political executives are top executives in major federal, state, and local agencies or programs. Although the specific nature of the terms of office vary, political executives are political appointees who, for the most part, serve at the pleasure of elected executives whether the president, governor, or mayor. Most have had little experience working in the agency or department they head; many have little knowledge of the policies they now administer. Most political executives, especially those in federal and state government, serve for only brief periods—a year or two.

Political executives must balance three conflicting roles. First, they are political aides. Many see their primary objective as helping their elected boss earn reelection. Second, they are major policy makers. Presidents, governors, and mayors can address only a small portion of the issues that fall within their responsibility. The rest of these become the responsibility of the political executive. Even in policy areas of personal concern to elected leaders, political executives are often charged with putting substance into broad policy mandates and political promises. Third, political executives are top administrators who must manage large organizations. Career civil servants who have spent years within the agency or on a specific policy domain may view political executives as visitors, often unwelcome visitors, in their organizations. Political executives must somehow engage the organizations they so briefly manage to serve the policy goals of the current administration.

Desktop administrators are public administration's middle managers. They are the career civil servants one step below the political executives, the directors of the individual programs, and the supervisors of the professionals and street-level bureaucrats. They are primarily concerned with assuring that the policy directives of elected and appointed officials are effectively translated into the actions of service providers and the decisions of regulators. In addition, they must guide policy implementation within the limitations of budget and organizational capacity. Desktop administrators have organizational careers. Most start near the bottom or in the middle of the hierarchy and work their way up.

Increasingly the work of public organizations depends on professionals. Professionals learn their trade and the values of their profession through certified education and supervised practice. Their education and professional conduct are guided by professional standards that are independent of the specific work expectations of their organization. The work of professionals involves their applying their general knowledge to the specific case or problem and requires considerable autonomy and flexibility. The professionals' desire to control their own work often conflicts with administrative demands for accountability.

Street-level bureaucrats work on the front lines of government service. Although working at the bottom of the hierarchy, their face-to-face contact with clients and citizens gives them considerable discretion over the delivery of government services. They screen clients for service and decide which laws or rules to enforce and ignore. Street-level bureaucrats rarely draft legislation or engage in policy debates, but their everyday actions and inactions alter policy as delivered to citizens. As Lipsky (1980, xii) writes, "Public policy is not best understood as made in legislatures or top-floor suites of high-ranking administrators, because in important ways it is actually made in the crowded offices and daily encounters of street-level workers."

The policy entrepreneur is a role-type that exists at all levels of the organization; entrepreneurs range from high-ranking and visible leaders to obscure activists working in middle- or low-level positions or far from the nation's capital. Policy entrepreneurs are committed to specific policy agendas and are strong managers. The role requires conceptual leadership, strategic planning, and political activism. The role of policy entrepreneur is both necessary and dangerous. Without energetic advocates few policy initiatives overcome barriers to change, yet single-minded policy entrepreneurs who bend the rules and bypass established policy processes pose a threat to government by law and legislative process.

CASE STUDY: FIVE INDIVIDUALS IN FIVE ROLES

Political Executive: Secretary James Baker

Secretary of State James A. Baker, III, is one of the government's top political executives.[1] He is the chief administrator of one of the nation's oldest, largest, and most complex bureaucracies. He earned this job not by success in lower-level management positions but because he was a long-term political ally of President Bush, who announced Baker's appointment within days of winning the 1988 election. Baker was treasury secretary during Reagan's second term, a position he left to become George Bush's campaign manager. Many observers credit Bush's election victory to Baker's political skills. Baker also managed Bush's first unsuccessful run for the presidency and then, with Bush's help, became chief of staff during Reagan's first term. A man of great skill and insight, and a close friend of the president, Baker is not a foreign policy expert; he is a politician.

The tension between the career foreign policy experts in the State Department and Secretary Baker is palpable. Part of this conflict is a representation of the inevitable clash of career civil servants and their political superiors, but others who held this job—Henry Kissinger and Cyrus Vance are examples—were foreign policy experts. Careerists look to the secretary as one who can translate their advice into the president's policy. They see the secretary as their ambassador in the White House. Baker has the opposite view. He sees himself as the president's representative in the State Department; his job is to get the careerists to conform to Bush's views. As Thomas Friedman (1989, 7) reports, "Mr. Baker and the aides he brought with him argued that the Foreign Service was great at giving seminars about the politics of Brunei, but was totally deaf to the politics of the United States Congress, and as a result had failed to achieve as much as they could have."

This emphasis on politics is perhaps best seen in an exchange through the press between Senator George Mitchell and Secretary Baker. Mitchell had criticized the Bush administration's conservative response to the political turmoil in eastern Europe in 1989. Baker responded as if the question asked who was ahead in the opinion polls; Mitchell insisted that policy, not politics, was the issue. Baker told the press, "When the President is rocking along with a 70 percent approval rating on his handling of foreign policy, if I were the leader of the opposition, I might have something similar to say." Mitchell responded, "I remind the Secretary that this is not a political campaign. This is an effort, in good faith, to deal with serious questions of public policy. He will better serve the nation and the President if he addresses the substance of my remarks, rather than resorting to accusations about politics" (quoted in Friedman 1989, 1,7).

Desktop Administrator: Bill Washington

Bill Washington is the director of the bureau of communicable diseases in the department of health in a populous midwestern state.[2] He directly supervises five programs with a total of sixty-five employees. He reports to the assistant secretary of health and is chairman of the AIDS Prevention Task Force, one of the department's major policy initiatives. Except for a few years working for an insurance company, Bill has worked in state government for his entire working life. He started as a nursing home inspector in a neighboring state and was promoted to a series of increasingly important management positions. He moved from program to program in both the welfare and health departments. Along the way he earned a master's degree in public administration (MPA) by attending night classes at a nearby state university. Although it took him nearly five years to complete the degree, at a time when his wife was working and his two children were young, he felt that the MPA degree was necessary if he was to win promotions.

His current position offers an important opportunity but one with real career risks. AIDS prevention is at the center of the public health policy agenda. His bureau has doubled its federal funding and his state allocations are growing. He has expanded his staff, attracting aggressive, creative professionals from other parts of the agency. He gets calls from the press, testifies before the legislature, attends policy sessions with the governor, participates in the agency's weekly executive meeting (the only bureau director attending) and has helped organize a national conference. If he plays his cards right, he could be the next under secretary or land a top position in Washington.

Bill also knows he is walking a tightrope and a misstep could mean reassignment to a less visible and less important job. One big mistake and his current position could be as high as he gets professionally, a hard thing to face for someone in his mid-forties. He's especially worried about the agency policy on elementary school sex education. The medical and public health professionals on his staff along with the AIDS activists demand an aggressive and explicit sex education program implemented in schools across the state, even in the conservative dairy farming region. He knows that if the professionals and activists accuse him of making political, not professional, decisions, his credibility is weakened. But this is a conservative state, and the governor and health secretary are nervous about the political dangers of explaining condoms to sixth graders. In the past, Bill rose in management by making careful, expert decisions and by working closely with his staff. Now he's worried that doing the right thing for AIDS prevention may be doing the wrong thing for his career.

Professional: Dr. Ellen Cooper

Ellen Cooper works on a different aspect of AIDS policy, the testing of AIDS drugs and treatments.[3] She is an unlikely enemy of AIDS activists, but in August 1988 she epitomized a slow and unresponsive government to those demanding the early release of treatments for AIDS. She was a heartless bureaucrat to her critics, a dedicated professional to her supporters.

In August 1988, Ellen Cooper at the age of thirty-seven was director of the Food and Drug Administration's Division of Anti-Viral Drug Products. A pediatrician in a mid-level managerial position, she supervised the tests of drugs promising cure or treatment of AIDS-related diseases. A mother of four, one with Down's syndrome, Ellen Cooper is a Phi Beta Kappa graduate of Swarthmore. She studied medicine at Yale and Case-Western Reserve and earned a master's in public health from Johns Hopkins. Several years earlier she had played an important role in the quick approval and release of AZT, the only proven treatment for AIDS-related diseases. She won praise from her agency supervisors and the drug manufacturers for expediting the AZT trials without compromising scientific standards.

As the AIDS epidemic continued and people with AIDS became more politically organized, Ellen Cooper became the target for complaints. She insisted that all drugs and treatments meet scientific standards—that tests show they are effective and their benefits outweigh their risks—before they are released to the public. Careful tests, even when expedited, take time, since many harmful side effects appear only after months or even years of treatment. AIDS advocates asked why anyone would deny dying patients promising drugs even if they were not proven. They demanded immediate access to experimental treatments while Dr. Cooper continued to insist that only safe and effective treatments would be approved by the FDA. Martin Delaney, codirector of Project Inform, which identifies and broadcasts news about potential AIDS treatments, found her scientific standards synonymous with indifference. He told a reporter, "She's really rigid and adamant in her beliefs. She's been adamantly opposed to the early release of experimental treatments. She clearly places the needs of the research process above the needs of compassion for patients" (Boffey 1988, 23).

But to a physician, compassion means providing effective treatment, not succumbing to the dying person's understandable panic. Dr. Cooper takes the position of most physicians and medical researchers: "The primary conflict here is between the individual who has a fatal illness and is willing to take a million-to-one or thousand-to-one shot, and larger public health considerations that require controlled studies to determine whether drugs are effective and can have a role or not. . . . We've got to think of what's best for most patients" (Boffey 1988, 23). Caving in to public opinion, even the anguished opinion of those with AIDS, is not her view of professional behavior or good public policy. Her stand was shared by others in the medical community. Dr. Dannie King, who helped develop AZT, told the reporter, "In my mind, she represents the ideal regulator. She has excellent credentials, is willing to work on a scientist-to-scientist level without taking an adversarial position from the start, and is intelligent, deliberate, and gutsy."

Street-Level Bureaucrat: Chris Zajac

Chris Zajac doesn't think of herself as a street-level bureaucrat—or any other kind of bureaucrat or public administrator.[4] She might even find the terms offensive. She is not, in her view, a policy maker. She is a fifth-grade public school teacher in a small Massachusetts town. Nevertheless, when she stands before her class of students of mostly Irish, Polish, and Puerto Rican descent, she is on the front line of education policy. It is here in the direct contact between public school teacher and student that education policy is delivered. How she does her job, and how thousands of other teachers do theirs, is education policy in its most concrete form. As Tracy Kidder (1989) observes, "Decades of research and reform have not altered the fundamental facts of teaching. The task of universal, public, elementary education is still usually being conducted by a woman alone in a little room."

What is it like on the front line of education policy? Chris Zajac daily faces a dilemma shared by all teachers and others providing human services. Her class is made up of individuals but she hasn't the time or resources to respond to the individual needs of all her students. If she focuses on the kid who is failing and indifferent then she may overlook the quiet, talented one. And then there's the disruptive, hyperactive, fight-prone boy who commands so much attention that it's easy to forget everything else. Can she risk her entire class or should she try to have him placed in a special class?

Chris Zajac's work is intimate. She spends six hours a day alone with the same twenty kids; there is no room for pretense or escape. When she's tired or disappointed, the kids know it; they also know what makes her happy or angry. Physically close, she knows when a student doesn't bathe; students, in turn, smell her perfume and experience her hugs, pats, encouragement, criticism, and jokes.

Chris Zajac's work is demanding—she often finds herself awake at night thinking about her class—and isolated—contact with other teachers is rare. Supplies are short and equipment only adequate. Her pay is modest and her career opportunities very limited. Although highly regarded, she will remain an elementary school teacher her entire work life unless she decides to leave teaching. She must, therefore, define her success not by the outward symbols of position and salary, but by her influence on children. But all too often her best efforts seem insignificant compared to the kids' needs and rarely does she see the fruits of her labor. Yet, despite the difficulty, she knows that hers is most important work. In her small classroom, she—not the principal, superintendent, school psychologist, or the secretary of education—determines how public education affects kids.

Policy Entrepreneur: Carl Bianchi, Court Administrator of Idaho

Carl Bianchi is a policy entrepreneur who developed, built support for, and then implemented a major reform of the Idaho court system. In his own words, this is his story.[5]

I am the state court administrator for Idaho. Under our state constitution the [Idaho] Supreme Court manages the entire court system and I manage the court system for the justices of the Supreme Court. It's kind of like a hospital administrator manages a hospital for doctors. Like a hospital administrator does not do surgery, I also do not decide the cases for the court. But I do just about everything else. . . .

The [Idaho] Supreme Court and I, recently, took on the legal-judicial establishment in Idaho. . . . We changed the legal culture of a state, I hope, forever. The problem we identified was one of court delay, a problem that's been identified down through history. It's something that was a problem in Idaho and every other state in the country. And the problem had some very practical implications. It hinged on farmers waiting for a decision on their water rights while their crops dried up in the field; businesses going bankrupt while they waited for litigation to end; people dying while they were waiting for the result of a court case and leaving a lawsuit to their heirs. . . . Mostly people aren't used to going to court, and the longer that litigation lasts, the worse the trauma gets.

Now what causes this kind of delay? The research has shown that the reason why we have court delay is because of the attitudes of the people involved in the system: the judges, the lawyers, and the courthouse people. . . . It's an attitude that the system exists for the lawyers and . . . that courts are [not] there to provide services to the public.

What's the solution to that delay? Well it's to make delay unacceptable. . . . It's to take the control of the pace of litigation away from the lawyers and to have the courts take control. And it's to look at the courts as an institution of government, who have a responsibility to the people, not to any private interest group.

Now what did we do in Idaho? Well first of all we went public with our problem. We identified the number of cases that were over ten years old in our court system. We pointed out the horror stories. This was a courageous step for the Supreme Court to take—to admit publicly that the courts weren't working well.

We hammered at the theme that the judges have a responsibility to control the pace of litigation, not the lawyers. We set time standards for how long it should take to have a case decided in the courts. We developed a very controversial computer tracking system which gave reports on individual judges to show what kind of progress they were making in reducing delay. And we adopted rules which required the judges to step in if the attorneys weren't moving their cases. . . .

Were we successful? We were successful beyond my wildest expectations. In a very short period of time we disposed of 90 percent of the older cases in the court system. Within a two-year time period we reduced the number of cases that were longer than the Supreme Court time standards by over 47 percent. . . . And we did all this without major bloodshed.

Were there risks? You bet. . . . First of all in order to do something about the problem we had to identify it, and that meant that we had to wash our dirty linen in public. . . . Another . . . risk was in attacking the legal establishment, which is powerful in every state. . . .

We could suffer as a result: funding cutbacks, pressure from the bar. . . . And we could also suffer in a more direct way, by challenges to the justices for reelection. Our judges are elected as most are around the country. We could wind up with some judges being defeated and perhaps a whole new Supreme Court.

There were personal risks involved also. First of all, if I created enough trouble for the Supreme Court, and in fact if I wound up getting some of them defeated for reelection, well you know when you have trouble on a ball club the first one to go is the manager and that would have been me. Since there are only 49 other positions like mine around the country, I would have been in big trouble.

But there were other kinds of personal risks even if I'd survived and one was the risk of failure. To fail in such a major undertaking, where I had become so identified, so personally identified with the program that many of the lawyers referred to this as "Bianchi's program." To fail in such an endeavor would have meant the loss of influence and effectiveness as a court administrator. . . .

What support did I marshal? Well first of all I marshaled the support of the people I work for, I had to have my Supreme Court behind me, and the justices were solidly in favor of the program, despite the risks. I knew, however, that if things didn't go well I was on my own. But I also found support in the other branches of government. I found that people in the executive and legislative branches were just as fed up as I was about court delay. In fact, the legislature was willing to hinge our appropriations and judges' salaries on reducing court delay, which was a tremendous boost for our effort. We built a small cadre of trial judges who believed as we did that we needed to do something about court delay, that we weren't doing our job, and they went to work. The support of our trial judges ultimately made the program successful. The State Bar Commissioners endorsed the effort and that brought acceptance from practicing lawyers.

Another thing we did was get some help from the public and the media. They supported our campaign. In fact the Associated Press in writing about our effort to reduce court delay said, in one of their articles, "If justice delayed is justice denied, then there's more justice in Idaho these days." I was very proud of that and if I ever have to have something on my tombstone, I wouldn't be unhappy with having that.

How about my thought process in evaluating risk and deciding on a course of action? To be very honest with you I was never hung up for very long on whether or not we should do it, once the Idaho Supreme Court gave me the green light. The only thing that I considered long and hard was how and when we ought to do it and how we could minimize the risks. . . . I found that if you can get people committed to an idea and get them going in the same direction you can unleash a tremendous amount of energy for constructive programs. But to do it you sometimes have to take some risks. As that old court administrator Yogi Berra says, "When you come to a fork in the road, take it." [6]

Discussion Questions

1. How does the nature of the role-types determine the conflicts experienced by each individual?
2. What elements of each role-type are present in each case?
3. In what ways do these individuals conform to the roles they play and in what ways do they change their roles?
4. Discuss how these role-types overlap.

NOTES

1. The details of this example are taken from Friedman (1989).
2. This example is fictitious.
3. The details of this example are taken from Boffey (1988).
4. Chris Zajac's story is told by Kidder (1989).

5. These quotes are taken from the transcript of Bianchi's talk at the National Academy of Public Administration Spring 1988 meeting in Kansas City.
6. On July 15, 1987, the American Judicature Society awarded the Supreme Court of Idaho a Special Merit Citation for Improvement of the Administration of Justice for "leadership in substantial and systematic reduction of unnecessary delay."

CHAPTER 6

Decision Making
and Leadership

At the height of the Cuban missile crisis in 1962, President John F. Kennedy was faced with an enormously difficult decision: Should he order an invasion of Cuba in order to remove forcefully the missiles the Russians were putting there? Should he order "surgical" air strikes to bomb the missile sites? Or, should he directly confront the Soviet Union to try to force the Russians to withdraw the missiles? Decision making and leadership—the topics of this chapter—conjure up images of powerful men and women, such as President Kennedy, comparing options and making the choices that guide nations. War and peace, national direction, and the future of the earth depend on the actions of a few. In the situation room of the White House, the president and his national security advisers review the latest satellite photographs before deciding to retaliate against terrorists. What are the options? What are the consequences? The director of the National Science Foundation consults with the nation's best scientists to choose a billion dollar physics experiment over other valuable research. More money to smash atoms means less money to study cancer. The Environmental Protection Agency must choose between the protection of wild coastlines and resort development. Should nature or jobs take precedent? Headlines daily repeat the major decisions facing national leaders.

Leadership and decision making are closely linked. Leaders must be both thoughtful and decisive. Leaders who act rashly with little thought of consequences do not inspire confidence, but those who endlessly mull options and postpone choices cannot provide direction. Intelligent choice and decisive action are two strongly held, if at times contradictory, values in American government. The image of powerful leaders taking decisive and important action does, however, distort the nature of government. Most decisions are small scale, incremental, and modified by those charged with their implementation. In fact, Carol Weiss and Michael Bucuvalas (1980) found that most federal executives do not believe they make decisions; they write memos, attend meetings, and hold discussions with others, but do not make policy decisions that are then executed. In addition, individuals and groups, even at the top, are constrained by uncertainty, short deadlines, past choices, history, and competing interests. Theories of decision making and leadership must add to our understanding of choices and actions made in such real-world circumstances.

DECISION MAKING

By ourselves and with others, we all make decisions all the time. Most are small; some will have ramifications throughout our lives. Sometimes we make snap judgments that in retrospect seem wise; a used sports car bought on impulse proves reliable. Other times we carefully weigh the pros and cons only to be betrayed by fate; the car rated most reliable by a consumer magazine proves to be a lemon. Often the most important decisions are *nondecisions:* We put things off, choose to ignore problems, or avoid situations or people only to discover that inaction has consequences just as important as those resulting from action.

Four Processes

Whether small or large, short- or long-term, studied or impulsive, deliberate or by default, decision making involves four major elements: problem definition, information search, choice, and evaluation. At first glance these four processes appear sequential, but, as will be discussed, they occur continually and simultaneously. Decision making is a discovery process, and judgments about the future and preferences are not preformed; they take shape and change throughout the decision process. Moreover, it is often difficult to identify when a decision process begins and ends since most important choices are ongoing.

Problem Definition.   At some point in the decision-making process a problem, question, or choice commands attention, however fleetingly. Of the nearly infinite list of policy concerns for government—military spending, the homeless, trade imbalances, acid rain, and on and on—only a few receive serious attention at any point in time (Hilgartner and Bosk 1988). Some, such as prison overcrowding, are deliberately ignored. Neither citizens nor elected officials want to spend money to provide adequate jails, and until prison riots or court orders force attention, most policy makers avoid this problem. At other times, a problem is just overlooked. Attention is focused on economic growth, and the growing problem of acid rain simply is not noticed until a report or headline commands attention. The first step in defining a problem is recognizing that it exists.

Clearly there are many more issues, questions, and problems than we as individuals or a society have the time or resources to confront. Problems are plentiful; attention is scarce. It is as if we were navigating a swamp, with a morass of issues or questions just below the surface. We can see shapes, but they lack definition. Are they rocks to be avoided or merely shadows? Then for a variety of reasons an issue rises to the surface, receives attention, takes shape, and becomes part of the public agenda (see Chapter 1).

Identifying and defining issues that warrant attention are, therefore, not passive acts that lay the groundwork for decision making; they are central decision-making processes (see Weiss, 1989, for an interesting case study). Problem recognition and definition alter decisions in two ways. First, selecting a problem or issue for attention precludes attention to other issues. John Kingdon (1984), in *Agendas, Alternatives, and Public Policies,* concludes that placing an item on the policy agenda is the most important element in policy making. He sees policy making as primarily a process of various actors and advocates vying to place their issues on the agenda. Once an issue is given attention, the specific choices and outcomes are determined by the nature of the problem. Once health insurance, air pollution, or naval strength are on the agenda, the various policy choices are limited by the nature of the problem. Placing the issue on the agenda in the first place is the more fundamental choice.

The second way recognition and definition alter decision making is more subtle. As a problem or issue emerges from the background and is given attention, it gains focus and takes shape. How a problem is defined affects how it is addressed. This process is difficult to describe without making it appear more deliberate than it often is. The problem of the homeless is a good example. People without homes have always been with us. Most often they have been seen as bums—people who because of their own weaknesses could not find work and afford homes. They were dismissed as drunks and drifters. So defined, the homeless remained a problem in the background—a problem for the Salvation Army, not the government. But as their numbers grew through the 1980s, we all began to take a closer look. We saw individuals discharged from mental institutions, the unemployed whose benefits had expired, and families unable to afford safe, decent homes. Increasingly, we see "the homeless" as people in desperate situations, and this change in our perception of them—from bums to people with whom we more readily identify—alters the decision process. Homelessness is now a focus of policy debate.

Clearly, how we see and define a problem greatly alters the way we treat it. Such perception is not fixed or mechanical, like a photograph; it is determined by our preconceived ideas and our knowledge. Perception is, therefore, shaped by the second process, information search.

Information Search.   The distinction between problem definition and information search is never sharp. When we are only vaguely aware that a problem exists, our first step is often to learn more about it, and this learning process gives a problem the form and identity that distinguishes it from others lurking in the background. Acid rain is a good example. First in Europe and then in North America, people noticed that trees were dying, and a few scientists began to ask why. Growth trends, changes in climate, and other explanations for decline were explored. Out of this active search for information the problem gained definition: Air pollution is killing trees. Information about the nature, scope, and source of the problem gave shape to vague concerns and largely defined the nature of the solutions considered. Reducing acid rain requires costly reduction in pollution created in regions and nations often at great distance from the dying trees. The information, therefore, defined the nature of the policy dilemma.

Nearly all decisions include information search, but the nature of that search varies considerably on several dimensions. The first dimension is the thoroughness or *breadth of the search*. Not all decisions benefit from detailed analysis. If time is short and the desired information not available, a careful search becomes procrastination. More important, only rarely do we have the time, resources, or energy to search thoroughly and find all the relevant information (Simon 1957). Most often, we search until we find an alternative that is marginally better—one that is satisfactory but not necessarily best. We *satisfice* rather than *optimize*. (See below for a further discussion of this.)

The federal and most state governments are vast storehouses of information on nearly every possible subject—from pig farming to violin making, from translations of ancient Chinese to the transmission of disease. The Library of Congress is one of the more visible signs of the importance of information in policy making. Founded in 1800, the Library of Congress was created to purchase and house "such books as may be necessary for the use of Congress" (2 Stat. 56). Even in much simpler times, information was central to governing. The library's nearly universal collection and research staff now serve the entire federal government.

Governments—federal, state, and local—are also primary sponsors of research. The government supports much basic research in the sciences and humanities. Such research is driven by the interests of scholars and may not have immediate relevance to policy debate. But basic research can have important policy implications. Advances in lasers and genetic engineering influence defense and social policy in ways unanticipated by scientists or their government sponsors. In addition, governments sponsor policy research. When faced with questions about the Soviet Union's military or how to deal with drug abuse, government decision makers ask their own research staffs to provide analyses. (Curiously enough, despite its image as a spy agency, the Central Intelligence Agency is primarily a research organization.) Governments also turn to independent scholars working in universities and think tanks for policy research.

In addition to breadth and depth, information search varies in the types and forms of information gathered. Although the distinction is not always clear, decision makers rely on two categories of information. Thoughtful choices—personal or collective—require both objective information about problems and outcomes and subjective information about preferences and values.

Stripped of tedious research and sleepless nights, any decision is an inference about achieving future results based on current understanding. Decision makers need information about the nature of the problem and the likely outcome of different choices. We have a strong preference for objective, even quantitative, information about problems and outcomes. The information provided from research and by experts is never objective, of course, in the sense of absolute truth. Inaccuracies and personal bias are present in the most scrupulous research, but such information is objective when it provides evidence for conclusions that can be evaluated by others.

Objective evidence about problems and consequences, however, is not enough to guide decisions. Decisions also require information about preferences. As Giandomenico Majone (1989) argues, public policy issues are "trans-scientific"; facts alone are not sufficient for making public policy decisions. As individuals and groups, we need to understand what we want in the future to guide our choices. Such choices are easy when our preferences do not conflict with the likely outcomes. For example, choices about applying for jobs are easy if the job you want is also the one you are most likely to receive. But when the job you really want is also the most difficult to land, then you are faced with a dilemma (Behn and Vaupel 1982, ch. 2). Do you go for the sure thing and compromise your aspirations or do you risk getting the job you want at the increased chance of remaining unemployed? How you balance preferences and judgments about outcomes depends not on any objective calculation but on a subjective balancing of these two different types of information. This balancing process is highly personal and depends in part on an individual's willingness to take or avoid risks.

Moreover, preferences are not always fixed nor are they clearly understood. They must be discovered and clarified to guide decisions. Preferences are, therefore, a form of information. Understanding preferences is difficult enough for individuals but extremely complex for groups and nations. Groups rarely have single preferences. The larger the group the more likely it is to contain diverse and conflicting values. Finding ways to combine these diverse preferences is central to government decision making.

Much political activity is a process for expressing and balancing preferences. Voting, hearings, special interest groups, mail campaigns, financial donations, and most political acts give voice to preferences. Scientific polling gives information about attitudes and opinions the appearance of objectivity, but individual and collective preferences are subjective value statements. Nevertheless, such information is central to decision making. If we as a society decide to do something about the homeless, it will not be solely because of careful studies of the problem's causes and consequences. We will address it when we decide that we do not want to live in a society marred by indifference.

Choice.   As problems are defined and information about problems, outcomes, and preferences is examined, choices emerge. Weighing options and selecting alternatives are the most visible decision-making processes. The common image of decision makers resembles a person ordering in a Chinese restaurant: Even if unfamiliar with the different items, the decisive eater chooses from column A or B and learns from experience. The most fundamental choice in policy making is to select problems for consideration—what is put on the menu—but once a problem enters the policy agenda, choices narrow to alternative solutions.

The choice process involves individual or group selection of a course of action. This selection process does not necessarily require reasoned judgments; the compromises of group decision making, whether by a small group or an entire community, often produce results few individuals prefer. One government leader commented that he knew he had made the right choice when nobody was happy, since satisfying single interests often means ignoring the interests of others.

Moreover, choices are rarely clear. Even when distinct alternatives can be identified—Do we negotiate with terrorists? Do we place a neglected child in foster care?—the results of different choices are often unpredictable. Our preferences can also remain unclear. Do we want to save the lives of hostages, as family members prefer, or do we want to eliminate any incentive for future terrorism, the preference of foreign policy professionals? Do we want to assure the safety of the child or do we want to preserve the family? These are difficult choices but not uncharacteristic of those facing decision makers at the highest and lowest reaches of government. Guided by uncertain preferences, the choice between options with uncertain outcomes is difficult—so difficult that different actors and groups within government often pursue conflicting policy choices. Such inconsistency testifies to both the complexity of the issues facing policy makers and the different interests served (Mitchell 1987).

Evaluation.   Decisions do not end with choices among alternatives; few choices are final and most are continually reconsidered. Moreover, even if the specific choice is not repeated, current choices become precedents for future ones. Decision making, therefore, involves evaluating the effects of choices and actions. At times this evaluation process is highly formal: A new government program is carefully studied to ascertain whether it produces the expected results. The professions of program and policy evaluation evolved to provide just such studies, and most government agencies have a division or department for planning and evaluation (see Chapter 11). Nevertheless, most evaluation is informal. Decision makers scan the news, talk to colleagues, and explore other sources of information about the impact of their actions.

Whether formal or informal, evaluation is basically another form of information gathering that occurs after the choice. This distinction between information search and evaluation is somewhat arbitrary, however. Before decision makers reach conclusions, most try to anticipate outcomes and the reactions of groups. In this manner, the evaluation process psychologically begins before the decision is made. At other times evaluation involves the search for information that justifies rather than scrutinizes past decisions, a process called *bolstering*.

The most difficult aspect of evaluating choices is establishing the criteria. The most common criterion is the result—if things turn out well then we feel that we made the right choice—but relying on outcomes, whether good or bad, ignores the uncertainty facing most decision makers and may confuse good luck with good decision making. Consider the decision to have surgery. All surgery involves risk, and if someone chooses to take the very slight risk to remove a small tumor and dies during surgery, was the decision wrong? Or if someone else recovers from cancer while relying on some quackery, was the decision correct? In either case the different outcomes were never certain, and choosing the option with the greatest chance of a positive result is never a guarantee. Since bad things happen to careful decision makers, results are not universal criteria for the quality of a decision.

As will become clearer in our discussion of different models of decision making, there is also no right or wrong way to make decisions. At times cautious deliberation is the best path; at other times risks are required. History, the availability of information and time, and the presence and interests of key actors all determine the appropriateness of a decision process for the situation and choice at hand. Thus, the process of decision making cannot serve as a universal criterion for decisions. The evaluation of any decision must involve looking at results and processes as well as the situation faced by decision makers. Evaluations must be tempered by an understanding of decision making and leadership, discussed in the remainder of this chapter.

Before we move on, however, we need to restate that these four decision processes—definition, information search, choice, and evaluation—often occur simultaneously. We are making choices when we select certain problems and solutions for consideration. Our search for information does not begin with a blank slate; our evaluations of past decisions and our expectations of certain results narrow our focus. These four processes help us think about decision making, but the distinctions among them are never sharp.

Normative and Descriptive Theories

In the sections that follow we examine two broad categories of models or theories of decision making: rational and nonrational models. Before examining both approaches, we need to dispel a false distinction between normative and descriptive theories. *Normative theories* suggest how, in the best of all worlds, decisions *should be* made. *Descriptive theories* explain how decisions *are* made. Traditionally, normative and descriptive have been considered more or less interchangeable with rational and nonrational: We should be rational but often are not. We choose to start from a different premise. We view rational and nonrational decision models as both normative and descriptive; there are times when people and groups should and do make rational decisions, and there are times when people and groups should and do make nonrational decisions. Irving Janis and Leon Mann (1977) remind us that "terms like *less rational, nonrational,* and *irrational* carry invidious connotations ('stupid,' 'crazy')" (p. 32) that often do not correspond to the quality of the decisions and that "the desirability of cool detachment as an ideal is highly questionable. A world dominated by Dr. Strangelove and like-minded . . . cost accountants might soon become devoid of acts of affection, conscience, and humanity, as well as passion" (p. 45).

Rational Theories of Decision Making

In this section we examine three different theoretical models of rational decision making: strict rationality, bounded rationality, and vigilant information processing. These models differ significantly but share a common foundation: Rational decisions are choices based on preferences and expected outcomes. Rational decisions do not always turn out best, nor are rational decision makers necessarily smart or diligent.

Suppose you want to buy a new record and you know from past experience that one store is more likely than another to have the new release. If you go to the store that offers the greatest chance of fulfilling your goal, the new record, you are making a rational decision. If that store is sold out and you learn that a friend has just bought the record at the other store, then you have still made the rational choice. If on the other hand you flipped a coin or checked your horoscope and as a result chose the store less likely to have the record, your choice was not a rational one, even if successful.

Rationality does not preclude taking risks. Sometimes your goal is so important that it is rational to choose an option with little promise of payoff. Opting for experimental surgery can be a rational choice over a life of pain. Whether or not the decision involves risk, rational decision making is the search for the option that best combines preferences and expectations.

Model I: Strict Rationality.   In this view of decision making, the four processes discussed earlier—problem definition, information search, choice, and evaluation—are
tightly connected and sequential. The problem is clearly and objectively defined. All
the necessary information about the dimensions of the problem and the consequences
of various alternatives is available and understood. Choices among these various alternatives are made exclusively on the facts presented and on expressed preferences.
The final choice is the one that produces the greatest benefit. This process is generally
called *optimizing*. After the decision, the results are carefully and objectively evaluated. James March (1982, 306) concludes that strict rationality has four characteristics: (1) knowledge of alternatives, (2) knowledge of consequences, (3) consistent
preference ordering, and (4) consistent decision rule for combining knowledge and
preferences for producing the optimal result.

Most decision theorists quickly add that the conditions for strict rationality
rarely exist. Strict rationality is more normative than descriptive; it describes how we
think we should make decisions, not how most decisions are made. Nevertheless,
strict rationality does describe how some decisions are made. After the space shuttle
Challenger exploded, the redesign of the booster rockets closely followed strict rationality. A range of options was examined, choices were made on engineering requirements, and tests were completed before the redesigned shuttle was launched. Such
care does not eliminate the possibility of failure; it does, however, reduce its likelihood.

Limits to Strict Rationality.   Admittedly, the four preconditions March listed for
strict rationality are rarely present. There are two fundamental limits to the model of
strict rationality that restrict its usefulness for describing choice. The first is uncertainty about both ends and means. Put simply, no matter how hard we may try, often
we cannot clearly ascertain the risks or the payoffs of certain options (March 1982,
307). Some uncertainty can be quantified in terms of probability: The risks of an
airplane crash or the probability that someone on parole will commit another crime
can be estimated. In many situations, the level of uncertainty is not definable, and if
we cannot define the risks we cannot include them in our calculation.

Second, preferences are often unformed and changing. Until faced with actual
choices, individuals have at best vague and often conflicting preferences: We want
better public schools and lower property taxes; we want to lock up criminals but do
not want to pay for prisons; we want inexpensive imported goods but decry the loss
of American jobs. In addition, preferences change over time. Rather than existing as
fixed goals, preferences evolve as we face different problems and situations.

The uncertainty and fluidity of preferences greatly increases as we move from
individual to group decision making. Even if an individual's preferences are firm,
when individual preferences are combined with others, certainty often gives way to
ambiguity and conflict.

Third, we often do not have the time, resources, energy, or ability to examine
all alternatives. For example, when the negative income tax was tried as a way of
providing welfare for the poor, it was necessary to evaluate the outcomes of experiments that were being conducted in New Jersey *before* they were fully implemented.

This tendency to have to act before all information is in is the typical way most public decisions are made.

Model II: Bounded Rationality.   The difference between strict and bounded rationality is a matter of degree, not fundamental concept. Bounded rationality is small-scale, short-term rationality. Rather than waiting for a clear and objective definition of problems and a thorough and complete information search, bounded rationality requires only adequate definition and sufficient information. When faced with a choice, most decision makers do not struggle to find the best solution (a process called *optimization).* Most are satisfied with the first acceptable solution. James March and Herbert Simon (1958, 140–141) named this decision criterion for bounded rationality *satisficing.*

If strict rationality admonishes decision makers to search for the ultimate solution, bounded rationality encourages them to make short-term reasonable choices and then to reconsider their options down the road. Such decisions are incremental, not once-and-for-all-time. Muddling through and tinkering replace strategic planning and radical changes. Bounded rationality remains purposeful but is myopic compared to strict rationality. Amitai Etzioni (1967, 397) uses the metaphor of two cameras to describe bounded rationality, or what he calls *mixed-scanning:* "a broad-angle camera that would cover all parts of the sky but not in great detail, and a second one which would zero in on those areas revealed by the first camera to require a more in-depth examination."[1]

Most thoughtful observers agree that bounded rationality more adequately describes most government decision making than does strict rationality, but some decry the loss of vision implicit in bounded rationality. Bruce Adams (1979, 547) complains that

> in time, the official can lose track of priorities. And this is where a conscientious official could be lulled into complacency by . . . incrementalism. . . . It often seems that in Washington it is enough to be busy. It does not always matter much what you are busy about.

Proponents of bounded rationality, Charles Lindblom (1979) for example, disagree with this criticism. They argue that bounded rationality provides a better approach to decision making in conditions of uncertainty; they make normative as well as descriptive claims for their model.[2] This claim is based on several observations.

First, theories of decision making should be based on human capacities. It would make little sense to design the perfect car if three hands were required to drive it. Decision-making processes and institutions should accommodate human capacities and limits, and a considerable body of research establishes very real limits to human rationality: We cannot consider large amounts of information and are prone to simplification. Herbert A. Simon (1957, 198), a principal architect of the bounded rationality theory, concludes that

> the capacity of the human mind for formulating and solving complex problems is very small compared with the size of the problems whose solution is required for

objectively rational behavior in the real world—or even for a reasonable approximation to such objective rationality.

Second, even if the thorough search and deliberate choice of strict rationality were possible for a given problem, the effort might not be worth the reward. The four decision processes require time and resources—what economists call *decision costs*. For example, one could spend months learning technical details and comparing costs before buying a compact disc (CD) player. While such a thorough decision may prove fun for the stereo buff, the investment of time and effort makes little sense for most people. It makes more sense to talk it over with a few knowledgeable friends, go to a reputable store, buy the CD player that satisfies your immediate needs, and turn to other decisions. The decision process should be appropriate to the problem. When designing the billion dollar space shuttle, attempting to achieve strict rationality is worth the costs to the designers, but for many other choices, strict rationality is overkill.

Third, if the information is simply not available, adhering to the canons of strict rationality only encourages delay. Bounded rationality is less ambitious. Accepting that a decision is only one of many small steps encourages actions even in conditions of uncertainty, and small changes are easier to implement, and, when necessary, reconsider. As Lindblom (1979, 517) observes, "Neither revolution, nor drastic policy change, nor even carefully planned big steps are ordinarily possible." Solid but not synoptic analysis and incremental rather than grand-scale changes are the best choices when understanding is limited.

Model III: Vigilant Information Processing.   Irving Janis and Leon Mann (1977) carefully avoid the term *rationality* in developing their model of decision making, preferring the less judgmental term *vigilant information processing*. Their theory of decision making is, nonetheless, a variation of rational decision making. They combine the core elements of strict and bounded rationality with a more detailed examination of the psychology of decision making.

Like strict rationality, vigilant information processing is based on a set of demanding standards, but, like bounded rationality, this model is grounded in the limits of individuals and the constraints of time and understanding. Fundamental to Janis and Mann's (1977, 11) view is the assumption that important decisions can be judged by how closely the decision maker adheres to their seven criteria: "Our first working assumption is that failure to meet any of these seven criteria when a person is making a fundamental decision (one with major consequences of attaining or failing to attain important values) constitutes a defect in the decision-making process."

Within the limits of time and ability, the vigilant decision maker strives to

1. examine a wide range of alternative courses of action;
2. review the full range of objectives and the values implicated by the choice;
3. weigh the costs, benefits, and risks of plausible positive and negative consequences;
4. search for new information relevant to further evaluation of the alternatives;

5. assimilate information and advice, even when it does not support pre-
    ferred options;
6. reexamine positive and negative consequences, including those previously
    disregarded, before making a final choice; and
7. plan for implementing the decision and for dealing with problems as they
    emerge.

In addition, Janis and Mann (1977) describe the situations that encourage fulfilling these seven demanding standards. Vigilance requires both discriminating judgment and open-minded review of supportive and opposing messages and is enhanced
by three conditions: awareness of serious risk, belief in the possibility of a satisfactory solution, and sufficient time. Reducing any of these conditions will allow decision makers to let down their guard and increase the chance that one or several of the
seven criteria will be violated. In their view, vigilance does not assume that every decision turns out right but rather that each one increases the long-run odds of achieving objectives. This is an assumption shared by all rational decision-making theories.

Nonrational Theories of Decision Making

Although different in details, the three rational models of decision making share a
common assumption: Rational decision making involves selecting alternatives based
on judgments about preferences and future outcomes. But close observation of many
government decisions reveals little evidence of outcome-oriented choice. Before we
discuss the two nonrational models of decision making, it is important to appreciate
the disorder of much governmental decision making. Graham Allison (1971) studied
presidential decision making after the Kennedy administration discovered Soviet nuclear weapons installations in Cuba. The situation was dramatic, but Allison suggests
that the process was typical.

When reading this excerpt from Allison's book, *Essence of Decision: Explaining the Cuban Missile Crisis,* keep two points in mind: First, note how little resem-
blance this description has to any of the rational theories of decision making discussed previously. Second, note the presence of the four decision processes. Although
not neatly ordered as in the rational theories, problems take form, information is
accumulated, and choices and evaluations are made.

Allison writes that

> in many governmental decisions there is no unitary actor but rather many actors as
> players—players who focus not on a single strategic issue . . .; players who act in
> terms of no consistent set of strategic objectives but rather according to various
> conceptions of national, organizational, and personal goals; players who make
> government decisions not by a single, rational choice but by the pulling and haul-
> ing that is politics (p. 144). . . .
>
> Most "issues" . . . emerge piecemeal over time, one lump in one context, a sec-
> ond in another. Hundreds of issues compete for players' attention every day. Each
> player is forced to fix upon his issues for that day, deal with them on their own
> terms, and rush on to the next. Thus the character of emerging issues and the pace

at which the game is played converge to yield government "decisions" and "actions" as collages.

Choices by one player . . ., resultants of minor games . . ., resultants of major games . . ., and "foul- ups"—these pieces, when stuck to the same canvas, constitute government behavior relevant to an issue. (p. 146)

Nonrational decision models attempt to explain such seemingly chaotic decision processes, and they differ fundamentally from rational models. The rational and nonrational approaches are not, however, inherently contradictory; subscribing to one theoretical framework does not require rejecting the other. The differences between rational and nonrational models are based, in part, on focusing on different aspects of the complex social process we call *choice* or *decision making*.

In nonrational models, the words *choice* and *decision* are somewhat misleading. Choices are made but they do not result from the deliberate balancing of pros and cons or costs and benefits. Nonrational models generally describe decision outcomes as the result of the interaction between two structures or sets of rules. *Decision structures* are sets of rules that determine what problems and solutions will be allowed for discussion and how disagreements will be resolved. Rules based on majority vote, consensus, or arbitrary authority will obviously yield different results. *Access structures* are sets of rules that define which individuals or groups will have "standing" or will be allowed to participate in the decision process. (In law, *standing* refers to the right to participate, that is, to stand before the court.) Nonrational models suggest that decision outcomes are determined by the interaction of these two sets of rules rather than by the calculation of expected utility.

Nonrational models suggest that determining and enforcing the rules of the game are more important to the decision process than is careful analysis. If we define politics broadly as the continual struggle over whose interests will be given voice (the access structure) and over the rules for arbitrating the differences (the decision structure), then nonrational decision models are political (Schattschneider 1960, ch. 8; March and Olsen 1984). For example, access rules such as literacy tests and poll taxes kept southern blacks from voting for many decades and had a greater effect on local policy making than any individual decision could have had.

Nonrational models share the assumption that the mix of rules and participants shapes choices. The amount of predictability or fluidity of rule following and participation is not constant, however, and the two nonrational decision models described below differ precisely in describing the amount of fluidity of the process. The first model stresses flux and unpredictability and the second rigidity.

Model IV: Garbage Can Model.   The most clearly articulated nonrational model for conditions of flux carries the unlikely name of the Garbage Can Model of Organization Choice. In their paper of the same title, Michael Cohen, James March, and Johan Olsen (1972) describe organizations as settings or collections of solutions, problems, procedures, and people.[3] In their words,

> An organization is a collection of choices looking for problems, issues and feelings looking for decision situations in which they might be aired, solutions looking for

issues to which they might be the answer, and decision makers looking for work. (p. 2)

These four elements or *streams*—choices, issues, solutions, and decision makers—enter and exit the setting or "garbage can" randomly, and decisions result from the varying mix of ingredients. Solutions and problems become attached to one another as varying groups vie for influence. The more open the setting is to different actors, problems, and solutions, the more unpredictable the results. In general, the garbage can model describes highly fluid and temporal decisions and suggests that the coupling of solutions, problems, and people—not reasoned choices among alternatives—creates the decision outcome. This coupling can result from deliberate action or from chance.

Describing such a turbulent and evanescent decision process is difficult. Cohen, March, and Olsen (1972, 16) summarize:

> The garbage can process is one in which problems, solutions, and participants move from one choice opportunity to another in such a way that the nature of the choice, the time it takes, and the problems it solves all depend on a relatively complicated intermeshing of elements. These include the mix of choices available at any one time, the mix of problems that have access to the organization, the mix of solutions looking for problems, and the outside demands on the decision makers.

These observations have several important implications for understanding governmental decisions. First, turf battles and other struggles over who has access to deliberations and who has the right to make choices are a central element in decision making. For example, in the late 1970s, controversy erupted over government sponsorship of medical research using aborted fetuses. When the decision was left to the medical community, policy favored the research. When the views of anti-abortion groups were seriously considered, policy restricted the research. The nature of the problems and the solutions considered were based more on who participated than on an objective review of evidence (Maynard-Moody 1984).

Second, solutions and problems may arise independently. At times, decision makers invent novel solutions for problems. But at other times, the existence of certain solutions encourages people to discover problems. People communicated adequately long before desktop publishing was developed. With the ability to produce elaborate charts and figures, however, managers are discovering all kinds of problems that require this new solution. Just as some problems are intentionally ignored, some solutions are considered unacceptable. Decriminalizing drug use to cut drug-related crime is not a socially acceptable solution in the United States, despite the long history of this solution in the garbage can. The garbage can model underscores the important point that decision making is more a process of connecting acknowledged problems with acceptable solutions than a process of deliberate choice.

Third, the garbage can model describes how decisions are guided or manipulated. The particular mix of problems, solutions, and actors involved in the decision process is not necessarily accidental. Chance plays a role, but so does deliberate action. When individuals and groups voice concern for AIDS or advocate tax cuts, they are forcefully adding their problems and solutions to the mix. As discussed earlier in this chapter, placing a problem or solution on the decision agenda is fundamental to political decision making.

Model V: Administrative Routine.   The garbage can model describes a level of fluidity and change that does not always exist in government decision making, especially as attention shifts from the legislative to the administrative sphere. Legislatures are arenas for pushing agendas and building coalitions. Even though over 90 percent of the incumbents in Congress and state legislatures win reelection, elections provide a mechanism for assuring fluid participation. The decision and access structures in administrative decision making are more formal and rigid, however. Michael Masuch and Perry LaPotin (1989) modified the garbage can model to include standard features of bureaucratic structure such as hierarchy and limited participation (see also Levitt and Nass 1989). With these characteristics of most public organizations added, decisions become more predictable and routine. Understanding the evolution of administrative routine is important to understanding government decision making.

A frequent outcome of many major policy decisions is the creation of a new administrative agency or program within an agency. The need for developing and implementing foreign policy created the State Department, and the decision to preserve and manage vast tracts of land gave birth to the Department of the Interior. Local, state, and federal departments on aging, economic development, management and budget, and many other policy areas were created through the legislative process, and this process often resembles the fluid model described above.

But once agencies are created, the decision process changes. Participation and decision making become more rule bound.[4] Consider, for example, welfare reform. Many states have adopted legislation instituting workfare programs; the decision to legislate these reforms was a relatively open, fluid process. However, when new or existing agencies began to implement these legislative directives, they quickly developed rules—both formal and informal—that began to determine both the extent of participation and the nature of the programs.

Over time, these rules will become accepted as givens, as simply the way things are done. This two-step process, called *institutionalization,* involves first codifying the rules of access and decision making, in the form both of written directives and unwritten norms, and then internalizing the rules to the point that they are no longer seen as choices to be reconsidered. As Lynne Zucker (1977, 726) writes, "For highly institutionalized acts, it is sufficient for one person simply to tell another that this is how things are done." The access and decision rules are no longer questioned; they become frozen.

As the decision process becomes rule bound, major choices begin to be based not on rational analysis nor on the fluid mix of solutions, problems, and participants but on what James March and Johan Olsen (1984) call the *political structure.*

By a political structure we mean a collection of institutions, rules of behavior, norms, roles, physical arrangements, buildings, and archives that are relatively invariant in the face of turnover of individuals and relatively resilient to the idiosyncratic preferences and expectations of individuals.

This institutionalized political structure often precludes many problems from consideration and many groups from influence. The systematic exclusion of policy problems and groups from consideration is a central—and often disturbing—result of administration routine. Peter Bachrach and Morton Baratz (1962, 44) suggest that this *nondecision making* is "a means by which demands for change in the existing allocation of benefits and privileges in the community can be suffocated before they are even voiced; or kept covert; or killed before they gain access to the relevant decision-making arena" (see also Lukes 1974).

Thus, in both nonrational models of decision making, outcomes are the result of a mix of actors, problems, and solutions. The administrative routine model, however, underscores the relative inflexibility of decision and access rules and, therefore, the greater predictability of decisions.

Criteria of Reasonable Choice

Both rational and nonrational models provide well-articulated theories of decision making, but both models are finally somewhat impersonal. Taken to extremes, rational models reduce human judgment to computation, and nonrational models portray decision outcomes as the result of forces beyond individual control. As Andrew Van de Ven (1983, 39) observes, such models "anesthetize . . . human reason by ignoring basic questions of value, morals, conflict, and teleology inherent in any significant issues in which human purpose is involved."

A less clearly articulated but emerging view of decision making places a stronger emphasis on decisions as value statements. Values enter rational decision models in the form of preferences, but such preferences are generally defined in terms of self-interest: Legislators vote for certain bills to increase their chances of reelection, not because they will enhance the public good. Both rational and nonrational models of the decision process are basically products of value-neutral social science.

Van de Ven argues that underneath our analyses of problems and outcomes are beliefs or values of which we may not be entirely aware, but which, like magnetic north, invisibly guide our decisions (see also Fischer 1980). The criterion for reasonable choice is the combination of short-term purposiveness (or bounded rationality) and values. This criterion is most clearly articulated in law. As Van de Ven (1983, 45) summarizes:

> Over the years, a theory of jurisprudence and negligence in torts emerged around the concept of a "reasonable man." . . . In law, the reasonable man must meet some uniform, collective standard of conduct. This standard is external and objective in the sense that it is determined with reference to a community valuation.

History as a Guide to Decision Making.   One of the clearest ways that values shape decisions is in our reliance on history. Our recollections, both personal and learned, have a strong grip on our perceptions. History, however, has a paradoxical effect on decision making, and this paradox is best captured by two oft-repeated aphorisms. We are told in some situations, that "those who ignore history are doomed to repeat the mistakes of the past," but in other situations, that "generals always fight the last war." To ignore history disregards the successes and failures of our predecessors and our heritage of values, but to assume that future events will repeat the past—that the next war will be like the last—overlooks contemporary changes and problems.

The positive and negative role of history in governmental decision making is examined by Richard Neustadt and Ernest May (1986) in *Thinking in Time: The Use of History for Decision-Makers*. Their book suggests that history guides choices by altering how problems and solutions are perceived. History guides decisions primarily through analogy; when we see an event we immediately compare it to some past event. For example, both opponents and supporters of aid to anticommunist rebels in Nicaragua see different analogies to the Vietnam War: Opponents fear foreign entanglements; supporters worry about weak commitments.

Neustadt and May (1986) observe that the choice of analogies is rarely conscious or subject to critical analysis. Historical analogies enter deliberations as interpretations of events based on personal and institutional histories. Further, Neustadt and May observe that our uses of history reflect our values, and they argue that governmental decisions could be improved if historical analogies and, by inference, values were more closely scrutinized. They suggest a closer examination of the similarities and differences between the current situation and historical analogies. Our view of history tells us a great deal about our current values, and examining history clarifies the values that guide reasonable choices.

Common Decision Flaws

In addition to developing different theoretical models of decision making, scholars have closely examined common errors in judgment. These errors are not simple mistakes; they are predictable individual and group biases or errors in judgment. We discuss five common judgment errors: stereotyping, cognitive bolstering, defensive avoidance, entrapment, and groupthink. All five can be thought of as too much of a good thing. Stereotyping results from oversimplification; cognitive bolstering is an extension of our need to move on after decisions are made; defensive avoidance results from overly thorough information search and analysis; entrapment can be a consequence of too much commitment; and groupthink is the negative result of too much group cohesion.

Stereotyping.   When faced with complex problems, we simplify. Simplification can help us determine the important outlines of a problem, but these simplifications become one-dimensional caricatures of people and problems that can also place blinders on decision makers, limiting decision making. Often simplifications become shared by a wide number of individuals and greatly narrow the possibility of collective wisdom. Examples abound. All recipients of government aid are lazy, welfare cheats. The Soviet Union is an evil empire. All liberals are muddled; all conservatives militaristic. The list of stereotypes—some comic, others cruel—is endless, but all reflect the human predisposition for substituting simplistic caricatures for complex appreciation. In nearly all significant policy questions, such stereotyping greatly reduces the quality of decision making. Stereotyping reduces complex choices to simplistic formulas.

Cognitive Bolstering.   The information search process is often narrowed by the need to justify or explain previous choices. This cognitive bolstering involves magnifying the value of the chosen action and denigrating the value of the rejected alternatives. This bolstering is achieved by exaggerating favorable consequences, minimizing unfavorable consequences, denying adverse feelings, minimizing personal responsibility, and other, similar means (Janis and Mann 1977, 60–63). Cognitive bolstering represents the abandonment of the critical evaluation of information and is increased by stress. When individuals feel pressured to make rapid choices based on uncertain information and are held accountable for results, they spend considerable effort highlighting information that supports their views and suppressing information that raises doubts.

Defensive Avoidance.   Individuals commonly avoid making decisions that require unpleasant choices or that entail risk. Decision theorists call this problem *defensive avoidance.* One form of defensive avoidance is similar to cognitive bolstering as it involves ignoring information that could require action. Defensive avoidance also involves continually avoiding decisions by obsessional mulling over information and options. Nearly all choices exist within deadlines, and when time is short, gathering more and more information can become a form of avoidance rather than evidence of diligence. It is important to restate that *not* making a decision is a choice with consequences just as significant as those that follow making a choice.

Entrapment.   Entrapment is the negative side of commitment. In general, commitment to groups and decisions is positive. (See Chapter 4.) Unfortunately individuals can become committed to failures as well as successes, and commitment to failing policies or poor choices is called entrapment or the *trapped administrator syndrome* (Fox and Staw 1979). When individuals publicly and unambiguously announce their choices it becomes difficult for them to change their minds, and when decision makers become committed to a certain course of action, their prestige and careers may become associated with its success or failure. Once the commitment is made, we make every effort to make it work.

As a result, commitment can restrict the evaluation of a choice. Without a careful evaluation of results and a willingness to acknowledge errors, committed decision makers often persist with those same errors. This course of action is especially common if, as is usually the case, the evidence of success or failure is not clear; when there is even a faint hope of success, commitment can encourage persistence. We admire "can do" administrators who push ahead despite doubts, but decision makers must also know when to stop and change course. Too often decision makers are trapped by the awareness that their choices are proving incorrect and the knowledge that they are held personally responsible for assuring success. If they persist they foresee failure; if they admit failure they are held accountable.

An extreme example of entrapment occurred at the turn of the century when a British team of explorers was racing to become the first to the South Pole. The leader of the British team, Sir Robert Scott, based the expedition on mechanical and horse-drawn sleds. The sleds broke down and the horses died, but Scott could not admit failure and continued to press forward. His team lost the race to the South Pole and froze to death. Their persistence was hailed by many as great courage (their freezing provided a literal example of maintaining a British stiff upper lip) rather than as mindless commitment to foolish choices.

Groupthink.   All four of the decision errors discussed are individual errors amplified by group processes. The last, groupthink, is primarily a group problem. As we discussed in Chapter 4, groups tend to seek and enforce unanimity. Dissent is suppressed, and conformity of behavior and ideas is encouraged. Irving Janis (1972) called the extreme suppression of minority or dissenting views *groupthink* (see Whyte, 1989, for a reevaluation of groupthink). Groupthink results when conformity pressures are so extreme that the group acts as if it had one mind. Groupthink robs the decision-making group of one of its primary assets, the critical faculties of its members.

Groupthink has eight symptoms. Note how these symptoms include the other four decision flaws. The end result of these eight symptoms is the atrophy of critical evaluation information and options.

- The group shares an illusion of its own superiority and invulnerability. Members see themselves as the "best and the brightest."
- The group collectively avoids and discounts information that calls into question either its choices or its own superiority. Members engage in collective cognitive bolstering.
- The group believes in the inherent morality of its goals. This is especially common with groups working for a specific cause—members equate their views with the public interest—or for important elected officials—who are fulfilling the mandate of the people.
- The group develops negative stereotypes of other groups and of dissenters. These stereotypes allow the group to dismiss out-of-hand legitimate challenges.
- The group attempts to silence internal dissenters. Dissenters are often the brunt of jokes that emphasize their disloyalty.
- Group members censor their own doubts; they internalize the group pressures to conform.
- Even though overt and self-censorship is prevalent, the group perceives the lack of dissent as unanimity.
- Certain members of the group take on the role of "mind guards" or watchmen who protect leaders and the group from dissenting views.

Any policy-making group showing these symptoms is destined for fiascoes, and the list is as long as recorded history. In recent times it includes such policy disasters as Kennedy's Bay of Pigs and Reagan's Iran-Contra. There are, however, ways to reduce the likelihood of groupthink. Assigning members to play the devil's advocate or subgroups to examine different options encourages constructive dissent and can increase the tolerance for dissent. Bringing in outside experts can also diffuse conformity pressures. Avoiding groupthink and the other predictable decision flaws depends, however, on the quality of leadership, which is the focus of the rest of this chapter.

LEADERSHIP

Leadership is paradoxical. We look for leadership in candidates for high office. When things go well or poorly we credit or blame the leader, whether president or baseball manager. Important historical events such as the civil rights movement may be the work of hundreds of forgotten men and women yet become associated with leaders, such as Martin Luther King. Leadership is important—we seek it, are moved by it, and use it to help understand current and past events—but leadership is difficult to define and its effects are elusive.

The difficulties contemporary social scientists have had in defining and measuring leadership have encouraged many to reject the usefulness of the concept. Some scholars argue that leadership is not a scientific concept (Meindl, Ehrlich, and Dukerich 1985), while others insist that rejecting the study of leadership impoverishes our understanding of governing (Doig and Hargrove 1987). Richard E. Neustadt (1987, ix) writes:

> [Leadership] is among the most challenging of human activities, stirring ambition, exciting admiration, arousing fear or pity (to one's taste), inspiring dramatists since literature began, ignored by almost nobody in all of human history—until the coming of American political science.

Leadership is also often confused with high position. The president, cabinet secretaries, and senior legislators are in powerful positions; they are visible and have the authority to make choices affecting thousands of people. Perhaps the starkest reminder of such authority is the briefcase with nuclear weapons codes that follows the president, but even the power to launch nuclear Armageddon is not leadership.

Leadership is the increment of influence or performance that goes beyond the authority of office. Leadership is the difference between the privilege of position and the ability to get things done (Kanter and Stein 1979, 5). Leadership takes performance beyond routine expectations. Holding high office does not guarantee impact. Large, complex organizations develop routines and procedures that blunt the will of even the most powerful. Leadership, therefore, involves adding to the influence of any position or role, at the top or bottom of the hierarchy. To help us understand leadership several distinctions are helpful.

Transactional versus Transformational Leadership

The first distinction contrasts transactional and transformational leadership—concepts conceived by James MacGregor Burns (1978) and developed by Bernard Bass (1985). The difference between the two forms of leadership is one of degree; most leaders exhibit a blend of both. *Transactional leaders* exchange rewards for services.

Such leaders guide subordinates in recognizing and clarifying roles and tasks. They give their subordinates the direction, support, and confidence to fulfill, and at times exceed, their role expectations. They also help subordinates understand and satisfy their own needs and desires. Transactional leaders are effective guides and good managers. They encourage better than average performance from their subordinates.

Transformational leadership is more dramatic. *Transformational leaders* change the relationship of the subordinate and the organization. They encourage subordinates to go well beyond their original commitments and expectations. If transactional leaders solicit diligence, transformational leaders foster devotion. Such involvement is encouraged by raising the level of awareness, motivating individuals to transcend self-interest, and raising aspirations (Bass 1985, 22). Transformational leadership requires a blend of charisma, individual relationships, and intellectual stimulation and involves symbolism as well as effective management. As Warren Bennis (1984, 70–71) summarizes,

> [Transformational leadership] is the ability of the leaders to reach the souls of others in a fashion which raises human consciousness, builds meanings, and inspires human intent that is the source of power. With transformative leadership, therefore, it is visions, purposes, beliefs, and other aspects of organizational culture that are of prime importance. Symbolic expression becomes the major tool of leadership. . . . Effectiveness is instead measured by the extent to which "compelling vision" empowers others to excel; the extent to which meanings are found in one's work; and the extent to which individual and organization are bonded together by common commitment in a mutually rewarding symbiotic relationship.

Several concepts discussed in Chapter 4 are relevant to understanding both forms of leadership. Levels of motivation and commitment and the nature of the psychological contract between individuals and organizations are not fixed. Leaders are not the only influence on these variables but they are an important influence. When people in positions of authority encourage subordinates to believe that their work is important—not merely a fair exchange of pay for work—motivation, commitment, and performance surpass routine expectations. This increment is the essence of leadership.

Ingredients of Leadership

The observation that authority of position does not assure leadership raises the difficult question, "What *does* distinguish leaders from others?" There is no simple nor single answer to this question; it appears, however, that leadership has several ingredients.

Personal Characteristics.   Early research on leadership focused on individual traits. Max Weber in describing the emergence of bureaucracy foresaw the decline of charisma in human affairs. He contrasted leadership based on authority with that based on religious inspiration, the latter he referred to as charismatic leadership. Nonetheless, *charisma* or a personal magic that arouses popularity and loyalty remains important. Charisma is, however, difficult to define. It involves a culturally determined set of traits and characteristics that engender devotion (Willner 1984), and this devotion is emotional, not rational. To conservatives President Reagan's John Wayne swagger was part of his mystique. Although it is important not to exaggerate such characteristics, it is equally important not to forget the emotional bonds that tie together even the most rationalistic organization.

In addition to charisma, providing *intellectual guidance* contributes to leadership. Some leaders articulate the mission of the organization in a way that convinces and moves followers. Others are innovators who find new solutions or chart new directions. Much of the work of public agencies is problem solving, and professionals respect leaders who provide constructive insight.

Leader-Follower-Situation Match.   Leadership does not exist in a vacuum; it requires followers and occurs in specific situations or settings. Just as leaders are more than individuals in authoritative positions, followers are not just subordinates. As we implied in the previous discussion, followers must grant the increased levels of motivation, commitment, and creativity called for by leadership. In addition, leaders become magnets for the credit or blame of subordinates. Even in situations in which chance rather than skill determines outcomes, people typically attribute success or failure to the leader (Staw 1984, 72).

The relationship between leaders and followers forms a dyad; both concepts are meaningless without the other. Leadership is what sociologists call a *socially constructed reality:* It exists because we tacitly agree to believe collectively that it exists. As Gary Hamilton and Nicole Biggart (1985) argue, concepts such as *leaders* and *followers* or *power* and *obedience* are not opposites or even conceptually distinct.

In addition, the leader-follower dyad occurs within specific situations. Both time and place shape this dyad as historical events create opportunities and problems for groups and individuals. The growing unpopularity of the Vietnam War in the late 1960s propelled political candidates opposing defense spending into leadership roles. By the late 1970s, war anguish was replaced by fears of Soviet aggression, and political leaders advocating greater defense spending achieved renewed prominence. In addition, the specific setting is important. An individual who arouses devotion in one setting may not do so in another. For example, highly successful business leaders who enter government are often unable to find the right symbolic gestures or to provide the intellectual guidance that motivates public organizations.

Research on small groups reinforces the importance of the leader-follower-situation match (for a review see Schein 1980, ch. 7 and 8). Early research asked whether directive leaders, who focused group attention on the task at hand, were more effective than participatory leaders, who helped group members deal with social and emotional issues. The answer was, "It all depends." Effective group leadership depends on the nature of the task: Is it routine or does it require a creative solution? It depends on the individuals in the group: Do they prefer strong direction or expect to share decision making? It depends on the perception of the group on the nature of the task, situation, and the various roles, and as Schein (1980, 112) writes, "These perceptions will be a *joint* function of the actual characteristics as they might be observed by an outsider and the leader's own predispositions, biases, defense mechanisms, and personality.'' Research on leadership emphasizes, to the dismay of social scientists looking for broad generalizations, the importance of individuals, their perceptions, and the uniqueness of time and place.

Leadership and Organizational Culture.   A third issue of growing interest to students of leadership is organizational culture. The relationship between organizational culture and leadership is a two-way street. As mentioned in the discussion of charisma, effective leaders define and articulate symbols that are important to followers. Much of the work in public organizations is practical and mundane, and effective leaders use culturally meaningful symbols to infuse this work with meaning and value. Doig and Hargrove (1987) call this use of symbols and language *rhetorical leadership.* As Laurence Lynn (1987, 39) observed:

> If ''creating favorable interpretations of governmental activity'' is the essence of policymaking, time spent in persuasion and reinforcement of favorable symbols, for example, may be more productive than time spent gathering information, designing internal structural changes, or motivating subordinates.

But leaders must also change cultures. Organizational cultures can become maladaptive to a changing world, and guiding cultural change requires both insight into existent values and a vision of direction that few individuals share. Edgar Schein (1985, 171) concludes, ''One might go so far as to say that a *unique* function of 'leadership,' as contrasted with 'management,' is the *creation and management of culture.* '' The founders of organizations and programs often put a stamp on organizations that long outlives their tenures. They create symbols that others manipulate to maintain the status quo or to encourage change.

Thus, even in the often mechanical, down-to-earth world of public bureaucracies symbols, language, and charisma matter. It is important to note in the context of the previous discussion of decision making that government and policy making is not just choice. Governing requires interpreting events and actions, and leadership involves guiding interpretations. As James March (1984, 32) writes:

> We live by the interpretations we make, becoming better or worse through the meanings we impute to events and institutions. Our lives change when our beliefs change. . . . *If we want to identify one single way in which administrators can affect organizations, it is through their effect on the world views that surround organization life.* (emphasis added)

How Much Does Leadership Matter?

This discussion of the elements of leadership leaves unanswered the question, ''How much does leadership matter?'' This question cannot be answered precisely, and the range of opinions depends, in part, on how the subject is examined (for a review see Thomas 1988). Scholars, such as Doig and Hargrove (1987), who look at the impact of specific individuals, stress leadership's importance, whereas others who look at a large number of organizations find little impact. William Gamson and Norman Scotch (1964) studied the impact of new managers on the success of baseball teams.

If leadership mattered, we would expect to find performance improvements with leadership changes. Gamson and Scotch found no evidence that new managers improved team standing and described the practice of replacing managers when a team was failing as "ritual scapegoating."

These two opposing answers to the question of the importance of leadership merely underscore a central observation. Leadership in government or baseball is rare; it has impact when it exists, but it cannot be relied on. In Gamson and Scotch's study the exceptionally poor new managers may have canceled out the impact of the exceptionally good ones. Average performance is always most predictable and therefore most reliable. If our government and society depended on leadership to operate, it would surely collapse. When Woodrow Wilson became ill and for an extended period was unable to carry out his functions as president the country did not collapse; with his wife running the White House, Wilson's illness was kept secret from the public. Ronald Reagan is reputed to have slept a great deal of the time and was not involved in the details of his office; yet he is considered to have helped change the direction of politics and policy in the United States. Nevertheless, leadership is required for major changes and new directions, and without leadership government easily stagnates.

This observation led James March (1984) to conclude that leadership was less important than the "density of administrative competence." Doing routine things well, not implementing bold new initiatives, may be the most important characteristic of productive organizations. He writes,

> Much of what distinguishes a good bureaucracy from a bad one is how well it accomplishes the trivia of day-to-day relations with clients and day-to-day problems in maintaining and operating its technology. Accomplishing these trivia may involve planning, complex coordination, and central direction, but it is more commonly linked to the effectiveness of large numbers of people doing minor things competently. (p. 23)

In concluding this chapter, it is important that we emphasize that government and policy must endure in a world of imperfect decisions, imperfect leaders, and imperfect organizations. Governments and agencies that depend on perfection do not endure, but systems that do not aspire to ideals in decision making and leadership stagnate.

SUMMARY

Outsiders see government as the place in which elected and appointed leaders make decisions; insiders, even those in high positions, see government decisions and leadership as highly constrained and limited to incremental actions. Decision making involves the mix of four processes: problem definition, information search, choice, and evaluation. Although we commonly associate decision making with choice—one of the four—all four processes shape the final outcome and are, therefore, aspects of decision making. There are many more issues or problems vying for government's attention than can be reasonably addressed, and recognizing and then defining a problem guides both what information is sought and what alternatives are considered. Information search also gives shape to our understanding of problems, possible outcome, and beliefs or preferences. Choice involves weighing options and selecting alternative policies or courses of actions. The choice not to act or even recognize a problem is decision making—although sometimes called nondecision making—and often has consequences of equal importance to overt decision making.

Several theoretical models of decision making were examined. The rational models included theories of strict and bounded rationality and vigilant information processing. Although these models vary in the extent of information search and the nature of the decision process, the rational decision models involve selecting alternatives based on judgments about preferences and future outcomes. Nonrational decision models describe decisions as the result of the mix of participants and the rules of deliberation: the access and decision structures. When these two sets of rules are loose and changing, the mix of problems, participants, and solutions becomes fluid and unpredictable—the conditions described by the garbage can model. When the rules of participation and deliberation are more rigid, decisions become far more predictable as described by the administrative routine model. These rational and nonrational models of decision making do not adequately account for the importance of values and beliefs in guiding decisions. Reasonable judgments about policy must often conform to community norms, and these norms are often evident in the way decision makers perceive and apply history.

Research on decision making has also focused on predictable individual and group biases or errors in judgment. Stereotyping occurs when we substitute simplistic caricatures for complex understanding. Cognitive bolstering involves magnifying the correctness of the chosen option while denigrating the value of the rejected alternatives. Either ignoring information that might require action or postponing decisions by obsessively gathering and considering information is defensive avoidance. Entrapment occurs when individuals persist with failing policies rather than change course, and groupthink occurs when pressure for conformity within groups eliminates dissent and thereby narrows the range of options considered.

Leadership is the increment of influence of performance that goes beyond the authority of office and is, almost by definition, rare. Transactional leaders exchange organizational rewards for better-than-expected performance, whereas transformational leaders raise the level of awareness and aspiration and encourage people to look beyond their self-interest. Leadership involves a mix of the personal characteristics of the leader, the needs and expectations of the followers, and the specific time and place. Leaders, especially transformational leaders, often call on the symbols and beliefs of a particular organizational culture to achieve the increment of performance. Leaders must also, however, guide the adaptation of culture when it is no longer suited to the needs the organization.

CASE STUDY: SWINE FLU FIASCO

On March 12, 1976,[5] President Gerald Ford announced on television a bold new public health program. Over the next six months he planned to "inoculate every man, woman, and child in the United States" against a threatened swine flu pandemic.[6] The side effects proved more dangerous than the pandemic that never came, Ford lost the election, and the immunization program was ended on December 16, 1976, before President Carter assumed office. The events and actions surrounding this case provide a window for viewing decision making and leadership in government.

The story begins in January, 1976, when 13 soldiers at Fort Dix, New Jersey, caught an unusual flu. On February 4, one flu sufferer, Private David Lewis, left the infirmary and joined a five-mile forced march. After the march, he collapsed and died. Later that month the Centers for Disease Control (CDC) identified the flu as a strain more common among pigs. On February 20 a news story linked this new swine flu to the 1918 flu pandemic that killed nearly 500,000 Americans—more Americans than were killed in World War I combat.

Public health experts became worried about the slight possibility of another major flu pandemic. Many thought that major influenza pandemics occurred in cycles and that one was overdue. Moreover, most recognized that the modest epidemics in 1957 and 1968 had caught the United States unprepared, and many public health agencies had been criticized as providing "too little, too late." As discussions about swine flu developed among health professions, the numerically slight risk of a major pandemic began to be described as a "strong possibility," and the CDC quickly developed a consensus that "with a pandemic possible and time to do something about it, and lacking the time to disprove it, then *something* would have to be done" (Neustadt and Fineberg 1978, 11).

Although pandemic fears were at least partially justified, swine flu was also a policy opportunity. Government public health professionals had been promoting prevention through immunization but had found little public or political support. Swine flu was a problem ready-made for their solution. Theodore Cooper, the assistant secretary for health, "had been seeking ways to raise the consciousness of private citizens—of voluntary agencies, of parents, of physicians—to prevention of diseases through immunization" (Neustadt and Fineberg 1978, 22) and swine flu was his first opportunity. In addition, public health experts saw swine flu as a way to increase their budgets and the visibility of CDC; swine flu satisfied bureaucratic as well as public health interests. CDC director, David Sencer, hoped to surpass the last great immunization effort, which was against polio, by doubling the number of immunizations and completing them in half the time. Borrowing from Chairman Mao, he spoke of the plan as the "great leap forward."

In March, President Ford convened a "blue-ribbon" panel of public health experts that included such medical luminaries as Dr. Jonas Salk and Dr. Albert Sabin, who had developed the polio vaccines. This panel of medical experts—there were no nonmedical people on the panel—argued that swine flu was a threat and that massive immunization was the appropriate response. President Ford, chided by the press and politicians as a bungler, was fighting off a primary challenge from Ronald Reagan and needed an issue to help him appear the decisive leader. In his March 20 press conference he cautioned that no one could predict the seriousness of the threatened pandemic, but despite uncertainty bold action was needed. He took charge and asked Congress for $135 million to vaccinate every American against swine flu. When he made this public announcement, Dr. Salk and Dr. Sabin stood at his side.

Not everyone thought such a mass immunization was appropriate. In early April, Richard Friedman, the Chicago regional director of the Department of Health, Education, and Welfare,[7] sent a memo to Cooper suggesting stockpiling of the vaccine rather than mass immunization. He warned against overstating the dangers of the pandemic and the use of "scare tactics." The tight-knit group of public health experts pushing the immunization ignored such dissent, however. The insurance companies were the only group that took a careful look at the possible risks of mass immunizations, and they warned pharmaceutical manufacturers that they would not cover the swine flu vaccine without further study of its actual risks.

The doubts of the insurance companies created the first political crisis: Congress was asked to pass a law that would shift the risk from the insurance companies to the federal government. Before taking on this obligation, Congress gave the program its first real vetting outside the public health community. Under congressional scrutiny, doubts emerged and some early proponents, such as Dr. Sabin, withdrew their support for mass inoculation. Chance intervened with an outbreak of an unknown but fatal virus in Philadelphia; several men died of this unknown disease after attending an American Legion convention. False fears about swine flu—Legionnaire's disease was later shown to have no relationship to flu—and a panicked public pushed the program through Congress.

After several false starts, the immunization program began on October 1. By October 13, fourteen persons in nine states died shortly after receiving the shots. In one instance three old men in a nursing home had heart attacks within a week of their flu shots. Public health officials insisted that these deaths were attributable to chance: People, especially old people, die, and with such an extensive program, some will die shortly after the shots. Press accounts and the public, however, began to associate the shots with the deaths. In November, a new problem emerged. An unexpectedly large number of cases of a rare and sometimes fatal nerve disease, Guillain-Barré syndrome, were associated with the shots. Although the syndrome had never before been associated with vaccinations, CDC established a slight statistical link between swine flu vaccination and Guillain-Barré syndrome: one death in two million shots. But such slight risks mean that approximately twenty deaths will occur when 40 million people are inoculated.

The public fear of both unfounded and slight risks was made worse by one central fact: the pandemic never occurred. Only a few more scattered cases of swine flu appeared. In November, President Ford lost the election and on December 16 the immunization plan was suspended never to be resumed. On one level, this effort was an administrative success, but as Neustadt and May (1986, 52) conclude, "In ten weeks more than 40 million persons had received flu shots, twice the number in any previous year. Everything considered, that will be viewed as an administrative wonder. In the absence of the flu, however, it seemed to most contemporaries but a waste, or worse."

Discussion Questions

1. In what ways did uncertainty alter the events and decisions?
2. Examine the events for evidence to support both the rational and nonrational models of decision making.
3. Were any of the common decision flaws evident in this case?
4. What can be said about leadership based on these events?
5. Is it fair to judge our government leaders based on the outcomes of their decisions?

NOTES

1. Bounded rationality and mixed scanning are not identical concepts, but both share the observation that individuals and governments make rational decisions only within limits and on narrow problems.
2. See Palumbo and Wright (1981) for an application of these ideas to program evaluation research.
3. The garbage can model is a computer simulation of organizational decision making.

Mohr (1982, 172–178) suggests that the model is broadly generalizable to public organizations, and Kingdon (1984) applied it to political agenda setting.

4. This, of course, is a matter of degree. Legislatures often follow strict parliamentary rules, and the seniority and committee structures create elements of hierarchy. Nonetheless, legislative decision making tends to be more fluid and less orderly and predictable than administrative decision making.

5. This case is based on Neustadt and Fineberg (1978) and Neustadt and May (1986).

6. A pandemic is a widespread epidemic that affects a large number of individuals.

7. HEW is now split into the Department of Health and Human Services and the Department of Education.

CHAPTER 7

Public Personnel
Administration

The National Aeronautics and Space Administration (NASA) faces a potential personnel crisis. In the early 1990s, 70 percent of the space agency's 2,500 top managers and engineers will be eligible to retire. (NASA employees can retire at age fifty-five, although not all those eligible will do so.) Many of these experienced public employees joined NASA in the early years of the space program. They guided the first astronauts into orbit and onto the moon; they monitored the control panels for the first space shuttles and watched the shuttle *Challenger* explode; and they put the shattered space program back together. Their knowledge and experience is a major asset of NASA, an asset soon to be spent and not replenished. Throughout the budget cutting years of the 1970s and 1980s, NASA could not hire and train new top-level employees.

In some desperation, NASA is attempting to teach a new generation of smart computers, rather than a new generation of engineers, the technical wisdom of these *Apollo*-era space veterans (Broad 1989, 1, 11). Smart computers may adequately replace some NASA engineers and may greatly enhance the work of many public organizations. Nevertheless, the personnel crisis at NASA underscores a central fact: People are the primary asset of public organizations.

The quality of government policy and service depends in large measure on the skill, energy, and creativity of the people working in government. Most public organizations spend well over 50 percent of their budget on personnel; for many—schools, service agencies, research labs—personnel costs can account for more than 90 percent. Even the defense department with its expensive weapons spends over half of its money on people. Spending on education, foreign affairs, social services, and research means issuing paychecks to teachers, diplomats, social workers, and scientists. Thus, a large part of public administration is personnel administration.

The personnel crisis at NASA is symptomatic of problems throughout public service. It is expected that during the 1990s the United States will lack the skilled and knowledgeable people needed to address our nation's problems (National Commission on the Public Service 1989). Who will find a cure for AIDS, improve schools, reduce homelessness, negotiate arms reductions, test foods, and manage prisons, if government can neither afford nor attract skilled, creative, and responsive public servants? In 1989, the National Commission on the Public Service (1989, 1) observed:

> Too many of our most talented public servants—those with the skills and dedication that are the hallmarks of an effective career service—are ready to leave. Too few of our brightest young people—those with the imagination and energy that are essential for the future—are willing to join.

As a result of the cuts during the 1980s and the constant criticisms of "bureaucrats," the U.S. government faces a personnel crisis in the 1990s.

Public personnel administration is a broad subject. It deals with placing individuals into public jobs; maintaining their interest, knowledge, skills, and commitment; and assuring that they are productive. Accomplishing these purposes involves numerous technical challenges, such as the design of valid entrance exams and the development of pay and fringe benefit programs.[1]

In this chapter, we stress the central role public personnel administration plays in building and maintaining an organization's capacity to implement public policy. Personnel administration simultaneously reflects and guides much public policy. As John Nalbandian and Don Klingner (1987, 4) write, "The real life dynamism in [public personnel administration] is found neither in policy arenas nor in personnel techniques. It is to be found on the metaphorical bridge where policy and techniques merge in debate." Selecting, guiding, evaluating, and encouraging public employees—the activities of personnel administration—define the setting in which the abstract issues of organization theory and public policy come to life; where principles confront individuals. Individual personnel decisions—a job description is rewritten to emphasize technical skills, a woman is promoted as police chief—reflect broad changes in society and government, such as growing professionalism and affirmative action.

Personnel administration is on the cutting edge of many social conflicts, and this edge is sharpened by the constant friction of two issues. First, public sector jobs are themselves valued and scarce resources. They consume much public spending and provide careers for countless citizens. Who wins the competition for public sector jobs molds the character of government and is a central theme in the history of civil service reform as well as in current debates over affirmative action. Second, how public employees do their jobs—what they emphasize and overlook, their level of knowledge and energy, and their values—largely determines the nature of policy as delivered to citizens. All of these factors are influenced by traditions and habits developed during the history of public personnel policy.

POLITICAL RESPONSIVENESS
VERSUS NEUTRAL EXPERTISE

Peter Colby (1984, 191) writes, "The history of public personnel administration in the United States usually is told as a morality play in which the forces for the evil spoils system are defeated by the champions of merit.'' According to this simple tale of good versus evil, in the early to mid-1800s elected officials paid back supporters and cronies with politically appointed jobs. The principle guiding personnel administration was ''to the victors go the spoils,'' with the public service raped and plundered by victorious political parties. Connections, not competence, were the basis of public employment.

The second act in this morality play begins in the late 1800s and early 1900s. In this period, good government reformers slowly defeated the party bosses and their system of spoils. They introduced merit principles into public personnel practices and fought for a government run by nonpolitical experts who earned their jobs based on skills, knowledge, and performance, not political opportunism.

The historical shift from political to nonpolitical appointment of public employees changed the character of American government. The increased reliance on nonpolitical appointment at all levels of government, from the nation's capital to small towns, replaced a government by average citizens with one of experts and professionals or in Hugh Heclo's (1977) term *strangers*. Yet, ironically, in the United States merit principles have become closely associated with democracy, not elitism (Mosher 1982a, 217).

This simplistic view of the history of public personnel administration as the triumph of merit over spoils is misleading on several levels. First, to identify political appointment with spoils obscures the inherent conflict of values in personnel administration. The more important conflict is not between good and corrupt government but between two positive values: responsiveness and competence. A highly efficient government staffed by the best and the brightest is not a triumph of good government unless it remains responsive to elected officials and the general public. Conversely, a government devoid of competence cannot respond to the needs and hopes of the public, no matter how well articulated these are by elected officials.

Spoils and merit systems are false opposites because the values of responsiveness and competence are central to democratic governance. As Kenneth Meier (1981, 559) writes,

> Although responsiveness and competence can be traded off, they are not necessarily mutually exclusive. Merit system agencies are often highly responsive to their clientele, political executives, or legislators. Patronage appointment can also be used to attract highly qualified persons to government.

Rather than the gradual triumph of merit over spoils, the history of personnel administration reflects the ongoing tension between the values of responsiveness and competence. This tension underscores an issue previously introduced: Who becomes a public servant makes a difference in governance. This issue is central to the concept of *representative bureaucracy*. In our large and complex society, most citizens must delegate concern for policy matters to elected and nonelected officials. In this sense, policy is always made by elites (Redford 1969). These elites who represent our interests are not generally representative of the population. For example, the U.S. Senate is often referred to as the ''millionaires' club.''

Samuel Krislov and David Rosenbloom (1981), in their book *Representative*

Bureaucracy and the American Political System, document that while public bureaucracies do not mirror the gender, education, racial, and other demographic characteristics of society, they are more representative of the U.S. public than are legislative bodies. Much of this representation is deliberate as public agencies have taken the lead in equal opportunity and affirmative action. Representative bureaucracy theoretically provides more responsive public service and reduces social and economic inequalities. It is important to note, however, that the bottom of public bureaucracies, the street-level bureaucrats, are more representative than the top. Hugh Heclo (1977, 100) reminds us that top public administrators are "disproportionately white, male, urban, affluent, middle-aged, well educated at prestige schools, and pursuers of high-status white collar careers."

TWO CENTURIES OF CHANGE

From Gentlemen to the Masses

Heclo's characterization of current top-level public administrators echoes the first years of our nation.[2] The period from 1789 to 1829, from the signing of the Constitution to the election of President Andrew Jackson, is often referred to as "Government by Gentlemen" (Mosher 1982a, 58–64). During this period, government officials holding elected and appointed office were predominantly members of the landed gentry, even though a few wealthy businessmen and professionals entered government service.

This government by gentlemen (women could not even vote until the twentieth century) was in part the historical continuation of the colonial tradition and in part a demographic necessity. Few except the landed gentry could read and write and understand laws and lawmaking. Only 2 percent of the population were professionals—clergy, lawyers, doctors, engineers, professors, and military officers—and they were the children of the gentry. During this period even well-paid craftsmen and farmers lacked the social standing and skills to govern. The American Revolution was not a social revolution that gave political power to the masses. In the early 1800s, the accepted prerequisites for governing—education, belief in public service, lack of conflict of interest—differed little from those of today, but during this period the landed gentry maintained a monopoly on these prerequisites. The influence of the gentry declined gradually during this period, as the rhetoric of self-government and equality began to catch up with the practice of government.

The period beginning with the election in 1829 of President Andrew Jackson and ending in 1883 with the Pendleton Act witnessed the marriage of political power and patronage, a marriage that produced two offspring. The first was a great increase in the rate of turnover in government jobs. By the end of this period nearly all government positions were filled by political appointment. This meant that when a political party lost control of the presidency or governor's or mayor's office, nearly all federal, state, or city employees could lose their jobs. During this period, public servants had a clear and personal incentive to see that their party stayed in power: Their livelihood depended on it. President Lincoln, who used patronage with great skill, complained that he was running an employment service, not a government. Robert Caro's (1974) description of New York City in the early 1900s characterizes government at all levels across the nation during the middle to late 1800s.

> There were in 1914, 50,000 city employees and this meant 50,000 men and women who owed their paychecks—and whose families owed the food and shelter those paychecks bought—not to merit but to the ward boss. Patronage was the coinage of power in New York City. And reforms of the civil service . . . were therefore daggers thrust at the heart of Tammany Hall [a corrupt and powerful political machine]. (p. 71)

A second result of increased patronage was a change in the relative emphasis on merit. President Jackson did not advocate a venal or incompetent public service. He was, however, distrustful of a permanent and elite government. He argued that

> the duties of all public offices are, or at least admit to being made, so plain and simple that men of intelligence may readily qualify themselves for their performance; and I cannot but believe that more is lost by the long continuance of men in office than is generally to be gained by their experience. (quoted in Mosher 1982a, 65)

During this period in American history, political appointment extended to most levels of public employment, and once appointed, public servants had little claim to their jobs. They served at the pleasure of elected officials who created political power by promising and then awarding jobs. Patronage also wrested control of the government from established elites who relied on merit and experience to maintain their position and authority. If responsiveness is defined narrowly as being responsive to the views and interests of elected officials, then extensive patronage creates a more responsive government. Public servants earn and retain their positions on the basis of loyalty to elected officials, not through the more abstract loyalty to public service.

As patronage dominated public personnel at all levels of government, the negative implications of Jackson's egalitarian views became increasingly apparent. A change in elected leaders meant chaos, not responsiveness. Incompetence and corruption spread, with public administrators increasingly seen as leeches rather than servants. Elected officials lost control of their own appointments as party bosses and local leaders demanded jobs for support.

Public disdain for government by patronage grew steadily throughout the mid-nineteenth and early twentieth century. Reform was gradual, taking root in some places and spreading eventually across the nation. Many local governments (local governments are often the source of political innovation) experimented with merit systems and civil service reforms. In the 1860s, President Lincoln complained bitterly about the spoils system but conformed to patronage demands. President Grant attempted but failed to pass civil service reform. By the 1870s, patronage was so entrenched in American government that it proved difficult to excise.

In the late nineteenth century, civil service reform became a popular cause for intellectuals, but it took an assassin's bullet to wound patronage, and in 1881, a disgruntled office seeker assassinated President James Garfield. The corrupt spoils system was increasingly seen as a threat to social order, and in 1883 Congress passed the first major civil service reform act, the Pendleton Act.

The Pendleton Act of 1883

The Pendleton Act of 1883 was the first of a century of federal civil service reform laws. Federal reforms were only the most visible signs of reform; changes gradually occurred at all levels of government. Although the full implementation of the Pendleton Act required years of development (Van Riper 1958), these federal reforms encouraged state and local reforms by both modeling and mandating change (Tolbert and Zucker 1983). The Pendleton Act created the Civil Service Commission to oversee the hiring and promotion of certain federal employees. In addition, entrance and advancement in those jobs included in the federal civil service were for the first time based on open, competitive examinations. The Civil Service Commission began to define and classify positions in order to facilitate merit practices.

Patronage was not eliminated, however. Many of the Pendleton Act reforms were based on contemporary reforms of the British Public Service (specifically, the Northcote-Trevelyan Report), but unlike the British reforms, the Pendleton Act allowed the American civil service to retain the political appointment of top officials (political executives). Many categories of federal jobs were only gradually included under civil service laws. Thus, despite the moral fervor behind the introduction of the merit system, responsiveness remained central to American public personnel administration. Throughout our history, the dividing line between political and merit appointment has remained a source of controversy.

Lloyd-Lafollett Act of 1912

Merit hiring and promotion were an essential first step, but as long as public employees can be arbitrarily dismissed, partisan interest can easily intrude on civil service. In 1912, the Lloyd-Lafollett Act provided federal civil servants with a measure of job tenure. This statute distinguished between probationary and tenured employees by granting job security to those who had successfully completed an often brief probationary period. After probation, employees cannot be fired without cause and have the right to notice of their discharge, and the right to learn the reasons for their discharge. In some cases employees also have the right to a hearing to review their dismissal.

Thus, the Lloyd-Lafollett Act extended merit principles to dismissal as well as to hiring and promotion. After the Lloyd-Lafollett Act federal civil service employees could lose their jobs only if their work fell below articulated standards of performance or ethical behavior. Taking unpopular or politically unfashionable stands was no longer grounds for dismissal. As with others aspects of civil service, some state and local governments led while others lagged in adopting merit based dismissal, but over time merit hiring, promotion, and dismissal have become accepted in principle, if not always in practice, throughout public personnel administration. Of course, patronage continued well into the twentieth century in many eastern and midwestern cities; even as late as the 1960s patronage was the backbone of Mayor Richard Daley's political machine in Chicago. However, merit rules at the federal and state levels and in many smaller cities that rely on professional, not political, management.

Hatch Acts of 1939 and 1940

Merit principles severely restricted the patronage system of getting and holding public jobs based on political allegiance. Merit-based personnel practices did not, however, sever the link between political power and public employment. As the number of federal, state, and local public employees grew, the temptation to use their numbers and influence to alter partisan elections also grew. Some public employees were assigned to election campaigns while still on the public payroll; others were forced to contribute money to campaigns. Partisan loyalty remained a key to successful government careers.

The Hatch Acts encouraged political neutrality among government officials by banning certain types of partisan activity. The 1939 act prohibited federal employees from actively taking part in the management or operation of partisan political campaigns. The 1940 act extended the same prohibitions to state and local employees whose salaries are partially paid by federal grants. The Hatch Act restrictions apply only to career civil servants; elected officials, such as sheriffs, and political appointees, such as cabinet secretaries, may remain active partisans. The Hatch Act restrictions are interpreted to include prohibitions against actively raising funds for political campaigns, running for elected office, actively working to help elect political leaders, and attending political conventions. Public employees are now expected to appear neutral and are free from pressures to provide political support to their elected bosses. Many state and local governments have passed similar prohibitions called "Little Hatch Acts."

This freedom from pressure has a serious trade-off, however. To neuter public organizations politically, the Hatch Acts have taken from public employees several basic citizen rights. Public employees can take leaves of absence to participate actively in political campaigns, can publicly express their own opinions, can voluntarily contribute their own money to political campaigns, and can vote, but the line between expressing personal views and active partisanship is not easily drawn. David Rosenbloom (1989, 217) notes that "federal employees have been disciplined for such behavior as stating 'unsubstantiated facts about the ancestry of a candidate' (calling him an S.O.B.?), failing to 'discourage a spouse's political activity,' and voicing 'disapproval of the treatment of veterans while acting as a Legion officer at a closed [American] Legion meeting.'" Despite the ambiguity of where free speech ends and partisanship begins, the Supreme Court has upheld these restrictions of political rights based on the overriding public interest in an efficient, nonpartisan civil service (*Civil Service Commission v. National Association of Letter Carriers* 1973; *Branti v. Finkel* 1980).

The principles of merit and neutrality began as a reform movement and have become fundamental to the American system of government. As Mosher (1982a, 217) comments, "A neutral, efficient civil service was viewed [by the reformers] as not merely desirable; it was essential to democracy itself." From the mid-eighteenth century to the present the reformers' views have become the foundation of public personnel administration.

Merit Reconsidered

The abuses of the patronage system that so alarmed civil service reformers were real. The value of responsiveness was corrupted to support the narrow interests of politicians and political elites, not the public. But the principles of merit and neutrality have created an increasingly inflexible and conservative civil service. Critics of merit systems argue that the emphases on testing and job security have created a system of mediocrity, not merit. By trying to prevent wrongdoing through procedural protection, reformers have created a system that does little. E. S. Savas and Sigmund Ginsburg (1973) overstate the failings but in so doing underscore several problems in contemporary public personnel administration. They write,

> In trying to prevent itself from doing the wrong things—nepotism, patronage, prejudice, favoritism, corruption—the civil service system has been warped and distorted to the point where it can do hardly anything at all. In an attempt to protect against past abuses, the "merit system" has been perverted and transformed into a closed and meritless seniority system. A true merit system must be constructed anew, one that provides the opportunity for any qualified person to gain access non-politically, to be recognized and rewarded for satisfactory performance, and even to be replaced for unsatisfactory service. (p. 80)

Merit systems limit the discretion managers have in hiring, rewarding, and firing employees. To the extent that top managers of public organizations are, ultimately, elected officials and political appointees, merit systems also separate administration from elected political officials. Patronage and spoils were the negative side of closely linking administration and political power, but increasingly commentators observe that without power there can be no governance. As Norton Long (1949, 257) wrote forty years ago, "The lifeblood of administration is power. Its attainment, maintenance, increase, dissipation, and loss are subjects the practitioner . . . can ill afford to neglect." Public bureaucracies isolated from elected officials become constraints on policy, not instruments for developing and implementing policy. Current reform efforts attempt to restrike the balance between responsiveness and competence—not to recreate patronage but to augment flexibility and innovation.

The Civil Service Reform Act of 1978

The Civil Service Reform Act of 1978 grew out of these concerns about the merit system. Perhaps the most striking characteristic of the 1978 reform is how little it changed the basic principles and practices of public personnel administration. Despite the often harsh critiques of the current system, the Civil Service Reform Act did not fundamentally alter the twin principles of merit and neutrality that are the foundations of public personnel administration; it tinkered with, rather than overhauled, the system. The Reform Act restated and elaborated nine merit principles, created or redefined numerous agencies involved in public personnel management, and created the Senior Executive Service. The Civil Service Reform Act's nine principles of merit (see list) provide the current working definition of merit.

Civil Service Reform Act (1978) Merit Principles

1. Recruitment should be from qualified individuals from appropriate sources in an endeavor to achieve a work force from all segments of society, and selection and advancement should be determined solely on the basis of relative ability, knowledge, and skills, after fair and open competition which assures that all receive equal opportunity.
2. All employees and applicants for employment should receive fair and equitable treatment in all aspects of personnel management without regard to political affiliation, race, color, religion, national origin, sex, marital status, age, nor handicapping condition, and with proper regard for their privacy and constitutional rights.
3. Equal pay should be provided for work of equal value with appropriate consideration of both national and local rates paid by employers in the private sector, and appropriate incentives and recognition should be provided for excellence in performance.
4. All employees should maintain high standards of integrity, conduct, and concern for the public interest.
5. The work force should be used efficiently and effectively.
6. Employees should be retained on the basis of the adequacy of their performance, inadequate performance should be corrected, and employees should be separated who cannot or will not improve their performance to meet required standards.
7. Employees should be provided effective education and training in cases in which such education and training would result in better organizational and individual performance.
8. Employees should be:
   a. protected against arbitrary action, personal favoritism, or coercion for partisan political purposes, and
   b. prohibited from using their official authority or influence for the purposes of interfering with or affecting the results of an election or a nomination for election.
9. Employees should be protected against reprisal for the lawful disclosure of information which the employees reasonably believe evidences:
   a. a violation of any law, rule, or regulation, or
   b. mismanagement, a gross waste of funds, an abuse of authority, or a substantial and specific danger to public health or safety. (Adapted from Klingner and Nalbandian 1985, 11)

Federal Personnel Management.   The Civil Service Reform Act reorganized the various agencies and commissions overseeing federal personnel administration. The bipartisan Civil Service Commission created by the Pendleton Act was redesigned and renamed the Office of Personnel Management. Unlike the Civil Service Commission, the Office of Personnel Management reports directly to the president and thereby strengthens executive control over federal personnel policy. In addition, the Reform Act delegates greater discretion to individual federal agencies to manage their own personnel practices. Other work of the Civil Service Commission was divided between two new agencies: The Merit Systems Protection Board assures compliance with the nine merit principles, and the Federal Labor Relations Authority oversees negotiations with unionized federal employees.

Senior Executive Service.   The most innovative aspect of the Civil Service Reform Act was the creation of the Senior Executive Service (SES), a new classification of public administrators at the highest levels of the federal government, which encompasses approximately 7,000 positions. The SES was promoted as a cure for two pervasive civil service ills: the lack of responsiveness, and the low performance levels in the highest ranks of public service. To increase political responsiveness the SES increases political appointments: Up to 10 percent of SES positions are open to political appointment, and political executives can more easily reassign career civil servants who enter the SES within and across agencies. To increase performance, SES executives receive extensive performance appraisals based on written goals and objectives. In principle, outstanding performance should lead to substantial merit rewards and below-average performance to demotion out of the SES.

Although it is perhaps too early to tell, the Civil Service Reform Act does not appear to have eliminated conflict between the values of responsiveness and competence. Conflict persists, especially in the Senior Executive Service. From the point of view of public executives, joining the SES involved a trade-off of increased political involvement in their work for greater performance rewards and work responsibilities. In the early years of Reagan's presidency, the SES became a tool for reshaping the civil service to serve better ideological and partisan interests. Geographic reassignments were used to punish or silence uncooperative senior public servants. Moreover, the promised pay raises for greater performance never materialized: Raises were modest and few performance distinctions were made. As one disgruntled senior official told Patricia Ingraham (1985, 34), "the [SES] is a litany of broken promises." Another added, "I've been had."

In the first years of the SES, partisanship, conflict, and job turnover increased. Just under half of the experienced and high-ranking career civil servants who joined SES in 1979 had left by 1983. Although the problems encountered in the early years of the SES were largely political, they also raise questions about the general impact of merit systems on motivation and performance.

Merit Rewards, Work Performance, and the Civil Service Reform Act.   The basic assumption of merit systems is that reward for performance increases work motivation and productivity. As we discussed in Chapter 4, expectancy theory argues that the relationship between reward and motivation is complex. Only if workers consider a reward rewarding, trust the system to reward performance, and believe that increased effort will improve performance do merit rewards encourage greater effort and productivity. The increased emphasis on performance appraisal and merit reward of the Civil Service Reform Act provides an opportunity to examine the linkage between merit systems and work behavior.

Shortly after the Civil Service Reform Act was implemented, Janice Beyer, Harrison Trice, and John Stevens (1980) examined the motivation of members of the Senior Executive Service. They found a major break in the motivational link described by expectancy theory. Federal managers perceived little connection between merit criteria and their own reward and promotion. Jone Pearce and James Perry (1983) studied a similar group of top federal executives and found no motivational differences between those working in merit and seniority pay systems. The failure of the merit reward system was due in part to the trivial and therefore unmotivating pay differences between top and average performers. Moreover, many federal employees saw the performance appraisal process as unfair.

In a recent follow-up study, James Perry, Beth Ann Petrakis, and Theodore Miller (1989) found another problem with performance appraisals. To motivate, merit rewards must be targeted to top performers, and as a result, the remaining employees—even highly productive ones—are identified as average or below average and may be discouraged rather than motivated. When a few are rewarded, the net effect may be reduced overall organizational performance. Perry, Petrakis, and Miller (1989, 34) observe,

> It is important to recognize that performance ratings affect an employee's understanding of the job by providing feedback about performance, self-image, organization commitment, and trust. Although normally-distributed performance ratings [that is, grading on a curve] may be desirable to meet the objectives of the compensation system, they could undermine other aspects of employees' organizational attachments, producing an overall negative effect on motivation. Evidence from several sources suggests that tradeoffs exist between the compensation objectives of performance ratings and employee self-image, performance feedback, and organizational commitment.

Merit reward systems that depend on overly fine distinctions between individuals may, therefore, reduce overall organizational effectiveness. If only the best are rewarded and the differences between the select few and others are trivial, then merit systems can dampen overall motivation and effectiveness. This problem is compounded by the modest salaries offered in government agencies.

Top performers in corporate and professional organizations are routinely paid salaries and benefits many times greater than their public sector peers. Supreme Court justices earn only a fraction of the salary of top corporate lawyers. Public resistance to high salaries for top government officials places severe limits on any merit reward system. Given these constraints, how much performance can we reasonably expect? Organizations, public or private, that consistently require extraordinary performance rarely endure. Public personnel management that encourages consistent, reliable, and, yes, average performance may, in the long run, prove more productive than a management system that rewards only exceptional performance. Attention to the intrinsic value of public sector work may also enhance public personnel management more than refinements in performance appraisals and merit rewards, since motivations for public and private employees often differ, and reward systems designed for the private sector may work less well in the public sector.

Increasing Professionalism

The growing emphasis on merit hiring and the increasingly technical nature of much public sector work has fostered the growth of professionalism in public personnel. The work of more and more public organizations depends on scientists, engineers, lawyers, and policy analysts. Rising to administrative positions often requires an employee to earn a master's degree in public or business administration. Professionalism has begun to alter street-level work, with social work, policing, and public health requiring advanced and continuous education. The role and work perspective of professionals was examined in Chapter 5. The important point to restate here is that professionalism and merit are closely linked. Entrance and promotion exams and stricter definitions of job qualifications have increased the educational prerequisites for public employment. The emphasis on merit has augmented the control of educated elites over public organizations.

Professionalism, as an extension of merit, further reduces the political responsiveness of public agencies. As Eugene McGregor (1984, 126) notes, "That democracy and professional public service are potentially inimical is one of the supreme ironies of government and public service." Professionals identify themselves more with their profession than with the specific organization within which they work. Professionals value public service but frequently define public service and public interest from a narrow and often technical point of view. At times they are more concerned with the professionally correct response than with solutions that are politically feasible or favored by their supervisors. Many professionals would rather lose their jobs than risk their professional standing. Lawyers, doctors, or engineers have more to lose if disbarred, unlicensed, or even sanctioned than if fired.

The public and government have increasingly turned to professionals precisely because we want policy guided by their knowledge and neutrality. Professionals, however, add an additional barrier between the public and public organizations. Although Richard Kearney and Chandan Sinha (1988) concluded that the conflict between professionalism and responsive government is often overstated, they summarize the opposing views held by others:

> In essence, these and other scholars have been concerned that an increasing professionalized public service tends to act in accordance with its own narrow self-interests, losing sight of its duty to respond to the public interest. . . . A self-serving, self-perpetuating bureaucracy would be the principal receptacle of power and knowledge, leading to a government of the technocrats, by the technocrats, and for the technocrats. (p. 571)

Balancing Responsiveness and Competence

The century of federal civil service reform, marked by the Pendleton Act of 1883 and the Civil Service Reform Act of 1978, has rebuilt public administration. The abuse of patronage, which once characterized hiring and promotion at all levels of public service, is now relatively rare. The complete reliance on the principles of merit and neutrality can, however, promote unresponsive government. The political appointment of top-level administrators and the values of political responsiveness remain important elements in American public personnel administration—not mere remnants of the spoils system but essential elements of democratic governance. Our current system is not based on the triumph of merit over politics but on a constantly adjusting balance between the principles of competence and responsiveness.

This balance is sustained by a number of structural features of public personnel administration. The most obvious one is the position of the political executive. Through the waves of civil service reform and moralistic condemnation of patronage and spoils, top management jobs in public organizations remain political appointments. The merit system and civil service start below the top layers of management. With all its failings, the Senior Executive Service further strengthened the political responsiveness of career federal agencies.

Political appointment is also prevalent in state and local governments. Many local governments rely on the *long ballot* that requires top administrators to run for office. The attorney general of the United States is appointed by the president, but the attorney generals of most states, like district attorneys in most cities, are elected. Communities with long ballots often elect treasurers, judges, sheriffs, and even the county engineer, even though their work is primarily administrative, not political (Sylvia 1989, 12). It is not uncommon for mayors and district attorneys to belong to different political parties. Such positions may have merit or professional qualification requirements—the county engineer must be a licensed engineer, the district attorney must be a member of the bar—but getting and holding these jobs requires a political base.

At all levels of government, getting, holding, and wielding political power is a necessary part of governance (Long 1949; Lowi 1979). Rewarding supporters and punishing (or withholding rewards from) opponents remains the main currency of political power. Even if civil service jobs are no longer awarded as spoils, government contracts and other forms of spending are becoming a new form of patronage. As more and more public services are provided indirectly through contracts and other forms of privatization, this new form of patronage may rival the traditional spoils system. For example, Anne Freedman (1988) documented the way that minority politicians relied on affirmative action and minority contracts to build a political organization in Chicago to rival the old patronage-based party machines.

> The Chicago experiences seems to lend support to the argument that patronage is an integral and ineradicable feature of American politics. Civil service may take jobs out of the patronage system, but patronage reappears in other guises. . . . As a result the army of patronage has shrunk although patronage, a very hardy bloom on the American political scene, still thrives in other forms, particularly in government contracts. (Freedman 1988, 857)

PUBLIC SECTOR UNIONS AND COLLECTIVE BARGAINING

Discussions of civil service reform and the needs for responsiveness leave out a major element of public personnel administration: A substantial portion of public employees belong to unions. At state and local levels, approximately half of all full-time government employees are union members. Fire fighters are the most unionized; 71 percent belong to a union. Sixty one percent of teachers, 53 percent of police officers, and 30 percent of hospital workers belong to public employee unions (U.S. Bureau of the Census 1981, quoted in Rosenbloom 1989). Their wages, responsibilities, and working conditions are set by collective bargaining. Union members are neither political appointees nor, strictly speaking, civil servants. They are a special case, and as

Frederick Mosher (1982a, 188) comments, ''The founders of the civil service did not bargain on collective bargaining.''

Union members are not free of the demands of political responsiveness or the standards of merit hiring and promotion. Nonetheless, through union membership public employees collectively influence political demands and merit requirements. Many of the groups now unionized—police, fire fighters, and highway and sanitation workers—were the backbone of the patronage system. In the past, they got their jobs through political influence and voted to sustain political machines. With direct patronage reformed out of most personnel decisions, elected officials have little direct influence over unionized employees.

Unions, however, have not abandoned their efforts to influence elected officials and political decisions. Many public sector unions represent large blocks of voters and form powerful lobbies. In statehouses across the nation, teachers' unions, such as the National Education Association, effectively lobby for higher wages and better working conditions. If unions strike, unplowed streets, uncollected garbage, and absent teachers contribute to election defeats, encouraging vote-conscious mayors to acquiesce to union demands. Budget-breaking union contracts contributed to New York City's bankruptcy in the mid-1970s. Thus, while unions protect workers from political control, they remain a source of partisan influence.

Unions also alter merit systems. Public sector employment in highly unionized jobs, such as fire fighting, still depends on merit considerations. Job candidates often take tests for entrance and promotion. Unions, however, have considerable influence on the content of the entrance and promotion exams and on the criteria for merit promotion and pay. For example, requiring certification for public school teachers limits the labor market (education majors, not English majors, become teachers), reduces job competition, and thereby increases the bargaining position of union members. Unions also stress collective rather than individual merit, seniority over performance criteria, cost-of-living over merit raises, and promotions from within rather than from outside the organization. In unionized systems, performance appraisals tend to contribute only to marginal differences in rewards. For that reason, it is more in the interest of union members to bargain collectively for higher wage contracts than to compete individually for merit raises.

Public sector unions, which collectively represent the private interests of members, are seen by many as a threat to democratic institutions. Public servants, the idealists say, should abandon their preoccupation with wages and working conditions and place the public interest over their own personal interests. But to the teachers, police officers, government scientists, and other public employees, public service also means a job performed in exchange for reasonable compensation, working conditions, and security.

The conflict between the public interest and the private interests of public employees poses difficult problems for public personnel administration. The general public depends on pubic employees for safety and basic services. When a union strikes and shuts down a private business, the public may be inconvenienced but can usually turn to a competitor for goods or services. Strikes by public unions, however, can threaten the social fabric. When teachers, trash collectors, or bus drivers strike, no matter how reasonable their demands, whole cities barely function. If police officers or fire fighters were allowed to strike, uncontrolled violence and economic ruin might result.

For these reasons, the right of public employees to strike is often severely limited. As long as such strikes do not threaten public health and safety, some states—California and Minnesota are examples—allow all public employees the right to strike. Most states and the federal government restrict this right. When the federal air traffic controllers walked off their jobs in the early 1980s, President Reagan fired them and decertified their union—an action from which the air traffic system has not yet fully recovered.

Frederick Mosher (1982a) writes that two main questions shape public sector unions. The first is "What is negotiable?" Some unions bargain over the entire range of personnel issues: wages, hours, benefits, position classification, promotions, training, discipline and grievance procedures, holidays, sick leave, seniority preferences, overtime, and working conditions. Others are restricted to a narrow scope of bargaining (Rosenbloom 1989, 233). In many public jobs, we should note, working conditions, wages, and hours are set by legislative bodies, not management.

Mosher's second question is "What tools or weapons are available?" With restricted rights to strike and the fact that elected officials, not managers, determine contracts, public employee unions depend more on direct political influence and less on job actions. Public sector unions are lobbies, and union leaders spend considerable time trying to influence elected officials. Even if Hatch Act restrictions prohibit direct involvement of individual government employees, unions raise money for political campaigns and often support specific candidates.

The tug-of-war between political responsiveness and independence, the need for skills and performance, and the growing presence of professional and unionized workers have shaped the development of American personnel administration. This evolution has not stopped, and public personnel administration faces several contemporary problems that will force further changes in both practice and theory.

CURRENT ISSUES IN PUBLIC PERSONNEL ADMINISTRATION

Conflicts over general issues in personnel administration are usually expressed as controversies over specific questions about policy or practice. The range of current issues is vast, and many lack clear and obvious solutions. Many of the most difficult issues facing personnel administration are hidden in what erroneously appear to be purely technical problems of measuring skills and performance. The day-to-day work experience of public employees and the problems of minorities and women also shape public personnel administration. Assuring that public servants serve the public, not their own personal or other narrow interests, remains a constant struggle, especially when public officials move in and out of careers in government.

Measurement for Selection and Reward

Merit principles are hollow if supervisors subjectively and arbitrarily choose who is hired, promoted, or rewarded. The increased reliance on tests of skills and performance and on credentials has, therefore, accompanied the increasing importance of merit criteria. In most cases the working definition of merit is a high score on an entrance exam or a performance appraisal. On the surface, reliance on objective measures of qualifications and performance appears uncontroversial. Who could argue with rewarding proven merit? The quantitative measurement of merit is, nonetheless, controversial for two reasons: the inherent limits of performance measurement, and the management problems created by overreliance on objective tests.

Basing merit decisions on test performance assumes that the exams accurately reflect the skills, knowledge, and performance of the individuals—that those with better scores demonstrate greater merit. To the extent that a test score accurately reflects actual skill and performance, the score is considered valid. Writing valid tests and demonstrating test validity is a highly technical problem, but the basic principles are straightforward. A valid test should reflect accurately the individual's level of skill, knowledge, and performance and should distinguish him or her from other individuals who demonstrate higher or lower levels of skill, knowledge, and performance. Valid tests must measure what they claim to measure and discriminate among different levels of performance.

However, since the choice of test items or questions becomes the working definition of merit, valid tests must meet an additional criterion. One could develop a valid test of someone's knowledge of calculus, but that would not be a valid screening device for jobs that require no math. Merit evaluations assume that the criteria are related to the nature of the job. Assuring the link between aptitude tests and actual work performance is essential to validity, and this issue has often proved controversial. For example, in many traditionally male occupations, such as police work and fire fighting, tests of physical strength have been used to deny women jobs. Such criteria are valid only if they are required to do the job.

The extensive reliance on objective tests can create management problems as well. No tests are unquestionably valid and few jobs can be reduced to purely objective criteria. Most hiring or promotion evaluations are to a degree subjective, and this subjectivity is necessary to both managerial flexibility and control. If supervisors cannot exercise judgment, cannot in some way alter hiring and promotion, then employees owe little to their bosses. Management depends on mutual obligation, and if jobs and rewards depend entirely on the objective measurement of aptitude and performance, then employees need not satisfy nor impress their supervisors to get ahead. Current practice in personnel administration allows for some discretion in hiring, promotion, and rewards. Rather than guaranteeing jobs to the top performers, tests are generally used to identify a pool of qualified applicants. Managers can then choose from this pool on the basis of their own judgment and preferences, as long as these preferences are based on work-related characteristics and are not discriminatory.

Quality of Public Sector Work Life

Merit principles have improved the working conditions of public employment. Getting and holding public jobs no longer requires partisan influence; you earn rather than buy jobs. Promotions and career advancement are, for the most part, based on what you do, not who you know, and public employees are protected from arbitrary firings. Nonetheless, the quality of the work experience of many public employees remains low. Pay for public sector jobs—especially technical, scientific, and managerial jobs in the federal government—lags behind similar jobs in business. A scientist working for the National Institutes of Health can expect a much lower salary than one working for a drug company.

In principle, public employees should earn pay that is comparable to similar work outside government. The Civil Service Reform Act asserts the principle of equal pay for equivalent work in private employment (see Principle 3, p. 170). Many worry that the low pay encourages only the least qualified to work for government and that this problem is most severe in professional jobs. The problem of relatively low pay was aggravated during the 1980s. Cutbacks in government spending limited salary increases at a time when private employers were increasing professional salaries. Anthony Fauci, director of the National Institutes of Health, reports, "Over the last decade, [the National Institutes of Health] have not been able to recruit a single senior research scientist from the private or academic sectors to engage in the independent conduct of a clinical or basic biomedical research program" (quoted in the National Commission on the Public Service 1989).

Low relative pay is not the only problem with public sector work; working conditions may also be poor. Equipment is often old and inadequate—government agencies lag far behind businesses in computer purchases, for example—and many offices are crowded, with desks separated by partitions filling large open halls. Public sector work can also involve danger: Teachers and diplomats, like police officers and fire fighters, increasingly risk their safety to do their jobs.

Adding to these very tangible problems, public service has often been the target of a barrage of political criticisms—from elected officials, political executives, and the public at large. Especially during the Reagan presidency, working for government was no longer described as a high calling, and civil servants were portrayed as ineffective, lazy, and parasitic. During the 1980s, government has had its share of scandals and incompetence. But as former defense secretary, Frank Carlucci, points out, those in government should take care when they denounce public employees: "If I as a CEO [chief executive officer of a business] were to say that I have loafers, laggards and petty thieves working for me, one could hardly expect my people to perform. Nor would such talk inspire customer confidence; indeed they would wonder about us as a company and me as a CEO" (quoted in the National Commission on the Public Service 1989, 12). The low pay, poor working conditions, and lack of respect have increased the burnout and job stress of many public sector jobs.

Rights on the Job

Merit principles give public employees certain proprietary rights to their jobs: Tenured public employees cannot be fired, demoted, or even in some cases reassigned without reason and due process.[3] Merit principles, however, do not assure that public employees have other rights on the job. The rights in question can be divided into three overlapping categories: general rights as citizens; the right to give honest, unbiased advice; and the right to dissent. The first suggests rights in the legal sense of the term. The second and third allow public employees to serve the public better but are not in all cases, strictly speaking, legal rights. There are several sources for these rights—the Constitution, state and federal statutes, specific agency and government-wide personnel manuals, and collective bargaining and job contracts—and these rights are continually reinterpreted by the courts.

General Rights as Citizens.   Accepting a job should not, of course, require abandoning legally protected rights. As we have seen, public employees do give up certain political rights, but the Hatch Act restrictions on partisan political activities are seen as a necessary—and protective—abridgment. But what about other rights, such as the presumption of innocence, or the right to privacy or free speech? For public employees, the nature of the employment often makes these rights controversial as well.

Presumption of Innocence.   When the honesty and loyalty of public employees is questioned, public servants are often presumed guilty—especially in press coverage—without trial or due process. Accusations of wrongdoing can force resignations or reassignments, even when the accusations eventually prove groundless. The recent attempt to impose lie detector tests on federal employees across the board by the Reagan administration also posed substantial threats to the rights of public employees. The plan was to test everyone, not just those suspected of wrongdoing. Random and indiscriminate use of lie detector tests—in this case, ostensibly to identify the sources of news leaks—raises profound questions about the presumption of innocence. The policy was never fully implemented, largely because Secretary of State George Schultz refused to take the test himself and threaten to resign if such testing were imposed on his department.

The Right to Privacy.   Random drug testing, like random lie detection, has been promoted for federal, state, and local employees as a deterrent to illegal or inappropriate behavior. But drug testing involves urinating in front of an observer (to prevent switching of samples)—a procedure with which many of us might feel understandably uncomfortable. Moreover, unless suspected of a crime, random drug testing is considered by many as an unreasonable search. The United States Supreme Court has approved random drug testing for certain occupations, like that of railroad engineer and customs official, which involve public safety; and many states require police and corrections officers to submit to drug testing when they apply for work. At this time approximately four million employees working directly or indirectly for federal, state, and local governments are potentially subject to drug tests: 538,000 employees of the Federal Aviation Administration, 3 million truck and bus drivers, 120,000 members of the Coast Guard, 90,000 railroad workers, and nearly 200,00 urban mass transit workers (Cushman 1989).

How far this kind of invasion of privacy may extend into other forms of public employment is uncertain, however. Federal District Judge John McNaught decided that rules requiring everyone seeking work in the post office to be tested for drugs were unconstitutional: ''I conclude that the required urinanalysis drug testing for all job applicants to the United States Postal Service without individualized suspicion is an unreasonable intrusion into the privacy of applicants and thus a violation of the Fourth Amendment" (quoted in Associated Press 1989, 12). In the case involving the U.S. Customs Service, Supreme Court Justice Scalia strongly disagreed with the court's approval of random drug testing. To underscore his dissent, he quoted Justice Brandeis:

> Experience should teach us to be most on our guard to protect liberty when the Government's purposes are beneficent. Men born to freedom are naturally alert to repel invasion of their liberty by evil-minded rulers. The greatest dangers to liberty lurk in insidious encroachment by men of zeal, well-meaning but without understanding." (quoted in Scalia 1989, 4346–4347)

The privacy of public officials is threatened in other ways as well. Many political executives, like their elected counterparts, must disclose their complete financial histories to assure a skeptical public that they are free from conflicts of interest. The public does have an interest, of course, in knowing whether the county administrator owns land near a proposed shopping mall. But information about income, debts, property, and investments is often highly personal, and the extent of the public's demand to know has grown to the point that qualified individuals hesitate to accept political appointments because they do not want to undergo the kind of examination that is now common.

Finally, the very nature of public decisions also reduces privacy for public employees. Controversy may thrust a mid-level bureaucrat—a professional or desktop manager—into the limelight. The civil servant who approves using dogs in cancer research may become the target for animal rights protests. Police officers complain that they are never really off duty. Other public servants feel constrained from legal but perhaps not exemplary behavior—renting an X-rated video, for example—because it does not measure up to public expectations. We often expect our public servants to conform to standards of public and private behavior that we do not demand from corporate executives or even ourselves.

Free Speech. Pressures to conform, and to suppress unpopular or controversial views, are present in virtually all groups or organizations. But the right to speak freely is, at times, denied public employees—who, ironically, are responsible for nurturing the basic rights of citizens. Let's look at three examples, all of which occurred far from the center of power.

During the height of the Vietnam War protest in 1969, Charles James, an eleventh-grade English teacher at Addison High School near Elmira, New York, wore a black armband to school. He made no references to the band in class; other teachers who supported the war sported flag lapel pins or "Peace With Honor" bumper stickers. But James was asked by his principal to remove the armband and was fired when he refused. "This is a political act," the principal said. "It is an illegal act. You are acting against the President of the United States" (quoted in Harris 1974, 46). A lawsuit filed by James eventually worked its way up to the United States Supreme Court, which upheld his right to free speech and ordered him reinstated—although he was then assigned a difficult schedule and soon fired for "unsatisfactory performance."

A second suit brought James back wages and a cash settlement, but the cost to James and his family throughout the legal battle was considerable; he, his wife, and four children lived on welfare, their garden, and part-time jobs.

In another instance, an employee in a district attorney's office was fired for "insubordination" when she circulated questionnaires to others in her office about transfer policies and morale. A divided Supreme Court upheld her dismissal, the majority arguing that free speech is not an issue when "a public employee speaks not as a citizen upon matters of public concern, but instead as an employee upon matters of personal interest" (*Connick v. Myers* 1983, 709). The dissenting opinion argued that "speech about the manner in which the government is operated or should be operated is an essential part of the communications for self-government the protection of which was a central purpose of the First Amendment" (*Connick v. Myers* 1983, 709).

Finally, a government office worker was fired for remarking, after the assassination attempt of President Reagan, "If they go for him again, I hope they get him." No matter how tasteless or offensive the remark, it was not grounds for dismissal, according to the Supreme Court, since it was not made publicly and was not meant to support assassination generally (*Rankin v. McPherson* 1987).

Although such situations can and do occur in private employment, these examples underscore the fragility of free speech in the public bureaucracy. Specifically, they raise the question of the extent to which public organizations, which are created to support and serve democratic values, can subvert those values internally and continue to carry out their functions.

The Right to Give Honest, Unbiased Advice.   The cases above deal with the right to express general opinions about national policy, government practices, or public officials. The right to give honest, professional, and sometimes controversial advice about policy deals directly with the work of public organizations, and it is not protected by the Constitution or the Bill of Rights. (Someone who has lost a job as a direct result of offering professional advice may of course claim a violation of the First Amendment: The line between protected political speech and unprotected nonpolitical speech is difficult to draw in public organizations.)

In the narrowest sense, offering appropriate professional advice is not a right but an obligation, demanded by the standards of most professional associations. Physicians, lawyers, engineers, and other members of strong professional associations are obligated to base their conduct on professional, not political, standards. Reagan administration surgeon general, Everett Koop, for example, concluded that there was no scientific evidence to support or reject the observation that abortions are psychologically harmful to women, a position in tune neither with the President's stated opinion nor with Dr. Koop's personal beliefs.

The right to state unpopular opinions publicly and to criticize superiors and policies may in fact be more important to the administrative development of policy than the more general (and more clearly protected) right to political expression. This case is best made by an example of lasting harm caused by the condemnation of honest, professional advice.

The 1949 victory of the Chinese Communists over the U.S.- supported troops of Chiang Kai-shek panicked many Americans, who were already alarmed at the growing communist presence throughout the world. Many politicians looked for scape-goats for "losing" China, and they found their targets among State Department specialists who had accurately described both the abuses and weaknesses of the anti-communists. The Foreign Service, which had long prided itself on clear and objective analysis, collided head-on with Senator Joseph McCarthy, who found their objectivity un-American. Many of the State Department's most competent China experts lost their jobs for having provided honest and perspicacious advice. Purging employees who were deemed disloyal for maintaining the standards of professionalism left lasting scars on the quality of analysis provided by the State Department. As Donald Warwick (1975, 20) reports:

> John Paton Davis, Jr., the most famous of the Foreign Service exiles wrote later: "The violence and subtlety of the purge and the intimidation left the Foreign Service intimidated and intellectually cowed . . ., it became a body of conformists." An entire generation of officers learned that innovation and departure from the normal were forms of bureaucratic suicide.

Thus, under pressure from Senator McCarthy and others, the State Department metaphorically shot the messengers; it dismissed those who had honestly and correctly warned of impending disaster. Punishing those who gave critical advice and observations taught those who remained to temper their opinions and robbed the public of the kind of professional analysis that is central to public service and sound policy.

Dissent. Objectivity is rarely criticized until it conflicts with popular or established views. In Chapter 4 we discussed the pressures that organizations put on individual members to conform, to keep dissent within the bounds of group norms and remain team players. For public employees, "blowing the whistle," or taking dissent public, has traditionally been an unprotected right. The Civil Service Reform Act (1978) does protect whistle-blowers, but dissenters nevertheless continue to pay personally for placing public interest over the demands to conform to their organization. Even when they are publicly exonerated and organizations are forced to change policy or procedures as a result of their revelations, whistle-blowers often remain outcasts. Rarely do dissenters rise to top positions in public organizations.

Equal Employment Opportunity and Affirmative Action

Having rights on the job presupposes having a job. Work is not considered a political right in the United States, yet most political rights are based on some measure of economic security. Even voting is difficult for those without income, housing, or access to transportation. Fear of losing one's job often restrains free speech; had Charles James anticipated his dismissal and years of hardship, he might not have chosen to wear his black armband. Few among us would consciously jeopardize careers to speak out on political or policy issues. But if Americans do not have the right to jobs, they increasingly do have the right to fair treatment in educational opportunity, hiring, and promotion.

Equal employment opportunity is the policy, sometimes legally mandated, that prohibits using a wide range of non-work-related criteria when making hiring or promotion decisions. It does not reduce hiring to a random lottery, but it does preclude consideration of race, national origin, gender, age, sexual proclivity, and disabilities in many hiring decisions. The specific list of protected classes remains controversial (the military continues to discriminate legally against homosexuals in enlistment and dismissal policies), but the concept of equal employment opportunity is now generally accepted. Even Representative David Duke of Alabama, a former Grand Dragon of the Ku Klux Klan, endorsed equal opportunity hiring during his congressional campaign in 1988.

Equal opportunity policies remove some of the barriers that have kept minorities, women, older people, and other groups from obtaining jobs and promotions based on merit, but they do not confront another, more subtle problem: how the long history of discrimination has created unequal merit. The removal of discriminatory hiring barriers still leaves many economically disadvantaged minorities far behind; past discrimination limits the models of proper work and school behavior and access to good schools, influential clubs, and organizations that define merit and create work opportunity.

Jobs and careers are like a race, with discrimination an extra burden carried by some competitors. A few of the strongest can compete even when carrying the extra weight and a few of the unburdened will fall behind no matter how advantaged. But overall, those carrying the burden of discrimination will persistently fall farther and farther behind. Equal employment opportunity is the equivalent of removing the burden, of everyone racing under the same conditions. Equal employment opportunity does not, however, make the race fair because the results are not the same for everyone.

Unlike a track event, the race for jobs, careers, and economic success is continuous; this race does not end nor is it restarted. Therefore, assuming an equal distribution of talent, equal opportunity assures that those who previously fell behind will forever remain behind and those up front will forever win the merit competition. As David Rosenbloom (1984, 36) comments, "Thus the merit system may short-circuit the ability of [discriminated against] groups to use public employment as a means for upward mobility because it tends to demand that one already be 'middle class' as criterion for entry into the civil service." Bringing victims of previous discrimination up to the point of fair competition requires affirmative action.

Affirmative action is a form of constructive discrimination designed to erase the historical disadvantage of negative discrimination. Rather than merely removing barriers, affirmative action looks to results: Are minorities and other discriminated against groups adequately represented in the work force? It is important to note that public sector employment has historically been a source of upward mobility for minorities. Francis Piven (1973, 380) reminds us that "public employment was a major channel of mobility for the Italian, the Irish, and the Jew, each of whom, by successively taking over whole sectors of the public service, gave various municipal agencies their distinctly ethnic coloration." Blacks, Hispanics (although both groups have been in North America from the beginning of European colonization), Asians, and women are merely the most recent waves staking a claim on public sector jobs.

Women, although not a minority in the population, are a minority in public sector jobs, especially in high-level positions.

Controversies over Affirmative Action.

Giving preferential treatment to groups previously hampered by discrimination is necessary, at this point in history, to create equal opportunity. Affirmative action is, nonetheless, much more controversial and contentious than equal employment opportunity. In practice, affirmative action requires that a *qualified* member of a protected group be given a job or a promotion before someone of equal or even greater demonstrated merit who is not a member of a protected group. A Hispanic police officer may be promoted to sergeant before an Anglo officer who scored marginally higher on the exam if the employer has reason to believe past discrimination has occurred. Affirmative action does not require hiring and promoting incompetents but does require preference for those who meet threshold standards and are members of protected groups.

Affirmative action is controversial precisely because giving preference to some groups disadvantages others. This controversy sharpened during the 1980s as budget cutbacks throughout the public sector heightened the competition for jobs and economic rewards. When employment opportunities expand, preferential treatment of minorities places only minor hardships on others. Postponing the promotion of a white social worker for six months or a year is a much smaller price to pay for affirmative action than a five- to ten-year wait. The problem becomes especially acute when funding cutbacks require layoffs. The general rule for layoffs, and one demanded by most unions, is "last hired, first fired," but in many public sector jobs the last hired were minorities and women. Should white men who have responsibly held jobs for many years be laid off to protect the jobs of more junior minorities?

Quotas are another source of controversy. Discrimination is subtle. Long after obvious discrimination has ended—the "colored" section of restaurants are closed, women are no longer excluded from top management—less visible forms remain. Minorities have long complained that entrance and promotions exams are culturally biased.[4] Subjective performance appraisals may also reinforce the stature of established groups. Thus, the ultimate proof of equal opportunity should be the results, and all too often hiring and promotion decisions made following strict equal opportunity guidelines do little to erase discrimination.

Quotas, like affirmative action, place the emphasis on results, not process. A quota is a specific target: 25 percent of police recruits will be black. The targets can be relatively flexible, used to measure the success of affirmative action efforts, and in such cases they are referred to as goals. At times quotas are implemented rigidly, creating two separate personnel processes whereby a percentage of the jobs is set aside for protected groups. Without specific quotas it is difficult to eliminate the effects of discrimination, but quotas also raise the alarm of *reverse discrimination*. The U.S. Supreme Court in *University of California Regents v. Bakke* (1978) insisted that setting aside a specific number of places in medical schools for minorities was unconstitutional discrimination if more qualified whites were rejected. But in *Steelworkers v. Weber* (1979), the court upheld temporary quotas in clear cases of past discrimination, as long as they did not create an absolute bar against the advancement of unprotected groups. In general, past discrimination against minority groups is now seen as a legitimate and constitutionally protected criterion for preferential hiring and promotion, but it should not be seen as the only criterion (Nalbandian 1989).

Quotas raise an additional question: "What are reasonable expectations for affirmative action?" Entering a top-level job, especially in a specialized field, is the product of a long chain of events, and discrimination at early stages can greatly alter opportunities at later stages. Take, for example, the district attorney's (DA's) office in a city with a large black population. Ideally the DA's office should mirror the population of the city, but the number of qualified black lawyers interested in working for the DA is relatively few. This is the final and unfortunate result of a long chain of events. A disproportionate number of blacks grow up in poverty; they lack the educational opportunity and money to enter the better colleges. This disadvantage means fewer enter law schools and are then available for hire by the DA. Clearly the DA's office is not responsible for this chain of events, but earlier disadvantage alters the ability of the office to achieve equal employment opportunity.

In general, the criterion used to set hiring guidelines is the ratio of minority (or "protected") to majority members in the qualified work force. The criterion for the DA's office, then, is not the ratio of blacks to whites in the community at large but the ratio of black lawyers to white lawyers. Although this approach may appear reasonable, it in fact reinforces rather than remedies the effects of discrimination and unequal opportunity at earlier stages of career development. When the ratios within the qualified population differ dramatically from the ratios in the general population, then grounds exist to assume that discrimination has occurred and that some form of affirmative action is required. First steps are often modest—recruitment targets, for example—but the final step may be a court-ordered quota.

Jobs and economic opportunity are so fundamental that affirmative action has also raised other difficult questions. For example, "Should affirmative action be applied to entire groups or only to individuals who have suffered disadvantage?" Clearly blacks as a group have endured generations of abuse and discrimination. Despite the social odds, many blacks have achieved economic and professional success and provide for their children the social and educational opportunities that enable them to succeed. Should affirmative action be extended to these blacks and to other minorities who have "beaten the odds" or only to those individuals whose social and economic position currently disadvantages them?

Since it is difficult to establish specific disadvantage, most affirmative action programs treat people as members of groups or protected classes, but this approach does not eliminate difficulties. Deciding what is a protected class and then who belongs is often problematic. Currently the groups identified by federal law for affirmative action are blacks, Hispanics, Native Americans, Asian Americans, Pacific Islanders, and women. Such classifications often combine subgroups with very different histories of disadvantage. Asian, for instance, is not a single category but comprises many groups from entirely different cultures.

Moreover, racial categories are not distinct.[5] Many Americans from Central and South America are white, Hispanic, Native American, and black. Who is and is not black is hardly a black and white question. In Boston, two blond twins were hired by the fire department after listing their race as "black;" one of their great-grandmothers was allegedly black. The courts rejected their racial claim, and the twins lost their jobs. The court was, however, unable to define precisely who is black. As John Eastman of the U.S. Commission on Civil Rights commented, how to define minority status is "one of the most touchy and buried questions, and the more we get into it the more intricate it becomes" (quoted in Diesenhouse 1988). What percentage of black ancestry makes someone black? Do we rely on visual inspection, on birth certificates, on changing community standards, or self-identification? When membership in a protected group can mean the difference between getting and holding a job, these difficult questions become relevant indeed.

Special Problems of Women

Working women are a different kind of minority. Women are not a minority numerically, nor do only a minority of women work. Women have historically been discouraged from all but the most menial white-collar jobs, and although women have made much progress, they remain an underrepresented group in management and professional positions and in other traditionally male jobs. A glance back one generation shows the barriers to women at work. A 1941 book, *Civil Service Careers for Girls* (Carlisle and McFerran 1941), mentions possibilities for lawyers and doctors but emphasizes careers as typists, teachers, and dietitians (and meeting husbands). This guidebook does mention the equal opportunity created by the merit system but encourages "girls" to seek subservient rather than managerial jobs. Even in the late 1980s, men held most top positions at all levels of government. The special problems of women fall into three categories: pay equity, balancing work and family, and sexual harassment.

Pay Equity.   The early rallying cry for working women was "Equal Pay for Equal Work." In the past, it was common for women doing the same job and with similar performance and experience to earn less than men. Such blatant discrimination is now considered a violation of equal rights and has been substantially eliminated from the workplace. Nevertheless, women, on average, earned substantially less than men in 1988,[6] even when the comparison was of men and women with similar educations and work experience. If men and women are paid similar wages for the same jobs, why do such large discrepancies remain?

One explanation of the different earnings of men and women is found in the different pay scales for traditionally men's and women's work. Women predominate in certain occupations and professions that have traditionally been low paid, such as nurses, elementary school teachers, and secretaries. Economists argue that the laws of supply and demand determine the pay level for different jobs—needed yet scarce skills demand higher wages—but the supposedly neutral market consistently pays higher wages to those jobs that are dominated by men. This fact cuts across the entire labor force: Urologists earn more than pediatricians, high school teachers earn more than preschool teachers, gardeners earn more than housekeepers, and so on. Although more and more women are taking traditionally male jobs and generally earn similar wages, the pay gap between men's and women's work remains a major equity problem.

One remedy is to revise pay scales based on *comparable worth,* not supply and demand. Advocates of comparable worth argue that pay scales should be based on the levels of skill, prior training and education, and level of responsibility, not simply supply and demand. Comparable worth does not require that all jobs receive similar pay; clerk-typists would still be paid less than administrators. According to comparable worth a clerk-typist or lab technician should earn the same as a worker in another skilled trade, such as a carpenter or painter.

Identifying and then applying the criteria to judge job comparability is often difficult and a source of conflict. Comparable worth may also greatly increase the cost of public services. Lowering wages for traditionally male jobs will only drive those employees out of the public service; few computer programmers would work at the wage of a secretary. Raising the wages of traditionally women's jobs would, however justly, add to the costs of government services (Kilborn, 1990). These problems have limited the actual effect of comparable worth. Elaine Johansen (1985, 631) concludes, "While the impact of comparable worth on the political imagination has been substantial, its actual accomplishments have been quite modest" (see also Johansen 1984 and Evans and Nelson 1989).

Conflicts of Career and Family.   Although men are slowly taking more responsibility for the work of raising children, women more acutely experience the conflicts between work and family roles. A small part of this is the result of biology, since pregnancy, nursing, and newborn care take time and effort from work. (Men in their fifties and at the peak of their careers are much more likely than women to miss work because of physical problems. Ironically, no one argues that men prone to heart attacks are unfit for promotions, even though many employers still worry about giving women responsible jobs during childbearing years.) The larger part of the conflict between work and family is social. Women who take jobs and work hours that allow for involvement with family must all too often accept limited careers—the "mommy track"—as supervisors do not consider them properly devoted to work.

Work schedules, structures, and, most important, perceptions are still based on the now dated assumption that work life and family life do not conflict because men work in the office and women work at home. Most women with families work. In the era of fax machines and video conferences, there is little reason to force parents to choose between an important business trip and a child's doctor's appointment. As government becomes more and more dependent on the knowledge and work of women and as men acknowledge in action their equal responsibility for family, both public and private personnel practices must find ways to reduce the role and time conflicts of work and family (Schwartz 1989).

Sexual Harassment.   Sexual relations are part of social and, therefore, work life. Although office romances can prove distracting, sexual harassment is more insidious. Sexual harassment does not necessarily involve sex and has two important elements. First, sexual comments and behavior become harassing when considered unwelcome by the recipient. As with racial or ethnic comments, it is properly the right of the recipient to define what is inappropriate; one person's flattering comment may be another's rude suggestion. Many women legitimately feel that constant remarks about their appearance is demeaning and distracts from the more proper emphasis on their work.

Sexual harassment becomes more disturbing with the addition of the second element, power. In most organizations and careers, success requires employees to please supervisors. Using positions of authority to demand or request sexual favors is a form of nonviolent rape. Holding someone's career or job in exchange for sex is less brutal than physical attack and does not receive the same criminal punishment, but it can have profound emotional effects. Sexual harassment comes in every form— including women harassing men and other women—but is overwhelmingly a crime men commit against women. In most organizations men are disproportionately in positions of authority, and in our culture men too often confuse masculinity with dominance and sex with power.

In most public organizations, sexual harassment is grounds for censure and dismissal, yet too many instances are unreported. Most women, unfortunately, experience some form of sexual harassment during their careers. Its effects are often subtle and therefore difficult to prove. Asking a woman who is a co-worker for a date is not harassment, but persistently pursuing a woman who tells you to leave her alone is, especially if one is in a position of authority over her. Defining sexual harassment is not easy because the legal doctrine in this area is new. Nevertheless, some instances are obvious, such as letting a woman know that her advancement or promotion depends on her sleeping with her boss.

Public Administration's Leadership Role

Before leaving the problems of minorities and women, we should underscore the leadership role of public personnel administration in equal employment opportunity and affirmative action. Although changing laws and procedures are only a first step to changing behavior, public organizations have more aggressively sought out and promoted minorities and women than have private firms. Public personnel administration will continue to lead by example in the struggle for equal opportunity. In addition, government has played a major role in requiring private firms to create equal and fair employment. Private firms resist the intrusion of government into their personnel practices. Nonetheless, racial, ethnic, and gender discrimination is now outlawed in all employment. Although businesses decry regulation, research shows that firms closely monitored by government, like drivers passing a radar trap, are more likely to comply with antidiscrimination laws and practices (Baron, Dobbin, and Jennings 1986). Public administration has played a constructive role in both stimulating and demanding equal work opportunity for citizens.

SUMMARY

The quality of government policy and service depends in large measure on the skill, energy, and creativity of the people working in government. Public personnel administration deals with placing individuals into public jobs; maintaining their interest, knowledge, skills, and commitment; and assuring that they are productive. Although many aspects of personnel administration are highly technical, these activities involve constant tension between the need for a government that is competent and one that is responsive. How this tension is resolved in the day-to-day administration of public personnel greatly alters the nature of government.

In the first decades of our nation's history, government officials holding elected and appointed office were predominantly members of the landed gentry. With the election of Andrew Jackson in 1829 the rule by gentlemen was diminished by the increased use of patronage appointment. Elected leaders and their political party awarded public jobs on the basis of loyalty rather than merit or social standing. The growing reliance on patronage appointment created a spoils system that equated responsiveness with political influence and deemphasized competence.

The Pendleton Act of 1883 was the first in a century of civil service reform that attempted to reassert the values of competence and political neutrality. The Pendleton Act began the development of a public personnel system based on merit hiring and promotion. The Lloyd-Lafollet Act of 1912 added protections against arbitrary and politically motivated dismissals, and the Hatch Acts of 1939 and 1940 prohibited federal employees, and state and local employees who were partially paid by federal grants, from taking leadership roles in political campaigns. The Civil Service Reform Act of 1978 attempted to increase the flexibility and managerial control over federal employees by several institutional reorganizations and the creation of the Senior Executive Service. The Senior Executive Service extends political appointment into higher levels of the civil service and allows greater control over the work assignments of career civil servants entering the Senior Executive Service. All of these federal reforms influenced (and were influenced by) personnel practices in state and local governments.

Public sector unions present a set of unique challenges to public personnel administration. At the state and local level, approximately half of all full-time government employees belong to unions. Public sector unions negotiate the entire range of personnel issues—from pay to hiring and promotion criteria—and greatly influence the nature and operations of merit systems. The right to strike, especially in essential jobs such as police work and fire fighting, is limited for public employee unions, and in many jobs elected officials, not agency directors, determine wages and working conditions. For these reasons, public employee unions spend considerable time and effort lobbying elected officials. Many public employee unions actively support political candidates who support their interests.

This chapter also examined several contemporary controversies in public personnel administration. The reliance on entrance and performance tests and other objective standards is a necessary element of merit systems. Such tests can prove controversial because of the difficulty in developing tests that measure with validity the skills and performance that are clearly related to the job. The quality of public sector work life is another contemporary problem. Public employees generally earn less and endure worse working conditions than comparable employees working for private businesses. In addition, public employees are the targets of undeserved political criticisms that devalue their work and contributions.

The general citizen rights of public employees and their rights to give honest, unbiased advice and to dissent are often challenged on the job. The expanded use of drug and lie detector tests in the absence of specific evidence of substance abuse or misdeeds conflicts with the presumption of innocence and the right to privacy. Free speech or the right to hold and express dissenting political views—one of our most basic political freedoms—is also challenged on the job. The right to give honest, professional, and, at times, dissenting views is related to free speech even though it is not restricted to political views. The right to disagree with supervisors is a constant source of conflict in public organizations.

The controversies over equal opportunity employment and affirmative action also affect public personnel administration. Equal opportunity employment removes all discriminatory barriers from hiring decisions that cannot be directly related to the work. Equal opportunity employment does not, however, erase the persistent effects of past discrimination. Once barriers are removed, minorities and other groups previously discriminated against cannot easily catch up. Affirmative action is a form of positive discrimination that gives an extra boost to those groups suffering from past discrimination. Because affirmative action requires preferential treatment it is more controversial than equal opportunity employment.

The special problems of women were also discussed. Although women are not a minority and a majority of women work, women remain a minority in managerial and professional positions and certain traditionally male jobs. In general women earn less than men, even when you account for differences in education and experience. This pay difference is due in part to lower pay scales in traditionally women's work, a problem that could be addressed by basing salary on comparable worth. Working women also experience greater conflict between career and family needs and greater sexual harassment. In all areas of personnel administration, from leadership in ensuring on-the-job rights to encouraging affirmative action, public administration has historically taken the lead.

CASE STUDY: AFFIRMATIVE ACTION AND THE DETROIT SYMPHONY

The Detroit Symphony was recently rocked by a controversy over affirmative action.[7] More than most arts organizations, the Detroit Symphony relies on state funding: It receives $2.5 million or 20 percent of its budget from the Michigan legislature. Although 60 percent of the population of Detroit is black, its symphony had until recently no minority members, a situation disturbing to several black legislators. When the state legislature withheld nearly $1.3 million in aid, the symphony waived its stringent audition process and hired Richard Robinson, a black bass player.

Although this case raises concerns about artistic freedom, it highlights numerous issues in affirmative action. Is the primary goal of the symphony, like any public agency, to provide the best service, in this case music, to the public, or must it accommodate other social policy goals? Can we expect any organization to make up for the long-term effects of discrimination and economic differences in the pool of qualified applicants for high-level positions? The primary audience for the Detroit Symphony drives into center city from the suburbs, but can a state-supported institution limit itself to such elite interests?

In many ways symphony auditions are paragons of equal opportunity employment. To eliminate discrimination and favoritism, the Detroit Symphony, like most symphonies, relies on blind auditions: Applicants perform behind screens so that the hiring decision is made on the performance, not the performer. There are, however, very few black classical musicians; less than 1 percent of the 4,000 musicians in major orchestras are black. The chances that any orchestra will have several black players, based on performance alone, is extremely remote. With such a small pool of possible candidates, for an orchestra to meet stringent affirmative action goals could require its hiring much less qualified performers. Moreover, abandoning blind auditions raises doubts about the quality of the minority performers. Although he earned the unanimous support of the bass section of the Detroit Symphony, Mr. Robinson said that the process made him feel like a second-class citizen, as if he were given his position because of his race, not his ability. He told the reporter, "I would have rather auditioned like everybody else. Somehow this devalues the audition and the worth of every other player" (Wilkerson 1989, 18).

But why are there so few black classical musicians? A disproportionate number of blacks grow up in families with low to moderate incomes and lack the resources for the years of expensive lessons that careers in classical music require. Moreover, when young black children are exposed to classical music either on school trips or on television, they don't see black musicians on stage; they see white men and a few white women playing primarily European music from the nineteenth century. Indirectly, the Detroit Symphony, like all other symphonies, in their current membership and repertoire contributes to the affirmative action problem they, when forced to hire from such a limited pool of minority musicians, cannot solve.

Discussion Questions

1. In what ways does this case illustrate the clash between affirmative action and equal opportunity employment?
2. What is the responsibility of institutions such as the Detroit Symphony to remedy the result of past discrimination?
3. What are the effects of affirmative action hiring on other majority and minority musicians?

NOTES

1. See Parts III and IV of Klingner and Nalbandian (1985) for a review of the techniques of personnel management.
2. It is interesting to note that the pattern of federal employment during this early period also reflects current decentralization. Of the 3,000 federal employees in 1800, all but 150 worked outside the capital (Mosher 1982a, 61).
3. Jobs are increasingly seen as a form of "new property." For a discussion see Rosenbloom (1989, 450–451).
4. For a discussion of creating unbiased tests see Quaintance (1984).
5. The concept of race is more social than biological. There is only one, interbreeding human race with minor, superficial physical variations. These biologically trivial differences have been the basis for major and life-altering social and economic distinctions. Nonetheless, there are no scientifically distinct racial groups, and it is not possible to identify discrete groups for affirmative action.
6. In the third quarter of 1988, the female-to-male earnings ratio for full-time work was 0.71. If there were no aggregate wage differences between men and women, the ratio would be 1.00. This figure changed little from the previous year (Bureau of Labor Statistics, 28 October, 1988, 1).
7. This case is based on a story by Isabel Wilkerson (1989).

CHAPTER 8

Budget Processes and Policy

Money is, with property, considered as the vital principle of the body politic: as that which sustains its life and motion, and enables it to perform its most essential functions. (Alexander Hamilton, *The Federalist,* Number 30)

The United States government is big business. Daily operations exceed $2 billion. The federal government has branch offices called embassies and military bases throughout the world, and state and local governments extend into every town and neighborhood. The government owns much of the nation's most valuable real estate, from 1600 Pennsylvania Avenue in Washington, D.C., to vast mineral deposits in the West. Its parks include the nation's most popular vacation resorts, and its research and development programs encompass all the sciences. Advances in medicine; inventions from teflon, the computer chip, to lasers; and applications from better highways to space exploration are all results of government-sponsored research. The government is also active in the service economy: Schools, post offices, police, sanitation, emergency relief, loans, pension funds, and insurance are only a few of the services provided by government.

Not only is the government diversified and involved in nearly every aspect of the national and world economy, it has a long history of growth. Figure 8.1 shows the growth of federal government activity from its founding in 1790 to 1970. Although in the 1970s and 1980s this growth leveled, the historical pattern is clear. On both measures of the size of government activity—dollars spent per person and number of employees per 1,000 citizens—the growth has been extensive and sustained. (During the 1920s there was a brief downturn that was reversed in the 1930s.) Sixty years ago, when Calvin Coolidge was president, the federal government spent approximately 3 percent of the Gross National Product (GNP).[1] It currently spends nearly 25 percent of the GNP.

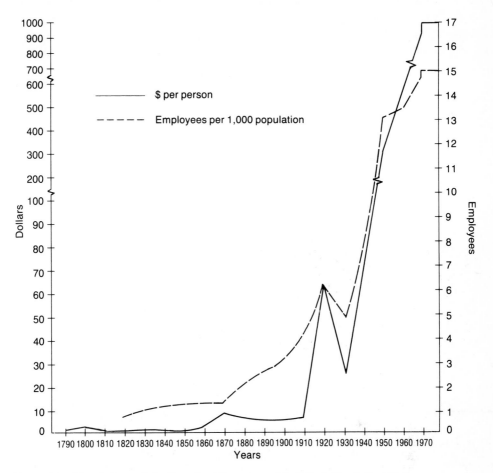

Figure 8.1. Two Indices of the Growth of Government Activity in the United States
SOURCE: Johnston, Ronald J. *The Geography of Federal Spending in the United States of America.* New York: John Wiley and Sons, 1980, p. 2.

With this increased size and scope of activity, the government's influence in the lives of citizens and on the direction of the economy has also grown. Changes in government spending, both in amounts and priorities, have ramifications throughout the economy. Government warnings about the dangers of radon gas in basements creates a new market for private radon detection and prevention firms. Increased funding for AIDS research changes the career direction and opportunities of thousands of scientists. When the nation's bank, the Federal Reserve Bank, raises its interest rates, fewer homes are built and carpenters lose jobs. When the federal, state, and local governments tax and spend; buy, sell, or lease; lend money or restrict credit, they have direct and immediate influence on our lives.

Many worry about the size and pervasiveness of government and call for reducing government's role. During the presidencies of both Carter and Reagan the rate of growth of many government activities, especially social programs, slowed. (Others, such as defense spending, greatly increased.) However, as economist Herbert Stein (1988, 2) states, "We can argue about whether this influence of the Government should be a little larger or a little smaller. It is never going back to being as small as it was even 25 years ago." Decisions about taxing and spending have always been central to understanding government. With the increased scale and scope of government activity, budget decisions now reverberate throughout the nation and echo around the world. Hidden in the complex and technical questions of budgeting are central questions of governing.

BUDGETS AND GOVERNING

The authority to tax and spend is a fundamental power of the state. Combined with the authority to make and enforce laws and regulations, these powers give the state its influence over citizens. The government budget process can make some individuals and businesses wealthier and others poorer; can help cure some illnesses while ignoring others; can provide services to some neighborhoods and not others. These are intentional or unintentional results of government allocation decisions. As Aaron Wildavsky (1988, 2) writes, "In the most general definition, budgeting is concerned with translating financial resources into human purposes." Because these decisions have such direct effects, the process of making budgetary decisions is as important as the results.

The Federal Budget Process

The founders of our nation were fearful of centralized government control and recognized the power of the purse. In drafting the Constitution, they deliberately placed the primary budget authority in the hands of Congress, not the presidency. The president is not excluded but his control over taxing and spending is restricted. The federal budget is a product of the deliberate conflict between these two branches of government. In recent years the courts have also become involved (Straussman 1986). Judicial decisions to close mental institutions, require better prisons, or desegregate schools have major budgetary implications for state and local governments. At various times in our history one institution gains the upper hand, but the other institutions counter to regain balance.

Budgeting is the decision-making process—and all too often the decision-avoidance process—that links revenues, spending, and policy. This decision process follows a set of rules and routines that are refined over time. The federal budgeting process of attaching spending to programs and authorizing off-budget expenditures is guided by the interaction of individuals and institutions, each with their own interests and norms. The specific actors and institutions differ with levels of government. In general, budgets are assembled by administrative specialists but shaped and redrafted by elected officials.

Actors and Institutions.   At the federal level the primary budgetary actors are the president and his Office of Management and Budget (OMB), the House and Senate, and their budgetary committees. The federal budget begins in the White House and the various government agencies. The OMB prepares economic forecasts; the various cabinet departments—Defense, Health and Human Services, etc.—calculate the projected costs of current and new programs. During November and December these projections and requests are continuously argued over, trimmed, and recalculated to conform to the president's spending and fiscal policies. To increase the chance of successfully passing a budget (as opposed to making symbolic gestures), presidents and administrative leaders generally work closely with congressional leaders when formulating the budget. In January all the compromises are packaged into the executive budget which is sent with the president's budget message to Congress.

When the executive budget reaches Congress the process begins anew. The Congressional Budget Office (CBO) prepares its own economic forecasts to test the revenue assumptions of the president's budget. In Congress, the House and Senate budget committees, first separately and then together in a conference committee, write the appropriations bill. The Congress must pass the appropriations bill before adjourning in July. The appropriations bill is then sent to the president who must sign or veto the entire bill. At this time he cannot veto specific items, a process called the *line-item veto* that will be discussed later in this chapter.

Although there are specific calendar dates on which the budget process becomes more visible to the public, this process is continuous. New negotiations begin before old negotiations conclude. The budget process is a continuous game of reciprocal expectations with different actors and institutions playing predictable parts. For example, the Office of Management and Budget under President Reagan continually developed overly optimistic economic forecasts (which were given the nickname "Rosy Scenario") to support his claim of presenting balanced budgets. Representatives and senators predictably add programs and expenditures that help their local constituencies (so-called pork barrel legislation), and agencies routinely pad their requests in the expectation of cuts. This predictable padding is kept within bounds so that agencies do not jeopardize their credibility and thereby invite closer scrutiny. As Aaron Wildavsky (1988, 87) notes, "Asking for too much may prejudice their chances, so it becomes apparent that the ability to estimate 'what will go' (a phrase of budget officials) is a crucial aspect of budgeting."

The budget process vacillates between conflict and cooperation, bluff and sober analysis, and does not end with the signed appropriations bill. Budgets change as they are implemented, since most budgetary allocations give some discretion to the agency charged with spending the money. This discretion can involve moving money across categories—from personnel to equipment, for example—and on the manner spent—by direct service or contracting out. Discretion can be a source of abuse (the government car used for personal travel) but overly strict accounting can lead to paralysis. Many expenses cannot be anticipated, and administrators need flexibility to respond to unanticipated circumstances. For example, in 1988 the National Parks Service needed to take money from other items to pay to extinguish unanticipated forest fires.

The budget process of most states is similar to the federal budget process: Agencies send their requests to the governor's office, governors propose a draft, legislatures modify the budget, and the governor either signs or vetoes the package. In some states, governors can veto individual items; they can approve the education items while rejecting money for a new prison. The budget process in local governments is more varied. In some jurisdictions the mayor and city council propose and refine budget proposals. In others, elected officials may never see the budget until it is presented for approval. In such jurisdictions, the professional staff and department heads retain considerable control over the budget process (Sokolow and Honadle 1984).

Policy Uses of Budgets

Budgets are policy documents. At the most obvious level, allocating money for one program and not another is a strong statement of policy preferences. When the federal government cuts funding for an infant nutrition program, the state does not provide adequate money for prisons, or a city does not pay for increased police protection, these are statements of policy priorities. Elected officials will rarely state opposition to infant health, prisons, or police. Their budget choices are often better evidence of their views than their public statements.

In addition, spending decisions have direct and indirect benefits. The decision to spend money on the Stealth Bomber has the *direct benefit* of adding a new weapon to our arsenal. It has the *indirect benefit* of providing jobs and corporate profits. At the price of $500 million per bomber, the indirect effect on jobs and profits may be greater than the direct effect of greater national security. Many argue that the primary benefit of defense spending, especially on the scale of the first term of Reagan's presidency, is to stimulate the economy.

Government spending has direct and indirect costs as well. Although the federal government borrows huge sums of money (the national debt in 1990 was $3.1 trillion), resources are not unlimited. The *direct cost* of spending in one area is the lack of spending in another: If we spend great amounts in space research there is less money available to fund AIDS research. *Indirect costs* are more difficult to identify. The decisions to cut prenatal nutrition programs can, for example, lead to increased numbers of premature and low-birth-weight babies. Such babies are at greater risk for both medical and emotional problems that may eventually cost the government much more in welfare and health care than was saved by the initial cuts.

Fiscal Policy.   In addition to spending for specific programs, budgets are important elements in fiscal policy. As the federal government's role in national affairs and its spending as a proportion of gross national product have grown, its impact on the general economy has greatly increased. Except for the scale, there is nothing new in this. Alexander Hamilton, George Washington's secretary of the treasury, felt that national government must play a constructive role in encouraging the economic growth of the new nation (Carroll 1987), and in the middle to late 1800s, government grants encouraged the building of the railroads and public universities.

Early in this century, the British economist John Maynard Keynes argued that government spending can play a positive role in guiding the economy. Government spending stimulates employment and consumption and can help push an economy out of recession or depression. By restricting spending and credit, the federal government can also dampen an overly active economy; boom economies can encourage too much speculation and inflation. The use of *countercyclical spending*—spending more during recession and less during recovery—can help keep the overall economy on an even growth rate. This is the goal of fiscal policy. Governments have found it easier, however, to spend during recessions than to save during booms, a policy that has led to ever increasing expenditures.

Tax Policy. Federal, state, and local government tax policy also influences the economy. For example, the part of a monthly mortgage that pays for loan interest is tax deductible; home owners pay less tax than renters. This policy encourages home ownership and helps support those who build and sell homes. Tax breaks, however, also reduce the revenues collected by the federal government. A tax deduction is a form of government spending, since not collecting taxes for specific expenses such as home loans is the equivalent of a government grant to encourage home ownership.

State and local governments also rely on tax breaks to implement policy. Cities and states routinely grant businesses tax breaks to expand or locate in their communities. The justification for reduced taxes is that business expansion helps the overall economy and, therefore, the community at large. Critics call these tax breaks *giveaways*. Many of these tax incentives go to the nation's wealthiest companies. In the late 1970s, 16 percent of the local tax-exempt bonds were raised to fund business expansions, renovations, and relocations of the top fifty wealthiest companies in the nation. Over half of the wealthiest 500 firms received some tax-exempt government support (Bennett and DiLorenzo 1983, 129).

Incrementalism and Retrenchment

The most prominent shared feature of budgets at all levels of government is *incrementalism*. Under most circumstances this year's budget is a slight change—usually a slight increase—from last year's budget. Budget battles are often heated, but the end result is most often a little more of the same. Budgetary incrementalism is an important form of governmental stability and is built into the structure of many budget items. For example, multiyear contracts make some incremental adjustment automatic. Few businesses would sign contracts with governments if they could not count on more than a one-year commitment. Stability has its costs, however. Bernard Pitsvada and Frank Draper (1984, 405–406) comment:

> If it can be assumed that popular wants do not change drastically from year to year, neither should the budget. . . . Incrementalism is reflective of stability, something that lawmakers and administrators like to project more often than not. At the same time incrementalism is a two-edged sword: with stability has also come a steady and inexorable growth in federal expenditures.

The gradual but unrelenting rise in taxes and government spending became a major political and economic problem in the late 1970s. The 1970s was a decade of general economic stagnation with inflation (the cost of things) exceeding growth. Beginning in the late 1970s during President Carter's four years in office and accelerating during President Reagan's two terms, federal domestic spending slowed and in many areas was actually reduced. The rate of growth in government spending declined during the 1980s, but the overall growth did not stop. The conservative revolution led by Reagan did not eliminate or even significantly reduce the size or role of government; overall government spending grew steadily during his eight-year presidency. However, the growth in domestic spending was significantly reduced, and in the 1980s, government leaders across the nation turned their attention to cutting rather than expanding programs; retrenchment, not expansion, guided policy and budgets. This change in direction is likely to continue well into the 1990s (Levine 1986).

Financial stringency changes the social consensus of budgeting. Budgets are instruments for allocating resources toward high-priority programs. During periods of increased spending, when incremental expansion is the norm, governments can alter priorities without major cutbacks. With an expanding budget, the National Institutes of Health could fund more AIDS research, for example, without having to cut funds for cancer research. When expenditures grow, priorities can be adjusted by allowing programs to grow at different rates (Schick 1988, 527), and in this way, incremental budgets foster social and political consensus. No-growth budgets challenge this consensus, however. Without additional resources, budgetary politics becomes a zero-sum game: For every winner there is a loser. And shrinking budgets change the political equation even further: More programs are cut than are maintained or expanded. When there are more losers than winners, the politics of budgeting becomes difficult.

Politics of Budgeting

The political conflicts over budgets are magnified during periods of slow growth and cutbacks because the benefits of government spending are so widespread. When we mention government benefits, welfare recipients come to mind—but welfare recipients are hardly the only beneficiaries of government spending. The poor may be more dependent on government for food, shelter, and health care than most of us, but *all* citizens benefit from government spending. The highly paid engineer working for a defense contractor is, indirectly, a government employee whose food, shelter, and health care are supported by tax dollars. Lester Thurow (Bell and Thurow 1985, 125) reminds us that "middle-class Americans tend to forget that most social-welfare spending goes to programs designed to keep middle-class Americans from falling out of the middle class when they become ill, elderly, or unemployed."

Over the last half-century, government's role in the economy and in the welfare of citizens has grown to the point that we all have a stake in budgetary politics. Moreover, it is important to stress that policy debates and political process shape budgets more than the budget process guides political institutions. Aaron Wildavsky (1988, 439) concludes: "Budgeting is a subsystem of politics, not vice versa."

Macro-budgeting.   The politics of budgeting are complex and generally exist on two levels: the macro or large-scale level and micro or small-scale level (Schick 1986, 1988). Macro-budgeting involves setting overall budget amounts for expected revenues and overall spending. It establishes priorities and is similar to a family allocating money for food, vacations, or cars on the basis of estimated income. Macro-budgeting decisions—overall estimates and priority decisions—are made at all levels of government: federal, state, and local.

We should note here that during Ronald Reagan's two terms as president, macro-budgeting decisions did not involve reducing the overall federal budget, as is generally thought. Rather, the federal macro-budget decisions made during the 1980s involved a dramatic shift from domestic to defense spending, as well as the reduction of government revenues through tax cuts. Cutting taxes without reducing overall spending contributed to both the economic growth of this period and the explosion of national debt.

The macro-budget decisions of the Reagan years at the federal level necessarily mandated some macro-budget decisions at state and local levels as well. With less federal money in the revenue column for social services, cities were forced to reexamine their own priorities—to up their contributions to social service programs from their own revenues, or to reduce their emphasis on such programs.

Micro-budgeting. Micro-budgeting involves making specific funding decisions within the rough framework of the macro-budget. If the national government decides, at the macro level, to shift spending from domestic to defense programs, precisely which programs will be cut and which ones enhanced? Will less money be spent on farm subsidies and more on the Strategic Defense Initiative (Star Wars)? Should military salaries be raised to enhance the professionalism of the traditional forces and funding for the National Institutes of Health be reduced?

At the local level in particular, micro-decisions can provide battlegrounds for involved citizens. Once a city has decided to cut spending for social services, what suffers—the Bookmobile program? Homeless shelters? AIDS hospices? Advocates of each program have reasonable claims on government spending. Accountants may remind governments at all levels that they cannot afford everything, but how do you decide between compelling but competing needs?

WHAT IS A BUDGET?

Narrowly defined, a budget is a listing of actual and projected revenues and expenses for different programs. For example, if you wanted to know how much the federal government spends for the prevention and control of infectious diseases, including AIDS, you could turn to the Budget of the U.S. Government: Fiscal Year 1988.[2] (This section of the budget is reproduced in Figure 8.2.) In the budget, you would find that the Center for Disease Control spent $102,074,000 in 1986 on the control of infectious diseases. In 1987 and 1988, the center estimated its expenditure for this item to reach $130,809,00 and $154,187,000. As we shall see, however, this budget entry hardly tells the whole story.

A budget usually shows not only the amount but also the source of revenues. (Revenue sources are described in detail later in this chapter.) In general, revenues for particular programs are *appropriated* by Congress, state legislators, or city commissioners who decide to spend a set amount on specific programs. Appropriations acts are laws that allow agencies to operate by giving them permission to spend and con-

DEPARTMENT OF HEALTH AND HUMAN SERVICES

CENTERS FOR DISEASE CONTROL

Federal Funds

General and special funds:

DISEASE CONTROL, RESEARCH, AND TRAINING

To carry out titles III[, XVII,] and XIX and section 1102 of the Public Health Service Act, sections 101, 102, 103, 201, 202, and 203 of the Federal Mine Safety and Health Act of 1977, and sections 20, 21, and 22 of the Occupational Safety and Health Act of 1970, including insurance of official motor vehicles in foreign countries, and hire, maintenance, and operation of aircraft, [$539,067,000] *$552,956,000,* of which [$11,800,000] *$2,000,000* shall remain available until expended for equipment and construction and renovation of facilities; *Provided,* That training [of employees of private agencies] shall be made subject to reimbursement or advances to this appropriation for *not in excess of the full cost of such training. Provided further, That funds appropriated under this heading shall be available for payment of the costs of medical care, related expenses, and burial expenses hereafter incurred by or on behalf of any person who had participated in the study of untreated syphilis initiated in Tuskegee, Alabama, in 1932, in such amounts and subject to such terms and conditions as prescribed by the Secretary of Health and Human Services and for payment, in such amounts and subject to such terms and conditions, of such costs and expenses hereafter incurred by or on behalf of such person's wife or offspring determined by the Secretary to have suffered injury or disease from syphilis contracted from such person. Provided further,* That collections from user fees, including collections from training and reimbursements and advances for the full cost of proficiency testing of private clinical laboratories, may be credited to this appropriation[. *Provided further,* That any unobligated balance of the $6,900,000 appropriated in fiscal year 1986, to remain available until September 30, 1987 for the purchase and distribution of drugs, shall remain available until expended] *(Additional authorizing legislation to be proposed for $215,924,000.)*

Note.—Public Laws 99-500 and 99-591, section 101(i), provide funds to the extent and in the manner provided for in the conference version of H.R. 5233, Departments of Labor, Health and Human Services, and Education, and Related Agencies Appropriations Act, 1987.

Program and Financing (in thousands of dollars)

Identification code 75-0943-0-1-550	1986 actual	1987 est	1988 est
Program by activities.			
Direct program			
00 01 Preventive health block grant	87,549	89,531	89,536
00 02 Prevention centers	1,436	1,500	
00 03 Sexually transmitted diseases	53,864	59,094	57,079
00 04 Immunization	56,876	86,976	93,504
00 05 Infectious diseases	102,074	130,809	154,187
00 06 Chronic and environmental diseases	29,064	31,003	31,932
Occupational safety and health			
00 08 Research	56,141	60,036	59,433
00 09 Training	8,383	7,472	6,600
00 12 Epidemic services	49,025	53,304	55,452
00 13 Buildings and facilities	22,795	16,843	2,000
00 14 Program management	2,959	3,161	3,233
00 91 Total direct program	470,166	539,729	552,956
01 01 Reimbursable program	29,107	40,000	40,000
10 00 Total obligations	499,273	579,729	592,956
Financing:			
Offsetting collections from:			
11 00 Federal funds	-28,391	-39,233	-39,233
14 00 Non-Federal sources	-715	-767	-767
21 40 Unobligated balance available, start of year	-34,249	-5,089	
24 40 Unobligated balance available, end of year	5,089		
25 00 Unobligated balance lapsing	10,517		
27 00 Reduction pursuant to P.L. 99-177 in resources derived from offsetting collections	47		
39 00 **Budget authority**	451,571	534,639	552,956
Budget authority:			
40 00 Appropriation	451,571	539,067	552,956
45 00 Transfer out for pay raises and retirement contributions		-4,428	
Relation of obligations to outlays:			
71 00 Obligations incurred, net	470,167	539,729	552,956

	1986	1987	1988
72 40 Obligated balance, start of year	161,571	201,299	253,182
74 40 Obligated balance, end of year	-201,299	-253,182	-266,029
77 00 Adjustments in expired accounts	-1,061		
90 00 Outlays	429,378	487,846	540,109

NOTES

Includes $3,466 thousand in 1988 for smoking and health activities transferred from the Office of the Assistant Secretary for Health. Comparable amounts for 1987 ($3,466) and 1986 ($3,372) are excluded above.
Includes $1,231 thousand in 1988 for activities transferred from Health Resources and Services Administration. Comparable amounts for 1987 ($708) and 1986 ($824) are excluded above.

Preventive health block grant.—Provides States with funds for preventive health services.

Sexually transmitted diseases.—Efforts are directed toward reducing morbidity and mortality from sexually transmitted diseases by preventing cases and complications.

Immunization.—The long-range goal is to eliminate poliomyelitis, rubella, mumps, diphtheria, pertussis, measles, tetanus and haemophilus influenza B (HIB) as significant public health problems.

Infectious diseases.—Supports efforts to develop new or improved prevention, diagnosis, and control methods for infectious diseases, including research, health education, and risk reduction on Acquired Immune Deficiency Syndrome (AIDS).

Chronic and environmental diseases.—Efforts are directed toward reducing or preventing illness associated with certain chronic diseases and conditions, and to reduce the adverse health impacts of environmental hazards.

Occupational safety and health.—These activities are directed toward the elimination or control of factors in the work environment which are harmful to the health and safety of workers.

Epidemic services.—Supports efforts to contain epidemic outbreaks by maintaining national disease surveillance systems, epidemic investigations, and laboratory services, and to prevent the importation of diseases from foreign countries.

Buildings and facilities.—This activity provides funds for projects related to repair, alteration, and improvement of facilities.

Program management.—This activity provides leadership and administrative management.

Object Classification (in thousands of dollars)

Identification code 75-0943-0-1-550	1986 actual	1987 est	1988 est
Direct obligations			
Personnel compensation:			
11 1 Full-time permanent	101,017	102,341	106,469
11 3 Other than full-time permanent	6,990	7,707	7,749
11 5 Other personnel compensation	4,113	4,172	4,179
11 9 Total personnel compensation	112,120	114,220	118,397
12 1 Personnel benefits: Civilian	21,956	23,120	31,346
13 0 Benefits for former personnel	7		
21 0 Travel and transportation of persons	5,597	6,198	6,487
22 0 Transportation of things	1,419	1,489	1,493
23 1 Rental payments to GSA	1,579	1,515	2,661
23 3 Communications, utilities, and miscellaneous charges	11,767	12,143	12,410
24 0 Printing and reproduction	1,422	1,233	2,535
25 0 Other services	33,585	50,839	59,370
26 0 Supplies and materials	30,445	25,914	26,507
31 0 Equipment	11,126	12,716	2,653
32 0 Lands and structures	23,475	10,661	864
41 0 Grants, subsidies, and contributions	215,646	279,681	288,233
42 0 Insurance claims and indemnities	22		
99 0 Subtotal, direct obligations	470,166	539,729	552,956

Figure 8.2. 1988 Budget Allocations for the Centers for Disease Control
SOURCE: Office of Management and Budget, 1988. *Budget of the United States Government: Fiscal Year 1988;* p. I-K9. Washington, D.C.: U.S. Government Printing Office.

tract for services. The primary revenue *source* for federal appropriations is taxes, but governments raise money from user fees (you drive on the highway, you pay a toll), insurance funds (Social Security or public pensions), and borrowing. Most often appropriations are tied to specific legislation; the federal budget, for instance, identifies the specific laws defining the Center for Disease Control's obligations and responsibilities in dealing with infectious diseases.

Budgets, however, involve more complexity than simply matching revenues and expenses. The first level of complexity is in the budget itself, in the vast scope of activities covered. The condensed federal budget is a large format book of small print over 1.5 inches thick. You could not, for example, gauge the federal government's effort to fight AIDS by looking solely at the Center for Disease Control's expenditures: The National Institutes of Health fund basic research on AIDS; the Food and Drug Administration evaluates and sponsors clinical trials of promising treatments; and the surgeon general's office and the Department of Education spend money on AIDS education.

Many government programs cut across numerous budget items, so it is nearly impossible to answer the apparently simple question, "How much does the federal government spend on AIDS research and prevention?" At times this scattering is intentional. For example, the food stamps program, one of the more important support programs for the poor, is administered by the Department of Agriculture, not Health and Human Services where most welfare programs reside. In other cases, such as AIDS research, problems do not neatly fit into established programmatic boxes. Such cross-cutting programs add to the enormous complexity of government budgets.

A second dimension of budgetary complexity is in the process of budgeting, the uncertainty in predicting both revenues and expenses. In general, budgets are based on *projected* revenues and expenses. The accounting is so cumbersome that the federal government is always one year behind. As shown in Figure 8.2, the expenses for both the next year and the current year are based on projections. This is largely due to the time frame required to develop the budget; the 1988 budget was developed in 1987. Not until months after the fiscal year ends does the government know how much is actually spent.

The amount of revenues collected are also based on projections. Governments at all levels can only estimate the amount of taxes they will collect. For example, the amount the federal government collects in income tax depends on how many people earned raises and the success taxpayers have in finding loopholes. Most state and local governments are highly dependent on sales tax revenues which go up and down with consumer spending.

The best government can do is to project income and expenses based on economic forecasts. These forecasts, in turn, are based on assumptions about the future performance of the economy—and therefore are open to manipulation (Light 1985); political leaders who want to spend more without increasing taxes encourage optimistic forecasts that predict unrealistic tax receipts. The difficulty in estimating expenses is made worse by budget items that are based on promises of payment to many qualified citizens. Clearly the government cannot refuse unemployment or disability or a host of need-based compensations to qualified citizens simply because the amount allocated was already spent. The reliance on estimates of both revenues and expenses adds greatly to the complexity of budgeting.

WHERE DOES THE MONEY COME FROM?

Although most budget debates center on how to *spend* money, it is equally important to know where the money is coming from—to identify and understand the sources of revenue. Collecting revenues, like appropriating and spending it, can be a political process; different sources of income have different effects on the wealth of individuals. To some degree, the balance of revenue sources indicates political priorities.

Revenue sources can be progressive, proportional, or regressive, although the distinctions are not always clear. *Progressive* revenue sources redistribute wealth downward. They take proportionately more from the wealthy and proportionately less from the poor. The federal and most state income taxes were designed to be progressive: As you earn more, not only do you pay more in absolute terms, but you pay a larger percentage of your income. For example, in 1978 the poorest Kansans, those earning less than $3,000 a year, paid only .2 percent of their income for the state income tax, while Kansans earning more than $25,000 paid nearly 2 percent (Daicoff and Glass 1978). A progressive tax is, in effect, a form of welfare payment. Many argue, however, that the federal income tax is not truly progressive since the wealthy use the tax laws to avoid or minimize payment.

Proportional revenue sources are designed to have no redistributive effects. An example would be payroll taxes, such as the social security tax: Up to the maximum payment, the proportion deducted for social security does not change with income, and there are no deductions for special groups.

Regressive revenue sources take proportionately more from the poor than from the wealthy. Sales taxes are regressive: While the poor and the rich pay the same amount of tax on any given purchase, the poor pay a larger percentage of their income for that purchase and therefore pay a larger percentage of their income in sales taxes. Kansans with incomes less than $3,000 paid .4 percent of their income for sales tax, while those earning more than $25,000 paid less than .1 percent in 1978 (Daicoff and Glass 1978). Lotteries are also regressive revenue sources, since the poor not only invest a larger portion of their income in a single ticket but tend to buy more tickets than the wealthy. Clearly, the nature of the revenue sources on which a government depends and the relative burden they require from different groups in the population alter the wealth of individual citizens.

Taxes

For 1988, the Office of Management and Budget (OMB) estimated the total on-budget receipts of the federal government to reach $916.6 billion (OMB 1988, 2–2). The major sources of these billions are shown in Figure 8.3.[3] Clearly most federal revenues come from individual (38 percent) and corporate income taxes (11 percent). Both forms of taxes are highly complex, providing jobs to scores of accountants and tax lawyers who interpret the rules to benefit clients. The idea is simple, however. Citizens and businesses pay a proportion of their earnings in taxes.

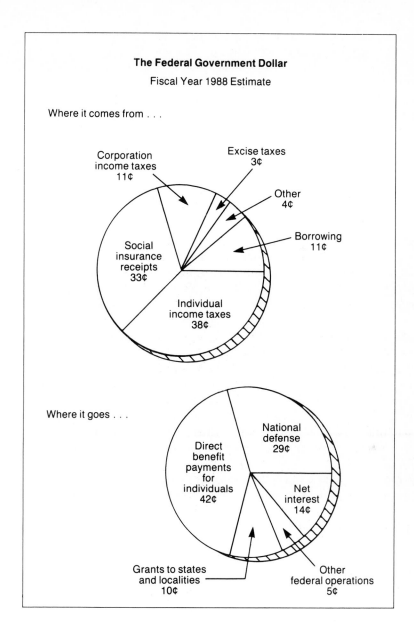

The Federal Government Dollar

Fiscal Year 1988 Estimate

Where it comes from . . .

Corporation income taxes 11¢

Excise taxes 3¢

Other 4¢

Borrowing 11¢

Social insurance receipts 33¢

Individual income taxes 38¢

Where it goes . . .

National defense 29¢

Direct benefit payments for individuals 42¢

Net interest 14¢

Grants to states and localities 10¢

Other federal operations 5¢

Figure 8.3. How the Federal Government Spends and Where it Gets its Money
SOURCE: Office of Management and Budget, 1988. *Budget of the United States Government.* Washington, D.C.: U.S. Government Printing Office, p. M–2.

Personal and corporate income taxes become complicated for two reasons. First, it is not always easy to define income. Income from a paycheck is easy, and tax forms for individuals with such standard income are quite simple. But income from investments and businesses is more difficult to define. Should the costs of word processors and editorial help be deducted from an author's income? In general, income is defined as what is left after expenses are paid, and individuals and corporations often deliberately increase their expenses to reduce their taxable income.

Second, income tax becomes complicated when it is used as a policy tool, not just as a means to collect revenue. Home owners can deduct the interest portion of their mortgage payment from their income tax. Until recently, expenses to reduce energy consumption through insulation or new equipment reduced the tax bill to both individuals and corporations. Donations to charities and nonprofit firms are also tax deductible. When individuals and corporations give money to public television their good will is rewarded by reduced taxes as well as good programs. Although tax simplification reforms have reduced the number and variety of deductions, tax provisions remain an important policy tool. Thus, as with all other areas of budgeting, income taxes serve both a narrow purpose of raising money and a broader purpose of encouraging individual choices to conform to policy goals.

The corporate income tax is more controversial than the personal income tax. Taxing corporations is appealing. Like Robin Hood, such taxes take from faceless organizations and wealthy stockholders rather than average citizens. Critics of corporate income taxes claim that their effect is the opposite of their appeal. Rather than reducing their profits and dividends to stockholders, corporations, whenever possible, pass expenses on to the consumer through increased prices. Average citizens, critics argue, pay twice: They pay their own income tax and then pay the corporate tax when they buy products and services (Bell and Thurow 1985, 103). The hidden tax of higher prices is, however, less painful than the more obvious income tax deducted from each paycheck.

Most states (Texas and Connecticut are exceptions) and some cities also levy income or wage taxes, but state and local governments get a larger proportion of their revenues from sales and property taxes. Many local government services, most prominently schools, are paid for from property taxes. The amount of property tax is a product of the tax rate (often called the mill levy) and the assessed value of the property. In most cases the assessed value of a property, your home for example, is much lower than the market value. One way state the local governments increase revenues without directly increasing taxes is to reassess the value of property at a higher level.

User Fees

In addition to taxes, governments raise money by charging for their services. These charges come in two closely related forms: user fees and excise taxes. Both are increasing in importance. User fees are direct charges for a government-provided service. When you enter a national, state, or even town park, you pay a fee. If the park ranger rescues you from a mountain top, the federal government sends you a bill. An excise tax is really a hidden or indirect user fee, such as the federal excise tax on airplane tickets, which helps pay for the maintenance and operation of airports, including the federally operated Air Traffic Control System.

The appeal of user fees and excise taxes is that they charge the user, not the general taxpayer, for the service. Why should someone who hates camping pay for national parks, or someone afraid of flying pay for airports? Charging users appears fair but has limits. Few government services can be supported entirely by user fees. In fact, those that could should theoretically be provided by private businesses, not government.[4] Therefore, most services that require fees—public transportation, public universities, parks, highways, trash pickup, and so on—are funded in part from general revenues. Tuition at a state university pays for only a fraction of the costs of education. The justification for paying for services out of general tax funds rather than entirely from user fees is they provide indirect benefits to nonusers. Public universities, for example, are a community asset even if your own children attend private universities—or no university at all.

Trust Funds

Another major source of government revenue is social insurance. As shown in Figure 8.3, 33 percent of federal receipts come from social insurance programs, primarily Social Security. All working Americans pay a portion of their income into the Social Security Trust Fund which pays them back a set income based on their earnings after their retirement. Government insurance programs at the non-national levels include employment insurance and various state and local pension funds.

Until recently, these funds have not been counted as revenue because they are targeted for specific programs. President Johnson began including them as receipts in a unified budget to obscure the costs of the Vietnam War. At this time the various trust funds add more to the budget than the various insurance programs pay out. They, therefore, mask the actual size of the federal deficit. Some trust funds, such as the highway trust fund, have actually lent money to other government agencies to make up for revenue shortfalls.

Borrowing

Another major source of revenue at all levels of government is borrowing. When the costs of programs and services exceeds receipts, or when the decision is made that future beneficiaries should help pay for particular projects—a new sports stadium or sewage treatment plant—governments borrow money. For the most part governments borrow from their own citizens, who, as individuals or in mutual funds, buy federal treasury, state or municipal bonds at set interest rates. Although governments can default on loans (as New York City did in the mid-1970s), government bonds generally represent a secure and profitable investment. Holders of federal government bonds own a portion of the national debt—a subject of some recent concern that we will discuss later in this chapter.

State and Local Revenue Sources

A major difference between federal revenues and those of smaller government units is that the smaller units receive a substantial portion of their revenues from governments "higher up" in the chain. Approximately 10 percent of federal government spending goes for grants to states and localities, and states spend much of their budget on local programs. For example, in 1990 nearly half the budget of the State of Kansas was spent as aid to local government units. (The proportion of revenues the state and local levels receive from the federal government varies widely, however.)

Some of these intergovernmental grants are broad and give local governments considerable discretion in spending, a few are very specific, and most are somewhere in the middle. Most state highways, for example, are substantially funded through federal tax dollars. The national government does not tell states where to build roads, but it does use the money to guide state policy. When President Nixon wanted to lower speed limits to fifty-five miles per hour, his administration simply changed funding rules so that highway funds were not available to states with higher speed limits. Needless to say, all states soon voluntarily lowered their limits. (In the mid-1980s these restrictions were modified, and most western states have returned to higher speed limits.)

In the past, state and cities were highly dependent on federal grants even to pay for such basic services as street repair. The amount of money available to states and local communities has dwindled in the 1980s and its form has changed somewhat—less money comes in the form of "block grants," which allow the recipient greater flexibility in spending, and more comes in the form of specific funds—but federal money remains an important source of revenue. In addition, states and local governments receive income from other miscellaneous sources, including state lotteries, which in recent years have brought in substantial funds to a number of states.

HOW IS THE MONEY SPENT? PART I: APPROPRIATIONS OR ON-BUDGET EXPENDITURES

Governments spend money in a variety of ways. The most obvious involve the direct dispersion of money. Social Security checks, government contracts and grants, and paychecks to the public employees are all direct payments that appear on government budgets. Even when they are "lost" on some obscure line in a massive budget, such expenditures are open: They are made through an appropriations process that requires the approval of elected officials. But the government spends in other ways as well. Governments spend when they take on debt or other financial liabilities, and governments spend when they consume or disburse assets (Leonard 1986). Such expenditures remain off budget and are rarely debated. We will look at visible expenditures first; hidden expenditures are examined in the section that follows. Visible or on-budget expenditures at the federal level take three general forms: grants to other governmental units, specific programs (annual appropriations and entitlements) and payment of debt.

Grants to Other Government Units

As we will discuss in Chapter 10 on federalism, the relationship between federal, state, and local governments is primarily financial. Spending at a higher level of government becomes a revenue source at a lower level. As we saw earlier, 10 percent of federal government expenditures goes to states and localities in the form of grants, funding everything from prison construction to computers in elementary school class-rooms. Although the amounts vary widely from state to state, approximately 20 percent of state revenues come from the federal government. These federal grants can shape policies at all levels of government. The federal government has reduced racial and gender discrimination in schools by withholding all federal grants, contracts, and tax deductions from schools and universities that violate federal antidiscrimination rules. The acceptance of grants establishes a pattern of obligation to conform to regulations that gives the grant-allocating agency considerable control over the grant recipient. The power of the purse goes both ways. It is not just the power to collect taxes; it is the power to shape policy through allocation and obligation.

Specific Programs, Entitlements

Specific programs make up the largest category of on-budget expenditures. Over 70 percent of federal spending goes for these programs, which cover the range of governmental activity from direct benefit payments for individuals to national defense. A glance at the 1988 federal budget shows the different allocations for different programs. For example, funds for research programs in space ($11.4 billion) and atomic weapons ($7.8 billion) far exceeded the support for research in basic science ($2.6 billion). Pollution control and abatement received an estimated $4.6 billion for fiscal year 1988; social services received $7.9 billion. A similar list could be drawn up in each state and local government, although the items would differ: Police would replace the military, sanitation would replace pollution control.

Overall state spending has increased an average of 8.5 percent a year through the 1980s. Some of this increase was necessary to offset the federal cuts in social programs. State spending is as diverse as the states themselves, but some general patterns are clear. In 1988, together the states spent $456 billion on specific programs. One-third, $150 billion, was spent on education, primarily as state support for local primary and secondary schools ($85 billion) and colleges and universities ($55 billion). Welfare programs received 17 percent ($78 billion) of the state spending; trust funds such as pensions for state employees received 10 percent ($43 billion); highways received 8 percent ($38 billion); health programs and hospitals, 7 percent ($32 billion); and the remaining 25 percent ($115 billion) went for all other functions and services.

At the federal, state, and local levels these specific on-budget programs are further subdivided into *entitlements* and annual *appropriations*. Both entitlements and appropriations are based in law and can, theoretically, be reversed or rescinded. Entitlements are programs or budget obligations that are determined by the needs of targeted citizens. The law now states that any citizen with black lung disease, a debilitating disease suffered by coal miners, qualifies for payment. That payment does not require additional legislative approval. If, based on criteria set in the legislation and administrative rules, you have black lung disease, you get a payment.

Specific appropriations require the direct approval of elected officials. This approval can extend beyond the single budget year; if Congress and the president decide to pay for the development of a new bomber, they can authorize a long-term effort. The military is not, however, *entitled* to a fixed number of airplanes that are automatically approved when the number falls below a threshold, a military "poverty line."

Entitlements pose budgetary problems very different from those of specific authorizations.

Characteristics of Entitlements.   Entitlements cover a wide range of programs. At the federal level, they include Social Security and social disability insurance; railroad, military, coast guard, and civil and foreign service retirement and disability; veterans' benefits; grants to states for Aid to Families with Dependent Children; food stamps; Medicare and Medicaid; unemployment compensation; trade adjustment assistance;[5] child nutrition and special milk programs; guaranteed student loans; coal miners' black lung disability benefits; agricultural subsidies; and many others. Some states and localities provide additional entitlements: California, for instance, provides an additional medical entitlement program called "MediCal," and free public education is a local entitlement program. Entitlements are for the most part social programs. They form the basic federal welfare programs for the poor, but some of the largest, such as Social Security and Medicare, provide service to middle- and upper-income citizens as well.

Entitlements are legislated obligations of governments—federal, state, and local—to all eligible citizens. Entitlement laws state that if individuals meet the requirements they are "entitled" to the benefit. Such benefits cannot be denied without a change in the law. If you are over retirement age, you get Social Security. If your income falls below a certain level, you qualify for food stamps. If your children are of school age, they are entitled to public education. The right to such benefits has been upheld in federal court challenges (Rosenbloom 1983, ch. 3). The allocations for entitlement are automatic; they do not require budget authorization. If entitlement expenditures exceed budget revenues, government leaders cannot withhold the benefit without changing the law. Once the amount earmarked for unemployment compensation is spent, government officials cannot deny your legitimate claim; if the school budget is exhausted, public schools cannot cut off enrollment.

Entitlements, therefore, remove substantial portions of government spending from the annual budget process. This has advantages and disadvantages. Many entitlement programs address basic needs: food, medical care, education, and disability and retirement income. The provision of these basic services demands predictability. If your Social Security benefits depended on decisions to be made by government officials in the year 2040, it would make little sense for you to contribute today. Entitlements are based on obligations that carry over from one administration to another and from one time to another, regardless of the short-term political or economic circumstances; they are part of the social contract between citizens and their government.

Eligibility.   What all entitlement programs share is the word *eligible,* although different entitlements vary in the breadth of eligibility. Some, such as Medicaid (a health insurance for the poor), require recipients to meet specific income requirements or "means tests," the most common form of which is income adjusted for family size. Some programs, such as unemployment compensation, serve broad populations, while others serve narrowly defined groups, such as beekeepers.

Funding. Entitlement programs also differ in funding source. Pension-based entitlements, such as Social Security, are at least partially funded by trust funds built by individual, business, and government contributions. Government pension funds are entitlements only to the extent that the benefits require support from general revenues. Other programs, such as Aid to Families with Dependent Children, are entirely funded from tax revenues.

Payments. Entitlement payments go directly to individuals, and their size depends on a variety of factors. Some entitlements are *indexed,* which means the amount of the benefit rises or falls depending on some measure of inflation. The most common measure of inflation is the cost-of-living index that charts the change in a wide range of consumer goods, such as food, housing, medical care, and transportation. Automatic *cost of living adjustments* or COLAs further remove entitlements from the control of elected officials. COLAs protect the standard of living of those dependent on entitlements, such as older Americans, but they are not entirely benign; as James Tobin (1985, 10) points out, "Indexation immunizes favored groups from inescapable national losses—in 1973/74 and 1979/80 the big rise in the cost of imported oil—and throws their costs onto unprotected fellow-citizens."

Political Base. Entitlement programs are the product of political action, but once in place they are removed from political scrutiny in two ways. First, although entitlements can be changed by law, they are, by definition, insulated from budget review, and the insulation is thicker when benefits are tied to COLAs. Second, entitlements create constituencies for programs. Once entitlements are in place, lawmakers must overcome considerable inertia to change benefits. For example, many government leaders and farmers consider agricultural subsidies wasteful and expensive; they distort the farm economy. But many farmers have bought land and equipment and planned crops based on these expected subsidies. Drastically altering farm entitlements would break a promise and create short-term hardships. In this way, recipients of entitlements become strong defenders of the status quo. The more entitlements become an expected part of many individuals' lives—whether it's the poor relying on food stamps or the elderly on Medicare—the more difficult they become to change. To achieve predictability, there is the cost of uncontrollability.

Entitlements during Hard Times.   By design, entitlements restrict the freedom of elected officials to alter or redirect the budget: Entitlements are long-term commitments. As Aaron Wildavsky (1988, 260) critically comments:

> Budgeting and entitlements are incompatible concepts. . . . Entitlement is mandatory resource-segregation. Nothing can be taken away; every person or entity who qualifies for payment—by meeting conditions for Unemployment Compensation, for agricultural subsidies, and so on—is entitled to receive the amount stipulated by the formulas in authorizing statutes, no matter what is happening elsewhere or to other people.

The inherent conflict between budgeting and entitlements causes few problems in times of revenue growth, but when government revenues remain constant or decline, then money committed to entitlements greatly reduces the freedom of elected officials to alter spending priorities. When entitlements are insulated from spending cuts, the amount that must be taken from nonentitlement programs grows proportionately.

During the Reagan presidency, the conflict between entitlements and budgeting was made worse by the government's commitment to increase substantially the largest area of nonentitlement spending, defense spending. With entitlements—which constitute 60 percent of total federal spending—excluded from budget cuts and defense spending increasing, other nonentitlement spending was sacrificed. Regardless of the specific budget decisions or the importance of entitlement programs, entitlements place barriers to controlling spending.

In addition to placing certain programs beyond consideration for cuts, the amount of entitlement spending varies in such a way as to compound budgeting problems. Because entitlement spending is defined not by allocation but by the number of eligible individuals, it can increase or decrease independently of government decisions. Some of these changes are predictable. When the baby boom generation retires the Social Security claims will increase. Unfortunately, entitlements predictably increase at the same time that government revenues decline. Economic slumps or recessions cause both the decline in tax revenues and the increase in demands for spending since more people are out of work and qualify for entitlement programs. Some entitlement spending is not predictable. For example, the severe drought in 1988 greatly increased the amount paid in farm price supports. The effect of predictable and unpredictable increases in the number of citizens qualified for entitlements is the same, however. Increases in entitlement spending tighten the knots that tie the hands of government officials trying to redirect or cut government spending.

Controlling Entitlements.   These characteristics of entitlements greatly increase the difficulty in controlling government spending. Entitlement spending can, at least theoretically, be controlled through changes in law and regulation. Such control can be achieved in three ways: elimination of programs, reductions in eligibility, and reduction in payments.

Entitlement programs can be eliminated. Although rare, it does occur. For example, General Revenue Sharing, an entitlement program established by President Nixon in 1972 which transferred federal revenue to qualified local communities, was canceled during Reagan's presidency. Budget cutters hunt for entitlement programs that serve narrow groups, such as the rural electrification program, for further cuts.

A second approach is to reduce eligibility. Narrowing the definition of a disability—how weak does your eyesight need to be for you to be considered blind—or raising income eligibility excludes people from qualifying and saves money. Most eligibility requirements for entitlements are based on complex administrative rules. For example, what counts as income for a means-tested program? During the Reagan administration loans were classified as income in determining the level of welfare payments. This administrative rule was changed after a welfare recipient brought a successful suit in federal court. She had borrowed $100 from a friend to make ends meet, reported the loan to her social worker, who, following the federal rules, cut her welfare payment by $100. Such strict interpretation of the Social Security Act reduces entitlement spending, but the federal district judge hearing the case found such penury "unconscionable" (Tolchin 1988, 37).

The third way to reduce entitlements is actually to cut the amount given. For years entitlements were cut indirectly through inflation. Inflation increases the cost of goods and services and reduces the actual value of the dollars paid out through entitlements, whereas tax revenues, such as those from the income and sales tax, go up with inflation. Holding entitlements constant or allowing them to rise at a rate lower than inflation reduces the real amount spent. This backdoor approach to cutting entitlements was well known to both critics and advocates of specific entitlement programs.

When in the late 1970s inflation reached an unprecedented peacetime rate—greater than 10 percent or double-digit inflation—advocates for entitlement spending, led by lobbies for older Americans, pressured for indexing. Indexing or cost-of-living adjustments protect the real income of those dependent on entitlements, but automatic COLAs also remove the most powerful tool for controlling entitlement spending: inflation. Current efforts to cut entitlement spending have started with controversial efforts to reduce automatic inflation adjustments. These so-called COLA Wars are hard fought, pitting the specific interests of one group, such as the elderly, against the general interest of controlling government spending.

Controlling entitlements is clearly difficult, and as a result, entitlement spending is growing 2.5 times faster than the gross national product. A major contributor to this growth is the rapid rise of medical expenses that are passed on to the taxpaying public through Medicare and Medicaid. Controlling entitlements while maintaining long-term commitments remains one of the greatest challenges facing government officials.

Specific Programs, Appropriations

After funds for entitlement programs are removed from the federal budget, remaining revenues are allocated by Congress in the form of appropriations, or specific funds allocated to specific departments or programs. Some appropriations are accompanied by restrictions on their disbursal; others may be spent more or less at the discretion of the department that receives them. Appropriated expenditures cover a wide range of programs including nonentitlement social programs, such as federally funded low-income housing projects; the many areas of research supported by government grants; and defense.

Defense Spending.   Federal spending for defense represents the largest single category of appropriations and is the second-largest budget item after entitlements. The proposed defense budgets for 1988 ($312 billion) and 1989 ($312.2 billion) constitute massive expenditures, between 25 and 30 percent of the federal budget, and cover a vast array of programs. Some are obvious: The largest proportion of the defense budgets goes to personnel, and another large percentage goes to maintaining nuclear and non-nuclear weapons in a state of both abundance and readiness. But some expenses are less obvious. The U.S. military funds numerous research and development projects. Two-thirds of all federal support for research and development comes from the defense department. In contrast, basic medical and science research sponsored by the National Institutes of Health and the National Science Foundation accounts for less than 15 percent of the federal research dollar (Garfield 1988, 9).

Controversy. Defense spending is controversial. It represents less than a third of the federal budget, but it includes roughly half of the nonentitlement or controllable budget. It is, therefore, a primary target for cuts for those who prefer spending on other needs, especially human services. For instance, the Defense Department plans to spend $70 to $100 billion for 132 Stealth Bombers—enough money virtually to eliminate homelessness. This conflict between spending for "guns or butter" often pits conservatives against liberals, Republicans against Democrats. Although not as inflexible as entitlements, defense spending is not as easy to cut as many critics would hope. The major items in the defense budget—personnel and weapons contracts—involve long-term contracts. Cutting defense, like cutting domestic spending, requires choosing not to fund new projects more than eliminating old ones.

The controversy over defense spending is heightened by the difficulty in knowing how much is enough. No one argues that defense should be less than what is necessary to protect the national security, but despite all the military simulations, no one can definitively set that level. Sometimes the budget itself becomes a surrogate answer: We need to spend as much as or more than the Russians to be secure, some argue.

Hidden in slogans are some important defense policy choices that affect the budget. Is the purpose of defense spending to protect the United States from war, or to protect our global economic interests? If the former, then a small but powerful nuclear force would do; if the latter, larger, more conventional forces are required. Do we design our military to win major, all-out conflicts, like World War II, or to effectively police smaller international conflicts? The type of forces to win major battles are often ill suited for constrained intervention. If we need a military ready for all possible missions, then we can never spend enough.

President Reagan's decision in 1987 to order the Navy to protect friendly oil tankers in the Persian Gulf during the Iran-Iraq War brought many of these conflicts to the surface. Our ships were designed for major open-sea conflicts, not for protecting commercial ships from mines and speedboats in a small sea. In addition, our advanced radar and computer-guided missiles proved unable to distinguish between civilian and military aircraft in a crowded sky. As a result, we shot down an Iranian civilian airplane. Moreover, our national interest in protecting the oil tankers was far from obvious. Although Europe and Japan are highly dependent on Persian Gulf oil, we are not. We acted in part as the protector of our allies (who are also our principal economic competitors) who spend far less on defense than we do, and in part to reinforce our general stature as a world power. Gunboat diplomacy remains an important if expensive part of our foreign policy.

Control. Missions such as the police action in the Persian Gulf—which may have contributed to the eventual cease-fire in the Iran-Iraq War—underscore another problem in defense spending. Like entitlements, defense spending is not predictable. Decisions to use force cannot be forseen by budget planners, and such incursions costs billions each day. In addition, with so many new defense contracts tied to developing and using the latest technology, procurements escalate with unanticipated costs. Some of these unanticipated costs, or cost overruns, result from poor management and graft. Most, however, result from working with unknown or unproved technology.

Controlling defense spending is also difficult because of its secondary effects. Defense spending is a major economic stimulus. Communities near military bases greatly benefit from defense spending (Thompson 1988). Corporations, from the nation's largest to the smallest, benefit from defense contracts. Some private corporations are almost entirely dependent on defense contracts; 99 percent of General Dynamic's sales are based on government contracts (Bozeman 1987, 8). Corporations are not alone; many major research universities, the Massachusetts Institute of Technology for example, are highly dependent on defense contracts for research money.

The political choice between spending for guns or butter is, therefore, complicated. Private individuals and corporations that design and build the guns and work in communities supporting military bases use their earnings to buy butter (and houses, videocassette recorders [VCRs], cars, and so on). From the late 1930s to the present defense spending has become a major element of fiscal policy, and many economists argue that defense spending was the major stimulus for the economic growth in 1980s. John Kenneth Galbraith (1971, 228) observed,

> If a large public sector of the economy, supported by personal and corporate income tax, is the fulcrum for the regulation of demand, plainly military expenditures are the pivot on which the fulcrum rests. Additionally they provide underwriting for advanced technology and, therewith, security for the planning of the industrial system in areas that would otherwise be excluded by cost and risk. And, to repeat, these expenditures have strong support from most businessmen. . . . From his pleas for public economy, defense expenditures are meticulously excluded.

In the late 1980s and early 1990s, tension between the United States and the Soviet Union eased, fracturing the consensus for the massive defense spending that dominated federal fiscal priorities of the late 1970s and 1980s. If as a nation we need to spend less on defense, the macro-budgeting controversy over other priorities will no doubt emerge. Seymour Melman (1989), chair of the National Commission for Economic Conversion and Disarmament, argues that the nation must reinvest in infrastructure to remain—and in many places, regain—our economic strength. This commission recommends spending $53 billion for schools and educational programs; $33.5 billion to clean up radioactive and toxic wastes; $30 billion on a comprehensive housing program; $26 billion to repair roads, bridges, water, and sewer systems; and $10 billion to electrify the U.S. rail system (p. F3). Felix Rohatyn (1989, E21), the chair of New York's Municipal Assistance Corporation, agrees: "The need for large-scale investment in public works is obvious to anyone who travels about the United States." Others hope to use the money that would have gone to defense to increase spending for social programs. Still others hope that decreased defense spending will allow lower taxes and reduction in debt, the last category of expenses.

Debt

The last major expense in the federal budget goes for interest payments on the national debt. Fourteen cents of every federal dollar spent in 1988 went to pay for interest on loans. Throughout this chapter, we highlight the painful trade-offs implicit in budgetary decisions. Government and the public want to spend for an endless array of positive programs—from defense to research to basic human services. Borrowing money allows government to avoid difficult choices, to spend more than we collectively have.

To cover the gap between spending and revenues, the federal government issues treasury bonds. Individuals and investment institutions buy these bonds because they offer secure and profitable investments. If the U.S. government goes out of business, we will have more to worry about than our worthless treasury bonds. But debts, or at least interest on the debts, have to be repaid and can become a drain on the treasury. Tax revenue spent to repay loans reduces the money available for other government programs. Our collective debt is, however, much larger than the cumulative gap between on-budget revenues and on-budget expenses. Debt is also one of several main components of the hidden budget.

HOW IS THE MONEY SPENT? PART II: OFF-BUDGET OR QUIET EXPENDITURES

Although they may be lost among the thousands of items and obscured by confusing categories, all specific programs, entitlements, and interest payments are defined somewhere in the budget. Appropriated expenses do not, however, exhaust the forms of government spending. Government officials, especially local government officials, increasingly turn to off-budget or quiet expenditures. Quiet spending is any form of government expenditure of resources without appropriation (Leonard 1986). The three most common forms of quiet spending are government loans and loan guarantees, off-budget enterprises, and tax preferences.

Guaranteed Loans

Many college students take out guaranteed and relatively low-cost loans, and these student loans are an example of quiet government spending. But how can loans be considered spending? Banks, after all, make large profits from lending money.

Here is how it works. Most citizens and, therefore, most elected officials believe that encouraging college education is good public policy. The commitment is expressed in a variety of federal and state programs to support colleges and universities. Attending college, however, remains an expensive investment and elected officials have decided that many student should receive help in paying these costs. Government support for college costs could come either as a direct supplement, an entitlement, or in the form of loans. A direct supplement would require appropriations, but a guaranteed loan program is theoretically not an expenditure, since students are required to repay the loans.

Such loans become a form of spending in two ways. The most obvious is that when students default, the government loses money. Private banks cover their losses from interest earnings, but the government provides students loans at below-market rates to encourage education and does not earn enough to cover losses. Second, and less obviously, loans tie up government resources, including credit, for specific programs. Giving low-interest guaranteed loans for students means there is less credit available for federally supported home loans, for instance.

Students are not the only recipients of government loans, and the extent of government lending at below-market rates can reduce the amount of money available to other individuals and businesses. Government borrowing can "crowd out" private sector borrowing. James Bennett and Thomas DiLorenzo (1983b, 144), two harsh critics of off-budget spending, observe,

> As an example of how private sector investments are crowded out in favor of governmentally sponsored investment consider the following: In 1980 when a 20 percent prime rate and a 16 percent consumer loan rate contributed to the bankruptcy of thousands of small businesses such as auto dealerships and grocery stores, the Rural Electrification Administration began a new program to provide 35-year loans at five percent interest to finance rural cable television systems; rural home mortgages were available at 3.3 percent; and insured student loans went for seven percent, to name just a few.

By providing loans to students, farmers, or failing corporations, the government becomes, in effect, a banker whose goal is not to make money but, however indirectly, to support public policy goals.

Off-Budget Enterprises

Governments often create separate corporations to pursue policy goals. These off-budget enterprises are the second major form of quiet spending and come in a wide variety of forms. Most off-budget enterprises (OBEs) are government agencies, established by law but financially independent from government control. They lie outside the traditional model of executive agencies that report to the president, governor, or other elected official. OBEs are most common at the state and local levels of government and cover a range of services; they include port and highway authorities, public utilities, finance corporations,[6] and special districts. These different forms of OBEs encompass nearly every public service from airports to cemeteries, sewage to libraries, and pipelines to parks. In Kansas, a state of fewer than 2.5 million people, there are over 4,000 governmental authorities; that is one governmental unit for every 625 citizens (Maynard-Moody and Nalbandian 1988).

Public authorities, such as highway or port authorities, are the most common form of OBEs. These organizations are independent corporations that are wholly owned by a governmental unit. Most public authorities can gather and use funds through user fees, such as bridge tolls, and by issuing government bonds (Doig 1983). Since their primary source of revenue is independent of the legislative budget process, public authorities escape much of the legislative oversight and control common in other public organizations. Such agencies are off budget to the extent their operations are independent of the appropriations process.

All off-budget enterprises are a form of quiet spending to the extent that the collection of fees falls short of costs. When this shortfall occurs, federal, state, or local tax dollars must be spent to make up the difference. Since OBEs often enter into services such as low-income housing that businesses shun because they are not profitable, the need for tax-based supplements to operations is common. Moreover, although many government bonds do not legally obligate the government to cover defaults, government agencies are often morally obligated to back the borrowing of OBEs. If these quasi-public agencies fail to pay back bond holders, the ability of the city or state to borrow in the future is jeopardized. As anyone who has lost the use of his credit card will tell you, credit is a valuable resource.

During periods of tax cuts or limits, OBEs become attractive solutions to providing services without appearing to increase spending. As Bennett and DiLorenzo (1983b, 6) underscore, "In effect, the OBE device permits the politicians to be magicians: Pubic sector activities can be made to disappear by the simple expedient of a corporate guise which moves the operations off the books and beyond the control and scrutiny of the taxpayer."

The cost of moving programs off budget is a great loss of accountability. In most cases, voters and their elected representatives have no control over the directors or managers of OBEs, who may make decisions that obligate citizens to pay for services. Although many OBEs are run efficiently and in the public interest, the potential for abuse is great. As Diana Henriques (1986) notes, the lack of accountability creates opportunities for favoritism, special interests, and corruption as well as simple inefficiency.

Tax Preferences or Loopholes

Tax preferences or loopholes are the third major form of quiet spending. A tax preference is a federal or state income tax deduction for specific expenses. If you qualify, your taxes are reduced. The interest payments for home mortgages are tax deductible thereby giving an indirect benefit to home owners. Tax deductions for charitable contributions, on certain types of investments, and for child care are other examples.

How is not collecting taxes the same as spending? Tax preferences are not a general tax reduction but are available only to those who qualify, and they are targeted to support specific policy goals. For example, during the energy crisis of the 1970s, federal government policy encouraged increased home insulation and greater reliance on solar heat. Rather than requiring that all houses meet certain standards or providing a government subsidy for energy conservation, the government provided tax breaks for insulation and alternative energy sources for families and businesses. If you insulated your house, you could enjoy lower taxes as well as lower heating bills. Such tax preferences can be considered spending in the sense that they deliberately reduce tax revenues to support policy aims. They are simply another way governments use their taxing and spending powers to change the way people behave.

Tax preferences are an attractive way to implement policy. They are noncoercive; they don't force people to buy homes or support public television. Moreover, they do not require massive bureaucracies to administer programs. Nonetheless, they do have problems. Because they are an attractive means for pursuing various policy goals, tax preferences tend to proliferate. The accumulation of preferences greatly complicates our tax laws and creates imbalances. People with equivalent incomes often pay dramatically different amounts of taxes (Thurow 1980, 170). Tax preferences are legal inequalities.

If they work, tax preferences also change the way people and corporations spend and invest their money. Such changes in spending may conform to policy goals but may also have unforeseen negative consequences. For example, a business may choose to invest in tax deductible energy conservation rather than plant expansion. This decision may eventually reduce the competitiveness of the firm and its long-term financial growth. Like other forms of spending, the scale of government budgetary decisions has ramifications throughout the national and world economy.

According to Herman Leonard (1986), all three forms of quiet expenditures share various characteristics. He uses the word *quiet* because information about such spending is either hidden or nonexistent. It is exceedingly difficult for citizens to uncover the extent to which their governments are obligated to repay loans or what their governments are losing on below-market oil leases on public lands. Sometimes the information is not public because of the nature of the contracts, but more often the extent of public obligation is obscured by the financial complexity of the arrangements. Moreover, unlike on-budget spending, quiet spending is not subject to the same level of legislative and public review. Once a loan program is authorized, officials in the agency, often a private, nonprofit agency, make the allocation decisions.

Quiet spending also obscures the relationship between who receives the benefits and who pays the bills. Guaranteed government bonds to pay for business expansions, such as industrial revenue bonds (IRBs), separate public and private interests. The taxpayer is obligated to pay off any loan defaults made to encourage private profit. Other quite expenditures separate economic classes: Low interest, guaranteed student loans are of greatest help to middle-income families, even though all taxpayers must make up any shortfall. The great appeal of quiet spending is that it gives the appearance of spending without paying. We experience the benefits—a college education or a new shopping center—but remain unaware of the costs. For these reasons, quiet spending is increasing.

REFORMS OF THE BUDGET PROCESS, PART I: BETTER MANAGEMENT

The budget process is continually being reformed. As spending priorities change, resources expand or contract, and as the balance of power between different actors and institutions shifts, the budget process, the fulcrum of governing, is modified. Often these reforms begin at the federal level and are then imitated by state and local governments. Recent reforms are described here in two parts with the first focusing on reforms to improve the management of budget creation and implementation, and the second on reducing expenditures.

In this century, a first wave of reform culminated in the Budget and Accounting Act of 1921. This law centralized federal budgeting in the Bureau of the Budget and created the congressional General Accounting Office to scrutinize spending. During the 1920s and 1930s budgets became more specific. Categories were more narrowly defined with expenditures attached to *line-items,* single items or lines on a budget sheet that link spending to programs. (In a family budget the amount spent for food is a line item.)

Good budgeting requires more than careful accounting; in addition to good bookkeeping we want results. The second wave of budget reforms was *performance budgeting,* which attempted to consider the results of spending in budgetary decisions. Performance budgeting was further refined by integrating it with planning, a reform called *planning, programming, and budgeting* (PPB), and management, a reform called *management by objectives* (MBO). PPB involves defining program objectives in measurable terms so that they can be compared with specific costs. In theory, PPB could guide choices between alternative programs based on relative cost-benefit ratios; the policy that provides the most benefit for the least money is, in this definition, best (see Chapter 11 for a more detailed discussion). MBO is less ambitious and involves stating clear and, when possible, measurable objectives and timetables for programs as a guide to efficient management.

While efforts to link spending to results remain important, experience has also emphasized difficulties. Many government programs produce benefits that are difficult to measure. How do you measure the value of learning, health, or wilderness? Can we put a dollar value on the support of historical research as a measure of the effectiveness of the National Endowment for the Humanities? Moreover, evidence that one program is more cost effective than another does not eliminate the difficult choices facing government decision makers. More Americans would benefit from a cure for arthritis than for AIDS and basic research into such a new disease as AIDS is rarely efficient, but government leaders can hardly dismiss the need for AIDS research simply because of a low cost-benefit ratio. For these reasons performance budgeting has not greatly altered government budgeting.

Budget reforms have also addressed the relationship among government institutions. The period following World War II saw the increased consolidation of budget authority in the presidency. Renamed the Office of Management and Budget (OMB), the Bureau of the Budget was moved out of the Treasury Department and into President Truman's expanded executive office. Increasingly the OMB has exerted dominance over the federal budget because of its control over information on revenue, spending, and the economy.

With the Congressional Budget Act of 1974, Congress attempted to reassert control by establishing a counterinstitution, the Congressional Budget Office, which hires its own economists and budget analysts. The Congressional Budget Office provides Congress with estimates of revenues, spending, and economic trends that are independent of the president's estimates. It has improved Congress's capacity to examine both program effectiveness and spending and thereby has increased the budgetary checks and balances. Critics of the Congressional Budget Office conclude that it added more process but not more control, however, since congressional pressure to spend to satisfy constituents has not been restrained by the Congressional Budget Office forecasts.

These budget reforms have increased governmental control over the information about spending. Nevertheless, these managerial reforms have done little to stem the rising incremental tide of expenditures. Despite progress in the management of budgets, decisions about taxing and spending are political, not technical, decisions. The managerial reforms of the past were designed to monitor and guide growth, but the budgetary conflicts of the late 1970s, 1980s, and 1990s present different problems. During this period the attention of budget reformers has focused on a single but extremely difficult problem, the federal deficit. Understanding the current budget reforms requires understanding the problem of federal deficits, which is examined next.

THE FEDERAL DEFICIT

The *federal deficit* (and theoretically the federal surplus) is the gap between spending and revenues. Annual deficits accumulate into the *national debt*. Deficits allow the government to spend more than it earns but also to force it to increase spending to pay off interest. Figure 8.4 shows the growth of the total federal debt from 1939 to 1988. During World War II, 1940–1945, the national debt rose sharply; world wars are expensive. It dropped slightly until the Korean War, then remained relatively constant until the Vietnam War, when in 1968 the total federal debt began its alarming growth. From 1948 to 1968, the federal debt grew from $252 billion to $369.8 billion, an increase of 150 percent. During the next ten years, from 1968 to 1978, the debt doubled to $740 billion. In the next six years, to 1984, the debt more than doubled again, growing to a staggering $1,577 billion.

These mind-boggling numbers do not, however, present an accurate picture of the size of the federal government's debt. Whether personal or national, the absolute dollar size of a debt is not important; debt must be viewed in relationship to wealth. When a millionaire borrows $40,000 for an expensive car, the impact on the family budget is less than when someone of modest means borrows the same amount. In addition, the reasons for debt make a big difference.

Figure 8.5 presents a very different picture of the size of the total federal debt. Rather than the absolute value, it shows the change in the size of the debt as a proportion of the gross national product (GNP). The GNP is a rough measure of the nation's wealth. In the years following World War II, the nation's wealth has grown much faster than its debt. During that war the federal government owed more than the nation was worth. In general, the debt as a proportion of GNP declined rapidly from a wartime high of 120 percent to a postwar low of 25 percent in 1974. This downward trend was interrupted by three events: the Korean and Vietnam Wars and the Reagan presidency. From 1980 to 1988, the total federal debt as a proportion of GNP rose sharply reversing the forty-year trend.

The most troubling aspect of the federal debt in the late 1980s is not its size. Even as a proportion of GNP, the total federal debt in the 1980s is not out of line with recent U.S. experience. Nor is the U.S. federal debt very different from the debt of other industrialized nations, such as West Germany or Japan. What is important and alarming is that the relative debt is growing during a time of peace and economic

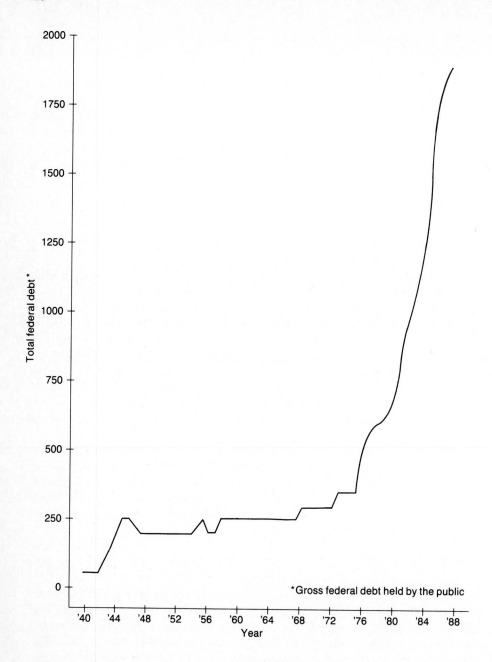

Figure 8.4. Total Federal Debt
SOURCE: *Economic Report of the President, February 1988,* Table B-76, p. 337.

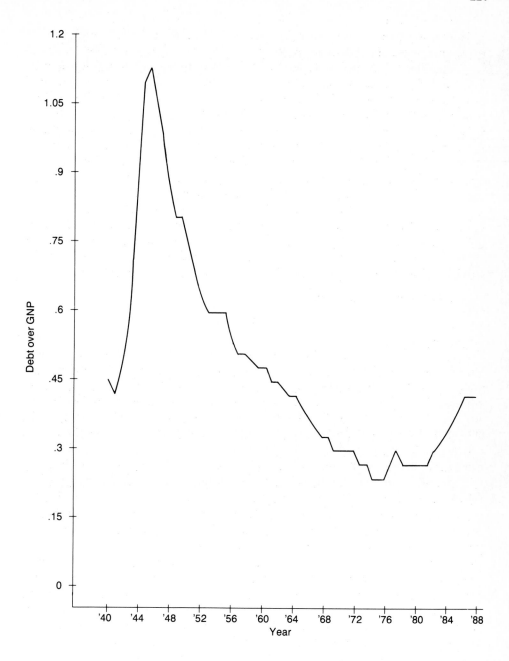

Figure 8.5. Gross Federal Debt as a Proportion of Gross National Product
SOURCE: *Economic Report of the President, February 1988,* Table B-76, p. 337.

expansion. During previous periods of prosperity the GNP growth was greater than the debt growth and relative debt declined.

The timing of the recent rise in relative debt is troubling because of the way debt affects the economy. The primary positive effect of the federal deficit is that it stimulates the economy. When, as a result of government spending, older people can afford to travel, corporations can receive defense contracts, farmers can purchase new equipment, and cities can finance a highway bypass, the economy gets a boost. In the past, the federal government used its spending power to push the nation out of recessions. By increasing spending during recessions—much of this increase is automatic due to entitlements—and by reducing spending during economic expansions, government spending can soften economic crashes and restrain booms.

During the 1980s, deficit spending fueled economic growth, yet growth did not exceed spending, leaving many worried about the impact of the next economic downturn. When a recession eventually comes (few economists feel our economy will ever be recession proof) will the relative debt grow even more rapidly or will the government refrain from spending to lessen its impact? These are troubling questions.

The growth of debt during economic expansion is only part of the problem, however. One individual's or nation's debt is another person's or some other nation's wealth. The federal government has not had trouble borrowing money; treasury bonds offer a good rate of return and are secure. In the past, the federal debt was primarily owned by U.S. citizens. When taxes were spent to pay interest on the debt, Americans—generally upper-income Americans—who owned the debt benefited. In the 1980s, however, an increasing proportion of the federal debt has been assumed by citizens and governments of other nations. The willingness of the Saudis, Japanese, and Germans to lend us money reflects our stature in the world, but foreign ownership of the federal debt also means that the U.S. tax dollars that pay for the interest on the debt are increasingly adding to the wealth of others. (Remember, 14 cents of every tax dollar is spent on interest payments.)

Moreover, our increasing dependence on foreign capital may eventually prove threatening to our national sovereignty. If foreign banks refuse to finance U.S. deficit spending further, our debt-stimulated economy could tumble into recession. When nations become indebted to others, their own domestic policies are often dictated by others. For example, the International Monetary Fund has required debtor nations like Mexico to curb social spending as a condition of continued loans.

The reason for the debt is also important. Borrowing money to spend is much more damaging in the long run than borrowing to invest. Government debt for careful investment in infrastructure such as roads, education, job training, and research can reap benefits in economic growth. When in the early 1800s the federal government spent money to send Lewis and Clark to explore the West and when later in that century government grants spurred railroad and canal construction, the government's investments paid dividends in economic growth.

Borrowing money to consume, however, does not create future wealth. Most defense spending and income transfers are a form of consumption, not investment. The value of a new aircraft carrier, depreciates and does not create new wealth. Consumption-oriented debt tends to increase inflation by creating more wealth than goods. Robert Eisner (1986, 179) stresses the importance of the reasons for debt:

Our future and our children's future is always a proper concern. The public has feared that budget deficits add to their own debt burden and that of future generations. What we really bequeath to the future, however, is our physical and human capital. A "deficit" which finances construction and maintenance of our roads, bridges, harbors, and airports is an investment in the future. So are expenditures to preserve and enhance our national resources, or to educate our people and keep them healthy.

Although the absolute size of the federal debt is less threatening than it would appear, the timing, ownership, and purpose for this debt are increasingly seen as a major national problem. It is a problem that the current budget processes with their incremental bias are ill equipped to address.

REFORMS OF THE BUDGET PROCESS, PART II: REDUCING GOVERNMENT SPENDING

Recent efforts to reform the budget process focus less on better management and more on restraint. Although better management can create some savings, real reductions in the growth of the federal debt require bringing spending more in line with resources (or resources more in line with spending). Unlike incremental decisions that award high-priority projects more than others, reducing spending or raising revenues is painful. Incrementalism has built expectations of growth into budgeting. Budget cutting, on the other hand, engenders conflicts among competing interests and institutions (Caiden 1984).

Critics of government blame the greed and lack of will of politicians and bureaucrats for the budget deficit. Bennett and DiLorenzo (1983b, 5) state the prosecution's case:

> There is no doubt that constraints on government behavior pose a major threat to politicians, public-sector employees, and powerful interest groups which benefit from political largess. Budget cuts endanger the income, power, perquisites, and prestige of politicians and bureaucrats. It is unrealistic to expect even grudging acceptance of fiscal restraints from those in the public sector.

It is easy to criticize government, but the problem of the deficit goes deeper, into the homes and businesses across the nation. As federal, state, and local government's activities grew over time, the variety and number of citizens with a stake in government spending grew. Although voters in the 1970s and 1980s consistently cast their ballots against taxes and for politicians promising fiscal restraint, the public does not want fewer government services. The extent to which government programs have permeated our lives highlights the difficulty in sustaining substantial cuts: To cut into the federal debt requires cutting services to ourselves, not just others.

Spending Cuts

There are two ways to cut deficits: raise revenue or cut spending. Realistic solutions to the problem will involve both and must focus on reversing growth trend rather than on short-term, draconian solutions. Tax increases or spending cuts that would quickly return debt or relative debt to 1980 levels would likely cause a dramatic economic recession. Although increased revenues are likely to prove necessary to reverse the debt growth, spending cuts are the more immediate focus of budgetary reform.

One area in which the federal government successfully cut spending was in aid to state and local governments. The General Revenue Sharing program was eliminated, and grants for roads, bridges, sewer treatment, schools, and community services were slashed. Cutting revenue transfers has reduced *federal* spending but it has not greatly reduced oveall *government* spending. In many areas, cuts in federal aid heightened pressure to increase state and local taxes. Local programs for low-income individuals and families, especially those provided by nonprofit community organizations, were the main target for cuts (Nathan, Doolittle, et al. 1983). Projects with strong local constituencies and communitywide support, such as local road improvements, were locally sustained. Often local government officials turned to nontax revenue sources, such as user fees, or to hiding increased spending off budget (Sharp and Elkins 1987).

Other easy targets for federal spending cuts are the many nonentitlement programs such as education, training, the weather bureau, and national parks. But these miscellaneous programs make up only 8 percent of federal spending and include some of the programs citizens value most. It also costs money to run the government and courts, but operational expenses are only 2 percent of spending. This leaves interest payments, which are fixed by the Federal Reserve Bank, defense spending, and transfer payments to individuals.

Clearly, serious talk about budget cutting must focus on defense and entitlements. As previously discussed, entitlement spending is difficult to cut. Entitlements are long-term commitments; cutting them means breaking a promise. Moreover, the largest proportion of entitlement spending goes to older Americans. Over a third of federal spending helps the elderly in pensions, welfare payments, and health care (Bell and Thurow 1985, 122).

Cuts in defense spending are attractive. Defense spending is the largest controllable portion of federal spending. Cutting defense spending requires reducing the size of the armed services (personnel are the most expensive part of the defense budget), postponing the development and purchase of major weapons systems, and retreating from committments abroad, principally in Europe and Asia. Defense-spending cuts require reduction of our role in the world, and like entitlement cuts, pose dilemmas.

Procedural Reforms

Making real spending cuts or even holding spending to less than revenue growth presents difficult choices. The growing debt is testimony to the failure of elected officials to address the problem. The Balanced Budget and Deficit Reduction Act of 1985 is one attempt to force reductions through procedural reforms. This legislation, referred to as the Gramm-Rudman Law after its principal sponsors, set deficit reduction targets. If Congress and the president failed to agree on a budget that met the targets, the budget would automatically be cut across the board until the targets were met—a process called a *sequester*. It is important to note that the Gramm-Rudman

Law requires only that the budget *estimates,* not the actual amounts, meet the targets. As Robert Kuttner (1989) points out, "This is, of course, an open invitation to cook the estimates. In 1988 the actual deficit, if anyone cares, came in at $155 billion. The Gramm-Rudman ceiling was $144 billion." Although it is not yet clear if the Gramm-Rudman Law will force a reluctant Congress or president to cut spending or raise taxes when they were unwilling to do so—at this point both Congress and the president have deftly avoided such hard choices—the law underscores the difficult choices.

A second proposed reform is the *line-item veto.* Under current procedures, the president and most governors must sign or veto the entire budget appropriations bill. The line-item veto would give them the right to veto specific appropriations. In theory this veto would reduce spending to the extent it is used. The item veto is allowed in several states, and experience raises doubts about its effectiveness as a budget-cutting tool. Line-item vetoes tend to increase the partisan struggle over the budget rather than reduce overall spending. James Gosling (1986) studied the use of the item veto in Wisconsin and found very modest reductions in spending, from a low of .006 percent to a high of 2.5 percent saved by exercising item vetoes. The item veto did increase the governor's power over the legislature, however, with roughly one-third of the item vetoes used to revise legislatively approved spending to conform to the governor's original request (p. 297).

A third proposed reform of the federal budget process is a *constitutional amendment* requiring a balanced budget. However attractive, forcing a balanced federal budget could create more problems than it solves. Deficit spending is an important fiscal policy tool. Unless the government can increase spending in economic hard times, the economy may remain trapped by stagnation or depression. Moreover, states with balanced budget requirements are often forced to build surpluses to provide a buffer against future losses. Over time, states with a surplus experience pressure to cut taxes and increase spending, an action which can leave the state with deficits during economic downturns. Such boom-and-bust spending discourages careful fiscal management.

Requiring balanced budgets has also encouraged states and localities to transfer more and more spending off budget. Constitutional amendments, like line-item vetoes, do not eliminate the difficult political choices that drive up deficits in the first place (Albritton and Dran 1987). To the extent that deficit-reduction reforms designed to reduce deficits drive more expenditures off budget, they may create more problems than they solve. Off-budget spending greatly undermines the accountability that is the foundation of our budget process. The politics of budgeting may be cumbersome and ill suited to confronting mounting deficits, but at least it is public. Leonard (1986, 253) calls off-budget spending a velvet trap: Without budgetary accountability there is no procedure to assure that public spending is for public purposes. Such reforms may in the end prove more damaging than the federal debt.

SUMMARY

The size and scope of government activity has steadily grown through our nation's history, and changes in the amount and priorities of government spending have direct effects on our daily lives. Although many worry about the size and pervasiveness of government, the scope and impact of government activities are not likely to shrink significantly. Thus, how and how much money the government collects and spends is fundamental to the process of governing.

Writing and then agreeing to a budget is often the most difficult task facing elected officials at all levels of government, from Congress to the school board. Budgeting is the decision-making process that links revenues, spending, and policy. It is difficult, in part, because of conflicts between the individuals and institutions involved. At the national level, the president and the executive office propose a budget that is then rewritten by Congress, leaving the president with the option of signing or vetoing the entire appropriations bill. The budget process in state and local governments is similar, with the executive and administrative agencies proposing budgets that are modified and approved by elected officials.

Budgets are policy documents with direct and indirect benefits and costs. Elected officials rarely state opposition to popular or reasonable programs; promises commonly exceed programs. The amounts actually allocated for different programs provide a clearer picture of actual policy preferences. Federal, state, and local governments also use their taxing and spending power to guide and alter the general economy, an activity called *fiscal policy*. Increasing government spending can push a nation out of recession while decreasing spending can reduce inflation. Tax policy also influences the economy. Tax deductions to homeowners help support those who build and sell homes, and tax breaks to lure businesses into a community can stimulate local economies.

At all levels of government, budget decisions are most often incremental: This year's budget is usually a slight increase over last year's. Incrementalism is a sign of stability and makes it possible to fund new programs without cutting existing ones. Incrementalism does, however, contribute to ever-increasing government spending. When budgets remain constant or are cut, political decisions become more difficult as programs and citizens' groups compete for limited resources. The political decisions about budgeting occur at two levels. Macro-decisions involve setting overall budget amounts and spending priorities, whereas micro-decisions involve decisions about specific programs.

The federal, state, and local governments get money from a wide array of sources: from personal and corporate income taxes, property taxes, fees, trust funds, and loans. State and local governments also get considerable revenue from the federal government in the form of grants. Governments spend money when they appropriate funds for specific programs; this is called on-budget spending. On-budget programs include entitlements, such as social security and workers' compensation, and endless specific programs sponsored by government, such as defense and research spending. Entitlements, especially those indexed to the cost of living, are difficult to cut and impose major constraints on budget decisions during periods of economic stagnation or decline. The government also spends money off budget. Off-budget expenditures involve raising and spending revenues or obligating credit without direct appropriation. The most common forms of quiet (or even invisible) spending are government loans and loan guarantees, off-budget enterprises (especially public authorities), and tax preferences.

The budget process is continually reformed. The first wave of budgetary reforms focused on improved management. At the federal level, the Budget and Accounting Act of 1921 created the Bureau of the Budget, the General Accounting Office, and divided expenditures into line items. The Bureau of the Budget was taken out of the Treasury Department during Truman's administration and renamed the Office of Management and Budget. In the 1960s new budgeting procedures, principally performance budgeting and management by objectives, tried to link expenditures with measures of results. In 1974, Congress created the Congressional Budget Office to provide legislators with independent economic and budgetary analysis to counter the growing dominance of the executive branch in budgetary politics. These various federal reforms were mirrored across the country at the various levels of government.

More recent efforts to reform government budgeting have turned to reducing, rather than managing, spending. The 1980s saw a rapid increase in the relative national debt at a time when our economy was expanding. (During times of economic growth, the relative debt—debt divided by GNP—usually declines.) Efforts to reduce spending are often thwarted by groups accustomed to receiving government services or tax breaks. Indexed entitlements and multiyear government contracts dull the knife of the most ardent spending cutters. Once interest payments, entitlements, and long-term contracts are removed from consideration, few programs—and many of the most popular, such as NASA or cancer research—are left to bear the brunt of cuts. The Gramm-Rudman Bill attempts to force spending cuts by mandating across-the-board cuts if the president and Congress fail to meet deficit-reduction targets. Some reformers suggest that the president should be allowed to veto specific budget items—the line-item veto—rather than merely sign or reject the entire appropriations bill. The line-item veto is allowed in some states and local governments but has not proved to reduce the overall size of budgets.

Other reformers insist that the only way to reduce the federal deficit is to mandate a balanced budget through a Constitutional amendment. Most states require balanced budgets and their experience raises doubts about this reform. Requiring balanced budgets forces states and localities to build a surplus which in turn increases pressures for more spending or tax cuts; these surpluses are rarely saved to buffer programs when tax revenues decline during recessions. In addition, balanced budget requirements encourage state and local governments to put more and more spending off budget and outside the control of elected officials.

CASE STUDY: THE SAVINGS AND LOAN BAILOUT

In less than a month after taking the oath of office, President George Bush, who won the election in part on a "no new taxes" pledge, was forced to announce an expensive new program. This program did not address any of the many social problems facing the nation but was necessary to make up for the regulatory failures, poor judgments, and recklessness of the savings and loan (S&L) industry. S&Ls were going bankrupt across the nation, depleting the reserves of the Federal Savings and Loan Insurance Corporation (FSLIC), and raising fears that a wave of bank failures could initiate an economic depression—not the way Bush wanted to begin his presidency. To calm fears, on February 7, 1989, Bush pledged, "We will see that the guarantee to depositors is forever honored."

The cost of living up to this pledge will not be known for many years, but the estimates are staggering. Although no one knows how many S&Ls will require help, estimates are that from 250 to 1,000 institutions will require major assistance within the next few years. The immediate costs are enormous: $50 billion is needed to shut down and sell off those S&Ls that are currently insolvent, $40 billion is needed to pay for 1988 bailouts, and $43 billion more is needed for future bailouts. A single S&L, the Lincoln Savings and Loan Association of Irvine, California, will likely cost the government more than $2 billion. The FSLIC does not have the reserves to reimburse even a small fraction of the depositors of failing S&Ls. If forced to borrow money, the estimated ten-year cost to the government is $166 billion, or more than the combined government bailouts of Lockheed, Chrysler, Penn Central, and New York City. If spread over thirty years, the costs will exceed $300 billion, leaving taxpayers responsible for $225 billion, or approximately $1,000 from every American citizen. How did the federal government get caught in such an expensive mess?

During the harsh depression of the 1930s, banks and S&Ls across the nation collapsed, stripping many Americans of their life savings. To rebuild faith in the banking system and to protect the savings of millions of small investors, the government entered the insurance business. In 1933 and 1934, the Federal Deposit Insurance Corporation (FDIC) and Federal Savings and Loan Insurance Corporation were created to guarantee deposits in banks and S&Ls. These savings institutions paid a small premium on deposits to these off-budget enterprises which would, in turn, pay depositors if their bank or S&L failed. As with other government insurance programs, the premiums were lower than would be required by a private insurance company and were backed by the "full faith and credit" of the federal government. The federal government also imposed regulations to reduce the chances of bank failures. S&Ls, for instance, were required to make most of their loans to help families buy, maintain, or repair homes. These two off-budget insurance corporations served several general policy goals, such as stabilizing the national banking system and stimulating home ownership.

For years the system worked well; federally insured deposits encouraged savings and, with rare bank failures, costs did not exceed reserves. For S&Ls, all this changed in the late 1970s. In the past, S&Ls generally provided long-term, fixed-rate home mortgages financed by short-term savings deposits. Throughout the 1950s, 1960s, and early 1970s, countless families received thirty-year house loans at rates fixed between 2 percent and 5 percent. The money for the loans came from savings in accounts paying one or two percentage points less. When inflation jumped from the 1 or 2 percent rate of this period to the more than 10 percent of the late 1970s, depositors began taking their money out of S&Ls and putting it into investments paying higher interest rates. S&Ls, which were profitable when the inflation and interest rates remained predictable, began to lose money; their earings were frozen in low-interest mortgages but their costs skyrocketed as they needed to pay escalating rates just to keep depositors.

S&Ls are politically influential institutions. Although some economists argue that they are no longer needed, they exist across the country, in nearly every small town and congressional district. In the 1970s, S&Ls lobbied for changes in regulations. In 1980, insurance coverage was expanded from $40,000 to $100,000 per account, and in 1982, the Garn-St. Germain Act removed nearly all regulatory barriers from S&Ls. S&Ls were no longer confined to conservative investments in home mortgages, and they began speculating in real estate and junk bonds. As with all investments, the greater the risk, the greater the potential gain, but the S&Ls had a special advantage: If they lost, the government would pay off their debts.

The effect [of deregulation] was to give operators of savings institutions a free hand in gambling with government-backed deposits. If the projects succeeded, they would reap huge profits as well as high fees. If they lost big and the industry insurance fund was wiped out, taxpayers would be forced to pick up the tab. (Hayes 1989, D5)

The philosophy of many of the newly deregulated S&Ls was "It's heads I win, tails the FSLIC loses," and in the late 1980s, for the FSLIC and taxpayers the coin toss was tails.

Like most policy fiascoes, the causes are many—from fraud to bad luck—with plenty of blame to share (for a detailed analysis, see Kane, 1989). Coming up with a practical yet politically acceptable solution proved difficult and touched on many of the issues we discussed in this chapter. One thing was clear, however: President Bush reaffirmed the government's commitment to pay for all insured deposits. Citizens were now entitled to federally insured deposits, whatever the cost. In the 1930s, the federal government had made the pledge and had set up the off-budget enterprises to administer that pledge, and in the 1990s someone would have to pay for those promises. The answers to the questions of who should pay and how to pay proved difficult, however.

Why shouldn't the people who benefit from the S&Ls pay for their bailout? Many individuals profited from the risky investments of the newly deregulated S&Ls, including a handful of crooks who took advantage of lax regulations. But if the stockholders and depositors in solvent S&Ls were forced to bear most of the costs of the bailout, then the entire industry would collapse. Even modest increases in costs, such as increasing the FSLIC insurance premium or requiring larger cash reserves, were fought by the industry as overburdening an already frail system. In the end, the only adequate source of money and the only way to save the S&Ls without causing great hardship on any segment of the population was to send the bill to everyone. When governments at any level pursue policy goals—in this case securing savings—by extending credit or providing insurance, the collateral is the taxpayer.

Once it became clear that ultimately taxpayers would have to pay the lion's share, the question remained how to pay. President Bush's "no new tax" pledge became a trap. Paying for the S&L bailout would require either new revenues, substantial spending cuts, adding to the deficit, or all three. Since both the president and Congress were publicly commited to cutting the deficit to meet Gramm-Rudman targets, they faced painful tax hikes, which the Republicans rejected, or painful spending cuts, which the Democrats rejected. To find a politically acceptable solution—one that addressed the problem, but did not overtly break campaign promises—Democrats and Republicans alike accepted unduly optimistic forecasts that minimized the problem. For example, OMB based its forecasts of the costs on the assumption that deposits in S&Ls would increase 7.2 percent a year even though they had been decreasing the past several years.

Although they agreed to accept these optimistic assumptions, the president and Congress diagreed on how to pay for the bailout. The president wanted to hide the costs. He proposed creating a new off-budget enterprise to sell bonds to pay for the bailout. The Congress, controlled by Democrats, arugued to keep the program on budget so that the public would see the actual costs. Moreover, they argued, off-budget borrowing to pay for the bailout, while not technically adding to the deficit, greatly increased the costs because the government would have to pay interest as well. But the Democrats were also trapped by the Gramm-Rudman budget ceiling; to keep the bailout on the budget would require drastic cuts in social programs. They therefore argued to keep the bailout on budget but to exclude it from the Gramm-Rudman limits.

The president and Congress wrestled with these problems through the spring and summer, and in August, the Financial Institutions Reform, Recovery, and Enforcement Act was passed and signed. This act created an off-budget enterprise, the Resolution Trust Corporation, to manage the merger or liquidation of insolvent S&Ls. The government, through this corporation, now owns the assets of the failed thrifts; it must, for example, find a way to sell the vacant and half-built real estate developments left over from the boom years. The law reintroduced some regulation—S&Ls must return to the home mortgage loan business—and raised insurance rates. With this bailout the government reinforced its promise to secure savings deposits, but the long-term budgetary implications of this promise are enormous.

Discussion Questions

1. How did the clash of institutions alter the budgetary policies?
2. What are the implications of dealing with the S&L bailout on and off budget?
3. How do assumptions about economic forecasts change budget politics?
4. How did individuals and small groups benefit from the general policy decisions affecting S&Ls?
5. Discuss the similarities of the use of credit and insurance and direct spending.
6. How did the efforts to reduce the federal deficit alter the policies on the S&L bailout?
7. In what ways is deposit insurance like other entitlement programs? What does deposit insurance tell us about the role of government in contemporary American society?

NOTES

1. The GNP is a measure of the total value of all the products produced in the nation that year. It is a rough estimate of the nation's economic output or worth.
2. Most budgets are annual but do not follow the calendar year. The federal fiscal year begins October 1, not January 1.
3. These figures are based on projections. Actual figures vary substantially, but the portions of sources of receipts and outlays remain approximately the same. These figures also change slightly from year to year, but the percentage of receipts and outlays in each category remains remarkably constant.
4. One theory about the proper role of government services states that government should provide only those services that are deemed important but cannot be provided on a for-profit basis. For a thorough discussion of this view see Weimer and Vining (1989, Chap. 3).
5. A program to help workers in industries suffering from unfair foreign competiton.
6. The loans granted to students, farmers, or corporations discussed above are often administered by OBEs.

PART FOUR

Macro-Administration— The Art and Science of Policy Making

CHAPTER 9

Administrative Policy Making: Macro- versus Micro-Administration

The importance of macro-administration and the difference between it and micro-administration have only recently been recognized in the field of public administation. Researchers have noted that successful implementation of public programs often involves many separate organizations and groups as well as several levels of government rather than a single agency. Successful administration, then, requires more than the traditional public administration skills, which emphasize management and policy making within a single agency.

The emphasis on macro-administration actually began in the implementation literature of the early 1970s (see Chapter 12). Pressman and Wildavsky (1984, 95–97, 103–106), for example, describe fifteen different participants (groups, agencies, and individuals) and thirty different decision points requiring a cumulative total of seventy agreements in order to complete the Economic Development Administration's public works program in Oakland, California. The term *macro-implementation* was coined by Berman (1978) in referring to implementation of programs involving the total federal system. In this book, we use the term to refer to administration that requires more than one agency or level of government to accomplish goals and objectives. This most certainly applies to the vast majority of administrative behavior. Particularly since 1980 in the United States there has been an increasing use of third-party agencies that actually implement many government programs (Salamon, 1981, 1989). Salamon notes that the range of responsibilities of the federal government has expanded since the 1960s while the number of federal government employees per 1,000 population has actually declined. This, he says, can only be explained by the rise of *third-party government*. Examples of this are private, profit and nonprofit agencies such as special districts, banks, hospitals, and corporations as well as state and city governments. Salamon calls these *third-party governments*. A 1984 survey of the International City Management Association of 1,780 local governments found that 23 percent of public safety services, 37 percent of health and human services, 24 percent of parks and recreation services, and 20 percent of support functions were being provided by the third party governments. (Valenti and Manchester 1984). Even when third parties are not involved, carrying out policy most often requires several agencies. For example, implementing a community corrections program in which nonviolent offenders are sentenced to a halfway house instead of prison requires the cooperation of the district or county attorney, judges, sheriffs, department of corrections, probation officers, and various community groups.

Administration in such situations requires some of the skills involved in microadministration (e.g., leadership, delegation) but it also involves much more (e.g., negotiation, bargaining, compromise). Administration is no longer simply and only a matter of planning, organizing, directing, staffing, and so on, but includes also negotiating with the numerous agencies whose cooperation is needed in order to achieve policy objectives. Because joint action is so complex, implementation requires mutual adaptation to succeed. Those who are closest to the clientele (i.e., street-level implementors) have the greatest ability to know what will work (Elmore 1979, Johnson and O'Connor 1979). Inevitably, this means that the goals of a program will be changed as it is being implemented (Palumbo and Harder 1981), a situation that is desirable because public agencies must be self-correcting and learn from their mistakes (Wildavsky 1972). We cannot assume that all problems have been thoroughly anticipated during program design and all that remains is mechanically putting the program into place.

To succeed in such an environment, administrators must understand policy making, not just how to manage people. Thus, it is essential for them to understand such models of decision making as the *garbage can* and *loosely coupled systems* (see Chapter 6) as well as the entire policy cycle (see Chapter 1). Most important, however, is acceptance of the idea that management in organizations is not simply a matter of the top-echelon people controlling those at the bottom (Stout, 1980), but understanding how to get people from all groups involved to support the program being implemented and to agree about what the goals of the program should be.

Bower and Christenson (1978, 1) say,

> The men and women who perform the general management function in the public sector . . . are not usually thought of as "policymakers" in the sense that newspapers discuss this topic. That label is usually reserved for the movers and shakers in elected executive or legislative roles. . . . But in selecting goals for their department or agency, the managers of public institutions interpret very broad and often contradictory mandates. In designing their detailed organizational arrangements, particularly in the allocation of personnel and budgeting, they shape what policy will be.

Lynn (1987) also emphasizes the policy-making components of public management. For Lynn, public managers are the executives in policy-making positions who manage public policy. They clarify the premises of organizational action, understand strategically significant issues, and exploit available opportunities. The manager's responsibilities and the skills required to be effective are more indeterminate the higher the manager is in the organizational hierarchy.

The vagueness and entrepreneurial nature of the public manager's task raise questions about what can be taught in classrooms. But some functions of public sector entrepreneurship have been described (Lewis 1980; Palumbo, Musheno, and Maynard-Moody 1986), and these can be learned. Behn (1987) compares effective managers with chess masters. Both have a repertoire of actions they can apply in appropriate situations, and both use intuition and inspiration. Bardach (1987) and Lynn (1987) both agree that the qualities that make the public manager effective can be identified, categorized, and taught to people who want to improve their public management abilities.

One of the most important functions of public sector entrepreneurs is to act as philosophical proponents and give the program bounded, focused goals that can be accomplished. Palumbo, Musheno, and Maynard-Moody (1986) found that the most successful community corrections programs were those in which there was agreement among the various stakeholders about the goals of the program, and it was the entrepreneur who succeeded in bringing this about.

Similar to private sector entrepreneurs, public sector entrepreneurs are risk takers who are alert to new opportunities, have the knowledge to exploit these opportunities, and are able to combine a number of production models in new ways (Gervitz 1984; Greenfield, Strickson, and Aubey 1979; Kirzner 1979). They are able to mobilize the winning combination of adopters, implementors, clients, and supporters needed to set successful implementation in action (Yin 1979).

Some of the successful characteristics of entrepreneurship can be learned, particularly flexibility, adaptability, and the ability to look for opportunities to bring together the key ingredients for program success. Of course, the skills needed to be a successful administrator at the micro-level also help at the macro-level, so there is overlap between the two. Perhaps the major difference is that at the macro-level, the successful administrator relies less on authority derived from his or her position and more on agreement and persuasion. Moreover, the focus at the macro-level is on policy making rather than on specific decisions about personnel or other matters internal to the organization.

POLICY MAKING VERSUS DECISION MAKING

We defined policy making in Chapter 1 and decision making in Chapter 6. We will add some additional points here about these concept to refresh your memory and to introduce the subsequent discussion.

Policy making and decision making are not the same even though they are heavily interrelated, interdependent, and overlapping. Classical decision-making theory in public administration closely adheres to the rational model. The theoretical assumptions underlying policy making are quite different from those of classical decision theory; the principal differences are as follows:[1]

1. Classical decision making usually assumes that there is a unitary or single actor (individual or group) who is faced with a distinct problem and needs to find ways of solving it.

- Policy making assumes that there is a multiplicity of stakeholders each of whom has a different perspective of what the problem is. These stakeholders also have conflicting interests about how the problem should be solved.

2. Classical decision making assumes there is a clearly defined goal (or goals) to be achieved and everyone agrees about what it is.
    - Policy making assumes there are multiple and conflicting goals involved, many of which are not clearly defined.

3. Classical decision making assumes that the problem can be defined so that everyone agrees about what the problem is.
    - Policy making assumes that defining the problem is problematic itself.

4. Classical decision making assumes that the goals of policies should be set by policy makers while the means for achieving the goals involve facts that can be determined by experts.
    - Policy making assumes that facts and values, ends and means are inherently intermingled.

5. Decision making assumes that decision making under conditions of uncertainty can be reduced to decisions with known probabilities so that rational choices can be made.
    - Policy making assumes that uncertainty abounds in choices and cannot be reduced to choices with known probabilities.

6. Decision making assumes a hierarchical organization in which choices made at the top are transmitted to and carried out by those at the street level of the organization.
    - Policy making assumes that there are many organizations or groups involved in making choices and that they are not hierarchically arranged.

7. Decision making assumes that administrative behavior is a fairly rational (or satisfying) activity.
    - Policy making is not conceived of as a rational activity but rather one in which a reverse cycle of activity is involved; this means that instead of first choosing goals and then finding the best means of achieving those goals, administrators act first (i.e., select a means) and then attach value and meaning to the conseqence of their action that puts them in a good light. This behavior has been characterized with the metaphor of Chinese baseball (Siu 1985). In this game, the bases are moved after the batter hits the ball and the rules of the game change while it proceeds.

8. Finally, and most important, decision making assumes that a policy maker actually makes decisions or choices that can be identified.
    - Policy making assumes that policy evolves and that actors do not actually make "decisions" but engage in a myriad of activities that add up to policy. Administrators do not decide whether convicts in prison should be rehabilitated or handicapped children should be educated in the least restrictive environment, and so on. But they are involved in policy making, even though their type of policy making is not the same as legislative policy making.

ADMINISTRATIVE VERSUS LEGISLATIVE POLICY MAKING

Although administators interact with legislators in a number of ways, and although administrators do make policy as we have said, administrative policy making is not the same as legislative policy making (Maynard-Moody 1989a).

One difference between the two is the organizational structures of each: Bureaucracies are much more hierarchical than legislatures. Individuals in bureaucracies are unequal in rank and in their ability to influence the direction that policy takes. Directors have greater opportunity, resources, and power to influence policy than those at the street level, but, of course, the latter are more numerous and also have a great deal of impact on policy (Lipsky 1980). Legislators, on the other hand, each have a vote and thus, in principle at least, are equal. Of course, some legislators are more powerful than others by virtue of their committee position or seniority, but when it comes time to vote on a bill, each has the same power.

A more important difference is that administrative policy making is more likely to be based on expertise, while legislative policy making is more likely to be based on political considerations. Of course, even this is a matter of degree, since politics plays a role in administrative policy making and expertise plays a role in legislative policy making. An administrative report being sent to the "higher ups" in the agency or to the legislature will be scrutinized for its political impact, but it is far more likely to be justified in terms of professional criteria.

A third difference is that administative policy making is less public than legislative policy making. For some, this is a negative fact of life; Hummel (1982, 213), for example, writes: "Politics seems to continue to exist within bureaucracy—except now citizens and the ordinary rank-and-file bureaucrat feel excluded from it. Bureaucracy conceals and denies the political experience." On the other hand, some see this as an advantage. Rourke (1984) believes that the nonpublic nature of administrative policy making enables bureaucrats to discuss proposals they could not discuss in public. Thus, they can reach an accommodation on controversial issues that legislators cannot because the participants do not have to go on the public record.

A fourth difference is that administrative policy making is often "process policy-making"; it occurs in the shaping of programs at the operational—or street—level, and those higher up, even presidents, sometimes cannot influence it. John F. Kennedy, for example, complained that by the time problems got to his desk, they had been "dissected, sanitized, and cast into a series of options—almost as though they were engraved in stone" (Harris 1973, 15). Of course, this should not be taken to mean that presidents, legislators, and the public are helpless in the face of bureaucrats. Ronald Reagan, for example, was a veritable master at influencing the implementation (or, more often, lack thereof) of programs. He succeeded in virtually crippling agencies whose programs he opposed. One example is the Consumer Product Safety Commission. First, he cut the commission's staff drastically, from 975 employees in 1981 to 519 in 1989. Then he reduced the agency's budget from $42 million in 1981 to $34.5 million in 1989 (which is equivalent to what it cost to run the Defense Department for one hour). And, most significantly, he stacked the commission with conservatives who had no background in public safety, including its chair, Terrence Scanlon, who was known to the agency's supporters as the "enemy within" (Russakoff 1989, 32). The result was a drop in the amount of support for consumer product safety.

So it is clear that administrative policy making can be used to thwart or further legislate policy making. We should hasten to add that legislatures are not single-minded monoliths either. Their members do not all agree about what the intent of policy is; they vote for or against a bill for a variety of reasons (their constituents are strongly opposed to it; they owe a debt to other legislators; they believe in it), only some of which are related to the ostensible purpose of the proposed law.

TYPES OF ADMINISTRATIVE POLICY MAKING

Administrative policy making is thus a separate, distinguishable process, not just a step in the overall policy process that begins with agenda setting, moves on to problem definition formulation, implementation, evaluation, and then termination. Policies can and do originate in administrative agencies and they can become part of administrative routine with little, if any, involvement of elected representatives (an example of this is given below). In addition, legislation may sometimes simply ratify policies begun in agencies rather than initiating them (Maynard-Moody 1989a). The following examples illustrate this process.

Vague Legislation

Often when they are faced with a controversial or difficult problem, legislators will skirt the issue and pass legislation that is not clear. This is done for the obvious political reason that by taking a stand on the issue legislators are bound to alienate some segment of their constituents. A former speaker of the House of Representatives advised newcomers to be quiet on issues because you can not be criticized for something you do not say, only for things you do say. The Food Stamp Program is a good example of this phenomenon.

During the lifetime of the Food Stamp Program, officials in the U.S. Department of Agriculture (USDA) determined who was eligible to receive food stamps, what the benefit structure should be, and the amount of coupons that would be available to each family because Congress was unable to reach a consensus (Berry 1984). The USDA staff members who made these decisions were experts who moved from one job to another in the policy network: One moved from USDA to the House Agriculture Committee, another went from a public interest advocacy group to the House Agriculture Committee, and several members had been with advocacy groups before joining USDA (Berry 1984, 134). The ambiguous legislation that allowed administrators to make policy was a deliberate choice the Congress made because legislators felt that the administrators were insulated from partisan pressures and thus could make better policy choices. This is a case in which the hidden nature of administrative policy making was considered an asset by the legislature. (However, the result was not a generous amount of assistance for poor families; see Berry 1984).

Administrative Policy Making without Legislative Involvement

In the early 1980s, a group of Arizona administrators began a project that they felt would fulfull a need left unmet by existing programs. Without any legislative involvement, they created a program called the Interagency Case Management Project, or ICMP. The administrators who initiated the ICMP all worked in agencies that were involved to a greater or lesser extent with juveniles; all of them felt that some of the youngsters with whom their agencies dealt had multiple problems that could not be handled by the Department of Corrections or the County Juvenile Court alone. Some children were physically or sexually abused by parents or relatives, some had been discarded by their parents, and some had parents who were alcohol or drug abusers. Many of the young clients had no place to live and thus lived on the streets. Putting them into detention at the Department of Corrections for whatever minor crimes they might have committed was no solution to their problems. They needed education, psychological help, and often placement in a residential facility or even a foster home.

The ICMP was created to fulfill these needs. Caseworkers were assigned to the new program from each of the participating agencies—the County Juvenile Court, the Department of Corrections, the Child Protective Services, the Department of Economic Security, and the Governor's Office for Children. Caseloads were much lower (perhaps fifteen children) than those workers carried in their parent agencies (perhaps eighty-five children). Most important, children who became wards of the Department of Corrections because they had been caught in a minor offense such as shoplifting could obtain service through another agency.

This program, of course, constituted a major policy change in the way many juveniles were handled. Children were recommended for the program by probation officers or court workers who felt that their multiple problems required such help, and ICMP case workers could decide whether or not to accept each child who was recommended. Because the staff of ICMP consisted of only eight caseworkers, many of the children who needed the help still could not receive it. But the situation certainly was an improvement over what had existed prior to ICMP. Seven years after it was begun, ICMP still was operating without the legislature having become involved in or sanctioning it.[2]

Legislative Ratification of Policy Initiated by Administrators

Community corrections in Kansas, Colorado, and Oregon illustrate a situation in which administrators initiated policy that was subsequently ratified by the legislature. All three states were faced with overcrowded prisons. In all three states, some officials felt that many offenders whose crimes were nonviolent and not sexual in nature were being put in prison when they could be handled much more effectively in halfway houses, where they could receive training for jobs, educational preparation, counseling and treatment for their drug or alcohol problems, and help in finding jobs. Programs doing these things on a limited basis were begun at the county level in each of these states.

Local officials then successfully lobbied state legislators to pass legislation making the programs a statewide endeavor. Thus, legislative policy making eventually legitimated the policy that was initiated by administrators and other local officials (including various reform groups such as church-affiliated groups).

This example is but one in which administrators initiate policies that legislatures later ratify. As Wilson (1982, 56) notes, administrative agencies at the state and national levels have developed their own "distinct locus of power" and have become "an independent source of political initiatives and problems." Wilson's discussion refers primarily to regulatory agencies which he felt had been extended "as far as or farther than that of most other liberal regimes . . . and the bureaus wielding this discretionary power are, once created, harder to change or redirect than would be the case if authority were more centralized" (Wilson 1982, 73). This situation is not due to the imperialistic designs of the bureaus themselves, Wilson believes, but the result of political decisions by elected representatives who were simply responding to popular demands for greater regulation of businesses. Whatever the reason, there is no doubt that governmental agencies initiate and shape policies. As Mosher (1982b, 12) says, since World War II, "it has become increasingly evident that most policies originated within the administration; that policy and value judgments were implicit in most significant administrative decisions; that many administrative officials worked on nothing except policy; and that insofar as public policies were controversial, such work inevitably involved administrators in politics."

Policy Making through Administrative Expertise

In areas in which the issues are technical in nature, administrators may be allowed to make policy because of their expertise. A case in point is the National Institutes of Health which funds research on in vitro fertilization. The decision to conduct such research is usually left to administrative agencies and in vitro fertilization research was conducted without legislative intervention for some years. Eventually, however, it resulted in controversy over surrogate parenting; several states then enacted legislation banning surrogate parenthood (Malcolm 1988). Legislative bans rarely challenge technical research of this kind.

Expertise has become a fairly standard component of policy making by administrators through agencies such as the Department of Health, and Human Services' Office of the Assistant Secretary for Policy, Budget, and Administration, the Congressional Research Service, the Office of Technology Assessment, the General Accounting Office, and numerous others.

Another example in which policy research experts attempted to influence policy are the negative income tax (NIT) experiments in the 1970s, which were initiated in Seattle and Denver (Rogers 1988, 111). Among the supporters of the experiments, which were designed to help relieve the burden on people in poverty, were some more interested in furthering scientific investigation than in advancing the cause of a negative income tax. In any case, the experiments were expected to legitimate the negative income tax by showing that tax reimbursements did not reduce the incentive of the poor to find a job. One Office of Economic Opportunity official remarked:

> Yes, it [the experiment] was an attempt to remove any doubt. It was thought if a 5% labor supply response can be shown that a NIT [negative income tax] could easily be had. There is no question about it. All the planner participants were predisposed to a NIT. (Quoted in Rogers 1988, 111)

The economists in the group liked NIT because it provided individuals with the ability to spend money as they saw fit; the ordinary welfare system did not. Moreover, these economists saw the welfare bureaucracy as inherently inept and believed NIT would reduce costs by bypassing it.

Experts favored NIT, but the public did not. A 1969 survey found that only 32 percent of the public favored it while 62 percent were opposed (Roger 1988, 118). Moreover, Health, Education and Welfare (HEW) officials did not agree with Department of Labor (DOL) officials about NIT, and they used the experiments to support their own point of view. The DOL wanted a jobs-based policy while HEW was strongly in favor of the NIT policy, and each agency omitted data from the experiments that did not support its position. Thus, HEW downplayed the amount of withdrawal from the labor force that NIT produced. But HEW lost because President Nixon wanted both a jobs and an income approach.

In the end, the experts did not have a direct impact on the outcome of NIT. The question of how much policy research is used in administrative policy making is a complex one (see Chapter 13). But there is no doubt that very often expertise plays a large role in policy making by administrators. Of course, this expertise is usually tempered with politics, but it is a part of the policy-making process.

LEGISLATIVE OVERSIGHT OF ADMINISTRATIVE POLICY MAKING

That administrators make policy creates a serious problem for both administrative theory and practice. As Mosher (1982b, 10) notes:

> The concept of a value-free, neutral administration is regarded by many as a thing of the past, but no fully satisfactory substitute has been offered. How to ensure that responsible and responsive policy decisions are made by career administrators, and how to coordinate their work with the policies of politically elected or appointed officials, remain vital problems, especially in democratic states.

One of the major devices that has been created to ensure that "responsible and responsive policy decisions" are made by career administrators is legislative oversight.

Legislative oversight is now considered to be one of the important functions that legislators perform (Ogul 1976; Keefe and Ogul 1969; Rosenthal 1974). It is a mechanism by which legislators attempt to maintain and enhance their own power and also to resist executive domination under our constitutional system (Keefe and Ogul 1969, 17). According to Ripley and Franklin (1984, 14), oversight acts "as a counterbalance to Congressional grants of policy-making authority to the bureaucracy. On the one hand, Congress gives away parts of its own powers to the executive branch. But, on the other hand, it reserves the right to monitor the way the executive branch is exercising that authority."

There are several constitutional bases of legislative control over administative agencies, including the following:

- Creation, continuance or disbandment of an agency or program
- Confirmation of gubernatorial or presidential appointments
- Setting limits on staff size
- Appropriations and budget authorizations
- Committee hearings and investigations
- Requirements for agencies to provide reports and data
- Legislated guidelines and requirements

Historical Development

Legislative oversight is a fairly recent phenomenon. It began at the federal level with the passage of the Legislative Reorganization Act of 1946. Section 13 of the act states:

> To assist the Congress in apprising the administration of the laws in developing such amendments or related legislation as it may deem necessary, each standing committee of the Senate and the House of Representatives shall exercise continuous watchfulness of the execution by the administrative agencies concerned of any laws the subject matter of which is in the jurisdiction of such committee; and for that purpose, shall study all pertinent reports and data submitted to the Congress by the agencies in the executive branch of the government.

Since the 1970s, the push for legislative oversight at the federal as well as state level has been fueled by political considerations. U.S. Senator Harrison A. Williams, Jr., summarized this sentiment (1981, 8):

> The credit or blame for govenment activity is leveled properly upon members of legislatures. We after all, created the administrative agencies and the programs they administer and we are expected in the normal course of events to cure their malfunctions. Administrators frequently are faceless. Legislators are never unknown.

Oversight requirements were extended by the Legislative Reorganization Act of 1970 when Congress required almost all of its committees to provide biannual reports on their oversight activities. This act also gave oversight capacity to the Congressional Research Service and the General Accounting Office (GAO).

The responsibilities for oversight have been divided among various committees and subcommittees (Riley 1987, 69). Fiscal responsibility, or "making sure that money is spent in the way Congress wants it spent," is designated to the appropriations committees (Riley 1987, 69), whereas accountability for achieving objectives, determining "whether particular programs work and . . . proposing remedies to problems they uncover" is given to the authorization committees (Dodd and Schott 1979, 157).

Legislative oversight at the state level varies widely. Some states require that executive agencies assess the programs they authorize (Rosenthal 1974, 68). About two-thirds of the states have created legislative postaudit agencies; the audit/evaluation mode of oversight is thus the predominant one at the state level (Rosenthal and Van Horn 1982, 1). The major products of these are performance audits, program evaluations, and sunset[3] and program reviews, which usually are presented to the legislators in a written report.

The purpose of this oversight is to determine whether a law has been properly implemented and what its impact has been. Oversight is thus an attempt to control and direct some of the policy-making activity of administrative agencies. In 90 percent of the states, the postaudit agencies are selected by and are responsible to the legislature (Rosenthal 1981, 316).

Assessment of Legislative Oversight

As a device for trying to control or guide administrative policy making, legislative oversight has not been greatly effective. There are several reasons for this (Oleszek 1984, 211):

> Too little time on the part of members of Congress to perform oversight along with all their other functions;
> alliances developed among committee members with agency staff and clientele groups;
> lack of clarity of legislative intent; and
> the huge size of the administration.

Oversight is likely to be most valued when members of Congress disagree with executive policy, or if a scandal occurs. But in the ordinary, day-to-day routine activity of administrative agencies, there is not likely to be much oversight. Most administrative policy making is hidden from public and legislative attention. As Rosenthal (1981, 321) remarks: "Oversight is at odds with the legislative environment and with legislative life. Making laws and devising new programs, and not examining whether old laws and programs are (or are not) working, is the meat of legislative activity." Legislators who have to be reelected every two years are more concerned with short-term factors than with long-term impacts of laws that may require years before their impact can be determined (Sundquist 1981, 327). Moreover, the dispersion of oversight responsibilities among many committees and subcommittees hinders systematic and rational oversight (Oleszek 1984; Riley 1987).

Political considerations also are very important. If the administration and the congressional majority are of the same political party, a committee will be reluctant to engage in oversight. Or, as Sundquist (1981, 327) observes, "Committee members might be deterred by the cozy relations that often exist between the overseer and the overseen."

Also, there is some question about the extent to which oversight reports are actually used by legislators. For example, in the savings and loans association scandal of 1989, audits of these institutions indicated that many of them were in financial trouble long before they were given attention by Congress. The reasons for non-initialization of oversight reports are similar to the reasons that program evaluations are used or not used, which is discussed in Chapter 11. If used at all, they are most likely to influence the way a legislator conceives of a program rather than to have a direct, immediate impact on the program. The impact and use of research on decisions is best summarized by Weiss (1981, 23):

> The use of research and evaluation is really a continuum. At one end are those few cases where research actually switches a decision from A to B by the power of its evidence and analysis. In the middle are the many cases where research evidence is taken into account but does not drive the decision—cases where users filter research evidence through their knowledge, judgment, and interests, and incorporate much besides research into decision making. At the far end are the large array of issues on which research contributes more diffusely to an understanding of issues, the cause of problems, and the dynamics of intervention. For people who are concerned with the effects of research and evaluation on social programming, most of the phenomena of interest probably lie in the large and unbounded middle ground.

However, researchers do not agree about how much research reports, whether produced by a legislative oversight committee or an outside research agency, are actually used. Thus, there may be many oversight agencies and many reports, but it is not clear exactly how much these constrain the policymaking activity of administrative agencies.

Finally, under conditions of macro-implementation, legislative oversight becomes more complex. What was once a link between a legislative oversight committee and a public bureaucracy is now complicated by the introduction of third parties that actually implement the program and whose primary goal may be profit maximization. Oversight is more complicated in these circumstances because usually the administrative agencies themselves rather than legislatures oversee the contract with the private agencies that provide government services. This relationship provides administrators with yet another opportunity to make policy. In the end, the reality is that administrators make policy, and it is not possible to control or reduce this activity to any great degree.

SUMMARY

Macro-administration involves many separate organizations and groups as well as several layers of government. Many public programs require more than one agency or level of government to accomplish goals and objectives. To succeed in such an environment, administrators must understand policy making as well as traditional management. Entrepreneurial skill, flexbility, argument, and persuasion are important in macro-administration.

Policy making can be distinguished from classical decision making in terms of how many actors are involved, the clarity of goals of public programs, problem definition, inclusion of values, the uncertainty involved, the structure of organizations, degree of rationality, and whether administrators make decisions. The difference between the two, however, shows that although administrators make policy, administrative policy making is different from legislative policy making. Administrative policy making takes place in a different organizational structure, is more likely to involve the use of expertise, is less public, and involves process policy making.

The major types of administrative policy making include policy making necessitated by vague legislation, policy making without legislative involvement, legislative ratification of policy initiated by administrators, and policy making through expertise.

Because administrators do make policy, a dilemma is created for democratic theory: Administrators are not elected and there is a need for them to be accountable for their actions. In recent years, legislative oversight has been developed as a solution to this dilemma. Legislative oversight has a constitutional basis. At the federal level it began with the 1946 Legislative Reorganization Act which divided responsibility for oversight among various congressional committees and subcommittees. At the state level, the method of oversight varies, with postaudit being the most predominant form.

Legislative oversight has not been very successful for a variety of reasons. It works only for highly visible programs when political considerations are crucial. Oversight reports produced by agencies are not often utilized by legislators and probably are only one and not the most important factor in policy making.

CASE STUDY: TREATMENT VERSUS SECURITY IN A STATE DEPARTMENT OF CORRECTIONS

In this case study there are two significant roles to be played. One is the director of the state's Department of Corrections and the other is the head of the Bureau of Community Services. The problem for the first is to please the legislative leaders who take a tough approach toward crime and believe that it is necessary to have harsh and long prison terms for offenders. In particular, the new laws concerning drug sales and driving while intoxicated call for presumptive sentences that are very severe. For example, a person who is convicted of selling narcotic drugs and who does not have a prior felony conviction receives a sentence of four years, and offenders who are convicted a third time for driving while intoxicated receive a sentence of two years. We should note, however, that not all legislators agree with this. Democrats, who are in a minority, disagree and believe the state is putting too many people in prison at too great a cost to taxpayers. The governor also is a Democrat but has not come out forcefully on the issue since it might make her appear to be "soft on crime."

The director believes that the principal function of the Department of Corrections is to lock up the offenders under tight security so that they do not cause trouble that gets into the media. He does not believe in rehabilitation or treatment. The head of the Bureau of Community Services, John Wright, does not agree with this policy. After reading the following scenario, take a position about what you would do regarding John Wright if you were director of the department.[4]

John Wright was upset by the way the Department of Corrections was handling nonviolent felony offenders. Sitting in his fairly spacious office on the third floor of the building that housed the Department of Corrections (DOC), he complained that the mandatory sentencing law passed ten years earlier had doubled the prison population, putting many minor drug offenders and burglars into expensive prison cells.

John is not an outsider; he is the director of DOC's Bureau of Community Services. He has been working for the DOC for over fifteen years in several capacities, including prison warden and director of the juvenile division. Currently, however, he is the DOC's most vocal critic of the criminal code revision that set up mandatory sentencing and also greatly increased penalties for most crimes (e.g., a young man who was twenty-three years old was given a sentence of forty years for selling one marijuana cigarette to a boy of fourteen. The sentence was so harsh because he had a previous conviction for selling stolen goods). The severe criminal code was authored by the attorney general's office and avidly supported by a number of legislative leaders. The ostensible reason for it was that it would reduce crime in the state, which had a criminal rate among the highest in the nation.

John Wright was doing what he could to change what he considered to be bad legislation that, in his words, "simply turns out embittered and potentially dangerous young men onto the streets rather than trying to help them." John was doing a number of different things in an attempt to change corrections policy in the state. He gave talks to numerous groups and wrote articles for the opinion page of the local newspaper. One example is a speech he gave before the state's probation, parole and correctional association, part of which is excerpted at the end of this narrative. Within the DOC he tried to increase the number of contracts the DOC had with private agencies; his reason was that these agencies provided treatment programs for juvenile offenders whereas the DOC's own juvenile programs did not. The director of the DOC was a strict advocate of maintaining security in the state's overcrowded prisons.

Particularly troublesome to John was the type of offenders being put into prison under the mandatory sentencing legislation. His favorite example was a sixty-seven-year-old man who was convicted of trafficking in stolen goods. The man, who owned a used goods store in a small town in the state, had loaned his pickup truck to a young man whom he knew slightly and who told him he had to move some furniture. Unknown to the store owner, the furniture was stolen. The old man was convicted of aiding the theft but, instead of being put on probation, he was required under the mandatory sentencing law to serve six years in prison because he had an earlier conviction for possession of marijuana. "The old guy," John said, "has emphysema, a bad heart, and needs extensive dental care. This is going to cost the state a lot of money and the old guy will have nowhere to go when he gets out because he lost his store. Now, I ask you, is this sensible policy?"

Although John is the director of a bureau within the DOC, he is, of course, unable to change policy by himself. But he can work indirectly with others to change things. In addition to promoting contracts with private agencies that provide treatment, he works with others to change the channels through which information is collected, evaluated, and disseminated in order to convince enough members of the policy-shaping community that the existing policy is wrong. In short, although John is an administrator, he is heavily involved in policy making.

Excerpts from Speech Given by John Wright before the Arizona Probation, Parole and Corrections Association

I have to say I was greatly flattered when asked to say a few words on professionalism. I immediately concluded, based on the Aristotelian principle that a thing cannot give what it does not have, that at least one person thought I was professional. Then it dawned on me that some teachers require students who lack certain qualities to do long papers examining the desired quality in the hope that the exposure will generate absorption. Finally, I decided it didn't really matter. I was given a chance to say something about a topic that I regard as extremely important.

My fear in addressing this topic with this group is that I am preaching to the choir. On the other hand, I have decided that it's acceptable to preach to the choir if you are asking them to recruit more altos, sopranos, and basses to strengthen and enrich the voices of that choir. As a consequence, I'll be focused on your role as correctional choir members engaged in harmony and building the professional corrections choir in Arizona. We want you tenors in probation to provide us with some drama in your presentation to the public, we want the basses in jails and institutions to discipline yourself so you can sustain those low notes in our training and education, and we want you sopranos in parole to top those high notes of commitment and good judgment without fear.

Our growth in both the community and institutions over the past ten years has been so rapid and unrelenting that we have been forced to use nearly all of our creative energies and thoughts to accommodate the growth. Our management skills have been strained beyond experience and training and have been devoted almost exclusively to planning alternatives in the cutback mode, juggling caseloads and bed space and doing our best professionally to manage the increasingly unskilled and inexperienced work force that is employed to supervise or hold the hordes of offenders sent to us. In brief, it has been difficult, if not impossible, for us to perform as proactive professionals. We have been in a reactive stance, responding to the results of the political demagoguery that manifests itself in an irrational criminal code replete with unnecessary and ineffective flat sentences.

During the ten-year period since establishment of the code, reported crime per 100,000 has remained relatively constant while state prison commitments have increased 300 percent. In this period, the percentage of those incarcerated for violent crime has dropped from 38 percent to 22 percent. Since 1980, the length of a prison stay for rape has increased four-tenths of 1 percent, while the increased stay for part-one property offenses is up 17.6 percent. The number of commitments for drug and alcohol offenses has increased from 213 in 1980 to nearly 1,900 in 1988. Obviously, the major impact of the revised sentencing code is to send property and drug offenders to prison for longer periods while violent offenders tend to receive about the same sentences they did prior to the new code. Clearly, both the logic and effect of the criminal code has to be a focus of a professional in the Arizona criminal justice system. The current state of the criminal code deserves your attention and your energy. The will of the citizens of Arizona in criminal justice matters is, I believe, only loosely reflected in legislative decision making because of the enormous power given to legislative committee chairs. Naturally, in criminal justice matters the current chair of the House Judiciary Committee comes to mind as well as the recent chair of the Senate Judiciary Committee. Both are fine men, but I fear in matters of criminal justice both have been successfully coached in their efforts by one more reflective of a Machiavellian system approach than the reasonable man of the law.

Because legislators act on citizen fears that are inflamed by prosecutors, we are being required to do some things that I consider to be counterproductive to the long-term public safety. I believe we are perpetuating an absurdity and I suffer cognitive dissonance from the effect.

Having described the context of our work, let me now elaborate on the professional challenge that the negative social conditions present to us and list here the pressure points for professionals in Arizona corrections.

First, we are challenged to increase both our individual and collective influence over the policies that give direction to the criminal justice system in Arizona in general and specifically corrections. Make no doubt about it, if you have not already realized it, you need to take note that you are involved in politics.

Our work is being driven by a coalition of legislators and prosecutors who are the components of the criminal justice system that are generally the most political, the least professional, and the least informed about corrections. There are sixteen elected prosecutors and ninety elected legislators in Arizona. There are in excess of 10,000 people employed in some aspect of Arizona corrections in adult jails, juvenile detention centers, prisons, probation and private agencies, psychology, parole, food service, medicine, and architecture. Most have one or more significant others. Some corrections staff have vast knowledge and considerable skill in the correctional process. Few, if any, have been invited or have chosen to have influence over the development of policy for corrections. Complex criminal justice and corrections policy is made by a legislature composed of retired colonels, real estate salesmen, utility consultants, housewives, farmers, and teachers. They are powerfully lobbied for criminal justice policy by the prosecutorial and law enforcement professions. Corrections professionals as a group are not represented because they are not organized. They are not organized because they have limited vision of their potential for affecting the system. Too many corrections staff view their employment as accidental or temporary, not as the outcome of a professional choice.

If the American Medical Association (AMA), the American Bar Association (ABA), and the National Education Association (NEA) had only 6 percent of their numbers in their professional organizations, their professions too would be driven by uninformed legislators. Organizations such as the Department of Public Safety have only about 1,500 employees, but they have a powerful lobby, good pay, and an excellent retirement system. They, however, work together through lobbyists. They alert legislators to their professional direction and the size of their membership. They know the wisdom of the concept that there is strength in numbers. Whether we deal with our challenge is to a large extent dependent upon our willingness to organize and undertake efforts to influence both the lawmaking and the legislative appropriations process, which too is political in nature.

The challenge to us is to find ways to link, constantly and directly, the corrections experience to the crime, the behavior that caused the corrections contact. At the same time, the challenge is to use our creativity to utilize the vast manpower capacity of the inmate population, especially the low-risk population, to meet the needs of society as compensation for the wrong done. If judges are going to continue sending offenders who owe restitution to prisons, the offender should pay restitution while in prison and we are the ones who need to generate a prison system in which that can occur.

It is patently unfair to allow victims to believe they will receive restitution when there is little or no opportunity for prisoners to earn and less probability they will pay once back in the community, supervised for only a brief period or not at all.

Finally, we are challenged to do a better job of release and postinstitutional management of the offender. Through the political process, we should promote a sentencing structure that ensures that those who go to prison are the ones who, on the basis of mathematical risk calculation, post the greatest danger to our well-being. We ought to promote legislation to ensure that all of the 5,500 offenders released each year are under some control and supervision in the community for some period following their release. Currently 70 percent of all sex offenders leave prison to live in your neighborhood without supervision. A total of 1,700 inmates, presumably the most dangerous, left prison last year without any supervision because the prosecutor has pressed the legislature to create flat sentences. Violent offenders should not leave prison until they have evidenced, by objective mathematical measurement, that they constitute a reduced or limited risk to society. There will, of course, be risk in every release, but we should apply our best professional effort to minimize it. The shift to an objective mathematical measurement of risk, based on actuarial findings, enhances sentencing and release and obviates the need for the Board of Pardons and Paroles except to override. Release will always require the human override for the special case, but in general, we ought to depend on the actuarial tables as do the Prudential, Metropolitan, and Allstate insurance companies.

As an organization, we ought to pursue the following specific objectives:

a. Improved image of all correctional personnel as professionals who reflect a well-organized, disciplined staff and who possess an accepted minimum body of knowledge and an accepted level of skills, support a standard of performance, embrace a high ethical standard, show concern for the public they serve, and are committed to improvement of their profession
b. Gain influence over policy development by
   - influencing legislators' image of corrections staff as professionals
   - impressing upon legislators that corrections is an integral and important part of the state's public safety team
   - indicating to legislators that corrections staffs throughout the state are numerous, well organized, and powerful at the ballot box
   - providing facts to legislators as a basis for their policy making
c. Create and maintain a constituency among the public by
   - consistently, publicly, and effectively indicating corrections staff's contribution to the protection of the public safety
   - demonstrating effectiveness in the management of offenders by ensuring that the correction policy and activity fit the risk of the offender, ensuring that the dangerous are held securely and the nondangerous are not turned into the dangerous.

Activities:
a. Educate corrections staff, legislators, victims, vested interest groups, and the public with pertinent understandable data, concepts, costs, and results utilizing
   - print media—preparation of press kits with updates on facts and successes
   - electronic media—prepared videos
   - service club publications and presentations
   - school and university presentations
   - speakers' bureau
   - legislative lobbying
b. Energize and expand the Arizona Probation, Parole and Corrections Association (APPCA) organization or start a new organization that reflects the specific goals and objectives detailed above
   - fund the organization by member dues (including agency memberships) foundation grants to improve the corrections system, magazine ads
   - hire an experienced lobbyist as executive director
   - solicit the participation and active support of the leadership of all correctional agencies in the state

-   promote the adoption of standards of inservice training for all employed in corrections, including private providers

Discussion Questions

1.   If you were director of the department, would you try to prevent Wright from taking the actions outlined above? If so, how would you do this?
2.   How would you expect the legislature to act in this situation? For example, would conservative legislators who favor the harsh criminal code try to get Wright fired?
3.   Is Wright's behavior proper and legitimate?

NOTES

1.   To a certain extent we are setting up a "straw man" here. Classical decision theory has a tendency to make these assumptions, although they are not always explicitly stated. Also, contemporary decision theory has moved away from the assumptions of classical theory.
2.   This example is based on an evaluation of ICMP that the senior author did in 1989.
3.   Sunset review is usually done at a specified time, say three years, after a program has been created in order to determine whether the program will continue or if the "sun will set" on it.
4.   This case study is based on research conducted by the first author. The speech by John Wright is excerpted with his permission, and we are grateful for his cooperation.

CHAPTER 10

Administrative Accountability

The Federal Bureau of Investigation (FBI) and the Central Intelligence Agency (CIA) are two bureaucratic agencies with long histories of what some might call abuses of power. At times, they do not seem to be accountable either to the public or to their elected representatives in Congress. The Irangate controversy, in which the CIA was involved in illegal supplies of arms to the Contras in Nicaragua, is one example of the CIA's taking action without being accountable to citizens through their elected representatives in Congress (see the case study at the end of this chapter for the details of this situation).

The FBI also has a long history of using its power to harass and intimidate those who opposed government policies in Vietnam, Nicaragua, and El Salvador. For example, in 1988, through the Freedom of Information Act, the FBI's role in a five-year probe of the Committee in Solidarity with the People of El Salvador (CISPES) came to light. As reported in the *Washington Post*, "A detailed reading of more than 1200 pages of FBI files recently made public suggests that many of the field officers took an exceedingly broad view of their right to investigate dissidents" (Kurtz 1988). During the five-year period, nuns, union members, and students were the target of an investigation that the FBI said was for the purpose of investigating terrorist activity of CISPES and because CISPES allegedly trained guerrillas in El Salvador. But CISPES political director Hugh Byrne said the charges were ludicrous and called them nonsense. Others said the investigations were politically motivated.

Through undercover agents, the FBI infiltrated the Sisters of Mercy Generalate in Silver Springs, Maryland, the Religious Society of Friends, the Maryknoll Sisters, and the Church of the Brothers. Much of the cable traffic between the FBI's Washington office and its field offices had a decided political tone. Kurtz (1988) noted that these communications included numerous messages in which FBI officials questioned the motivation of those opposed to administration policy (p. 32).

The FBI abandoned its investigation of CISPES in 1985 when it concluded that the group was not involved in international terrorism but in political activities protected by the First Amendment. But FBI director William S. Sessions admitted in 1988 that the probe was not properly directed in all instances. During congressional hearings into the FBI investigation, the executive assistant FBI director Oliver B. Revell, admitted that the conduct of some of the FBI agents was "very close to the line" and that there may have been "some wandering over the line" (Associated Press 1988).

Instances of administrative agencies acting at odds with the directives and purposes of elected representatives and citizens, while not as sensational as the Irangate and FBI CISPES activities, are nevertheless pervasive. For example, a 1988 survey of the public, and of public school superintendents and principals, revealed a wide disparity in their respective views of how good a job the superintendents and principals were doing. According to the survey, 87 percent of superintendents and 75 percent of public school principals said that schools in their communities had improved in the past five years, but only 25 percent of the public shared that view. The nationwide survey of 1,704 superintendents, 1,349 public school principals and 524 private school principals showed that the overwhelming majority were white males: 96 percent of the superintendents were men and 97 percent were white, while 76 percent of the principals were men and 90 percent were white. They therefore were hardly representative of the ethnic composition of the population in general or in their schools, and not representative in their views of how well the schools were doing. The report called them "an ingrown, self-satisfied group" (Feinberg 1988, 37).

Examples such as these fuel the flames for more control of bureaucracies. But it is not just a question of bureaucrats abusing their power, as in the case of the FBI, nor of their being out of touch with the public, as in the case of public school administrators. It is a particularly perplexing dilemma in democratic nations; these nations have governments that are "based on nineteenth century ideals and political developments . . . which manifest systems of power, rule, authority, and legitimacy that are markedly opposed to bureaucratic domination" (Krislov and Rosenbloom 1981, 1). Yet, bureaucracies dominate government in all Western democracies; they are "control instruments of unparalleled power" (Hummel 1982, 26).

They have gotten this way because of their technical superiority over other forms of organization and because they claim to be rational and scientific in their activities (Weber 1946). (See Chapter 2.) The great German social scientist, Max Weber, noted that "once rational-legal authority becomes the dominant mode of exercising political power bureaucracy becomes central to the political community. Its expansion is assured as a result of external and internal pressure" (p. 7).

Bureaucracies also are powerful because they know how to use information. Johnson and Altheide (1980) observe "The practical use of truth is characteristic of most organizations in our modern age. They have found the cultural values of science and objectivity to be very useful in presenting information about their efficiency and overall necessity to the whole society" (p. 23). In the modern information age, attempting to "look good" may be more important than the quality of products and the efficiency with which they are produced. Those who control information in modern society—and bureaucracies do—control policy. Palumbo (1987) notes that "information is a representation of social virtue to an administrator for it enhances the perception that the administrator is competent and inspires confidence" (p. 25). Research in modern organizations, such as police departments, the Pentagon, big business, and a host of other government agencies, "reveals how they use information in the form of official reports as a 'front' to present public images of issues, problems, and efficiency" (Douglas and Johnson 1977, 35; see also Feldman and March 1981).

But the image that developed in the late 1970s and 1980s was of government officials who had gotten out of control. Presidential candidates Jimmy Carter and Ronald Reagan successfully ran for office on a campaign that promised to "get the government off our backs," and to oppose the "Washington establishment." This strain of antigovernment populism runs deep in the American political culture, and it doesn't take much to convince people to vote for those who promise to make government bureaucrats accountable.

WHAT IS ACCOUNTABILITY?

In the classical theory of democratic government, the line of accountability is clear and straightforward: The people elect their representatives and chief executives on the basis of their stand on issues. These officials then make policy in accord with their campaign promises, and administrative agencies carry out these policies to the letter. Carl Pinkele (1985) notes that "democracy rests upon two notions: that the authority for making political decisions is derived from the sovereignty of the citizenry, and that interests as reflected in policy decisions shall not supplant or countervail the broad and general interests of the public" (p. 8).

Not until recent years was it discovered that this simple chain of accountability does not work. Writing in 1940, Carl Friedrich noted how unrealistic the theory was, stating the "public policy, to put it flatly, is a continuous process, the formulation of which *is* inseparable from its execution" (p. 6). Administrators do not simply see to it that the laws are faithfully executed; they also make policy. This reality poses major problems for democratic theory because it reduces the relevance of elections in influencing the direction of policy. Policy is not dependent on election outcomes, as political scientists Samuel Krislov and David Rosenbloom (1981) note: "Elections remain 'media events' and grist for political science in journals. Yet their growing irrelevance in terms of accountability of public bureaucrats and the formulating of public policy is widely recognized" (p.16).

The problem can be traced back to the Founding Fathers for they did not take the bureaucracy into account when framing the Constitution. Of course, at the time there was no bureaucracy and hardly any government administration (except for the Post Office and Defense Department), so they can hardly be faulted for not seeing how a large bureaucracy would develop more than a century later. In the nineteenth century, positions in administration were handed out as the spoils of elections, and administration entailed work that "any average person could do."

American administrative theory has been plagued by this problem ever since. There stil is no theory of how to achieve accountability or even how it should be defined in the contemporary bureaucratic age. Janowitz, Wright, and Delany (1977) noted that "a system of political theory which would outline the desired relations between government bureaucracy and the public in a democratic political system is relatively undeveloped.'' Frederick Mosher (1982b) called this the central problem of our bureaucratic age: "How can a public service so constituted be made to operate in a manner compatible with democracy?'' (pp. 3–4).

The myth of a neutral administration faithfully executing the laws has persisted even in the face of the reality that it is not true. It persists because it serves the interests of administrators and representatives alike. It allows administrators to engage in politics and policy making without the bother of having to stand for election, and it allows politicians to remove many important public decisions as far as possible from "politics" and to blame "those bureaucrats" if things go wrong (Peters 1989). Most administrators are eager to buy the politics-administration distinction. According to Judith Gruber (1987), "In their eyes, policy-making consists of specifying the most general outcomes the agency is to achieve; all the rest is administration" (p. 110).

The problem of defining accountability in a bureaucratic age is not just a constitutional problem; it also is a question of values and, more important, whose values are served. As political scientists Douglas Yates (1982) notes, "The issue of [bureaucratic] control . . . looks like one of standard politics of who gets what, when, and how" (p. 151). It depends on who is looking at it. For example, Lockean liberalism holds that people (and consequently administrators) are not to be trusted because they will not cooperate or work in the public interest unless it furthers their own self-interests. According to this view of human nature, bureaucrats are expected to do things that ensure their survival and the constant expansion of the bureaucracy. But whether this is so has never really been proven (and can't be since it depends on one's values). In general, conservatives tend to hold this view of human nature and do not trust governmental bureaucrats. In this nineteenth-century view, we should either do away with bureaucrats, or, failing this, hedge them in with strict rules that guide their behavior. Such a position is expressed by K. C. Davis (1972) who argues that "the desirability of administrative rules extends as far as discretionary power extends. Whenever any agency or officer has discretionary power, rule making is appropriate" (p. 221). But realistically, as we shall show below, it is not possible to control completely the behavior of administrators. How, then, can they be made accountable for their actions?

There are two separate dimensions to accountability that must be kept distinct: One pertains to the substance of the concept, and the other pertains to the methods of achieving accountability. Most of the literature deals with the latter, but the former is just as crucial. In substantive terms, accountability means being responsive to the public. But this can mean doing exactly what the people say and no more (i.e., the delegate position), or it can mean acting as a trustee, wherein administrators let their own judgment about what the people want and need guide their action. Most legislators conceive of themselves as trustees rather than delegates, feeling that it is their duty to do what is right and just even if it does not conform exactly to the expressed wishes of the public. It is their duty to lead rather than just follow public opinion.

Administrators tend to hold the same views not only of the public but of elected officials as well. "If anything," Judith Gruber (1987) writes, "[administrators] see their role as guarding the public weal against the designs of politicians, and not as achieving it through those designs" (p. 115). Nor do administrators have high opinions about the ability of citizens. Many agree with those scholars who believe that citizens do not know enough to direct the detailed activity of administrators (Lindsay 1962). Government is so complex, some scholars say, that only experts can make the correct decisions (Friedrich 1940; Schumpeter 1962).

Of course, there are those who disagree with this view. Herman Finer (1941), for example, writes:

> I again insist upon subservience [of administators to elected officials], for I still am of the belief with Rousseau that the people can be unwise but cannot be wrong . . . the servants of the public are not to decide their own course; they are to be responsible to the elected representatives of the public, and these are to determine the course of action of the public servants to the most minute degree that is technically feasible. (p. 336)

It is very democratic to trust the people as Finer does, but it is not realistic to believe that it is possible to determine the course of action of the public servants to a minute degree. Moreover, as Mashaw (1983) notes, attempting to do this may be more dysfunctional than allowing bureaucrats to have discretion because it may and often does produce the very bureaucratic red tape and rule-bound rigidity that we so often criticize. In addition, the elected representatives of the people may be more interested in their *own* aggrandizement than in doing the public's will when they give directions to administrators. Finally, in the pluralist conception of democracy, there is no single public interest to be carried out but various public interests and these may be in conflict (Yates 1982). Who is to decide which is the correct one? In pluralist theory, administrators can be considered as another legitimate interest to be heard. The result is better policy since a wide range of interests are included. Nevertheless, there are times when administrators may abuse their power, and thus it still is necessary to find a mechanism for making them answerable when they do. If it is not possible to agree on the substantive meaning of accountability, let us see if we can discover what methods of control might work.

METHODS OF ACHIEVING ADMINISTRATIVE ACCOUNTABILITY

There are two major approaches to making bureaucracy accountable. One is *external*; this involves controls by legislatures through such mechanisms as legislative oversight, by the courts through review of decisions and administrative law, or by citizen participation. The second method is through *internal* controls; this includes development of professional standards and ethics, the use of rules, whistle-blowers, representative bureaucracy, and opening up administrative proceedings. We shall discuss each method in turn.

External Controls

Legislative Oversight.   Since the 1960s and early 1970s, legislatures at the national and state levels have increased their attempts to control bureaucracies. The 1968 Intergovernmental Cooperation Act required congressional committees to oversee the operation of federal grant-in-aid programs to states and localities. In 1970, Congress revised the 1946 Legislative Reorganization Act by reshaping the Library of Congress's Legislative Reference Service into the Congressional Research Service, giving new responsibilities to the General Accounting Office (GAO) for overseeing the executive agencies and adding more congressional research staff. At the national level, Congress's power vis-à-vis the executive branch reached a low point in 1972. Richard Nixon openly defied Congress when he impounded funds that Congress had appropriated. Nixon decided to cut spending for aid to cities and public works. Congress reasserted itself when it passed the Budget and Impoundment Control Act in 1974 that attempted to streamline congressional budgetary procedures. In 1972, Congress created the Office of Technology Assessment, and the Congressional Budget Office in 1974. Also in 1974, the GAO created the Program Evaluation and Methodology Division which was charged with the responsibility of conducting evaluations of executive agency programs and helping other GAO divisions in their evaluations. And the House of Representatives in 1974 modified its rules and procedures by establishing general and specific oversight responsibilities for committees and subcommittees (Ogul 1976, 318). By the early 1980s, more than 228 agencies were conducting evaluations of executive agencies. A total of 1,353 full-time professionals conducted 2,362 evaluations, 60 percent of which were under contract with external organizations (Palumbo 1988, 126).

At the state level, legislative oversight became one of the major functions of legislatures in the 1970s (Ogul 1976; Rosenthal 1974). Through oversight, the legislature is able to "resist executive domination and strengthen its overall position in the Constitutional system" (Keefe and Ogul 1969, 17). But perhaps more important was the public demand that legislators be more responsive. During the late 1970s the public mood was antigovernmental. Citizens were inclined to cut government. Former Senator Harrison Williams (1981) noted:

> The credit or blame for government activity is leveled properly upon members of legislatures. We, after all, created the administrative agencies and the programs they administer and we are expected in the normal course of events to cure their misfunctions. Administrators frequently are faceless. Legislators are never unknown. (p. 8)

About two-thirds of the states allow state legislatures to establish oversight agencies. The most common are postaudit agencies which have both *audit* and *evaluation* responsibilites (Rosenthal and Van Horn 1982). Auditing focuses on whether the administrative agency is spending funds for legislatively authorized activity, while evaluation is concerned with the way programs are being implemented and whether they are achieving legislative goals (see Chapter 11 for a more detailed discussion of evaluation).

Oversight is essentially backward looking; it is meant to assess the way in which programs have been working and whether changes can be made so they will work better (Rosenthal 1981, 320). In the late 1970s, legislatures went further, aiming at entire agencies, when they passed *sunset legislation*. Within a few years, almost forty states had passed sunset laws that mandated "on a cyclical basis automatic termination of programs, agencies, and in particular, professional and regulatory boards and commissions" (Rosenthal 1974, 317). The purpose of the laws was to force agencies to demonstrate their utility in order to avoid being terminated. This method of oversight proved to be impractical and relatively few agencies have been terminated through sunset laws.

All of this activity should have increased the accountability of administrative agencies. But according to Krislov and Rosenbloom (1981), legislatures have not been very effective: "Throughout the world the twentieth century has witnessed the decline in the effectiveness of legislatures as supervisors of bureaucracy" (p.121). There simply are too many administrative agencies, and they are involved in too many activities for legislatures to be very effective. "The GAO," say Krislov and Rosenbloom, "has yet to develop a notion of sampling or other techniques for sytematically assaying the government's total operations. . . . It suffers from the difficulties of the casual investigator needed as a gadfly but not coming from or getting to the heart of the matter" (p. 135). Because its review is so cursory and episodic, Krislov and Rosenbloom contend, Congress is a highly limited instrument of control. This is even more true at the state level where legislators work only a few months of the year and have less professional staff than the Congress.

Control by Courts.   If legislatures are ineffective in their ability to control bureaucracy, the courts are even less effective. The Administrative Procedures Act of 1946 was an attempt to establish uniformity, fairness, and rules for adjudication by regulatory agencies, giving the victim of unfair administrative procedures the right to appeal to the courts for relief. Under this act, the courts may review agency decisions and overrule them not only on the basis of legal jurisdiction but also on the basis of the facts in a particular case.

Following the passage of the Administrative Procedures Act, a complicated area of administrative law has developed, much of it concerned with the conditions under which interested parties may appeal rulings by administrative agencies. But agencies still remain the final power in most matters. Administrative decisions will not be overturned by the court when there is substantial evidence on the whole record to justify the outcome. Krislov and Rosenbloom (1981) conclude that "deference is thus paid to the expertise and authority of the bureaucrat while making that person reviewable and, on occasion, reversible" (p. 137). Although the rate at which courts reverse administrative decisions depends on which agency is involved, the courts provide relatively little limit on policy. They have not been able to develop any patterned review of agencies. The essential weakness of the courts is that they can take only the cases that are brought to them and their rulings apply only to the case before them, not to all similar cases. "It is a terrible way to monitor another system," write Krislov and Rosenbloom (p. 145).

Jerry Mashaw (1983) notes that the courts review a very small percentage of cases handled by agencies. For example, the Social Security Administration (SSA) handles a million and a half disability cases a year and judicial review touches less than 1 percent of this caseload. Court decisions affect only the cases involved in the ruling. The SSA believes that court decisions that are at variance with the secretary's interpretation are not binding on future cases or on cases in other regions. The SSA feels that it has as much legitimacy to interpret the intent of Congress as do the courts. "The courts, as they themselves often maintain," Mashaw (1983) notes, "are truly incompetent to deal with the complexities and subtleties of engineering and managing a large adminstrative decision process" (p. 193). For example, in the area of prisoners' rights, although the courts repeatedly ruled in favor of prisoners in the 1970s and ordered officials to correct the problems, their orders were seldom implemented (Levine, Musheno, and Palumbo 1986).

However, the courts have been more successful in making administrators accountable in another way. Since *Wood v. Strickland* (1975) officials no longer have absolute sovereign immunity; they are not immune from legal liability for actions that violate the constitutional rights of citizens, whether this is done out of ignorance or malice. This ruling was extended in *Owen v. the City of Independence* (1980), in which the Supreme Court said that knowledge that a city will be liable for its imperious conduct, "whether committed in good faith or not, should create an incentive for officials who may harbor doubts about the lawfulness of their intended actions to err on the side of protecting citizens' constitutional rights" (p. B1768).

Ombudspersons.   Another aspect of external review of agencies is the ombudsperson, a development of the 1970s. The system of having an outside reviewer (either ombudsperson or civilian review board in police agencies) has been more symbolic than real in its impact. The outside reviewer finds for the bureaucracy and against the complainant about 90 percent of the time. These offices generally process a small number of cases and they lack the power to force an agency to change its behavior; they cannot channel or control the bulk of the bureaucracy (Krislov and Rosenbloom 1981, 152).

Citizen Participation.   Citizen participation in administrative agencies also was touted in the late 1960s as an important method of making them more responsive (Kotler 1969). A prime example is the New York City Board of Education, which was broken into thirty-three separate districts in the late 1960s. Each district had its own elected board (Gittell 1967). However, citizen turnout in the elections was exceedingly low. The boards were ultimately controlled by teachers' unions and church representatives, and the influence of ordinary citizens on school policy was negligible. In general, citizen control has not been very effective (Morgan and England 1987).

Public Interest Groups.   Public interest groups have been more effective in their influence, primarily because of the 1966 Freedom of Information Act that enables them to keep informed about bureaucratic policy making. It was this act that helped reveal the FBI's actions in its investigation of CISPES, discussed at the beginning of this chapter.

By challenging and monitoring agency policy through this legislation, public interest groups are able to bring their influence to bear on agencies. Groups such as Ralph Nader's and Common Cause have forced some agencies to act in the public interest rather than strictly in the interests of the industries they are supposed to regulate.

Privatization.   Finally, although it has existed throughout American history, in the mid- and late-1980s, privatization was pushed by conservatives as a way of keeping bureaucracies efficient and responsive. Privatization is a complicated concept with many meanings (Palumbo and Maupin 1989), but its main component involves turning over or allowing (through contracting out) private, profit-making firms to deliver government goods and services. The economic theory underlying privatization is that through competition, private firms will deliver services more efficiently and effectively than will public agencies because they must be accountable directly to the public. The latter, because they have a monopoly on producing services, such as education, do not have an incentive to be efficient or to respond to citizen interests (Bennett and DiLorenzo 1983a). On the other hand, privatization places agencies one step further down the line of accountability. For example, if an administrative agency contracts with a private firm to provide a service such as institutional confinement of juvenile delinquents, the agency must ensure that public goals are being served. In order to do this, it must have feedback on what is being done by the firm. Then it must write detailed specifications into the program to make sure that the firm is doing what is expected of it (Kettl 1988).

Contracting grew tremendously under the Reagan administration. In 1985, the federal government had 21.5 million contracts totaling $200 billion, which was 21 percent of all federal spending that year (Kettl 1988, 24). As with legislative oversight, determining whether a firm is doing what it is supposed to do is easy if the government can define what it wants in a way that clearly tells a contractor what is expected. This can take many pages of detailed description, as was the case in the eighteen pages of specifications used by the military to describe the requirements for fruit cakes for the armed services, down to the size of the nuts and raisins (Kettl 1988, 33).

The problem with such third-party government (Salamon, 1981) is that it greatly complicates the accountability problem. Political scientist Donald Kettl (1988) writes: "The paradoxical result is that programs contracted out to reduce the size and scope of governmental action often become even more encrusted with governmental controls" (p. 37). Particularly in the area of defense contracting, Kettl found much abuse and shoddy work. But the government was unable to impose meaningful penalties on the defense firms. Canceling the contract is too severe because there may not be an alternative: Not many firms are able to build a nuclear submarine or a jet fighter plane. Moreover, it is difficult to make penalties stick, and the very complexity of the system, built on interwoven and inconsistent goals, makes it even more difficult to manage programs well and to make them responsive to the needs of citizens (Kettl 1988, 54).

No event in recent history brought home this problem as dramatically as the *Challenger* disaster on January 28, 1986. The problem was that NASA did not know about the potential dangers of launching the *Challenger* in cold weather. They had all the information, which was passed along the proper channels from the engineers in the Morton Thiokol Corporation (which built the *Challenger*), but the pressures of getting the launch off on schedule overshadowed this. It was a case of subordinates not wanting unpleasant information to rise to the top and of those at the top not wanting to hear information that would cause further delays in the launch and further embarrassment for NASA (Peters 1989). NASA did not adequately monitor the contracts that accounted for 88 percent of its $7.5 billion annual budget. According to a former NASA contract monitor, the "cozy relationship" of the agency and its contractors made discovery of problems extremely difficult (*New York Times*, April 23, 1986, p. A14-15). As Kettl (1988) notes: "The predicament of having too much information or too little of the right information comes with a program of any complexity and with a bureaucracy of any size. Government by proxy aggravates the distortion" (p. 142).

In summary, external methods of controlling or making the bureaucracy accountable do not work very well. Certainly they have some impact, but it is very limited. Do internal methods of control work any better?

Internal Methods of Control

The principal internal mechanisms of controlling bureaucracy are the use of rules by the hierarchy, representative bureaucracy, professionalism, whistle-blowing, and opening up administrative proceedings.

Hierarchical Control.   The classical method of control is to centralize authority in an agency and adopt rules that are supposed to govern the behavior of administrators and reduce their discretion. The classic example of successful controls in an agency concerns the forest rangers in the U.S. Forest Service (Kaufman 1960). Forest rangers have great powers over the issuance of permits that assign valuable rights for private use of public lands. Yet, the agency is untouched by scandal. According to Kaufman, this was accomplished by its ability to transmit an image of pride to its workers, plus the existence of detailed regulations and a requirement for elaborate logging of all transactions. However, there are only a few agencies whose functions can be standardized in this manner. As Judith Gruber (1987, 68) writes, because "most problems in public policy . . . abound in uncertainty," it is difficult to know when and why controls work or do not work.

In general, hierarchical controls cannot work, particularly in federal relations, because they would require elaborate monitoring of agencies that is impossible to accomplish. Mashaw (1983) remarks that in the area of federal disability decisions, the federal regional offices monitor the state agencies, but they behave more like U.S. embassies abroad; they mediate conflict and misunderstanding rather than enforce mandates. To achieve a unified culture of adjudication among state disability claims adjudication offices was not possible, Mashaw says, because of the ambiguity of norms, the limitations of management techniques, and competition among divergent state agencies. Furthermore, it is impossible to focus on all dimensions of the decision process at once. Worse yet, attempts to standardize decisions conflict with the need for individualized treatment. Justice requires that all cases be treated fairly, but fairness does not mean exact similarity because each case is unique is some ways. Hence, hierarchical control, or pure bureaucratic justice, is impossible. Mashaw (1983, 49) writes that to be perfectly rational in disability determinations requires (1) internalization of an appropriate definition of disability, (2) collection of information sufficient to allow a determination of whether a particular claimant meets that definition, and (3) understanding of the way in which a particular decision to grant or to deny

disability benfits furthers the statutory goal of income support for the disabled population. But achieving these aims is not possible because of the ambiguity and incoher-
ence of the goals of the disability benefits program and because of the uncertainties
that infect the factual concepts presented to adjudicators for authoritative resolution.

Representative Bureaucracy. If hierarchical controls cannot work in most situations, perhaps bureaucracies could be made more responsive and accountable if they
were representative of the general population (in terms of ethnicity, race, gender, age,
and education) (Mosher 1982a). As Krislov and Rosenbloom (1981) note, if "public
bureaucracies could be constituted so as to provide political representation of the
general public, their power could be made to comport substantially with democratic
values" (p.21).

What is a representative bureaucracy? Does the term mean that the bureaucracy
should consist of exactly 12 percent blacks, 51 percent women, and so on, if those are
the proportions of those groups in the general population? The answer is no, partly
because there is no assurance that the specific blacks, women, and so on, in agencies
will, in fact, reflect the needs, interests, and desires of those groups; and partly because observing such strict percentages conflicts with functional requirements of the
agencies (Meier and Nigro 1976).

Rather than demographic representation, American bureaucracies have represented major interests in society such as labor, business, agriculture, and the urban
poor. National bureaucracies are thus often highly representative of (some would say
captured by) interest groups. "In fact," Krislov and Rosenbloom (1981) note, "representation may be so pronounced that government agencies come to speak for private interests" (p.103). The unorganized, who usually are the poor and less powerful,
go unrepresented. Such representation shuts out these people at the most creative and
important place of policy making—the phase in which the problem is defined. Moreover, the agencies are accountable only to the interest groups (Lowi 1979), and, in the
absence of public scrutiny, policy is made by "iron triangles" consisting of the agencies, interest groups, and legislative committees (Meltsner and Bellavita 1983; Heclo
1978).

Representation by interest groups thus creates privilege and is conservative in
almost every sense (Krislov and Rosenbloom 1981, 106). This bias cannot be corrected short of trying to organize all interests and ensuring that they are run democratically, a formidable and all but impossible task given the "Iron Law of Oligar-
chy" (Michels 1915). This law says that any organization, even one that espouses the
most egalitarian democratic goals, will be controlled by a small elite that is not representative of the broader membership. Krislov and Rosenbloom (1981) conclude that
representativeness by itself is not sufficient to provide a responsive, controlled bureaucracy: "A bureaucracy drawn from all walks of life, but all powerful and unaccountable would be practically speaking as dangerous as any other uncontrolled
group. . . . Without constraints, other behaviors will be easily learned" (p. 196).

Professionalism. One of the more crucial developments of the twentieth century has
been the decline of patronage and rise of professionalism in the public service (see
Chapter 7). Some scholars see this as the best and least costly way of achieving bu-

reaucratic democracy (Bailey 1965; Friedrich 1940). The idea here is that professional administrators are more likely to make decisions in the general "public interest" than are people appointed on the basis of patronage. There is some evidence that this is the case. For example, Mashaw found that disability claims were more effectively processed in states in which the agency was located in the education department rather than in the welfare department. This is because in the former, examiners are classified as *counselors* and are required to work toward or hold a master's degree in vocational counseling. The examiners were thus better qualified and paid, and more professional. Mashaw (1983, 161) found that they were more thoughtful about their work, resourceful, and energetic in developing claims files. The personnel in the welfare department, on the other hand, were not as well paid and their entry qualifications were low. They tended to take the path of least resistance and decide cases very quickly.

The other side of the coin is that professionals may feel that they know more than the public (see Chapter 5). They speak to a limited group of citizens but distrust elected representatives (Gruber 1987, 110). Such zealousness may lead to the belief that they are above the law and its legal representatives, and produce the kind of behavior illustrated in the FBI and Irangate cases discussed in this chapter. Moreover, in the New York City school controversy in the 1960s, the highly professional city board of education and teachers found themselves out of touch with the parents and children in the ghetto communities (Berube and Gittel 1969). Thus, to the extent to which professionals are recruited from the ranks of the well educated, they may fail to be responsive to the poorer segments of society.

Whistle-Blowing.   Whistle-blowing occurs when an employee discovers wrongdoing in a company or agency, and exposes it by informing the media or other agencies in the hope of correcting the wrongdoing. While whistle-blowing may at times be effective in correcting administrative wrongdoing, whistle-blowers almost invariably suffer; usually they are persecuted or fired by the agency and have a difficult time securing comparable employment by other agencies. For example, an army officer who uncovered the theft of more than $118 million in war material was pressured to resign from the service and forced to undergo psychiatric evaluation under charges that he was unstable (Anderson 1988). Incidents such as this are not atypical; in fact, whistle-blowing can be dangerous to one's future employment (see Chapter 4). A number of states have passed laws protecting whistle-blowers in an attempt to encourage people to become watchdogs. But there is little information about the effectiveness of these laws. Most important, because very few individuals are willing to take the risks involved in whistle-blowing, it is neither a very systematic nor effective way of achieving administrative accountability. As the experience during the Holocaust in Germany demonstrated, people involved in wrongdoing are most likely to fall back on the claim that they were "just following orders" and felt that as individuals they could not resist administrative pressures (see Chapter 2).

Opening Up Administrative Proceedings.   The freedom of Information Act, under which the FBI role in the CISPES affair described above was uncovered, was based on the assumption that if administrative agencies are forced to provide an open, public accounting of their decisions, they are likely to be more careful and responsible in their actions. Citizen participation in administration also is based on somewhat the same assumption. Sociologists John Johnson and David Altheide (1980) believe that "only when individual members of the various audiences susceptible to efforts at bureaucratic impression management become more knowledgeable of this information war, and of the weapons used, will the organizational context of such information become more identifiable, and therefore less susceptible of manipulation" (p. 238).

No doubt, exposing what administrators do improves their accountability. Operating in a fishbowl is conducive to getting agencies to act more responsibly. But, of course, it is not a panacea. There are just too many agencies and decisions involved to be adequately covered by a public that is not very attentive to government in the first place (Yates 1982, 167). Hence, some strategic selection is necessary. Moreover, attempts to have policy formulated in a more democratic forum may have the negative consequence of pushing agencies in more bureaucratic directions. Mashaw (1983) believes that attempts to make the Social Security Administration more accountable to the legislature made it more bureaucratic; he concludes: "Improving the democratic connection as a device for administrative reform thus seems to imagine a politics that we do not have."

THE INEVITABILITY AND DESIRABILITY OF ADMINISTRATIVE DISCRETION

The principal proponents of bureaucratic accountability during the 1980s were conservative Republicans. In their view, government was the problem, not the solution to social problems. They therefore worked to end government regulations, privatize government, and reduce the size of government wherever possible (except in the area of defense). Reducing the size and responsibilities of government and privatizing many functions creates a need for less oversight.

A large part of the conservative agenda of the Reagan presidency was a reaction to the governmental regulations concerning worker safety, environmental pollution, and discrimination that were adopted in the early 1970s. These social regulations were in areas in which governmental regulation had not intruded previously (Wilson 1982).

But the clamor to reduce governmental size and restrict the discretion of government agencies was not the agenda of Republicans alone. Democratic candidate Jimmy Carter ran for president in 1976 on a platform that called for restraining government, and a number of liberal intellectuals also called for limitations on the discretion of government officials. But conservative Democrats and liberals tended to focus on restricting discretion in criminal justice agencies rather than in the areas of social and economic regulation favored by conservatives. As a result of pressure by liberals, a number of laws were passed in the 1970s aimed at restricting the discretion of prosecutors and judges. The most important of these was the 1978 Criminal Code Reform Act that created a rational and comprehensive system of sentencing. In particular, it established determinate sentencing, thereby reducing discretion of prosecutors and judges who, liberals felt, were using their powers discriminatorily against minorities. Conservatives supported the legislation also because they felt that judges were being too lenient in sentencing. The 1975 Federal Rules of Criminal Procedure Act further restricted plea bargaining, and the Parole Reform Act in 1976 limited the discretionary power of parole boards.

Although conservatives joined with liberals in supporting restrictions on the discretion of judges, there was a fundamental difference between them: Liberals were in favor of broad discretion for regulatory agencies aimed at social and economic regulations while conservatives were against this. On the other hand, liberals tended to favor restrictions on the discretion of police agencies (e.g., the Miranda warning and exclusionary rule), while conservatives decried these.

Thus, while the targets of limiting administrative discretion were different for conservatives and liberals, the cumulative result of pressure from both sides was a general attack on governmental administrative discretion. Both sides ignored the reality that administrative discretion is inevitable, cannot be eliminated, and can actually be desirable and beneficial. Government has a positive and crucial role to play in criminal justice, economic affairs, and social regulation, a role that cannot be dispensed with. For example, environmental pollution is considered an "externality" from the perspective of the firm or individual doing the polluting. Consequently, if government does not act, the environment will be damaged because there is no incentive for firms or individuals to take the responsibility or assume the costs of avoiding polluting the environment. Thus, governmental regulation is necessary to correct these *market failures*. The question then becomes this: How much discretion should regulatory agencies have in making decisions about specific firms? In handling individual firms or individuals, it is necessary to treat each case differently. As Pinkele (1985) notes, "Justice blind to the human facts of a case runs a very great risk of being blind justice" (p.11). Treating unequals in the exact same manner is unjust. It is essential for administrators to have the discretion necessary to adapt general rules to the specific circumstances of each individual case.

Even aside from the normative argument in favor of discretion, there is the realistic recognition that it is impossible to control the behavior of administrators completely. Of course, some controls do work (Bardach and Kagan 1982), and administrative behavior can and should be constrained by the general intent of policy and of Congress. Bardach and Kagan (1982) describe how the discretion of food inspectors was successfully restricted:

> An inspector's judgment always is at work in fitting a rule to the details of what he sees, in deciding, for example, whether a dirty rail on a conveyer in a meat packing plant poses a risk of "remote product contamination" or "direct product contamination," the latter requiring a tougher response. But discretion for inspectors to overlook obvious or clear rule violations, to grant extended time for abatement, to "forget" citations after they have been written up, seems by all accounts to have been restricted. (p. 76)

But heavy-handed attempts to control administrators completely usually has negative consequences (Fesler 1980; Knott and Miller 1986; Mashaw 1983). The classic dilemma of public administration is to balance the requirements for responsibility and accountability with those of effective and efficient administrative action. Any attempt to move to one or the other end of this dilemma is bound to have negative consequences. Moreover, it is impossible to control discretion completely because street-level bureaucrats cannot be constantly supervised while performing their jobs. Police on the beat, nurses making home visits, teachers in the classroom, probation officers working with offenders, prosecutors negotiating with defendants, sanitarians checking restuarants, and the multitude of other street-level bureaucrats work without direct supervision. They can be given general rules for how they should behave, but when push comes to shove in any specific case, there is an area of discretionary behavior that cannot be codified (see Chapter 5). It is impossible to specify what constitutes good and correct behavior in every case. How a police officer should handle a specific case of domestic disturbance or how a teacher should handle a particular difficult child, in the end, will be decided by the person on the scene.

If lower-echelon workers do not want to cooperate with rules that try to tell them how to handle each specific case, they can use various tactics to avoid or negate them. They can engage in slowdowns, or follow each detail so closely that the larger purpose of the rules is defeated. As Michael Lipsky (1980) notes: "The management challenge . . . at the heart of the problem is how to make the worker's need for personal, material, or psychological gratification mesh with the organzation's needs" (p. 17). If management fails to do this, street-level bureaucrats can use their discretion to defeat what management wants to achieve.

Balance can best be found through a combination of institutional design and trust. Krislov and Rosenbloom (1981) conclude that "continuing emphasis on decentralization, on flexible regulatory policies, and on review of existing structures will help restore a sense of accountability. . . . Above all, a sense of purpose and integrity, a sense of mission within the agencies, is needed" (p. 198). The institutional context in which American bureaucracies operate is conducive to administrative responsibility. "Institutionai arrangements that fragment power," Aberbach, Putnam, and Rockman write (1981), "create conditions of mutual dependence, and mutual dependence in turn encourages interaction between politicians and bureaucrats, because each holds resources valued by the other" (p. 236). Hence, it is essential to support the structure that facilitates these exchanges, rather than centralizing agencies in accord with the traditional politics-administration dichotomy. In an exchange model, "control results not from political actors telling bureaucrats what to do but from constructing conditions in which bureaucratic behavior is constrained in exchange for resources that bureaucrats seek. Such control emanates from a process of interaction; not from one of orders from above" (Gruber 1987, 211).

SUMMARY

Some governmental agencies, particularly the CIA and FBI, have been known to act at odds with the directives of elected representatives and citizens. In the 1980s distrust of government and calls for curbs on its powers mounted.

In modern societies, bureaucracies have come to dominate government through a variety of means. One of the most important is their control and use of information, and this presents a dilemma for democratic government that needs to make bureaucracy accountable.

In classical democratic theory, accountability is supposed to be ensured by direct control emanating from citizens to elected officials and thence to the bureaucracy. But we have known for some time that this simple chain does not work because policy is not dependent on election outcomes.

The problem originates with the founding fathers since they did not envision the development of a large bureaucracy that would make policy. The problem has plagued American administrative theory ever since. The myth of a neutral administration faithfully executing the laws has persisted in the face of the reality that administrators also make policy as well as administer it.

The task of defining accountability is not simply a technical one for it also involves values. In Lockean liberalism, bureaucrats are not to be trusted since their principal motive is to feather their own nests, often at the expense of the public interest. Thus, they should be hedged in with strict rules and guidelines. In the trustee view, however, administrators can and should use their own judgment about what is best for the public, but they can be wrong and uninformed. Others say that the people may be unwise but never wrong.

It is not realistic, however, to believe that all administrative discretion can be controlled. Moreover, attempts to do so can result in rigidity and massive red tape. And in a pluralist system, administrators may be considered as another legitimate interest to be heard. Still, it is necessary to find a mechanism to make administrators accountable when they abuse their power.

There are two major approaches to making administrators accountable; one is through external and the other through internal mechanisms. External controls include legislative oversight. A number of agencies have been created for this at the national as well as state level. However, this method has not been very effective.

A second means of external control is through the courts. Following passage of the Administrative Procedures Act of 1946, a complicated area of administrative law has developed. But the courts still defer to the expertise of administrative agencies most of the time, and courts are able to review only a small percentage of cases handled by agencies.

Other means of external controls are ombudspersons, citizen participation, public interest groups, and privatization. None of these works very well.

Internal methods of control include centralizing authority in agencies. These cannot work, particularly in the federal system, because federal agencies are not able nor should they be able to dictate to state and local agencies.

A second method of internal control is representative bureaucracy. The meaning of this concept is not exactly clear; it is not certain that members of ethnic groups will in fact represent the interests of their groups; and interest group representation, which is characteristic of the American system, tends to create privileges and is conservative in almost every sense.

Professionalism is seen by some scholars as the best and least costly way of achieving accountability. There is evidence that professional administrators are more likely to be resourceful, energetic, and thoughtful about their work. The downside is that professionals may feel they may know more than legislators.

Whistle-blowing has helped point out dishonesty and malfeasance, but whistle-blowers usually suffer losses, and laws to protect them have not been very effective. Finally, opening up administrative proceedings to public scrutiny does improve accountability, but it certainly is not a panacea.

Liberals, as well as conservatives, have both called for limiting adminstrative discretion. But discretion in administration is inevitable and essential. Decentralization, professionalism, and some of the other means of control will improve accountability. But in the end administrators should and will have a role in public policy making and this is perfectly appropriate in the American pluralistic system of democracy.

CASE STUDY: THE IRAN-CONTRA AFFAIR

Introduction

President Ronald Reagan was reputed to have been one of the nation's most inattentive presidents. He often did not work a full day, took long vacations, delegated broad powers, and frequently allowed his subordinates on the White House staff to make policy decisions. His press secretary, Larry Speakes (soon after resigning from this post), said that he often made up quotes that he then attributed to the president. Thus, a "hidden bureaucracy" in the White House, rather than the democratically elected officials, seems to have made major policy decisions during Reagan's presidency.[1]

This hidden bureaucracy consisted of 322 members in 1988—an all-time high in the size of the White House staff. One part of this White House bureaucracy is the National Security Council (NSC). The NSC is composed of the president, vice-president, the secretaries of state and defense, the director of the Office of Emergency Preparedness, the national security adviser, and a number of staff aides. The NSC was created by the National Security Act of 1947. It was intended to be the central, but not sole, machinery for advising the president and helping in the coordination of U.S. military and foreign policies.

The NSC Act recognizes that the primary responsibility for the formulation and implementation of national security policy falls on the president. It further accords the president the position as customary source of innovation and responsiveness in this field. The president's task, through the NSC, is to provide leadership and direction in order to bring his perspective to bear on those independent bureaucracies (departments and agencies) that are the instruments for executing various national security policies. The system that has developed under the NSC is intended to afford the president special resources for implementing the important role required by the NSC Act. These include the members of the NSC. They provide the means through which the creative impulses of the president are brought to bear on the permanent government (Tower Commission, 1987: Part V, V–1).

The NSC has varied in significance with different presidents. For instance, Eisenhower used it extensively and regularly, especially during his last term in office; Kennedy seldom used it; Nixon, who had been a member of the NSC under Eisenhower, restored it to prominence. Reagan also used it extensively, and as this case study illustrates, significant questions remain about the extent to which the NSC bureaucrats were held accountable for the decisions they made.

The NSC is supposed to be the central mechanism for *coordinating* foreign policy and, therefore, it is but one of a number of independent agencies that formulate foreign policies. Other agencies include the Joint Chiefs of Staff, the State Department, the Central

Intelligence Agency (CIA), and the Congress. But in the Iran-Contra affair, foreign policy was made without the concurrent checks and balances against abuse and accountability of the unelected bureaucracy. Consequently, it seems that the NSC staff, without the explicit approval of the president, made policy to divert profits from arms sales to Iran to the Contras in Nicaragua at the very time that Congress prohibited arms shipments to them. These staff members are people who are unelected, some of them unconfirmed, and unaccountable or, in principle, remotely accountable to the public. Their actions largely compromised professional standards and evaded the external instruments that tend to control and ensure bureaucratic accountability. Internal control mechanisms, given the president's management style, also failed.

Events Leading up to "Irangate"

A Lebanese weekly on November 3, 1986, reported that the United States had secretly sold arms to the Iranian government. Subsequent press reports corroborating this story claimed that the purpose of the sale was to win the release of American hostages in Beirut, Lebanon. The groups holding these American hostages reportedly had political ties to the revolutionary regime of Iran's Ayatollah Khomeini. These reports of arms sales seemed incredible in light of U.S. policy that no arms should be supplied to the government of Ayatollah Khomeini, especially coming on the heels of the 1979 Iran hostage crisis. In addition, Iran was considered to be among the terrorist nations whose activities were directed against U.S. citizens. The prohibition of arms exports to Iran was also consistent with the American policy and principle of neutrality between Iran and Iraq, which had been at war since 1981. Another amazing side of this continued arms sales story was the professed policy by the United States, emphasized by President Reagan, that other nations, especially the Western nations, should not give in to terrorist demands. But at the same time that the United States was pressuring its allies not to supply Iran with arms, it was secretly negotiating an arms-for-hostages deal with Iran. This revelation greatly embarrassed the United States in world public opinion,

Shortly after this first disclosure, another even more startling revelation related to the arms sales was made by the then–Attorney General Ed Meese. On November 25, 1986, Meese announced that profits from the Iran arms sales had been "diverted" to the Nicaraguan resistance group (the Contras), at a time when U.S. military aid to this organization was prohibited by Congress through the 1985 Boland Amendment (U.S. Congress 1987, 3). These two events in U.S. foreign policy came to be called the *Iran-Contra Scandal.*

The diversion of funds to the Contras was tied to the president's vow to keep the Contras together in "body and soul" during a time that Congress had explicitly prohibited such support. After the deals were uncovered, the public and members of Congress both expressed strong concerns over the propriety and legality of the actions taken by some members of the NSC. The serious implications for foreign policy and the rule of law in a democracy led the president to appoint an executive review board, the Tower Commission, and led the Congress to establish a congressional investigative committee to assess all aspects of this operation and report necessary findings and recommendations to the various responsible arms of government.

The Origins

The Iran-Contra affair had its origins in two unrelated revolutions in Iran and Nicaragua. In Iran, the pro-Western government of the Shah Mohammed Reza Pahlavi was crushed in a 1979 revolution by Islamic fundamentalists led by the Ayatollah Khomeini. This revolutionary government was ardently anti-American because of U.S. support of the Shah. In the eyes of the Ayatollah, the United States was the "Great Satan" that deserved retaliation and hatred. Following the revolution, Iran soon became a supporter and sponsor of terrorism, especially against American interests, notably in the Mideast.

In 1979, Iranians seized the U.S. embassy in Teheran and took forty-seven Americans as hostages. The hostage crisis dragged on for many months, punctuated by an ill-fated rescue attempt in which American helicopters and the charred remains of several U.S. servicemen were abandoned in the Iranian desert. In retaliation, the United States froze Iranian assets in the United States and prohibited arms sales to the Khomeini regime. These sanctions were broadened and strengthened in subsequent years as the Iran-Iraq war intensified and anti-American sentiment became highly charged in Iran and in the Mideast.

The U.S. policy that introduced the U.S. Marines in Lebanon in 1983 at the peak of its civil war exacerbated these anti-American sentiments. The intense dislike of the United States led to several kidnappings of Americans in Lebanon, reportedly by a group of Islamic fundamentalists loyal to Khomeini, who saw the United States equally as their enemy. Even after the marines had been pulled out of Lebanon, several more Americans were kidnapped and were still being held hostage in 1988 by various "terrorist" groups reported by the Central Intelligence Agency to have links to Iran. The relatives of the kidnapped hostages pressured the president and Congress to help secure the release of their family members. At the same time, the hostages provided Iran with a bargaining chip in its war with Iraq. This set the stage for the president's vulnerability to Iran's demands for arms (including spare parts for their U.S.-made weapons, which Iran had procured before the arms embargo), as the main condition for releasing the U.S. hostages.

The second revolution, unrelated to Iran's, is the one that occurred in Nicaragua. The long-time president of Nicaragua, General Anastasio Somoza Debayle, was overthrown in 1979 and replaced by a leftist government, the Sandinistas. The U.S. policy toward the new Sandinista regime at the time was to encourage it to keep its pledge of "pluralism and democracy." To the contrary, the Sandinista government became increasingly anti-American and autocratic. It outlawed the opposition political party, closed the press, and turned toward Cuba and the Soviet Union for political, military, and economic assistance. In 1981, the CIA alleged that the Sandinista regime was spreading communism throughout Latin and Central America (U.S. Congress 1987, 3). These allegations were enough to justify American concerns and action, particularly among the conservative Reagan administration, on the basis that U.S. national security interests and the stability of her allies in the region were being threatened. The Monroe Doctrine was invoked by President Reagan in opposing the Sandinista regime, but there was sharp disagreement between the president and Congress over the proper course of U.S. foreign policy in Nicaragua.

By 1981, the United States, through the CIA, had begun supporting the Contras. Most public opinion polls showed a substantial majority of Americans did not support giving military aid to the Contras, mainly out of fear of another Vietnam. The Congress reflected a similar policy stand when it refused to provide the military aid requested by the Reagan administration. The Boland Amendment, which was contained in the fiscal 1985 Omnibus Appropriations Act, prohibited all funds for the Contras' military and paramilitary operations. Congress expressed fears that such funds would constitute interference in the internal workings of a sovereign nation. President Reagan, nonetheless, was not about to give up on the Contras. Whenever Congress voted against military aid for the resistance, the president literally went over the head of Congress to seek funds from other sources.

A White House advisory group and select members of the NSC became the operational entity that secretly ran the Contra assistance effort, and later the Iran-Contra initiative. When Congress denied funding for the Contras, the NSC turned to third countries and private sources for funds. This concentrated effort within the executive arm generated over $34 million in aid between June 1984 and early 1986 (U.S. Congress 1987, 4). Some of these funds were controlled by private accounts and used for covert operations to support the Contras. When news of this activity began to leak out in the summer of 1985, the president and his then–National Security Adviser Robert C. McFarlane, assured the public and committees of Congress that the law was being followed. The diversion of the proceeds from the Iran arms sales to the Contras was an integral part of the president's policy to sustain pressure on the Sandinista regime until, in the president's phrase, they "cried uncle." However, President Reagan denied having knowledge about the diversion of funds to the Contras.

The Network

The NSC staff, led by Lt. Col. Oliver North and Admiral William Poindexter (NSC Adviser), were already engaged in covert operations through retired Air Force General Richard V. Secord, when, in the summer of 1985, the government of Israel proposed that missiles be sold to Iran. This proposed arms sales, they said, would lead to the release of American hostages held in Lebanon and the prospect of improved relations with some "moderates" in the Iranian government. These moderates, it was reasoned, could be very useful for the U.S. security interests in the Mideast if the regime of Khomeini, who was old and reported to be in ill health, were to lose power. A discussion among members of the White House staff and cabinet members reportedly took place in the summer of 1985, during which the secretaries of state and defense strongly objected to this Israeli proposal. Their objections were based on the U.S. policy not to give in to terrorist demands and the possibility that such a sale might violate the legal arms embargo against Iran.

The president, however, authorized Israel to proceed with the sales (U.S. Congress 1987, 6). The NSC staff conducting the Contra effort also took operational control of implementing the president's decision to sell arms to Iran. By executive order and national security directive, all covert operations must be approved personally by the president in written form. By statute, Congress must be notified about each covert operation. The funds used for such operations, as with all government funds, must be accounted for. But the president did not sign a Finding (a presidential decision and authorization) for this covert operation, nor did he notify Congress. In early December, 1985, the president signed a retroactive Finding, purporting to support the November arms sales to Iran. Subsequent shipments of arms to Iran led to the release of only one American hostage, but the president persisted in believing that more hostages would be released. The president's persistence was based on the advice of Admiral Poindexter and then–CIA Director William Casey, despite contrary recommendations by former NSC Adviser Robert McFarlane, which McFarlane made after his London meetings with the Iranian and Israeli middlemen.

The president signed other Findings on January 6 and 17, 1986, authorizing further shipment of arms to Iran. An outside agency for U.S. covert operations called "Enterprise," that was created by Secord and his business associate, Albert Hakim, was used for most of the transactions involved in the arms sales. Lt. Col. Oliver North had earlier, on December 6, told Israeli Defense Ministry officials that he planned to generate profits on future arms sales for activities in Nicaragua. Although North had become skeptical that the arms sales would lead to the release of all the hostages or a new relationship with Iran, he believed that the prospect of generating funds for the Contras was attractive enough to continue the Iran initiative (U.S. Congress 1987, 7).

In February, 1986, the United States sold 1,000 Tactical Operational Warheads (TOWS) to the Iranians, and also provided the Iranians with military intelligence about Iraq. All of the hostages were supposed to have been released long before then, yet none were. For North, the operation's productive aspect was the diversion of some of the profits from the arms sales to the Contras and other covert operations. According to North's testimony before the congressional investigative committee on this scandal, CIA Director William Casey saw the "diversion" as part of a "more grandiose plan to use the Enterprise as a 'stand-alone,' 'off-the-shelf' covert capacity that would act throughout the world while evading Congressional review."

As an unofficial "ambassador" under the auspices of Secord and North, businessman Albert Hakim produced a nine-point plan that was subsequently approved by North and Poindexter. Under this plan, the United States would receive *one* hostage if the United States would not only sell more arms to Iran but also induce the Kuwaiti government to release the terrorists held in Kuwaiti prison for their part in the December 12, 1983, attacks in Kuwait on the U.S. embassy, the French embassy, and several Kuwaiti government facilities. The release of the prisoners did not succeed, but the arms (TOW missiles) were sold to the Iranians. The release of two other American hostages followed soon after but at different periods, and more profit was generated for the Enterprise. The Iran initiative to that point had brought about the release of three hostages, but three more Americans were kidnapped within the same period. The third hostage, David Jacobsen, was released on November 2, 1986.

In all, about $48 million was realized from the arms sales to Iran and in contributions by foreign governments and American citizens directed to the Enterprise by North. The Contras received about $16.5 million, $15.2 million was spent on arms for Iran, and $6.6 million went to Hakim, Secord, and their associates as commissions and profits. In addition, $4.2 million was held in reserves for use in further operations, $1.2 million remained in Swiss bank accounts of the Enterprise, and several thousand dollars were used to pay for a security system at North's residence. Hakim and Secord also established the "B. Button" investment account in the amount of $200,000 to persuade North to remain in his White House position. The funds purportedly were to be used for the education of North's children. In his testimony to the investigative committee, North denied any knowledge of this fund.

The Cover-Up

As the story of the Iran-Contra plan became known, the officials who were responsible for creating and implementing it devised several strategies to answer to the public. In his first public statement on the subject on November 6, 1986, the president said that the arms sales reports had "no foundation." On November 13, 1986, he conceded that there was an arms sale, but branded as "utterly false" allegations that the sales were a direct swap for the hostages. At his news conference on November 19, 1986, the president denied U.S. involvement in the Israeli sales that occurred prior to January 17, 1986. At a news conference on November 25, 1986, Attorney General Ed Meese, with the president at his side, announced that the president knew of the Israeli shipments only after they had occurred. In spite of all this, the president continued to deny vehemently that his actions were illegal.

Meanwhile, the president's subordinates, North and Poindexter, were engaged in strategies to conceal any incriminating documents. Because of concerns that the 1985 sales violated the Arms Export Control Act, they agreed on a cover story if the operation was exposed. The president's assistant secretary of state for the Central American region, Eliot Abrams, also professed no knowledge of these operations. He later stated that he had been "careful not to ask North a lot of questions" and confessed to having lied to Congress.

North, Poindexter, Casey, and McFarlane told conforming false stories about U.S. involvement in these shipments. McFarlane and North rewrote NSC chronologies on November 19 and 20, 1986, in a manner that denied knowledge by the administration of Israeli's shipments to Iran in 1985. The NSC members asserted at one point that the United States believed the November 1985 shipment consisted only of oil-drilling equipment. At a congressional committee's public hearing in December 1986, North conceded that he had participated in "making false, misleading, evasive and wrong" statements to Congress.

On November 21, 1986, Poindexter told congressional committees that the United States had disapproved of the Israeli shipments and that, until the day before his briefing, he believed that administration officials did not know about them until after they had occurred. He then destroyed the only Finding signed by the president that showed otherwise. According to North, a "fall guy" plan was proposed by Casey in which North and, if necessary, Poindexter would be the scapegoats of the operation. On November 22, 1986, in the effort to conceal their actions, Poindexter had a two-and-one-half-hour lunch with Casey, but Poindexter could not recall any of their substantive discussions.

Upon learning that the president had asked the attorney general to gather the relevant facts, North and Poindexter shredded and altered official documents. North's secretary, Fawn Hall, concealed classified documents in her clothing and, with North's knowledge, removed them from the White House.

Prior to the discovery of the diversion of funds, each interview by the attorney general's fact-finding team had been conducted in the presence of two witnesses and careful notes had been taken in accordance with standard professional practices. A series of important interviews were conducted with Poindexter, Casey, Reagan, and Bush by the attorney general alone after the diversion discovery, but no notes were taken. Poindexter testified before the congressional investigative committee that the president knew nothing of the diversion. North testified that he had assumed the president authorized each diversion until Poindexter told him the opposite on November 21, 1986. The attorney general had earlier stated that the president had not known of the Israeli shipment before he signed the President's Finding. He further said that the proceeds from the arms sales were diverted directly to the Contras by Israel. The congressional investigative report described the attorney general's account [about the pre-Finding shipment] and direct Israeli involvement in the diversion of funds to the Contras as "both mistaken and inconsistent with information that had been received during the Attorney General's fact-finding inquiry" (U.S. Congress, 1987, 11).

The congressional investigative committee on the Iran-Contra Affair described the plan as having "the common ingredients of . . . secrecy, deception and disdain for the law." It further stated,

The United States Constitution specifies the process by which laws and policy are to be made and executed. Constitutional process is the essence of our Democracy and our Democratic form of Government is the basis of our strength. . . . We have learned that a flawed process leads to bad results and that a lawless process leads to worse (U.S. Congress, 1987, 11).

Analysis

The Iran-Contra affair could be read in a political sense, as a sensational, unique event, or as reflective of an unauthorized delegation of authority and bureaucratic unaccountability in a democracy. The activities of the NSC staff involved in the scandal clearly illustrated abuse and misuse of discretionary powers. The role of ascription in public policy administration is invaluable and unavoidable. However, such power should be professionally managed with a great deference to ethics and the law.

The Tower Commission and the congressional investigative committee report described the Iran-Contra scandal as characteristic of a "flawed policy process." The president's departure from the democratic processes (by evading congressional and public scrutiny) created the conditions for policy failure. These conditions also led to contradictions, confusion, secrecy, and dishonesty, which undermined the credibility of the president and the United States. The use of private citizens in such an important, major foreign policy endeavor, they said, is a mockery of the doctrine of "representative bureaucracy." It seemed that the private motives for profits and self-aggrandizement took precedence over national security interest. Does this notion of a "flawed policy process" relieve the president or those to whom he delegated powers of any accountability?

An integral constitutional issue at the heart of this Iran-Contra plan concerns the principle of "separation of powers" and "checks and balances" between the legislative and executive branches. An example is the president's power in foreign affairs; the president is preeminent, but he also shares those powers with the Congress. The president justified this inherent power because of the intelligence information involved in the Iran-Contra plan. The need for secrecy and confidentiality of the intelligence were the mitigating circumstances that led to the president's decision not to inform the Congress. Would the president's rationalization hold in light of the private businessmen who acted as the unofficial "ambassadors" of the United States? Or does the president's rationale imply an inherent distrust between the legislature and the executive? Would there be exceptions to complying with this democratic process or the shared-powers principle?

The Tower Commission recommended that the president "must at the outset provide guidelines to the members of the NSC . . . , and its staff," and that the president should intervene when his advisers are not performing according to his guidelines and procedures. It further recommended that the NSC adviser should be a person who is "skilled, sensitive, and with integrity" for managing this process of policy execution on a daily basis. The commission also called for NSC staff that are "highly competent, and experienced in the making of public policy. Staff members should be drawn from within and outside of government" (*Tower Commission Report* 1987, 12).

The congressional investigative committee recommended that oversight capabilities of the intelligence committees of Congress be strengthened by acquiring an audit staff and that this staff should conduct reviews of sole-source contracts entered into by executive agencies so that it could identify possible abuses. The report called for uniform and secure procedures for handling classified information by Congress, and for prescribing clear and strong sanctions for abuse of intelligence information by its members. The report also called on the president to uphold the constitutional oath "to take care that the laws are faithfully executed" as a moral and legal responsibility.

Are the above recommendations adequate for addressing the problems of bureaucratic accountability? Are these recommended controls (internal, external, professionalism, and wide bureaucratic representation) compatible with the inevitability of administrative discretion? Was the Iran-Contra affair a problem created by the president's management style, as the Tower Commission said?

In March, 1988, Lt. Col. Oliver North was indicted by a special prosecutor along with Poindexter, Hakim, Secord, and others, for crimes related to the operation of the Iran initiative, the diversion of funds, and other related activities that led to the possible violations of laws. McFarlane pleaded guilty to similar charges earlier. North was convicted in 1989, and Poindexter in 1990, on these charges. Both received relatively light sentences. The president was politically hurt and embarrassed by the hypocrisy of this episode and for pleading ignorance about activities related to his policy. He put himself in a no-win situation. If he said he didn't know what was going on in the NSC and in the White House basement, he was guilty of lax leadership and bad management; if he did know about it, he was guilty of violating the laws and his own expressed policy about terrorism. Was there any way out of this dilemma?

Discussion Questions
1. How can members of the White House staff be made more accountable?
2. What *external* mechanisms can be established to increase control and accountability of the White House staff?
3. What *internal* mechanisms can be created for this purpose?
4. What ethical and professional standards are relevant in this particular situation?
5. Should there have been greater control by and accountability to Congress by those involved in this policy formulation and implementation, or did they behave in a justifiable manner?

NOTE

1. Much of the research for this case study was done by Ernest Uwazie, a Ph.D. candidate in Justice Studies at Arizona State University. We are indebted to him for his excellent assistance. The Iran-Contra case is used in Chapter 2 to deal with questions of organizational structure. Here we focus on the accountability aspects of this historically rich case study.

CHAPTER 11

Program Evaluation and Public Management

Evaluations can have a large impact on public policies and programs. For example, an evaluation of a program aimed at reducing crime in a Bronx, New York, public housing project through the use of television monitoring by tenants was found to be ineffective (Musheno, Levine, and Palumbo 1978). As a result of this evaluation (and probably other factors as well), the U.S. Department of Housing and Urban Development decided not to use any of the $30 million allocated by Congress to improve security in public housing for projects such as the one in the Bronx (Newman 1980).

Of course, not all evaluations have an immediate and direct impact such as this. In fact, the general conclusion is that evaluations do not have immediate direct and instrumental use (Weiss 1981). There is some question about exactly what role evaluations should play in shaping public programs (Nachmias and Felbinger 1982; Palumbo and Nachmias 1984). We discuss this issue in more detail later in the chapter, but whatever role evaluations play, it is generally agreed that they cannot be the only factor in deciding whether a program should be continued. This position reflects the most recent development in a field that has undergone several changes since it began.

Since the 1960s, evaluation has gone through several stages. During the 1960s, the field was in its infancy and just beginning to develop. During the 1970s, the concern was to build consensus on evaluation purposes and standards. During the 1980s, the focus was on utilization of evaluations and the role of evaluation in public management (Chelimsky 1985). There was considerable doubt during the period about the effectiveness of evaluation, but to the extent to which public management aims at helping managers produce results, evaluation can play a crucial role for them. For example, Wholey (1979) would have managers specify substantive goals and objectives and make evaluation an integral part of managing a program to stay on that course. This idealistic notion of public management is not often put into pracice, nor can it be, for public management involves more than achieving measurable and specific results: It also is a human activity that involves the careers, lives, hopes, and expectations of those who work for governments and those who are affected by government (which could mean all of us). Public management is a rational activity, but is also a symbolic, political, ritualistic, power-oriented, and representational activity. So, while public management must be concerned with program planning, design, implementation, and evaluation, these are not the be-all and end-all of public management. Nevertheless, they are important functions of public management. In this chapter we focus specifically on the role of program evaluation in public management. Implementation is the subject of Chapter 12.

THE DEVELOPMENT OF PROGRAM EVALUATION

Evaluating programs has been a significant activity and responsibility of public administrators since the early 1960s. Although evaluating is a human activity that has been going on for centuries, not until the late 1950s in education, and the 1960s in other policy areas, has scientific evaluation played a systematic role in public administration.

One of the major forerunners of evaluation are the program planning and budgeting techniques that were introduced into the Defense Department by President Kennedy's secretary of defense, Robert McNamara. While he was at the Ford Motor Company, McNamara was one of the principal proponents of using quantitative methods and statistics to make production decisions. Part of a group that was known as the "Whiz Kids," McNamara belonged to the new class in American business who did not believe that knowledge was concrete about a product but abstract about systems. He pioneered a new kind of economic and managerial philosophy that he believed would make Ford Motor Company a better company. McNamara sought rationality in an irrational world. Journalist David Halberstam (1986, 210) says of McNamara:

> He was the forerunner of a revolution. He was a manager who was also a genius with numbers. He could see their meaning, indeed their truth, long before others around him; he could see the relationships betweem numbers where others saw nothing. At his best he was dazzling, and the rigors of meeting his standards forced a generation of his subordinates to be far more exacting in their own use of numbers, to become experts who could scan a sheet and pick out the one number that was wrong.

When he arrived in Washington, McNamara brought with him the same passion for numbers that he had used at Ford. He helped develop decision methods that became known as program planning and budgeting systems (PPBS). The goal was to convince managers to think in terms of concrete objectives to be achieved and the amount of resources that would be needed to achieve different levels of these objectives. Decisions about the combination of resources needed to achieve a greater amount of units of program objectives were to be made through sophisticated mathematical modeling and computer simulation.

President Lyndon B. Johnson was so enamored of PPBS that he encouraged all federal departments to adopt it. But these attempts at replacing the old line-item budgeting procedures with more synoptic, rational procedures failed and by the late 1960s, attempts to extend and routinize PPBS at the federal level were abandoned.

In its early formation in universities, evaluation was considered to be a part of applied social science research, a way that social scientists could contribute to improving social conditions. In the general social and political turmoil in which evaluation research developed in the 1960s, social scientists were urged by some of their more socially active colleagues to come out of their academic ivory towers and help solve the many social problems besetting the country. They were told that their research and teaching should be "relevant" to the problems of the times. No longer should they engage in research simply for the sake of seeking knowledge; it was their responsibility, these activists said, to find solutions to social problems.

Researchers believed that it was possible to discover the "facts" in the real world that existed independently of the researcher, and that the researcher doing the evaluation could be an objective, natural observer of these facts. Thus, evaluators and policy analysts could not say anything about values or goals; the most they could do was to provide decision makers with information about the most efficient way of achieving given goals. One of the leading policy analysts at the time, Russell Ackoff (1969, viii), said about the book he wrote: "It is a book on planning or designing the use of science in the pursuit of objectives. It leaves open the questions of what objectives ought to be pursued, what problems should be sovled, and what questions should be answered."

Another strand or approach to evaluating programs had been developing simultaneously with operations research. This kind of program evaluation was used primarily in evaluating educational and teaching programs. It has its roots in early studies of educational effectiveness. During the 1930s, the landmark Eight Year Study developed by Ralph Tyler conceptualized the objectives-based approach to educational evaluation and developed instruments to measure a wide range of educational outcomes (Worthen and Sanders 1987, 15). But the greatest impact for educational evaluation came in the 1960s with the Coleman study in 1965–1966 of equal educational opportunity for minority children. Coleman (1966) looked at variations among a set of schools in staffing levels, finances, student composition, and physical plants. They found that differences in these variables were not related very strongly to student achievement. The Elementary and Secondary Education Act (ESEA) of 1965 further fueled evaluation in its requirement that educators file an evaluation report for each grant showing what was achieved with the federal funds.

In the late 1960s, social psychologist Donald Campbell proposed what became known as "the experimenting society." He wrote an article entitled "Reforms as Experiments" (1971) in which he argued that we ought to treat government programs as "natural experiments" to test whether they worked. The example he used was a crackdown on speeders in Connecticut. The objective was to determine whether changes in highway fatality rates could be attributed to tougher enforcement of speeding laws in Connecticut. Year-by-year statistics about the number of highway fatalities were plotted on a graph. The question was whether a statistically significant drop in fatalities occurred after the crackdown was implemented and whether the drop could be attributed to the crackdown or other, uncontrolled factors. Since the question could not be answered using regular experimental methods, Campbell proposed developing a new set of methods called quasi-experimental design.

Early policy analysis and program evaluation emphasized methodological concerns. The early emphasis of Campbell and Stanley (1966) and Cook and Campbell (1979) was on ways to make findings valid. In the early development of the concept, two aspects of validity were distinguished: *internal* and *external* validity. The former refers to all the variables other than the intervention itself that might explain the outcome. For example, in a crackdown on speeders initiated for the purpose of reducing the number of highway fatalities, suppose that a statistically significant decrease is seen in the number of highway fatalities after the crackdown is implemented (the intervention). Because we do not have a controlled experiment, the observed drop in fatalities could be the result of a number of other variables in addition to the crackdown. The number of fatalities might have reached a peak from which it would drop without the intervention simply because it had become very high and there always are natural swings in such events. This is called *regression* and it is not caused by the intervention. Or, the drop may be due to changes in weather or road conditions, or new safety features on cars (such as better shoulder belts or air bags). To achieve internal validity so that we might say the drop in fatalities could be attributed to the crackdown, it would be necessary to rule out these and similar explanations.

External validity is concerned with generalizing to similar crackdowns in other states at other times. External validity asks: "What have we learned? Are the findings relevant for other situations and places or are they limited to the specific cases studied?" Campbell and Cook developed a number of methods for achieving a degree of internal and external validity but put most of their stress on internal validity.

In recent years, the emphasis on internal validity has been severely criticized by evaluation researchers (Lincoln and Guba 1985; Cronbach et al. 1980) and even by the originators of the concepts of internal and external validity (Cook 1985; Campbell 1987). Leading evaluators (Cronbach et al. 1980) said that the role of evaluation is not to produce authoritative truths but to clarify, raise questions, and create new perspectives. Evaluations should be judged by their contribution to public thinking. Thus, the stress on internal validity is misplaced, said psychologist L. J. Cronbach and associates (1980) and more attention should be paid to external validity.

Even more significantly, other evaluators began to question whether evaluating actually is research (Guba and Lincoln 1987, 1990; Patton 1986). The two are to be distinguished in this view because they have different goals, audiences, and intended outcomes. Table 11.1 lists a number of dimensions on which the two activities differ.

As the table shows, there are several dimensions on which the two activities differ, at least in an ideal sense. Hence, evaluations cannot be judged by the usual academic standards. Moreover, evaluations usually require a multidisciplinary approach because policy problems do not respect disciplinary boundaries.

The idea of an experimenting society caught on in the 1970s and spawned a whole new approach to reaching valid conclusions about the impact of public programs. Program evaluation took off rapidly in the 1970s. Several new books appeared (Weiss 1972a, 1972b; Caro 1971), the Evaluation Research Society was formed in 1971, and the federal government began to require that a certain portion of funds appropriated for programs be set aside for evaluation. By the late 1970s, the

TABLE 11.1. Differences between Evaluation and Research

Evaluation	Research
1. Problems originate outside the academic description	Problems originate among the community of scholars
2. The audience is the world of action	The audience is fellow scholars
3. There are explicit deadlines and time constraints	There are no deadlines or time constraints
4. Cannot be neutral	Attempts to be objective
5. Goal is control or change of programs or decisions	Goal is to add to knowledge
6. Language should be simple and based on common sense	Language is esoteric and jargonistic
7. Redundancy is required	Parsimony is desired
8. Studies are not replicated or even replicable	Studies must be replicated

federal government was spending hundreds of millions of dollars on evaluation. The Program Evaluation and Methodology Division (PEMD) of the U.S. General Accounting Office (GAO) was created in 1974. It was charged with the responsibility of conducting program evaluations and helping other GAO divisions in their program evaluations. By the early 1980s, there were some 228 federal agencies conducting evaluations. In 1980 alone, nondefense cabinet department agencies spent more than $177 million for program evaluation. A total of 1,353 full-time professionals conducted 2,362 evaluations, 60 percent of which were under contract with external organizations (Institution of Program Evaluation 1982, 3).

State governments also developed an interest in program evaluation in the 1970s. By 1980, forty states had accepted a commitment to program evaluation. Between 1976 and 1979, thirty-four states adopted "sunset" laws (Henry and Smiley 1981). These laws required that an agency prove it was accomplishing its objectives; otherwise the agency would be eliminated.

The experimenting society approach to evaluation differed from PPBS and policy analysis in several ways. First, its disciplinary base was psychology and educational psychology rather than economics. Second, program evaluation takes place after a program has been designed and implemented rather than before. PPBS and policy analysis are techniques for determining which alternatives will achieve given objectives most efficiently. Analysis is done before decisions are made although data about existing programs may be used in the analysis. Program evaluation is done after a program has been implemented; in its initial formulation, it was concerned with whether a program achieved its objectives. Finally, policy analysis and program evaluation are different in the techniques they use. The former relies mostly on econometric and operations research methods such as cost-benefit analysis, while the latter uses interrupted time-series analysis and quasi-experimental methods (we describe some of these methods later in this chapter).

Not only are there differences between policy analysis and program evaluation, but there are numerous types of program evaluations and a variety of approaches to evaluation. In fact, *evaluation* does not have a single meaning.

THE DIFFERENT TYPES OF EVALUATION

Like the blind people touching different parts of the elephant, each analyst sees a different model, approach, or paradigm when he or she engages in evaluation. There are numerous types of evaluations. We shall not attempt to describe them all here. Instead, we will describe seven major types that we believe include all the important ones.

Objectives Oriented

The earliest, most practiced, but most heavily criticized approach is the objectives-oriented approach.[1] Sometimes called summative evaluation, or impact analysis (Mohr 1988), this type of evaluation identifies the objectives of the program and its specific purposes, and through rigorous scientific research methods it attempts to determine the extent to which they have been achieved. The approach is logical, scientific, and rationalist. Although its methods are complex, the objectives-oriented approach is clear and consistent, and thus has been the dominant paradigm in evaluations. The methods are highly quantitative and the practitioner using this model must be trained in advanced statistics, mathematics, and computer analysis. Because of the technical nature of this approach it has great legitimacy, particularly among administrators and professionals. It requires a considerable amount of expertise.

At the same time, the objectives-oriented approach has serious flaws. The most glaring is the misfit between its dependence on clear and attainable goals to evaluate and the reality that policy and program goals usually are ambiguous, multiple, and conflicting. This ambiguity often results from legislators' need to be vague about goals in order to build the coalitions needed to pass a bill. For example, in order to pass the Elementary and Secondary Act in 1965, the Congress had to say it was aimed at benefiting children rather than schools. Various groups were opposed to federal aid to schools: Catholic groups opposed the bill unless the aid was given to parochial schools as well as public schools, but various educational groups opposed giving aid to parochial schools. Others opposed giving aid only to disadvantaged children, which was the main purpose of the bill. The concept of child benefit was a way around this, but it created problems during implementation. Because the legislation was so general, many states used the funds for general purposes rather than specifically for disadvantaged children, and the federal government did not have grounds to stop them. Thus it would be difficult to do a summative evaluation of this act because it does not have specific goals. When evaluators try to get an agency to be specific about the goals they are supposed to achieve, agency people fall into what Patton (1986) calls the "goal trap." This is an exercise agency personnel hate to engage in and one that they lose since it is usually the evaluators who ultimately specify the program's goals.

Another problem with the objectives approach is that goals often are not attainable; they serve symbolic purposes for policy makers: something that will win votes and support for them (Edelman 1964, 1988). The War on Poverty, for example, was full of overblown rhetoric. Regardless of whether this Johnson-era program actually reduced poverty (Palumbo 1988), to eliminate poverty completely is impossible and we know very little about how even to reduce it. In fact, most social problems do not have solutions; at best, public policy can only ameliorate the major negative ramifications of problems. Regarding programs to end welfare dependency, a prominent evaluation researcher, Carol Weiss (1987, 63), writes that "whatever eager sponsors may say, day-care centers will not end welfare dependency, and neighborhood government will not create widespread feelings of citizen efficacy. Programs should have more modest expectations (helping people to cope is not an unimportant contribution), and they should be evaluated against more reasonable goals."

The problem is in deciding who will determine what these "more reasonable goals" are. One way out of this dilemma is to follow the advice of a former president of the American Evaluation Association and do a "goal-free" evaluation (Scriven, 1972). In goal-free evaluation, the evaluator avoids specifying what the program goals are prior to the evaluation; instead, the evaluator attempts to determine what the program is actually achieving, and then decides whether it is meeting important societal needs. However, one critic of this approach says that "Scriven's goal-free model eliminates only one group from the game—local project staff. He directs data only in one clear direction—away from the stated concerns of people who run the program. . . . I am unconvinced that the standards he applies are other than his own preferences about what program effects are appropriate and morally defensible." (Patton 1986, iii)

Management Oriented

Several years after the initial surge of enthusiasm and optimism about objectives-oriented evaluation, evaluators began to realize that whether and how the program was being implemented was important in understanding *why* a program was or was not achieving its goals. Sometimes called "formative" evaluation, the purpose of management-oriented evaluation is to get inside the "black box" of a program. The black box contains the inputs and processes by which the inputs are converted into outputs (not outcomes, which are the impact of a program). In short, it is aimed at understanding how a program is being implemented.

Evaluating the implementation of a program involves the extent to which the program has been implemented as well as the process by which it has been evaluated. The extent has at least two components (Scheirer 1987). One is the accuracy (is it serving the right clients?) and the other is the scope (is it serving a sufficient proportion of those in need?).

The *process* of implementing concerns the organizational and administrative arrangements by which the program is being implemented. Programs can be implemented by top-down or bottom-up approaches, or a combination of the two, the interactive approach. Top down refers to attempts of those at the top of an organization to control and direct the behavior of those lower down so that the program achieves the goals those at the top believe are legitimate. Bottom-up implementation refers to a situation in which those who have contact with clients—the street-level bureaucrats—determine what should be done. Those who favor this approach believe that those who interact with clients know best what their needs are. (For a more complete discussion of these and other theories about the process of implementation see Chapter 12.) Interactive implementation involves both the top and bottom levels of an agency in determining what objectives are to be achieved.

A management-oriented evaluation provides managers with information they can use about the kinds of clients the program is serving, and what might be done to improve this service. For example, it can help to determine whether a program is being managed properly and whether it is getting the support of those at the street level. At the same time, formative or management-oriented evaluation can have the defect of being used by the upper echelon of an organization to identify dissenters or those who do not agree with what is being done (see Chapter 10 on administrative accountability and whistle-blowing). Evaluators in this situation are little more than hired guns. There are many stakeholders for a program besides its managers, and they all have a legitimate interest in specifying how a program should be implemented, particularly with regard to the extent, accuracy, and scope of implementation. For example, a community corrections program has as stakeholders probation officers, judges, prosecutors, sheriffs, corrections department officials, service providers, community board members, halfway house personnel, and the offenders themselves (Palumbo 1987).

Stakeholder Evaluation

When the views of all stakeholders, not just top management, are included in an evaluation, the evaluation is called a *stakeholder evaluation* (Stake 1975). All programs have a number of different stakeholders—that is, individuals and groups who have a stake in the success or failure of the program. These include legislators, administrators, various interest groups, citizens at large, supporters and opponents of the program, and clients. When the views and perspectives of all these groups are included in the planning and execution of an evaluation, we have a stakeholder evaluation.

Such an evaluation has the advantage of considering the views and needs of a large group of individuals and groups rather than a limited audience. It is thus more in accord with pluralist concepts of democracy since all stakeholders are deemed to have a legitimate voice and perspective to contribute. The principal disadvantage of such evaluations lies in the difficultly of resolving competing views about which program goals are most (and which are least) important. Thus, reaching a consensus about how well a program is being implemented may be difficult. A stakeholder evaluation may produce a variety of perspectives about how well the program is doing, leaving it to the agency that commissioned the evaluation to balance them.

Consumer Oriented

Consumer-oriented evaluations are used primarily for evaluating physical products such as computer software, supplies, or police vehicles. This is generally done through performance testing. Tests are run with the specific needs of the particular consumer in mind (e.g., how do police use their vehicles). The principal goal is to verify the claims of the manufacturer.

Expertise Oriented

For some purposes the views of experts are used to determine the merit and worth of a program. Professional experts are used to judge an institution or program such as a medical school or neonatal care program. The National Association of Schools of Public Administration is one such organization. It inspects the facilities, professors, and curriculum of member institutions to determine whether they measure up to the standards set by the organization. In some cases, certification by the experts is necessary to the survival of the institution (similar to accreditation for a college).

Experts also can be used to estimate values of variables in techniques such as cost-benefit analysis (described below). Expert judgment might be used to estimate how many injuries would be avoided if all automobiles were equipped with passive restraint devices. This estimation could be used in conjunction with studies or experiments or in lieu of such studies.

Experts also are used in areas such as determining whether discrimination has occurred in hiring or firing of employees and in malpractice sutis against professionals. Because courts have used statistical data as prima facie evidence of discrimination, statistical experts are hired by lawyers in discrimination cases.

Adversarial Oriented

Because evaluations cannot really be impartial and objective, it may be possible to achieve a degree of objectivity through adversarial evaluation. In this type of evaluation, both positive and negative views of a program are sought out. This could be done by assigning one part of the evaluation team the responsibility of uncovering negative things and another the responsibility of uncovering positive things about the program. The two views can be given to a panel of judges who will resolve them into a single view. In other cases alternatives by both sides can be presented to the decision makers who will decide which has more credibility. Another approach is to assign a resident critic to each evaluation; the critic's function is to challenge each bit of information turned up by the evaluators.

Adversarial evaluation has several advantages. It provides a broader range of information than other approaches. Since it presents conflicting views, it heightens interest; it can also be combined with other approaches. It is open to all stakeholders—the opponents as well as the supporters of a program. It anticipates and therefore blunts criticisms of the evaluation. Its use is appropriate when the program affects many people and generates wide interest, and when there are sufficient resources to conduct this kind of evaluation.

Adversarial evaluation has a number of disadvantages as well. It is not oriented toward compromise, the forensic skill of each adversary may be more important than the data in influencing a decision, it is polemical, and there is no supreme court to which to appeal for a definitive view.

Naturalistic

Naturalistic evaluation[2] is an alternative to the objectives-oriented, quantitative approach. Its advocates argue that the conventional approach does not tell us enough about the substance of programs. Because the conventional approach breaks programs into bits called *variables,* it sometimes obscures a broad, encompassing view of the whole program (Lincoln and Guba 1985). A naturalistic approach aims at describing the specific components and setting of a program; this type of information will be more useful to decision makers than to those who are trying to find general factors applicable to all programs (McClintock 1987).

The most important aspect of the naturalistic approach is its approach to knowledge. In the view of its proponents, there is no single truth or reality "out there" waiting to be discovered by a detached scientist. Instead, evaluations "create" reality through the research involved. The reality created is multiple, reflecting the views of all stakeholders rather than just a limited set of them.

Designing an evaluation through a naturalistic method is never static. An evaluation design evolves as it proceeds, like a "smart bomb"; it constantly changes course to home in on its target. The design of the evaluation keeps changing in response to stakeholders. The evaluator, therefore, is both learner and teacher, not an expert authority who imposes his or her view on the program.

A naturalistic evaluation is judged by its credibility rather than its truth (see Bozeman and Landsbergen 1989). Stakeholders for whom an evaluation is done have some preconceived notions about the program. An evaluation will be more or less credible to them to the extent it fits with and expands on these notions. Because it avoids technical jargon, the result of a naturalistic evaluation will be easier to communicate to decision makers.

Naturalistic inquiry has been criticized on several grounds. It is too subjective, say some critics, and therefore not as credible with decision makers. Because it canot be specific about the design of an evaluation, it is not as easily taught as conventional evaluation methods. Findings about a program are too context-specific and cannot be generalized to other possible applications.

Each of the seven approaches to evaluation described above has advantages and disadvantages. Some (e.g., consumer oriented) fit better in some situations (e.g., evaluating products) than others (e.g., evaluating a Head Start program). As we will see when we describe evaluation methods, a mixture of approaches is better than any single one.

EVALUABILITY ASSESSMENT (EA)

One of the first things to do when conducting an evaluation is an evaluability assessment. As originally developed, the concept meant determining which parts of a program actually could be evaluated (Wholey 1979). The assumption is that not all parts of a program can be evaluated because the objectives may not be clear or even known, or they may not have been implemented sufficiently. Evaluability assessment is meant to identify those parts of a program that are amenable to being evaluated and to allow the evaluators and those being evaluated to reach agreement about what it is that will be evaluated.

It is not always possible to do an evaluability assessment first, and then to proceed with the actual evaluation. Borrowing from the naturalistic approach, evaluators can conduct an evaluability assessment as they conduct the first stage of the evaluation.

The initial step in evaluability assessment is to diagram the program by collecting information about it. The various components and activities of the program should be linked together to show the outputs and outcomes that are expected to be related to the program inputs (see Chapter 2). In Figure 11.1, a juvenile delinquency program is diagrammed showing that after juveniles are committed to the department of corrections by the courts, they are diagnosed and assigned to one of two different facilities. Each facility provides various but somewhat different services, based on the diagnosed needs of the juveniles. The services are provided by staff counselors, psychologists, and educational specialists. In addition, each facility has a security staff and administrators. After spending a specified period of time in the facility (usually three to four months) the juveniles are released into the community with the expectation that they will avoid criminal behavior, get a job, and return to school. The purpose of the evaluation is first to describe how the programs are being implemented at each facility and to determine whether the desired outcomes occur as a result of the treatment provided in each facility. Other factors, such as maturation or the kind of family situation the child faces, can also influence what happens to the juveniles after they leave the facility (this example is expanded on in the case study for this chapter). These factors would be controlled in analyzing the data collected during the evaluation.

The purpose of the evaluation assessment is to determine which program performance measures are feasible. For example, can the kind of therapy being provided in the juvenile facility be measured and a how will this be measured? It is also necessary to identify the realistic objectives of the program and how they can be measured. For example, if the juveniles are in the facility for only three months, can we realistically expect that their behavior, once they are released, will be influenced by the treatment provided in the institution? These questions and suggestions about what objectives should be measured are then presented to program managers and other stakeholders with the purpose of reaching agreement on an evaluation plan.

An important component of evaluation assessment is to determine the purpose of the evaluation. (As we will see below, this step moves us into the politics of program evaluation.) The relevant questions are these: Who needs the evaluation and what do they want to know? Perhaps the program managers want to know only the kinds of services being delivered, or what the staff and clients think of the program.

In addition, the evaluator should try to determine the use to which the evaluation will be put and by whom. This is an important component of utilization-focused evaluation (Patton 1986). According to its leading proponent, utilization-focused evaluation sets up a task force consisting of representatives of the various groups and constituencies that have a stake in the evaluation findings and their utilization. Members of the task force should be people "who have authority and power to use evaluation findings in decision making, or to influence others who do have such power and

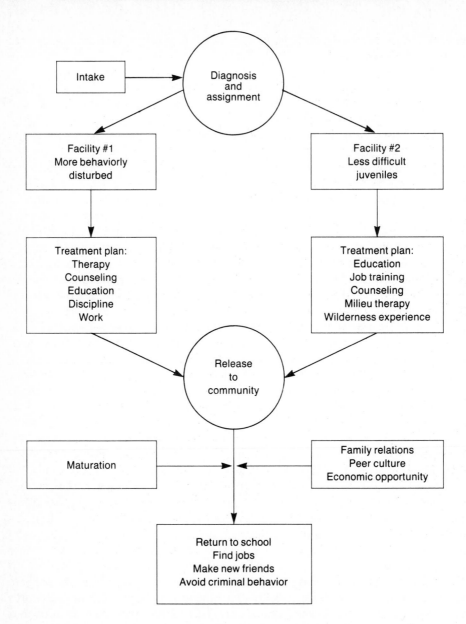

Figure 11.1. Program Diagram for Juvenile Delinquency Program

authority.'' (Patton 1987, 124). The task force would conceptualize the issues, consider ways of conducting the evaluation and measuring the variables, design the evaluation and review the instrument, and help interpret the data.

It is also important at this stage to begin identifying the political context surrounding the evaluation. All evaluations are political in the sense that they are commissioned by individuals with a political stake in their outcome, they are fed into a political decision-making process, and they take a stand on program success or failure (Palumbo 1987; Weiss 1987). However, it is not possible to uncover the political context entirely at the beginning of an evaluation. Details are discovered as the evaluation proceeds. The important point is for the evaluator to know the political realities that surround the evaluation. Otherwise the evaluation is likely to have little impact or it will be used negatively by politicians who oppose the program (Palumbo 1987, 13). We will discuss the politics of evaluation in more detail later in the chapter.

IMPACT ANALYSIS

Impact (or summative) evaluation is concerned with the accomplishments of a program relative to its goals (Mohr 1988). In this sense, it is quite the opposite of goal-free evaluation, which is concerned primarily with what the program has done regardless of its goals. In doing an impact analysis, one must assume that there is a theory underlying the program and one must identify that theory (Chen and Rossi 1983). Impact analysis is a test of this theory. For example, in the juvenile delinquency program diagrammed in Figure 11.1, we have listed components of the program, but by themselves they do not tell us what the theory is underlying the program. The theory links the components together and tells us how the program is supposed to affect the problem (Bickman 1987). To return to the juvenile delinquency example, there are several major theories about the causes of juvenile delinquency. Some are biological. These assert that nutritional problems (e.g., too much sugar) lead to aggressive behavior. Others are psychological. These are the heart and soul of the medical model of treatment that has dominated juvenile corrections for years. These theories assert that problem behavior in juveniles is linked to personality pathology. There are several treatment approaches to correcting this, including psychotherapy and behavior modification. Psychotherapy involves one-on-one "talk" therapy and is expensive. Moreover, it is not very successful with troubled youth. Behavior modification is more popular because it has scientific credibility, is simple to implement, and is inexpensive. Behavior modification involves setting up a system of rewards and greater degrees of freedom which individuals earn for behaving in the desired fashion.

In doing an impact assessment, the evaluator must determine what theory is being used (sometimes a number of different theories may be used) (see Chen and Rossi 1983). The goal is to determine what happened to the clients after the theory was implemented compared to what would have happened if the theory had not been implemented. There are several sophisticated statistical methods that are used to do this; they will not be described here (see Mohr 1988; Bingham and Felbinger 1989). We should mention, however, that it usually is difficult to determine unequivocally if there is actually a difference in outcomes and if the difference that is observed is due to the program as opposed to other, uncontrolled variables. A major dilemma of impact assessment is that in order to determine whether the observed difference is due to the program, it is necessary to create an artificial laboratory situation in which all variables other than the treatment are controlled. However, results of such an assessment cannot be generalized with confidence to other populations or treatments because the study situation is so unique. This is the trade-off problem between internal and external validity. The more internal validity we get, the less external validity we have. For this reason, many evaluation professionals have argued that impact assessment should not be the principal type of evaluation conducted (Cronbach et al., 1980). Moreover, while program managers and other stakeholders are interested in whether the program is achieving its objectives, they also are interested in learning how a program is being implemented and how it may be improved. This is the goal of process or formative evaluation.

PROCESS EVALUATION

Regardless of whether it is possible to do an *impact* evaluation, it is desirable to do a *process* evaluation because this will tell us what aspects of the program were responsible for producing the program outputs and outcomes. Moreover, there are several possible reasons for an evaluation to show that a program is a success or a failure. If an evaluation indicates that a program has failed, the program may be based on an inappropriate theory, the program implementation may be flawed, or the evaluation itself may be designed poorly. For example, if juvenile delinquency is caused by social factors such as family relations, inadequate job opportunities, or peer influence, using psychological therapy on the child won't do much good. Another reason for program failure may be inadequate implementation. Process evaluation will help determine whether this is the case, providing the evaluation is done correctly. The third cause for a finding of program failure may be a faulty evaluation rather than a problem with the program. A poorly designed evaluation may indicate that a program is not working when in fact it is.

The purpose of a process evaluation is to get inside the program and examine the linkage between its inputs and outputs. The inputs are the human and material resources used in the program and the outputs are the things that are done with these resources. How these resources are put together to produce the outputs is important to evaluation; it concerns how a program is being implemented. As we said above, this involves the scope as well as the process of implementation.

The scope questions pertain to whether the appropriate clients are being targeted as well as whether all of those in need are being included. The process questions pertain to the management style and organizational structure through which the program is implemented. Thus, a process evaluation will try to answer the following questions:

1. Who are the clients in the program?
2. Are they the ones who should be in the program?
3. What proportion of those in need of the service are in the program?
4. Do the staff and clients participate in making decisions about the services?
5. How much agreement is there among all levels of the organization about the goals of the program?
6. Is the program flexible so that it can be adapted to local circumstances?

A process evaluation contributes to construct validity. Following are four types of validity in evaluation:

1. *Internal:* This is achieved if all of the variables other than the treatment or intervention are controlled.
2. *External:* This is achieved if it is possible to generalize to other settings about what factors will contribute to program success.
3. *Construct:* This is achieved if there is a demonstrable relationship between theoretical constructs and their measurement.
4. *Statistical Conclusion:* This is achieved if the probability of errors (type I, rejecting a true hypothesis, and type 2, accepting a false hypothesis) is kept at acceptable levels.

Many evaluations use causal models to explain the relationships among variables. These models are used to answer the question: "Did the intervention or treatment cause the specific outcomes?" The reasoning is that if the causal factors can be isolated, the program can be put in place in another location. But even if something works in one place, it might not in other locations. Suppose one evaluation indicated that a juvenile delinquency program was successful primarily because it had full cooperation from the local school. The same program might not work in another location if the local school there were not so cooperative. In addition, even though a program produces good results in one location, we may not want to replicate it in a second location because of the way it has to be implemented. To illustrate, suppose we find that a community development program works (i.e., results in new buildings and businesses) in one location because the elite control it. We would not necessarily want to use this same model in another location; we may want to improve it to allow the less fortunate to have some control over it. In the first program, perhaps most of the new jobs went to the middle class instead of the poor who were supposed to be one of the target groups. We might want to change this outcome in future applications. Replication is important in scientific research when we are trying to determine whether a particular relationship holds. But it is not always appropriate in social programs if we want to improve future applications and learn from past mistakes.

COST-BENEFIT ANALYSIS

Cost-benefit analysis has the potential for being an important instrument of policy analysis. Some would say that it *is* policy analysis. Certainly, the terminology of cost-benefit analysis and, even more so, cost-effectiveness, is a standard part of the vocabulary of public officials and the mass media. A program that is not declared to be cost effective could hardly be supported in American culture.

Yet, for all its promise, cost-benefit analysis has many, many flaws.

- It applies only to policies and programs in which goals are clear and implementation is a technical and automatic matter. Not many programs are like this.

- It cannot be used in human service programs because we cannot translate goals in these areas into monetary terms (as we will see below, it is difficult to measure the economic value of worker safety).
- It can be manipulated easily so that the results are determined by whoever is doing the analysis.

However, it does have some use because its analytical rigor makes us think through policy problems in ways that we would not if we did not use it. It is important to recognize that policy decisions should not be based on cost-benefit analysis alone. As we will discuss in the last section of this chapter on utilization, political feasibility and practical concerns also are important factors in shaping policy decisions.

The General Theory

Cost-benefit analysis is an economist's tool. The philosophical assumption is that rational individuals will pursue their own self-interests. The same notion applies even if we are talking about an agency or a bureaucracy. For example, micro-economic theory tells us that bureaucracies will attempt to grow and ensure their survival because that is in their self-interest, and they have no incentive to be efficient because they do not face competition (Bennett and DiLorenzo 1983a).

The assumptions of cost-benefit analysis are as follows:

1. Policy makers are aware of all possible policy options.
2. It is possible to quantify the costs and benefits of each policy option.
3. There are no political constraints on adopting the preferred policy option.
4. The costs of each option are commensurable and can be expressed in monetary terms.
5. The benefits of each option are commensurable and can be expressed in monetary terms.

Micro-economic theory says that government intervention is justifiable only if there has been market failure; otherwise, the market mechanism is the best way to allocate resources among competing uses. Market failure can occur if there are barriers to entry (e.g., a monopoly), if externalities are excluded (e.g., an industry that does not pay the cost of cleaning the environment that it pollutes); and if we are dealing with public goods (i.e., a good which if produced people cannot be excluded from enjoying even if they do not pay; an example is clean air). The role of the policy analyst is to try to replicate the decision that would be made if the market were fully operating.

The criterion that is used in making the decision to adopt or not to adopt the policy is called the Pareto criterion (after the Italian sociologist and economist Vilfredo Pareto). The criterion says that if some individuals win and no one loses by the adoption of a policy, it should be adopted. The criterion has been criticized on the grounds that it does not take into account the distribution of the benefits; thus, by this test, if the group that benefits is the rich and the group that is simply not disadvantaged is the poor, the policy option would be considered desirable. In order to try to get around this problem, economists have proposed a substitute criterion that says a policy should be adopted even if it benefits only one group as long as those who gain can fully compensate the losers and still be better off (Weimer and Vining 1989, 243). This is known as the Kaldor-Hicks criterion after the economists who developed it (Kaldor, 1939; Hicks, 1940).

Cost-Benefit Analysis versus Cost-Effectiveness Analysis.   Cost-effectiveness analysis is a substitute for cost-benefit analysis when it is not possible to measure benefits in monetary terms. Suppose we cannot measure monetarily the benefits of rehabilitating juvenile offenders in a juvenile delinquency program. Cost-effectiveness analysis would simply measure the cost per juvenile who is rehabilitated. Measuring rehabilitation, of course, is difficult by itself, and we shall deal with this issue in the case study for this chapter. Here we want to note that cost-effectiveness analysis is not as informative as cost-benefit analysis because it simply tells us how much it costs for each unit of output; it does not tell us whether the costs are excessive.

Steps in Cost-Benefit Analysis

The first step in cost-benefit analysis is to specify goals. If the policy problem pertains to automobile safety, the goal might be lives saved by various policy options (e.g., mandatory seatbelt laws, use of air bags, safer automobiles, better designed roads, more driver education). In some programs it is not easy to specify and quantify goals. In a juvenile delinquency program, a goal may be to rehabilitate children. But what does that mean and how do we quantify it? There is a tendency to focus on narrow goals that can be quantified, such as recidivism (i.e., whether the person commits a crime or is returned to detention facilities within a specific time period). There are, however, many problems associated with using recidivism as a goal—problems which we cannot discuss here—and so the use of cost-benefit analysis in this case becomes questionable.

The next step is to assess the costs of each policy option. This is very difficult to do in most cases because there are different accounting approaches that can be used in assessing costs. The three below are often used:

1. *Operations Perspective.* Here the actual costs of personnel, facilities, equipment, and material are taken from the accounting ledgers of the agencies. But the accounting practices of different programs may not always be commensurable. Also, the agencies may hide some costs, and they may ignore the time that volunteers contribute to a program (which can be large in some social programs). Moreover, in certain programs some personnel may be paid less than they are worth. Critics claim that these are the circumstances that occur under privatization; they argue that private, for-profit agencies can deliver public goals and services cheaper than private agencies because they pay lower wages.

2. *Societal Perspective.* In this perspective, the value of all resources is estimated in terms of opportunity costs, that is, the costs of the other things that the money could be spent on if it were not spent on the program. This concept is very difficult to apply in a purely objective way, particularly if there is no market value for the options. For example, what is the cost of providing driver education in public schools? In these cases "shadow"

prices are used; these are estimates of what the prices would be if a market did exist. Obviously, there is a large subjective component in these estimates.

3. *Client Perspective.* This perspective can be used if the clients or target groups of a program pay for the program services. For example, in automobile safety, how much extra money would consumers pay for automobiles equipped with air bags? Again, it is difficult to determine this value because the actual cost could be determined only if air bags were being sold on the market on a wide basis.

Once the costs of each option are computed (using any of the three methods just described), the next step is to assess benefits. Many social programs have intangible benefits or benefits for which it is difficult to give a dollar value. Suppose we have two policy options; one saves 15,000 lives at a cost of $3 billion (or $200,000 a life) and the other saves 8,000 lives at a cost of $1 billion (or $125,000 a life). Which is to be preferred? On cost-effectiveness grounds, the second policy is to be preferred. But should we select the more cost-effective option when it saves far fewer lives? The answer depends on the monetary value we put on a life. If we set a high enough monetary value on each life saved, the first option will produce a better ratio. (Try this by assigning various monetary values to life, such as $100,000 per life and $300,000 per life). As we shall see in the section on politics and evaluation, the result usually depends on the political values of those who set the monetary values on the benefits and the situation to which cost-benefit analysis is being applied. For example, in the area of occupational safety, the Reagan administration downplayed the value of the lives and health of workers by assigning lower dollar values to these, and emphasized the costs to industry of making the workplace safe (Tolchin 1987). Thus, cost-benefit analysis is not merely an objective, technical matter; it is a political one as well.

Making Decisions with Cost-Benefit Ratios. A cost-benefit ratio is an appealing decision mechanism. It is simple to use; a ratio of more than 1 indicates that the benefits exceed the costs and a ratio of less than 1 means the costs exceed the benefits. Thus, the higher the ratio, the more desirable the option. Suppose the cost-benefit ratio for the option previously discussed that saves 15,000 lives is 1.8, and the ratio for the one that saves 8,000 lives is 3.4. The second is preferable if a decision is to be based solely on economic considerations. However, as we said above, policy decisions should not be based on economic criteria alone. Like program evaluations, cost-benefit ratios should be only one factor in a decision. Also, even if economic criteria are paramount, cost-benefit ratios have several drawbacks. One is that they hide information. Suppose two policy options have cost-benefit ratios of 4.2 and 4.8, respectively. The latter is better on the basis of cost-benefit alone. But suppose that its cost per client were $100,000 compared to $10,000 for the first option. In this case, even though the cost-benefit ratio is better, we might prefer the first option because the total costs would be much less if the same number of clients are in each program. Net benefits are a slightly better decision-making tool than cost-benefit analysis but they also do not take into account the total costs of each option. For example, suppose each of the two policy options just mentioned serves 100 clients; the total cost for the first would be $1,000,000, and for the second, it would be $10,000,000. The benefits for each would be $4,200,000 and $48,000,000, respectively. Thus, the net benefits would be $3,200,000 and $38,000,000. Obviously the second is still preferred. But if we are operating under a tight budget so that the $10 million required for the second option is not available, then the first would have to be selected. Thus, the raw data should be reported in any cost-benefit analysis.

POLITICS AND PROGRAM EVALUATION

According to Tolchin (1987), the Reagan administration used cost-benefit analysis as window dressing for its real purpose of deregulating and overturning Occupational Safety and Health Administration (OSHA) regulations. In cases such as the cotton-dust standards that OSHA adopted for the textile industry (breathing cotton dust may cause byssinosis, a lung disease), OSHA took the position that worker health and safety should be given priority as long as reaching the standard was feasible, even if the costs to industry were substantial. The Reagan administration gave higher priority to the cost to industry of decreasing cotton dust in the air and trivialized the benefits of better worker health. Most significantly, Tolchin found that the results of cost-benefit analysis differed depending on who was doing it.

Cost-benefit analysis is not the only kind of policy analysis that is used politically. All types of evaluation are inevitably political in several ways. They are political because the programs with which evaluations deal are the creatures of political decisions. Evaluations make judgments about these programs and therefore become a part of the politics surrounding them (Weiss 1987, 47–48). Evaluations are political, no matter how objective or neutral evaluators think they are, because they serve the interests of persons involved in the policy process (Lindblom and Cohen 1979, 62). "When evaluators argue that a nutrition program reduces the number of low weight births," Bellavita writes (1986, 239), "they are making an implicit claim that future policy actions should be influenced by this information. They are entering the political debate."

How should evaluators and administrators respond to the inherently political nature of evaluation? Evaluators should recognize that they cannot and should not be "objective." At the same time, they should avoid becoming the tools of one particular interest. They can do this by making sure that various stakeholders are included in the design, execution, and analysis of the evaluation (Patton 1987). In addition, they can attempt to represent interests that are not or cannot be involved (such as those of the clients or targets of the program or the general public) (Palumbo 1987). Evaluators and policy analysts also should recognize that evaluations are limited in what they can do. They are but one element of the policy process and by no means the most important (Weiss 1987).

UTILIZATION OF EVALUATIONS

When the evaluation profession was young, evaluators expected that there would be direct and immediate use of the fruits of their labors. These expectations were soon dashed. Seldom, if ever, were policy or administrative changes made as a result of program evaluations. Attempts to explain this lack of immediate and direct use focused on several thories.

The Two-Culture Theory

According to the two-culture theory, evaluators and administrators operate in two disparate worlds that have quite different and conflicting imperatives (Dunn 1980; Caplan 1979). Evaluators are interested in finding the facts, the truth (Wildavsky 1979), and in generalizing about programs and the process of evaluation. Administrators, on the other hand, are interested in specific information about populations in certain situations (Meltsner and Bellavia 1983, 18) and, of course, in avoiding the appearance of failure. Because these goals are in conflict, the results of evaluations are not used unless they can be turned to the advantage of program managers (Banner, Doctors, and Gordon 1975; Palumbo 1987, 22–26).

Methodological Flaws

Some studies have found that many if not most evaluations have had serious methodological flaws. It has been assumed that this lack of reliability has limited their use. But another study (Fritschler 1983) found that the methodologically weakest studies were the most likely to be used, and they were used in strictly political ways to bolster support for a program.

Instrumental versus Conceptual Use

A major breakthrough in understanding utilization came when the distinction between instrumental and conceptual use was recognized (Weiss and Bucuvalas 1980). Instead of being used to make immediate program alterations, (i.e., instrumental use), program evaluation changes the way managers think about the program (i.e., conceptual use). This shift in perspective could have an impact on the program at some later time, long after the evaluation was completed, but to show that the changes were the direct results of the evaluation is difficult. In fact, many program administrators do not think they make decisions that affect a program (Weiss and Bucuvalas 1980); they see themselves as writing memos, having conversations with supervisors, signing letters, but not actually making decisions that have much impact on program policy.

In order to understand utilization, it is necessary to understand the decision process (see Chapter 6). When utilization does occur, it is only an additional piece of information in a complex puzzle (Patton 1987). There is no direct link between an evaluation and program changes. Evaluation results feed into the slow evolutionary process of program development. They make a small and momentary splash in the large pool of policy.

Specific Factors

A whole of series of studies have pointed to a number of specific factors that affect utilization, including the context, how the information is communicated (Maynard-Moody 1989b), and how plausible the evaluation findings are in the eyes of the users.

Most research points to the importance of the personal factor (Patton 1987). Managers are very busy people who spend relatively little time on a lot of different problems, moving from one to another rather rapidly. To have an impact, evaluation results should be communicated in short and easy-to-digest form, preferably orally, rather than in a large technical report. They also should be communicated to those who care about the information. Thus, to improve utilization the evaluator should find the strategically located persons and answer the questions they want rather than the questions the evaluators are interested in.

All programs and policies are continuously changing. They have supporters and opponents. Opposition to a program by those who diasgree with it will continue no matter what an evaluation shows. Programs serve symbolic and political as well as substantive ends. They are not terminated or changed for technical or analytical reasons, but for ideological and political reasons. As Majone (1989) notes, policy issues are trans-scientific; they cannot be decided on the basis of "facts" alone. Realistic evaluators will recognize this and not expect the crucial factor in administrative decisions to be whether a program is achieving its goals. Most administrators understand this. Evaluations will continue to be done and to be useful to administrators because "there are no values closer to the core of western ideology than these ideas of intelligent choice, and there is no institution more prototypically committed to the systematic application of information to decisions than the modern bureaucratic organization" (Feldman and March 1981, 77). So evaluation will remain an important component of a manager's job. As long as citizens, elected officials, and administrators ask questions about the effectiveness of government programs, program evaluation will remain crucial to administration.

SUMMARY

Evaluations can have a large impact on public programs, although this may not always be direct and immediate. It is now recognized that evaluations cannot be the only factor influencing programs, a position that has evolved over time since evaluation became recognized as a formal endeavor in the early 1960s.

The main forerunners of evaluation are operations research and the progrm planning and budgeting techniques of the 1960s. President Johnson was so enamored of these techniques that he ordered all governmental agencies to use them.

In its early forms in universities, evaluation was considered to be a part of applied social science research. Researchers believed that it was possible to be objective. Evaluators should have nothing to say about goals.

Another strand of evaluation was developing at the same time in education in the 1930s, but it had the greatest impact in the 1960s with James Coleman's study of equal educational opportunity for minority children and with the work of social psychologist Donald Campbell on the "experimenting society."

These early efforts emphasized methodological concerns. The concepts of internal and external validity were developed. In recent years, however, the emphasis on internal validity has been severely criticized, and some scholars have even questioned whether evaluation could be considered *research* in the traditional meaning of that term. A number of important distinctions exist between evaluation and research.

The notion of an experimenting society caught on in the 1970s and spawned a whole new approach to research. The Evaluation Research Society was formed in 1971, several major evaluation books were published, the federal government created the Program Evaluation and Methodology Division in the U.S. General Accounting Office in 1974, and numerous federal and state agencies began requiring evaluations of government programs.

The experimenting society approach differed from PPBS and policy analysis in several ways. Moreover, a number of different approaches to evaluation were created within program evauation itself.

The major approaches to evaluation include:

1. *Objectives Oriented.* The earliest form of evaluation—also called summative evaluation—the objectives-oriented approach has been criticized on several grounds. The most significant criticism is that program objectives, which must be clearly defined for this approach to be used successfully, are difficult, if not impossible, to identify in public programs. One solution is to do a "goal-free" evaluation.

2. *Management Oriented.* Also called "process" or "formative evaluation," the management-oriented approach is concerned with determining how a program is being implemented. This involves questions about the extent and process of evaluation. The purpose is to provide managers with information about whether the program is being managed properly and what can be done to improve it. However, there are many stakeholders in addition to managers. The wider concerns of these groups are not always considered in this approach.

3. *Stakeholder Evaluation.* When the views of all stakeholders, not just those of top management, are included in an evaluation, the approach is called a stakeholder evaluation.

4. *Consumer Oriented.* This approach is used primarily for evaluating physical products such as police vehicles.

5. *Expertise Oriented.* In this approach experts are used to determine the merit of a program.

6. *Adversarial Oriented.* In this type of evaluation both positive and negative views about a program are sought.

7. *Naturalistic.* This approach aims at describing the program in its complete setting.

Evaluations usually begin with an evaluability assessment. This procedure is used to identify the parts of a program that actually can be evaulated and to come to an agreement with program managers about the goals of the evaluation.

Impact analysis attempts to determine whether a program is achieving its objectives. In this type, the evaluator must identify the theory that underlies the program. Various statistical methods are used in this approach. Process evaluation should usually be done in conjunction with impact evaluation.

Cost-benefit analysis is the principal tool of policy analysis, although it has a number of flaws. The assumptions of cost-benefit analysis are the basis of rational decision making. This type of analysis is different from cost-effectiveness analysis in that in the former it is necessary to measure benefits in monetary terms, whereas in the latter only the units of output are measured.

The first step in cost-benefit analysis is to specify goals. The next step is to assess the costs of each policy option and then attach monetary figures to the benefits. The option with the highest cost-benefit ratio is the preferred one.

Program evaluation and policy analysis methods, such as cost-benefit analysis, are unavoidably political in that they support one as opposed to another position about a program and thus become a part of the political debate.

Evaluations are not often used in an immediate and direct way; instead, they influence the way public officials conceive a program and are usually but one factor in policy decisions.

CASE STUDY: EVALUATION OF A PRIVATELY VERSUS PUBLICLY OPERATED JUVENILE FACILITY

In this case[3] you have two separate roles to play. One is that of director of the Community Services Division (CSD) of a state department of corrections and the other is that of the head of the evaluation team. In the first role you are confronted with the following management problem. The department of corrections (DOC) has been emphasizing prison building for a number of years and had done little in the way of providing adequate resources for community services, which includes work release, home furlough, transitional services for released prisoners,and halfway houses. Also, you know that the state-run juvenile facility for girls is headed by a person who used to be assistant to the director of DOC. She was appointed to emphasize security, discipline, and authority in the state-run facility. Treatment is to be downplayed. You feel this is not the right emphasis and there should be an attempt to build the self-esteem of the girls as well as to provide education and training for them while they are in the facility. Since you have funds in your budget for contracting with private, for-profit firms, you decided over a year ago to contract with a firm to provide institutional care for some of the juveniles. The firm is required to emphasize treatment and training rather than security and discipline.

Based on the feedback you have received from the manager of your contracts division and from the parole officers who are in charge of the juveniles after they are released from the facility, you believe that the privately run facility is doing a better job than the state-run facility. Moreover, there are plans in the director's office to open a new, larger institution for female juvenile offenders that would be a state-run facility. Since it is not likely that the director of the DOC will resign his position, it can be expected that the new facility will follow his philosophy of secure detention and discipline and minimal treatment.

The contract provisions for the privately run facility require that it be evaluated. The state-run facility, however, has not been evaluated, and several legislators, who are in favor of privatization, have pressured to have such an evaluation conducted. Thus, you feel that it is a perfect opportunity for you to have an evaluation of both facilities, especially since you believe that such an examination will produce good results for the private facility, which is what you want. Therefore, you contract with an evaluator from the local university to do a comparative evaluation of both facilities.

In your role of evaluator, you have no particular position with regard to this contract, although in your research as a university professor you have written several pieces that were critical of privatization. Of course, you are not aware of the internal politics in the DOC at the time you begin the project and thus have no preconceived views about the privately run facility in this case. You will work with two other people, one of whom is a former student of yours. Both of these people have their own consulting businesses.

The number of juveniles being detained in this state has been increasing steadily. Five years before the evaluation was undertaken a total of 3,062 juveniles were detained out of a total of 14,246 juveniles involved in incorrigibility and delinquency complaints. At the time the study was conducted five years later, 4,557 out of 17,770 children were being detained. The DOC administrators have asked you to evaluate the two residential facilities.

During an initial meeting with the administrators of both facilities, you found them to be somewhat vague about exactly what they wanted in the evaluation. They said they would like cost-effectiveness information and something about how the programs were being implemented. They also were emphatic in saying they did not want recidivism data. They knew what the recidivism figures were (about 40 percent of the girls were returned to one or the other of the state's three facilities).

In order to set up an evaluation design, the evaluators conducted an evaluability assessment. The various components and activities of the juvenile detention program were diagrammed showing what outputs were supposed to be related to program inputs (see Figure 11.1). The diagram was discussed with the administrators to determine what program performance measures should be used in the evaluation. The administrators agreed that these should include an assessment of the facility environment, such as the kind of education, counseling, and recreational activities the juveniles were offered. They also agreed that the evaluators should try to determine whether the juveniles went back to school, got part-time jobs, and associated with their old friends after being released. It also began to be clear that the person most interested in the evaluation was the woman who was in charge of the contracts of DOC and therefore in a position to contract with private facilities. But it was not possible to learn specifically how the evaluation results would be used. The only information that could be elicited was that an evaluation of the state-run facility had been mandated, but no one was sure who had ordered it. At the same time, the administrator said, it would be useful to compare that facility with the private one. It was clear that the administrators with whom the evaluators met had the power to use the evaluation findings.

In the discussions, some of the facts about the political context surrounding the program became clearer. The director of the Community Services Division revealed that the DOC was planning to open a very large facility in six months and that the contract for the private facility would be allowed to expire. The large facility was to house 80 to 100 juveniles and would be run by the state. The director of CSD did not look too favorably on this.

An impact analysis was ruled out because the conditions under which the evaluation was being conducted did not allow for it. Random assignment of the girls to each facility was not possible and there was no way to control for all of the other variables related to outcomes. Moreover, the administrators were more interested in a process evaluation.

Since they also were interested in comparing the two facilities it was necessary to determine the degree of similarity of the girls who were housed in each facility. The evaluators

Table 11.2. Demographic Profile of the Girls in the Two Facilities

	State Run	Privately Run
Mean age at present	16.5 years	15.8 years
Percent black	25%	8%
Percent Caucasian	58%	75%
Percent Mexican American	17%	17%
Mean age at first contact	12.7 years	15.8 years
Mean number of prior complaints	6.5	6.1

looked at the files on each girl in each facility. The girls in the private facility were slightly younger (see Table 11.2) than those in the state facility.

The girls at the state facility were younger when they first had contact with authorities, had slightly more prior complaints, and represented a smaller percentage of minorities. This finding seemed to substantiate the claim made by the head of the state facility that her facility received the more difficult cases. In particular, the girls in the state facility had gotten into trouble with authorities at a much earlier age than those in the private facility; age at first offense is an important predictor of whether a person will became a persistent offender. In addition, a much larger percentage (87%) of the girls at the private facility were first-time offenders compared with those at the state facility (only 23%). Thus, some of the differences in how well each facility is performing might be attributed to the differences in the populations at each facility.

The evaluation staff interviewed DOC administrators, parole officers, judges, administrators, and staff at each facility, juveniles in each facility, girls released from each facility, and the parents of these girls. The purpose was to develop a descriptive account of what was done at each facility and how the respective groups rated each program.

From the perspective of administrators, staff, and juveniles at the state facility, there was no consistent program philosophy or treatment theory there. There was no attempt to provide therapy. They felt the DOC administrative leadership was not interested in this and the principal purpose of the program was to maintain security. As one staff member remarked, "There is a prison atmosphere here, just lock 'em up. We can't change them, there isn't enough time." While there were positive comments about the education program in the facility and it was rated 9.17 on a 1 to 10 scale (where 10 is very successful), there also was criticism that the program was limited to helping girls obtain a general educational development (GED) diploma and nothing else.

The administrators, staff, and residents of the private facility all agreed there was an attempt to provide treatment there. A special plan was developed for each girl upon entry and the program was based on the assumption that the girls possessed the capacity to change. One administrator said, "At this facility, we try to get them to assimilate self-consciousness and self-reliance." Behavioral modification is used as the main treatment mode. But there were problems in implementing the philosophy. The security staff was disgruntled because of low pay, lack of promotions, little input into decision making, and an uncertain future (the security staff was aware the facility was to be closed). The education program at the private facility also recieved high marks (9.17 on the 1 to 10 scale).

The private facility was scored higher on self-rating by the administrators, staff, and residents. A far larger precentage at the private facility asserted that the program was successful in achieving its goals (80% of the residents and 100% of the staff) than was the case for the state facility (66% of the residents and 75%of the staff). Also, on items designed to measure the correctional environmnet (Moos 1974), the public facility appeared to be much more control oriented than the private one. For example, 60 percent of the public facility respondents said residents will be transferred from the unit if they do not obey the rules, compared to only 33 percent of the private facility respondents who gave this reply. One hundred percent of the state facility residents stated that the staff punishes them by restricting them while only 47 percent of the private facility residents stated this.

Although it was not possible to do a complete cost-effectiveness analysis (and a cost-benefit analysis was out of the question) because the accounting practices at each facility were quite different, some rough cost data were collected.

The total cost for running the state facility for a twelve-month period was $1,254,000 compared to $802,884 for the private facility. The costs at the state facility were higher in every category except for food and other operating expenditures. However, the state facility had an average of 38 juveniles per day, while the private one had an average of 26. Also, the state facility had a staff of 37 compared to 27 for the private one. Nonetheless, the state facility paid significantly higher salaries on the average ($21,000 per year) than did the private facility ($15,800). Also, employee-related expenditures for the state facility (25% of personal services costs) were significantly higher than in the private facility. A contributing factor in the comparison was substantially lower medical benefits in the private facility. Hence, the greater cost-effectiveness of the private facility ($84.43 per juvenile) as compared to the state facility ($91.27 per juvenile) was largely due to lower salaries and employee benefits. This situation was reflected in the low morale of the security staff at the private facility.

When these results were discussed with the DOC administrators who commissioned the evaluation, it became clear that they were hoping for and expecting that the evaluation results would be favorable to the private facility. The woman who directed the contracts components of the Community Services Division made it clear that she favored contracting because it gave her more flexibility and control. She and her boss did not like the security and discipline orientation of the DOC, which was the policy of the DOC director, and felt that the planned new facility would have a prison and security orientation rather than a treatment one. The evaluation seemed to support their position, although they were not too enthusiastic about the findings that there was not much discipline at the private facility and that some of the parents of the released girls did not like this. As the director of the Community Services Division noted, "Some legislators could view the evaluation as very supportive of the state facility, especially those who felt that security and discipline were necessary."

Discussion Questions

1. Do you expect the evaluation to be utilized?
2. Were the evaluation or results more favorable to the private facility than to the public facility?
3. Was the cost-effectiveness component of the evauation helpful and in what way?
4. What are the main political aspects of the evaluation?
5. How would you use the evaluation if you were the director of the Community Services Division of DOC? Would you ask the evaluators to change any parts?
6. What are the major flaws in the evaluation?

NOTES

1. This approach is closely associated with the goal achievement model of organization effectiveness discussed in Chapter 3. The criticism of the goal-achievement model also applies to this approach to program evaluation (see Maynard-Moody and McClintock, 1987).
2. In their most recent work, Guba and Lincoln (1989) refer to their approach as "constructivist." They use this term rather than "naturalistic" to emphasize that "reality" about programs is *constructed* by those who observe it, including the evaluators, and that there isn't a set of "facts" out there to be discovered by a scientific, objective researcher.
3. This case is based on research conducted by the first author. It is an actual case.

CHAPTER 12

Program Implementation

Policy making is a continuous process; it does not begin when legislators consider an issue and it does not stop when legislators pass a bill and the president or governor signs it. Policy making continues while the legislation is being implemented by administrators. Laurence Lynn (1987, 214), a professor of public administration, notes that "implementation is the continuation of policy-making by administrative means." Moreover, it is not just those at the top—the political executives—who make policy during implementation; middle- and street-level administrators, those who actually deliver public services (e.g., police officers, school teachers, prosecutors, judges, social workers, probation officers) also make policy during implementation (see Chapter 5).

Policy formulation is clearly only one part of policy making (Palumbo 1988). Much policy is made during implementation itself. Although this occurs in various ways, the principal way is that street-level bureaucrats create policy when they make the multitude of decisions required of them when interacting with the public (Lipsky 1980). They possess discretion that cannot be completely controlled because there are never enough resources to provide close, frequent, and direct supervision of the numbers of street-level bureaucrats, and also because they are physically separated from their superiors. There are no precise performance standards in existence that specify exactly how a teacher, cop, parole officer, prosecutor, judge, public health nurse, social worker, and the many other street-level bureaucrats should do their jobs. In sum, policy making occurs during implementation by bureaucrats developing routines and shortcuts for coping with their everyday jobs.

One reaction to this fact of bureaucratic life is that executives frequently try to control the behavior of those lower down in the hierarchy by issuing rules and guidelines, but this often results in more rigidity and red tape than greater effectiveness (Knott and Miller 1986). Brookings Institute scholar Herbert Kaufman (1981) believes that no part of an administrative agency can act without the cooperation, or at least the acquiescence, of other parts. When managers attempt to get this cooperation through commands or rules, the units become more rigid and rule oriented, a condi-- tion that leads to more controls and then more rigidity.

Skillful management does not simply involve attempts to control subordinates; it involves bargaining, learning and listening, and compromising on some points while standing firm on others, as well as being able to handle ambiguity and uncertainty. Being successful at implementing programs involves assembling numerous and diverse program elements, not only within the agency, but outside it as well. Doing this right requires political skills, not just authority. As Lynn (1981, 223) notes: "The notion that public executives acting in their own right can move government in directions of their own choosing seems unrealistic." As we shall see in this chapter, successful implementation is a complex matter involving different elements and skills.

DEFINING POLICY IMPLEMENTATION

Policy implementation involves two major dimensions: (1) the extent and (2) the process of implementation. The extent of implementation has two components: One is whether the *right* individuals are receiving the services, and the second is whether a *sufficient number* are receiving the services. For example, the Family Security Act (FSA) passed by Congress in 1988 was aimed at breaking the cycle of dependency by removing welfare recipients from the rolls (we describe this in more detail below). The extent of implementation of FSA can be measured by determining whether the right individuals are receiving the services and how many are involved.

The process of implementation involves the organizational structure and arrangement for delivering a program, about which we can ask the following questions:

- How centralized is the agency that delivers the program?
- Is a top-down or bottom-up management approach being taken? (These are described below.)
- How much support for the program exists among those who must implement it?
- How much do lower-level administrators participate in decisions about the program?
- How many agencies, groups, and levels of government must be involved in implementing the program?

Implementation is multidimensional and quite complex; it is not simply a matter of command and authority. As a result, measuring successful implementation in a quantitative way is difficult. As we will see in the next section, there are conflicting views about what constitutes successful implementation.

IMPLEMENTATION AND PROGRAM SUCCESS

In the fall of 1988, the U.S. Congress passed the Family Security Act (FSA) that was described as a break with the past. Its supporters claimed that it would "break the cycle of dependency.'' The act required that people receiving welfare assistance (there were 3.7 million adults receiving Aid to Families with Dependent Children in 1988) enter a program called Job Opportunities and Basic Skills (JOBS). The legislation did not require them actually to work because that would mean that jobs would have to be available as well as day-care facilities for the children of the welfare recipients (80 percent of whom were women).[1] Instead, they would be required to undergo remedial education, job training, and counseling. In order to make the bill palatable to conservatives in Congress, it was called a ''workfare'' program.

What will determine whether this legislation will be successfully implemented? Conventional wisdom says that its implementation will be successful if (1) the bill correctly identifies the reasons people go on welfare, (2) the bill contains unambiguous directives that structure implementation so as to maximize the likelihood that the 3.7 million welfare recipients will behave as desired, (3) the administrators doing the implementing possess the necessary managerial and political skills and are committed to its goals, (4) the program is actively supported by organized constituency groups and key legislators throughout the implementation process, and (5) the relative priority of statutory objectives is not undermined over time by conflicting public policies or by changes in relevant socioeconomic conditions that undermine the statute's purposes or political support (Sabatier and Mazmanian 1979).

Only one of these five conditions of successful implementation—number three—is related to the performance of administrators. Yet, administrators often take the blame when there is a gap between promise and performance in a policy, and such a gap almost always exists because the other four conditions seldom hold. There are several reasons that such gaps occur. The main ones are listed below:

1. Much legislation passed at the national, state, and local levels is symbolic; it is usually a *promise* that something can be done about an intractable social problem that has lingered on the public agenda for years (e.g., welfare dependency).
2. Legislation is often not based on a sound program theory that correctly identifies the conditions that will convince the target groups to behave in the desired fashion.
3. Socioeconomic and political conditions change so that the solution promised in the legislation may not be appropriate a few years later (e.g., the economy loses unskilled manufacturing jobs that welfare recipients could fill).
4. Administrators discover during implementation that a different kind of program would work better than the one envisioned in the legislation.
5. Insufficient resources are committed to the program.
6. Implementors don't have the know-how to make the policy work.

Implementation Studies and Policy Failure

Because a gap almost inevitably exists between the promises in legislation and the program actually delivered, early implementation studies concluded that most government programs failed. Pressman and Wildavsky (1984) expressed the problem well in the third edition of their landmark study—"How Great Expectations in Washington are Dashed in Oakland: or Why It's Amazing that Federal Programs Work At All. . . ." Unfortunately, many conservatives took this to mean that government couldn't do anything right (Bardach, 1977). Administrators were often blamed for program failure, and "bureaucrat bashing" became popular during the conservative 1980s. Implementation was called the "Achilles' heel" of government (Williams, 1980) and implementors were accused of playing the "easy life" or "diversion of resources" games (Bardach 1977).

But by the late 1980s, more than fifteen years after the initial implementation studies, researchers discovered that these earlier views were wrong (Fox 1987; Schwartz 1983). They were wrong, first, because of their assumption that policy implementation could be separated from formulation as a matter of carrying out decisions made at a prior point in time. They were based on the traditional politics-administration dichotomy. As Robert Denhardt (1984, 133) noted:

> The study of policy implementation represents a regression in the study of public organizations: the distinction between policy-making and policy implementation exactly parallels the old politics-administration dichotomy; and the uncritical acceptance of such a distinction by many students of the policy process neither recognizes the role of bureaucracy in framing public values nor addresses the issues of democratic accountability.

It is now accepted doctrine that administrators, as much as if not more than legislators, are a part of the policy-making process. Administrators and legislators in American government often play tug-of-war over which direction to take in policy issues. (We discuss below one such tug-of-war in regard to the Environmental Protection Agency.) The point to be emphasized here is that gaps between legislative promises and implementation performance may be the result of differences in political party ideology, bad policy design, or group and personal attitudes and perceptions about what a policy should be. This is a normal part of the American constitutional design (see Ferman 1989), not an illegitimate usurpation of power by "bureaucrats."

Another reason the earlier implementation studies were wrong stems from their placing the blame for program failure on implementation alone. These studies assumed that problem definition and policy design were usually clear and unambiguous. But this is seldom the case. Problem definition and policy design are political activities; as such, they are the products of conflict, bargaining, and compromise. They do not often correctly identify the causes of the social problem that the policy is supposed to help cure. Moreover, what is identified as a cause of a social problem depends on the ideology of the person or groups doing the identifying. In the War on Poverty programs, for example, policy makers (including some legislators running for office) expressed the belief that poverty resulted when individuals lacked the necessary training and education. (Some, more conservative, legislators suggested that it was caused by character flaws such as laziness and even defective genes, although they were reluctant to say so publicly.) Poor people, on the other hand, saw their situations as resulting from racial discrimination and lack of jobs (Ingraham 1987). Seldom is there a perfect fit among a problem as defined by legislators, the design of a policy aimed at alleviating it, and implementation of that policy. Instead, implementation is an "exercise in continuous problem solving" (Ingraham 1987, 149). Viewed in this way, the role of implementors is one of actively shaping publcy policy. And it should be; the traditional view that implementors (i.e., administrators and bureaucrats) should not be involved in making policy is false. Public administrators cannot be properly understood as the deliverers of decisions made earlier by separate groups or bodies of "real policy makers." Moreover, when policies are adapted through political and organizational conditioning, and given more specific content during implementation, this does not necessarily connote policy failure.

Policy failure comes from several sources; it results as much from inadequate problem definition or policy design as from administrative misfeasance, malfeasance, or nonfeasance. Moreover, administrative failure may be due to the inattention paid by legislators to program constraints (there may be community opposition to the program; busing is an example). Problems, or failures, in implementation, therefore, can be as much a consequence of flaws in the overall policy-making process as they are to "bureaucratic incompetence."

To the extent that implementation success or failure is attributable to administration alone, turning to traditional micro-administrative knowledge can help us understand how to improve implementation. This involves such topics as leadership, management styles, and strategic planning. But to the extent that implementation success or failure is a part of the policy-making process in general, such knowledge is no longer adequate; macro-administrative knowledge is needed as well. Implementation research has provided some of this knowledge and it has, therefore, somewhat opened up the "black box" of the policy-making process. One of the major developments is the recognition that implementation is a political matter, not just an administrative one.

THE POLITICAL NATURE OF IMPLEMENTATION

A great deal of the early research on policy implementation ignored politics. The researchers seemed to assume that implementation took place in a political vacuum. There are some exceptions. Nakamura and Smallwood (1980), for example, focused on politics in the broadest sense—on "the conflicts over values which permeate many, if not all, aspects of public life, and the role of politics in resolving these conflicts" (1980, 2). They described the various policy environments in which implementation occurs, such as the policy formulation, implementation, and evaluation environments.

Implementation is political in several ways. One involves the politics that takes place within the issue networks that influence implementation (Kingdon 1984; Heclo 1978). These networks consist of a variety of groups and individuals such as congressional committee members, staff, administrators, professionals in the field, academicians, clientele groups, and members of the media. Implementors are a key part of these policy networks and play a major role in interpreting policy directives.

A second way politics enters implementation is in the trading that occurs among the "tiny interlocking personal relationships and dependencies" within each bureaucracy (public and private) involved in implementing policies. There are loyalists who are complete supporters of what they think the directors want, and there are deviants who put their own spin on policy. The latter may include those who knowingly undermine or counteract the policy, those who say they advocate more effective ways to achieve the policy's goals, and others who are passive and indifferent and for whom inaction secures their stake against those seeking changes. There also are those who exploit a particular interpretation of policy goals as a way of attaining power.

Implementation must contend with this multiplicity of behaviors. Administrators will be ineffective if they act as if they are carrying out policy objectives as stated "on the books." Pure technocrats think that organizations exist only for the purpose of achieving goals, but organizations also are social enterprises that exist to serve human needs (see Chapter 4). Administrators no less than legislators seek power, esteem, and monetary rewards that invariably shape how and which goals are achieved.

The Environmental Protection Agency's Superfund

The Reagan administration seems to have understood the political nature of implementation better than previous administrations. It sought to change many policies in the direction it wanted by emphasizing implementation rather than seeking new legislation. The Environmental Protection Agency (EPA) is a case in point.

The 1970 legislation that created EPA was vague. Although the EPA functioned in what can be viewed as a technical area that presumably constrained bureaucratic discretion, the articulation and interpretation of acceptable guidelines proved to be enormously complex. Implementors had wide discretionary powers that could not be controlled by Congress and President Reagan was able to achieve his goal of reducing the government's role in protecting the environment through his appointments to EPA rather than through legislation.

EPA was a favorite target of Reagan's 1980 campaign rhetoric and he vowed to change it. After Reagan's election in 1980, the civil servants in EPA were in an uncomfortable position. On the one hand, they were members of the executive branch of government whose chief officer was President Reagan and they thus should be responsive on his policy preferences. He opposed serious enforcement of environmental laws. On the other hand, they were responsible for carrying out the environmental laws that had been passed during the previous decade by Congress, which presumably wanted to reduce environmental pollution. Moreover, Congress in 1980 wanted EPA to implement vigorously the Superfund Cleanup provisions of the law and also to issue air quality regulations according to the timetable established in 1970 (see Barnett 1988). That legislation stated explicitly that Congress did not want costs to be taken into consideration during implementation of the Superfund. The Reagan White House disagreed (Marcus 1980, 86).

The EPA became involved in this political battle. The atmosphere created by Reagan appointees who headed the EPA discouraged civil servants from serious enforcement of the environmental laws. They were encouraged to use their discretion to reduce the scope of effective enforcement (Rohr 1988, 171).

Thus, the EPA served two political masters. It could not be a single, monolithic public servant in which all members agreed on or fulfilled the same goals and objectives. This fissure between the president and Congress paralleled the public's disagreements about what was most important. Marcus notes:

> The goals of public health—lessening the impact of common cardiovascular illnesses, such as emphysema and heart disease—were in conflict with the average driver's concern to get to work, go shopping, visit friends, and use his automobile without restriction. (1980, 136)

The various deadlines set by EPA were not met, not only because of these conflicts, but because the EPA also had to rely on other agencies to carry out its regulations. It depended on an uncooperative Justice Department to bring compliance lawsuits forward. It also had to contend with the decreasing resistance of its counterpart state agencies, many of whose administrators worried about losing industries and therefore dragged their feet. In other words, the macro-implementation conditions, over which EPA administrators had no control, precluded effective implementation. But the micro-implementation conditions were not favorable toward implementation either. Not only were the Reagan appointees uncommitted to the goals of the legislation, they were downright hostile toward other EPA career administrators. Reagan's EPA administrators relied on their allies in Congress and lobby groups to prevent legislative goals from being completely eviscerated. As Rohr notes:

> Eventually, high-ranking officials from the EPA's political leadership became so flagrant in disregarding their agency's mission to clean up toxic waste sites that career officials were able to "blow the whistle" to key congressional committees which undertook investigations that led to the resignation of four officials and a criminal conviction for a fifth. (1988, 171)

EPA implementation, although outrageous, is nonetheless somewhat typical. The Reagan administration succeeded in changing agency goals by reshaping implementation in a number of other policy areas as well. These actions included changes in the policy of the Office of Surface Mining, which allowed stripping to take place on a large scale; and in the National Highway Traffic Safety Administration, which rescinded the requirement for all motor vehicles made after 1982 to be equipped with passive restraints.

Whether these cases are viewed as implementation successes or failures is a matter of political and ideological perspective. Implementation success cannot be objectively assessed solely by measuring differences between implementation and policy intentions. Implementation is not a matter of technical fulfillment of some clearly stated policy objectives. Instead, implementation helps policy intentions unfold in the ongoing political and organizational contexts of public administration. By opening up these contexts to the realities of politics, implementation research has shown how the "inputs" of policy design are translated into "outputs" of policy redesign. Not only is goal modification unavoidable (Stone 1980), it actually is desirable in certain circumstances (Berman 1980). Of course, from the purely formal-legal perspective (see Burke 1989), goal modification poses problems about policy making by bureaucracies. But accountability is not a simple matter (see Chapter 10). Bureaucrats are directly responsive to the policy preferences of the chief executive as well as the legislature even though the preferences of the executives and legislature may disagree. In the EPA case discussed above, bureaucrats tried to implement executive preferences while also remaining attuned to the counterdemands of Congress. It is hard to say whose goals were the "legitimate" goals for implementation in these cases. Implementation, then, remains a matter of perspective in that public administration must create the appearance of agreement on goals while reality dictates balancing competing views of policy priorities. In turn, accountability becomes muddled as public administrators negotiate their way through those differences.

Nevertheless, the problem of the responsible use of administrative discretion remains the central moral concern of the literature in public administration (Rohr 1988, 170; Burke 1989). Implementation research cannot really solve this moral concern; it simply concludes that policy making during implementation is inevitable. The problem with stating "ideal" implementation conditions described at the beginning of this chapter is that they are essentially static. They spell out how implementation responsibility can be achieved according to the old formal-legalistic view, but these conditions seldom, if ever, can be met. Therefore, policy will continue to be redesigned during implementation.

TOP-DOWN VERSUS BOTTOM-UP IMPLEMENTATION

A large number of studies, particularly those done in the early stages of implementation research, take a top-down approach. This approach assumes that the goals and perspectives of those at the top of an organization are the only legitimate ones, and deviations from these goals are considered to be implementation failures. The top-down approach recommends that to avoid failure, we should have fewer and clearer goals and less complex organizations (Mazmanian and Sabatier 1983; Edwards 1980). But according to other implementation scholars (Winter 1983, 2), this is "the same as denying and renouncing the very existence of politics."

In contrast to the top-down view is the bottom-up view. According to its adherents, workers at the bottom can find more effective ways of realizing organizational goals and objectives than can officials at the top. One team of researchers found that street-level workers in the Pennsylvania Department of Public Welfare who did not follow the directives of those at the top did not produce implementation failures because they were more likely to serve their clients' needs than were workers who rigidly followed directives. They concluded that "clients' needs come first, and field personnel in a bureaucracy have important policy insights that central management lacks" (Johnson and O'Connor 1979). A similar approach is called *backward mapping*. In this view, those at the street level are more familiar with the problems encountered during implementation and they, therefore, should have a large role in policy making (Elmore, 1979). Of course, field-level personnel can be wrong. Police on the street, for instance, may not be the best source for determining how to handle minority communities. Thus, it is dangerous to take the descriptive finding that street-level personnel have a great deal of discretion and use it to make policy, and establish this as a normative premise for proper and effective administration (Linder and Peters 1987).

Moreover, the bottom-up view counsels us to do only those things that can be implemented. In this regard it is a cautious and conservative view.

Thus, considerable disagreement exists about which approach to implementation is best—top-down or bottom-up. Some believe that an accommodation between the two is not likely to be achieved (Fox 1989). However, an interactive approach may be a way of reconciling the two. In such an approach to implementation, both the top and the bottom, as well as the middle levels, all contribute to decisions about the program (Musheno et al. 1989). Such a cooperative approach may not be easy to realize in an organization because of organizational traditions or culture that may inhibit this. But the evidence indicates that when an interactive approach is used, implementation is more successful (Palumbo, Musheno, and Maynard-Moody 1986).

EVOLUTIONARY IMPLEMENTATION AND ADAPTATION

Another dimension of the top-down versus bottom-up debate concerns whether a policy should be changed during implementation. One school of thought holds that we need to encourage habits of flexibility, of continuous learning, and of acceptance of change as normal (Brassier 1985; Drucker 1985; Majone and Wildavsky 1984). Others argue that changing or adapting to local circumstances may result in subverting the intentions of policy makers (Calsyn, Tornatsky, and Dittmar 1977). However, the adaptive implementation school has the most support (Baum 1976). Orfield (1975) found that in order to make desegregation work, it was necessary for teachers to adapt their teaching methods to accommodate the new types of students in their classes. Another scholar (Lowry 1985, 289) found that adaptation was necessary in implementing federal coastal policy. He concluded that

> many of the most challenging planning issues . . . involve policy problems that are only partially understood or require the achievement of multiple objectives . . . for which acceptable intervention strategies have not been identified. Such issues challenge implementation theory and planning practice to identify and create conditions in which adaptation, experimentation, and collaboration can flourish as implementation strategies.

European scholars have reached similar conclusions. In an application of the adaptive implementation hypothesis in England, Lewis and Wallace (1984) found that most situations called for an adaptive rather than a programmed implementation strategy, even in the case of implementing food standards in the European Economic Community. Since these standards involve fairly clear objectives and technologies, one might think that a straightforward, top-down approach could be used. But Wallace (1984, 142) concluded that these policies "need to be skewed and to some extent distorted to carry along different governments with diverse requirements and often contrary interests; this suggests that adaptiveness is the only sensible strategy to pursue." The same conclusion was reached by a Swedish scholar who looked at transportation programs:

> The assumption in the programmed paradigm of a controlled setting for evaluation and implementation does not fit the reality of the decision making environment, which is often turbulent and filled with conflict . . . when priorities have to be set between different transportation modes and when the relationship between transportation and other social phenomena have to be considered, such a methodology is simply not adequate. (Flyvbjerg 1984, 296–297)

But not everyone agrees with the adaptive implementation position. Some scholars believe that the adaptive view results in a tautology for evaluation. That is, whatever adaptations are made in a program constitute policy; therefore, the adaptive approach does not provide standards against which to measure success or failure. The evaluation approach most suited to the adaptive view is goal-free evaluation (Scriven 1972) because we do not begin with objectives in this kind of evaluation. Instead, we simply find out what the program has accomplished and then determine if this is socially worthwhile.

Of course, the problem with this approach is that the evaluator's standards and values are used to measure success rather than those of the implementors or legislators (Patton 1986).

IMPLEMENTATION AND EVAULATION

Program evaluation, also, has progressed in the past decade from the simple input-output model of evaluation to a model that includes "throughputs," in an effort to make clear what actually goes on in a program (Cook and Shadish 1986). This has been done by focusing on implementation questions rather than strictly on outcome or impact questions.

Evaluators have discovered that before we can conclude that implementation is a distortion or a failure, we need to learn what program theory has informed policy intentions. Program theory connects policy intentions to tacit assumptions about implementation. Policy formulation, then, requires understanding that implementation is a multifaceted and not a unitary phenomenon. For instance, as Bickman (1987) observes: "The policy-maker must know if the multiple ways a program was implemented at different sites provide similar feedback on validity of the program," and this can be known only if the theory underlying the program is understood. Nor can the prevailing notion that a policy's implementation led to "unintended outcomes" be treated as a distortion or failure; if a program has been only partially implemented, it cannot be judged either a failure or a success until we find out *why* it has not been fully implemented. Those consequences can be treated as unintended if causes other than poor implementation have been eliminated; such causes include the appropriateness of the underlying theory informing policy formation as well as the adequacy of the evaluation design. Poor evaluation design may erroneously conclude that a program has failed when it has not.

Extent of Implementation

Implementation research has gone a long way toward opening up the black box of program evaluation. This opening focuses on the two distinct elements mentioned at the beginning of this chapter. One is the *extent of implementation*—whether the program's elements were actually acquired and used, served the right clients, and were provided to a sufficient proportion of them. The primary concern regarding the extent of implementation is who—and how many clients—are actually experiencing the program's services. Again, it is necessary to specify the program theory in order to determine whether the right clients are participating in the program (Bickman 1987).

Process of Implementation

The second opening of the black box focuses on the *process of implementation*—the organizational processes that deliver a program (Scheirer 1987). These can be further subdivided into macro- and micro-implementation. Macro-implementation refers to the variety of organizations involved in implementing a program. For example, implementing a community corrections program requires the efforts of the courts, district or county attorney, sheriff, probation department, state department of corrections, and community groups; macro-implementation can also include federal agencies. Micro-implementation refers to what goes on inside the local agency primarily responsible for program implementation; macro-implementation refers to intergovernmental and interagency relations.

Macro-Implementation

The major theme that emerges from the literature on macro-implementation is that program objectives are often interpreted differently by those at the various levels of an implementation chain; these levels include federal agencies, officials of state and local governments, and community and business groups (Scheirer and Griffith 1989; Pressman and Wildavsky 1984; Salamon 1981). The many voices raised by these groups during implementation underscore the fact that policies are both interpreted and influenced by the character of those implementing organizations (Love and Sederberg 1987; Yanow 1987). Implementation outcomes, then, represent a confluence of actions among parties who may only superficially agree about mutual objectives. Implementation research has helped us understand this process of macro-level program implementation, but macro-implementation also creates problems for evaluation. In a system in which multiple actors and voices each claim to have the legitimate interpretation of the policy, there are no criteria or standards against which to measure policy success or failure (Linder and Peters 1987). What a policy is, then, cannot be known until the aggregation of intentions and implementation unfold (Lynn 1987).

Micro-Implementation

At the micro-implementation level the unfolding process involves adaptive implementation. As we mentioned above, this concept has grown largely out of the conflicts between the top-down and bottom-up views of implementation. While attempts have been made to integrate the two perspectives, no easy solution has emerged; implementors cannot simultaneously adhere faithfully to policy directives given in legislation and adapt the directives at the lower levels to fit what street-level bureaucrats see as the most appropriate clients or client needs. For example, the Elementary and Secondary Education Act of 1965, and the 1967 and 1974 amendments, were passed as antipoverty legislation aimed at helping the poor and disadvantaged. But the categories of aid were so inclusive that many school districts used the funds as general aid to education. Similarly, the Education for Handicapped Act of 1975 was aimed at providing financial incentives for states to enroll and educate handicapped children, and particularly at providing education in the least restrictive environment appropriate to the handicapped child's needs. But in implementation, schools took shortcuts and did not always follow the mandate of the law (Weatherly 1979).

As we have now learned to expect, federal programs seldom are carried out in the exact way specified by the legislation. This is true partially because legislation often has broad and vague mandates, but also partially because local jurisdictions adapt legislation to fit their needs, and the fedeal government can do little to force them to act otherwise. This variation in implementation is also a function of organizational relationships; most federally initiated programs are "loosely coupled" (Weick 1976), and such systems do not act in a tight, top-down manner. As Salamon (1981, 160) notes, most federal programs are implemented through "third parties such as special districts, banks, hospitals, corporations, states, and cities. Instead of a hierarchical relationship between the federal government and its agents, therefore, what frequently exists in practice is a far more complex bargaining relationship in which the federal agency often has the weaker hand." This factual reality reflects the normative basis for understanding implementation in the American federal system (see Chapter 13). At all stages—from design to redesign—public policy represents a mixture of levels of government as well as private and quasi-private agencies involved in implementing programs (Grodzins 1963).

These findings do not mean that adaptive implementation necessarily violates normative expectations about maintaining democratic controls over administrators and bureaucrats. Implementation research has shown not only that the politics-administration dichotomy is untenable empirically, but also that the political character of democratic policy making is both normal and legitimate. On one hand, adaptive implementation increases (analytically and politically) the chances that policy intentions will not be achievable *because* they must be operationalized as goals. On the other hand, adaptive implementation creates achievable operational goals *despite* the flaws of policy design (Calista 1986).

Because adaptive implementation (Berman 1980) is normal and not an aberration, to generalize findings from one evaluation to other programs is difficult (Palumbo and Oliverio 1989). Clearly if adaptation is a necessary element of implementation, then what works in one context or location may not work in another. As Palumbo and Oliverio (1989, 342) note: "Moreover, even if a program works fairly well in one location, we usually want to improve it in the next location." Adaptive implementation thus creates problems for evaluation as well as for the traditional constitutional issue of bureaucratic responsibility.

IMPLICATIONS: PREDICTING FSA'S FUTURE

At the beginning of this chapter we asked a question: What will determine whether the Family Security Act (FSA) of 1988 will be successfully implemented? Now we are in a position to answer this. From the vantage point of top-down implementation as an "ideal type," the FSA is disadvantaged.

Extent of Implementation

The FSA funding target was set at $3.34 billion over a period of five years—about $668 million a year. If success means acquiring bona fide employment for a large percentage of the 3.7 million people on welfare, then the funding is inadequate (i.e., the extent of implementation will be inadequate). If only 3 million of the 3.7 million who were on AFDC in 1988 qualify for aid under the FSA, and the funds are spent on them (assuming no replacements over these first five years), then there will be roughly $223 per individual plus whatever the states contribute—which we will assume to be an equal amount. How much can be bought for about $446 per person? Not much.

The only way to increase the amount of funds per individual is to greatly decrease the extent of implementation, which, of course, will also defeat the goals of the legislation. Some states will employ what amounts to a voucher system, providing funds directly to some recipients. These funds will do little except provide for some training for low-paying jobs such as office help. Gaining such employment will provide psychological rather than economic benefits, for the training will provide employment that moves families just above the poverty line and not much higher. These circumstances, among others, have led the FSA's sponsors to express reservations about not raising hopes too high regarding any near-term success.

Process of Implementation

To their credit, the sponsors of the FSA favored giving states considerable latitude in generating programs and structuring actions. This flexibility certainly satisfies the adaptive implementation requirement to encourage states to establish favorable administrative and managerial climates. Some states have already moved along the frontier contained in the legislation: The objective for these states would be to continue to raise their efforts and to support more experimentation through incentives such as demonstration projects. The results will be positive if these states provide additional programs, rather than replace their existing funding with the new federal funds. In other states, the federal funds will provide start-up incentives; these states have an opportunity to be innovative in creating new programs.

At the same time, however, such opportunity to adapt FSA to local circumstances can be used to defeat its purposes. Several possibilities exist. One is that some states, pressed for funds due to budget shortfalls, may try to use the federal funds to replace existing efforts rather than add to them. To the extent to which they do this there will be no increase in the effort to help people on welfare—an outcome that is certainly contrary to the law's intentions. A second possible negative adaptation is "creaming." Some localities may elect to spend their funds on the most trainable and employable individuals. While this may help particular individuals, it will greatly reduce the extent of implementation. It also seems contrary to the intentions of the FSA, although some might argue that this outcome is really a part of the intentions of some policy formulators (Robertson 1984).

On the positive side, some jurisdictions may use the funds to provide programs in addition to their existing efforts, thereby exceeding the extent of implementation over what they would have done without the federal incentive. Some may even find innovative ways of training some clients and removing them from the welfare roles. To the extent to which these constructive ways of implementing the FSA occur, the intentions of the policy will be fulfilled or even exceeded. Whether the positive and constructive adaptations are sufficiently great to offset the negative adaptations is impossible to say. There is no doubt, however, that both forms of adaptation will occur.

From a political perspective, the interesting question is how these adaptations are perceived by the Congress, the president, and the states and localities. To be sure, some of the adaptation we labeled *negative* will not be *seen* that way by all the groups, organizations, and individuals involved. While the programs may fail to achieve the substantive goal of reducing the number of people on welfare, they may still succeed politically by maintaining the support of key actors. We can be sure that there will not be agreement about the outcomes nor about who is to blame for what some observers will call negative outcomes. Implementation is a political act; therefore, the conclusions about whether implementation has succeeded will also be political. What an observer sees will be a function of the observer's political persuasion *and* the political circumstances surrounding implementation.

Judging Success

At the broadest level, the success of the legislation's implementation depends on the accuracy of the program theory underlying it. Similar to most welfare policies, the FSA is based on the theory that individuals are the cause of their own welfare dependency. It is designed to correct problems such as inadequate education, job skills, motivation, and lack of day-care facilities for welfare-dependent women. But it rejects a conflicting theory: that a major cause of welfare dependency is the lack of adequate jobs in the changing American economy (Wilson 1987). To the extent to which this conflicting theory is correct, the FSA will fail during implementation. The failure will be due not to faulty implementation but to faulty problem definition and policy design. All stakeholders, however, will certainly not agree that the failure, if such occurs, is due to policy design aspects of the policy-making process. Indeed, if antitax and antigovernment sentiment still abounds, it will be "those incompetent bureaucrats" who will shoulder most of the blame.

Since implementation as well as policy formulation involves the politics of symbolism, there will be instances in which the appearance of success will occur. Such instances may be sufficient to justify politically the continuation of the policy and even to vindicate its program theory in the minds of some stakeholders. Nevertheless, we can be sure that the FSA will not end welfare dependency. No existing theory identifies the causes of welfare dependency nor the incentives and tools that are sufficient to get the intended target groups to behave in the way the legislation wants. We do not mean to counsel despair, for we may discover the correct theories and methods if we attempt enough programs and experiments.

For the FSA, however, there also is the question of political feasibility. In the past, only job training programs that are distributed widely and evenly among jurisdictions have won broad political support (Chubb 1985). Moreover, the federal government has consistently used a grant-in-aid strategy in trying to achieve its policy objectives. Such "government by proxy" (Kettl 1988) has made it very unlikely that the grant money will be spent in accord with congressional intentions (Anton 1984; Salamon 1981). Particularly in the welfare and employment areas, federal implementation strategy increases the opportunities for delay, failure, and policy embarrassments.

The attempt to reduce the number of people on welfare has been going on for a number of years. In 1960, over three million people received Aid to Dependent Children (U.S. Department of Commerce 1975, 356). In 1967, President Lyndon Johnson advocated the Work Incentive Program (WIN) which required employable welfare recipients to enroll in job training programs. Able-bodied recipients had to register with state employment service agencies and risked the loss of their welfare funds if they refused to take suitable jobs or enroll in training programs.

The insistence that job training accompany any welfare plan continued in the Nixon administration. President Nixon conceded that such a job training approach would "cost more than welfare. But, unlike welfare, it is designed to correct the condition it deals with and, thus, to lessen the long-range burden and cost." His proposed job training reform included "provisions specifically designed to help move people off welfare rolls and onto payrolls" (Nixon 1969).

By the late 1970s, one of the Johnson War on Poverty programs, the Comprehensive Employment and Training Act, ran into severe criticism. Many local areas were using CETA money to ease their budgetary crises by including it in their regular payrolls. One U.S. representative said that the national government was utterly unable to control the program because state and local governments subcontracted to an "estimated 30,000 to 50,000 subgrantees," but no one could estimate within 10,000 how many organizations were actually receiving CETA money (U.S. House of Representatives 1980, 1, 30–33).

The macro-implementation structure utilized by the federal government, with its severe fragmentation and multiple veto points (Pressman and Wildavsky 1984; Kettl 1988; Salamon 1981; Robertson 1989), almost assures that federal policies will be drastically altered during implementation. It is this implementation structure that is blamed when these programs are perceived to be failures. However, the experience of over thirty years indicates that it isn't the implementation structure alone that is to blame. Even though there have been some local successes in poverty programs (Levin and Ferman, 1985), for the most part we simply do not have the knowledge or technology that will enable us to eliminate poverty completely. Thus, policy failure in this and in other areas as well, is as much a result of poor policy design as it is of faulty implementation.

SUMMARY

Policy making is a continuous process that takes place during implementation as well as formulation. In order for a program to be successfully implemented, widespread cooperation is necessary—from all parts of the agency as well as from the variety of groups and organizations usually involved in implementation.

Implementation encompasses extent as well as process. The former is a question of whether the right clients and a sufficient number of them have received the services of the program. The latter concerns the organizational arrangements for implementing the program.

There are two views of successful implementation. One is top-down and assumes that goals can be defined and the behavior of individuals within and outside an agency, including clients, can be effectively directed toward achieving these goals. This is seldom possible. There are several reasons why it is not possible to do this.

Implementation is an exercise in continuous problem solving in which those at the street level are as much involved as those at the top. Moreover, program failure results from poor policy design equally as often as from faulty implementation.

Implementation is not solely a neutral technical matter; it is also political. Politics influences the implementing agencies as well as the other numerous agencies involved.

One major factor in the politics of administration at the national level is the difference that often exists between the president and Congress about programs. The president can use implementation to thwart or change congressional wishes. The Reagan EPA is a case in point.

The top-down approach to implementation was predominant in early implementation research. The bottom-up or "backward mapping" approach was developed later. The second approach reflects the assumption that those who have contact with clients are in a better position than those at the top to assess what should be done to improve a program. An interactive approach may be a way of reconciling these opposing positions.

Other approaches include the evolutionary and adaptive approaches that reflect the view that programs must change and adapt to local circumstances as they are being implemented.

Implementation has become an important component of program evaluation. Understanding how a program is being implemented is crucial because this knowledge can help program personnel make adjustments to improve program performance. Adjustments in the extent and process of implementation are involved. In the latter, a crucial dimension is macro-administration. The major theme in macro-administration is that program performance is interpreted differently by its various stakeholders.

Our increasing knowledge of the implementation process can be applied to determine whether a program such as the Family Security Act of 1988 can be successful. It is clear that policies contained in this legislation are more symbolic than real attempts to solve welfare dependency problems because the legislation does not contain the conditions for successful implementation.

CASE STUDY: THE ENVIRONMENTAL PROTECTION AGENCY AND THE SUPERFUND

President Reagan was opposed to strong enforcement of environmental protection legislation. He attempted to limit enforcement through his appointments to top positions in the Environmental Protection Agency (EPA) and by getting the EPA administrators to slow down strict enforcement.[2]

The EPA was an outgrowth of the 1969 National Environmental Policy Act, which enabled President Nixon to create the EPA through an executive order. Because he feared that the agency would be influenced by militant antipollution forces to set water and air pollution standards without regard to costs, Nixon also put numerous environmental programs under the Department of Commerce. Thus "he carefully balanced the potentially anti-business EPA with an enhanced environmental program in the probusiness Department of Commerce" (Marcus 1980, 44).

EPA is headed by an administrator who is appointed by the president and confirmed by the Senate (see Figure 12.1).

The EPA has had to balance two competing national policy goals since its inception. On the one hand, it must prevent pollution of the environment that threatens the health and even the very existence of life. On the other hand, it has to avoid placing burdens on commerce and industry that would prevent them from operating at a profit. No wonder, then, that the EPA has been subjected to heavy criticism since its inception.

This case study focuses on implementation of the Comprehensive Environmental Response, Compensation, and Liability Act (CERCLA), known as the Superfund, which was passed in 1980. The primary goal of this legislation was to minimize the risk to health posed by the nation's uncontrolled waste sites. A $1.6 billion fund was established to cover the cost of cleaning up sites placed on a National Priorities List. At least 40 percent of the cost of cleanup was to be financed by the operators, generators, and haulers who were responsible for the hazardous waste.

Responsible parties were induced to contribute to cleanup through negotiated settlement or, if this failed, through litigation. Treble damages were to be assessed against those parties who did not comply with an EPA order. Furthermore, the EPA could finance cleanups in the face of recalcitrance on the part of a responsible party, and then sue them for cost recovery and treble damages.

In this case study, you play the role of EPA administrator appointed by the president. The questions you should answer after reading the rest of the case study are as follows:

1. What would you have done in implementing CERCLA?
2. How would you balance the competing interests of industry profits and a cleaner environment?
3. How could you satisfy the political demands on your position?

The Superfund

Although modern technology has produced economic development miracles, its increasing generation of hazardous substances presents an imminent and serious danger to public health and the environment. In an influential article, a Superfund proponent, Senator Robert T. Stafford, lamented the danger to humans posed by dependency on synthetic chemicals for "health, livelihood, housing, transportation, food, and for our funerals . . . there has been a realization that what is our meat may also be our poison" (*EPA Journal* 1981, 9). Stafford cited several studies and reports by the Congress, a Presiden-

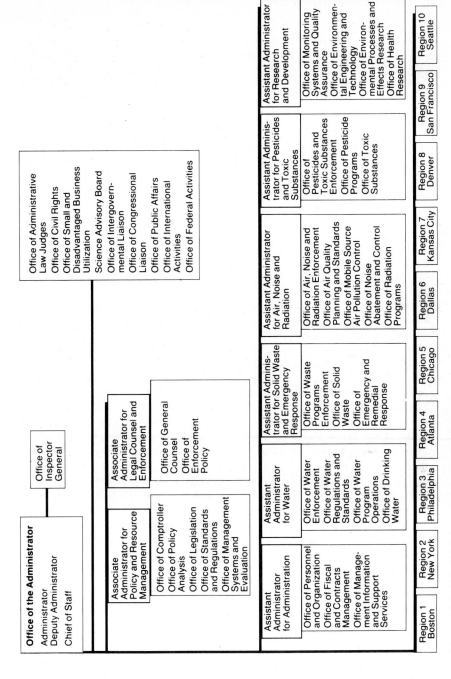

Figure 12.1. U.S. Environmental Protection Agency

SOURCE: *U.S. Government Manual*. July 1, 1989, p. 554.

tial Committee on Toxic Substances Strategy, the EPA, and independent, public agencies, which have reached a similar conclusion: Hazardous chemical substances imminently and seriously threaten humans and the environment. Testifying before the Senate Subcommittee on Environmental Pollution and Resource Protection in 1979, an EPA administrator cited actual studies showing that

there are about 3,500 incidents involving chemicals per year from sources which have the potential of releasing significant quantities of hazardous substances either onto land or into water. Of these, it is estimated that about 50 percent, or 1,700 spills, would reach navigable waters . . . there are about 700–1,200 significant spills per year.

These studies and reports about the nation's environment seemed at first to be a remote call for a legislative initiative to correct and avert a public health as well as an environmental disaster. There were, of course, protests and counterprotests by affected interest groups, commonly identified as "environmentalists" and "industrialists." The interests of these groups are in conflict, and this clash is reflected in the political agenda.

Jolted by the incident of Love Canal—site of the first abandoned hazardous chemical dump to receive wide public attention—as well as other incidents, Congress adopted the Superfund Act. The Superfund was "a trust fund of up to $1.6 billion during a 5-year period beginning in 1981, to provide emergency and long-term cleanup by the U.S. government of chemical spills and abandoned hazardous waste sites that threaten people or the environment" (*EPA Journal* June 1981, 13). Eighty-seven percent of the Superfund is derived from taxes imposed on oil (source of raw material for many synthetic chemicals) and on forty-two other specific chemical compounds. About 13 percent of the trust fund money comes from general tax revenues. The Superfund law requires states to pay for some of the costs undertaken under the Superfund, and to clean up some uncontrolled hazardous sites on their own. The federal-state effort envisioned in the Superfund was to complement reparative actions by those responsible for creating the hazardous dump sites.

After defining the objectives and goals of the Superfund, Congress mandated the EPA to formulate appropriate policies to implement the overall goal, but with few guidelines. EPA was to develop a national contingency plan that detailed (1) methods for identifying and investigating dump sites; (2) cleanup and evaluation procedures; (3) federal, state, and local government roles in these actions; (4) criteria for assuring cost-effective remedial plans; and (5) priority standards for cleaning up dump sites. In addition, Congress required that at least one dump site from each state be identified among the 100 sites that were designated in the National Priorities List (NPL).

In keeping with congressional intent, the implementation tasks of EPA include (1) discovery and identification of hazardous dump sites, (2) classifying these on a National Priorities List, (3) cleanup, and (4) evaluation. The tools available to EPA to accomplish these tasks are administrative orders, imposition of fines, negotiations, and court litigation.

The EPA's implementation structure is typical of federal programs. It includes regional offices (see Figure 12.1), state and local governments, and private business firms and groups. During the first two years of the program (1981–1983), EPA adopted a nonconfrontational compliance strategy. The EPA made minimimal use of the fund-option threat or of cleanup orders with their treble damage penalties for noncompliance. It attempted to conserve the Superfund as a means of reducing the federal budget deficit and imposed heavy cleanup burdens on the states. By 1983 EPA was waist-deep in scandals.

Its administrator, Anne Burford, was charged with political favoritism, conflict of interest, and mismanagement.

A congressional investigation in 1983 revealed that one chemical company had been allowed to edit an EPA report about dioxin contamination of two rivers and a bay near its plant and to delete critical statements that implicated it as the major source of the contamination (*Time* 28 March 1983, 18). In addition, the EPA official in charge of the solid waste program, Rita Lavelle, participated in a Superfund cleanup case in which the responsible industry, Aerojet General Corporation, was her former employer. Lavelle frequently had lunches and dinners with chemical industry officials and was warned about the appearent impropriety of this by congressional officials. In addition, EPA was unable to account for over $53.6 million of the 1982 Superfund appropriation.

Anne Burford refused to hand over certain documents to the congressional investigating committee, invoking executive privilege. She was supported by President Reagan in this. Rita Lavelle also invoked executive privilege when she was asked to testify before Congress. Determined to get to the bottom of the scandal, Congress cited both officials for contempt. Congressional hearings revealed that EPA officials were involved in shredding documents, deceiving Congress, and committing perjury. The scandal (called "sewergate" by some) put EPA on the defensive.

In late 1983, after Burford was removed, EPA adopted an aggressive enforcement strategy. It delegated increased enforcement discretion to its regional offices. EPA severely limited offers of release from future liability of responsible companies, invoked its fund-option threat, and emphasized court litigation to compel responsible party action.

While the Burford strategy was characterized as placing too much emphasis on negotiated compliance and favoritism toward industry, the post-Burford strategy was characterized by its critics as placing an excessive emphasis on threats and heavy costs to industry. Industry argued that the aggressive enforcement strategy would not be effective because many companies could not afford the cleanup costs.

Which strategy do you think would result in more settlements and cleanups? Which implementation strategy would you expect to be more effective and why? What standard are you using to determine effectiveness?

One economist who investigated these questions found that there were settlements for cleanup at thirteen sites in the Burford period and settlements equivalent to cleanup at thirty-three sites in the two years after Burford (Barnett 1988). He also found that the standards during the Burford era were more lax than those of the later period, and that the requirements for placing limits on and for addressing soil and groundwater contamination were more lenient.

Which of the two constituted successful implementation of the CERCLA? If congressional intentions are taken as the standard, the post-Burford strategy was more successful; however, it also fell short of getting 40 percent of cleanup costs financed by the responsible parties (it achieved a 28.7 percent rate in the post-Burford era compared to about 7.8 percent under Burford) (Barnett 1988, 20). Hence, while there was some improvement after Burford, the EPA still fell far short of cleaning up the hazardous waste sites that threatened the lives of those living near them.

The EPA record had not improved much by the end of the 1980s. In early 1989 it was reported that those responsible for cleaning up the sites were private contractors who had virtually taken control of the Superfund program, "reaping hefty profits for work that is often sloppy and costs too much, according to the Office of Technology Assessment" (Weisskopf 1989, 32). The report of the Office of Technology Assessment (OTA) said that only forty-three of the thousands of toxic waste sites nationwide were cleaned up in the eight years of Superfund. The private contractors were given a strong role by

Congress when Superfund was initiated because they assumed that private firms had the expertise to remove toxic wastes quickly and effectively without the need for a huge bureaucracy. "But as contractors received 80 percent to 90 percent of Superfund's annual budget—$4 billion since 1980—their responsibilities grew from testing and cleanup to the development of policy positions and the drafting of key documents, the OTA says" (Weisskopf 1989, 32). The firms, which made huge profits, got contracts to implement cleanup projects they helped to formulate. They also recommended cleanup techniques offered by companies in which they had a financial interest.

The OTA recommended a major restructuring of EPA. It also estimated that the total cleanup costs over the next fifty years would be $500 billion. OTA criticized EPA's organization; the EPA's Washington headquarters does not even have complete records of actions taken at each site. Cleanup standards varied widely from site to site. For example, the cleanup standard for benzene at one South Carolina site was seven times more stringent than the standard for benzene at a New Hampshire site (Carpenter 1989, 49).

Discussion Questions
1. Is the Superfund a case of failed implementation?
2. Would the Reagan administration say it failed?
3. What are the main defects in implementing Superfund?
4. What would you have done if you had been EPA director?

NOTES

1. The FSA depends in large part on the availability of day care. A bill to provide federal assistance for day care was not passed during the 1989 session, making implementation of FSA just about impossible (Johnson 1989, AI).
2. We are indebted to Ernest Uwazie, a Ph.D. candidate in Justice Studies at Arizona State University for doing much of the research for this case study.

CHAPTER 13

Federalism and Public Administration

INTERGOVERNMENTAL RELATIONS ARE EVERYWHERE

Almost every policy area, from railroads to zoos, involves an intricate web of intergovernmental and private organizational agencies. Nice (1987) describes how Amtrak is structured. Through the National Railroad Passenger Corporation, passed in 1970, the federal government operates all of the long-distance passenger trains in the United States. Much of the track on which the trains run is owned by private railroad companies. Revenues for the operation of the trains is provided by a combination of customers and federal and state subsidies. Local governments contribute money to build and repair stations. We have passenger railroads in the United States because of this system; each agency by itself could not do it. As another close observer of the federal system notes (Kettl 1986, 73), "Nearly everything has become intergovernmental; it has become far more difficult to differentiate national from state and local functions." Wildavsky (1984, 7) adds: "Along the way, participation in making and implementing policy by all sorts of private interests and levels of government has markedly increased."

The American federal system is incredibly diverse. In addition to the 50 states, there are over 3,000 counties, 18,800 municipalities, 16,800 townships, 15,000 school districts, and 2,600 special service districts. Along with numerous interest groups, nonprofit organizations, and for-profit business firms, these many governments are all part of the complex yet amazingly flexible system through which policy is implemented.

The U.S. Constitutional Basis

This system has been made possible through the structure created by the U.S. Constitution. Actually, only two levels of government are recognized by the Constitution:

federal and state. All the rest are created through legislation of state governments. Certain specific powers are expressly reserved to the national government by Article 1, Section 8, of the Constitution. These include levying and collecting taxes, borrowing money, regulating commerce, coining money, and declaring war, among others. The so-called "elastic clause" of Section 8 also gives the Congress all the implied powers necessary to carry out those functions expressly reserved to the national government. The Tenth Amendment to the Constitution reserves to the states all powers not delegated to the federal government nor prohibited by the Constitution.

These constitutional provisions have been the source of immense controversy throughout American history. The Civil War was fought over the relative authority of the federal and state governments. Much of this controversy has focused on the old questions: Which level of government should handle what policy? Are states or the national government closer to the people? Is there too much or too little national government? Are the states capable of exercising the functions they perform? We shall address some of these questions later in this chapter. However, we need to stress here that these are only a few of the issues involved in administering policy in a federal system. The interrelations among all the numerous units of government and private organizations are crucial because all these units are intimately involved in making and implementing public policy. Thus, the system we call federalism might be more appropriately labeled *intergovernmental relations.* We will continue to use the terms interchangeably, however, because it is the constitutional structure of federalism that makes the multifaceted intergovernmental system possible.

THE FEDERAL GRANT-IN-AID SYSTEM

The principal way the federal government makes policy in the federal system is through grants-in-aid to the states.

Types of Federal Grants

There are three major types of federal grants and several subtypes within these. The three major types are categorical, block, and revenue-sharing grants. *Categorical* grants, which were used heavily during the Great Society years (1966–1970), are given for specific purposes, such as compensatory education. Categorical as opposed to other types of grants are used when state and local governments do not or cannot provide a public service at a sufficiently high level without the help of the federal government. Categorical grants are mostly redistributive, and local governments have less discretion in how the money will be spent than is the case with block grants.

A *block* grant gives local governments great discretion in how the money will be spent and generally is used for a wide range of purposes within a broad policy area such as education. *Revenue sharing,* which gives recipients the greatest latitude, is similar to the block grant; in both cases, the federal government simply acts as a conduit for money it collects from citizens, returning it to them via the state and local governments. Block grants and revenue sharing are thus favored by those who believe in local control.

There are two major funding models by which grant monies can be allocated. In one, money is distributed by formula (e.g., in accord with the percentage of the population below the official poverty line); in the other, money is provided for a specific project (e.g., to acquire land for a planned park). The proportion of the total cost of the program that the federal government bears under formula grants can vary from 100 percent to just a small share. Grants can be open- or closed-ended, and have no ceiling or a specified amount that can be spent.

Federal grants-in-aid to states and localities, although declining during the Reagan administration, still amounted to $102.6 billion in 1986 and accounted for almost a quarter of all state and local revenue (see Table 13.1). The federal government is heavily involved in many policy matters, but that does not mean that management in the system is a one-way street; it involves both top-down and bottom-up lines of influence and power.

At the top levels federal officials try to ensure that recipients of federal monies carry out programs in a way that is at least somewhat consistent with the objectives set in Washington. Most of this is done indirectly through bargaining rather than by issuing mandates, rules, or regulations (Ingram 1977; Salamon 1981). At the bottom level (i.e., state and local governments), officials try to make programs work for their own government's purposes while still satisfying federal requirements. Much adaptation and adjustment in policy from place to place occurs as a result.

ADMINISTRATION IN THE FEDERAL SYSTEM

Administration in the federal system is a delicate process that takes place among policy professionals more than through formal channels. Policy professionals work at all levels of government. They help create the cohesiveness necessary for conjoint intergovernmental action. Peterson, Rabe, and Wong (1986, 160–161) describe policy professionals as follows:

> In their chosen areas of expertise they form a unified corps by virtue of similar values and orientations, similar educational experiences, common expectations of pursuing a career within a policy domain . . . , reinforcement of ties and values at meetings of professional associations, reading professional journals, and participating in career training programs.

The emergence of policy professionals is a recent occurrence. For most of American history, there were few professionally educated and trained administrators, particularly at the state and local levels. However, since 1970, the professional competence of administrators at the state and local levels of government has improved dramatically, and this has had a significant impact on the administration of public policy. According to political scientists Peterson, Rabe, and Wong (1986, 189), policy professionals have made the federal system run smoothly; they believe that "in most cases federal redistributive programs are implemented more successfully if they can be buried within the routines of established organizations controlled by professionals

TABLE 13.1. Federal Grants-in-Aid in Relation to State-Local Receipts from Own Sources, Total Federal Outlays, and Gross National Product, 1955–1987 (Dollar Amounts in Billions)

| Fiscal Year | Federal Grants-in-Aid (Current Dollars) | | As a Percentage of— | | | Federal Grants in Constant Dollars, (1972 Dollars, GNP Deflator) | |
	Amount	Percent Increase or Decrease (−)	State-Local Receipts From Own Sources	Total Federal Outlays	Gross National Product	Amount	Percent Real Increase or Decrease (−)
1955	$ 3.2	4.9%	11.8%	4.7%	0.8%	$ 5.6	3.7%
1956	3.7	15.6	12.3	5.0	0.9	6.2	10.7
1957	4.0	8.1	12.1	5.2	0.9	6.5	4.8
1958	4.9	22.5	14.0	6.0	1.1	7.8	20.0
1959	6.5	32.7	17.2	7.0	1.4	10.0	28.2
1960	7.0	7.7	16.8	7.6	1.4	10.8	8.0
1961	7.1	1.4	15.8	7.3	1.4	10.9	0.9
1962	7.9	11.3	16.2	7.4	1.4	11.9	9.2
1963	8.6	8.9	16.5	7.7	1.5	12.6	5.9
1964	10.1	17.4	17.9	8.6	1.6	14.7	16.7
1965	10.9	7.9	17.7	9.2	1.7	15.5	5.4
1966	13.0	19.3	19.3	9.6	1.8	17.9	19.3
1967	15.2	16.9	20.6	9.7	2.0	20.3	13.4
1968	18.6	22.4	22.4	10.4	2.2	23.6	16.3
1969	20.3	9.1	21.6	11.0	2.2	24.2	2.5
1970	24.0	18.2	22.9	12.3	2.5	27.0	11.6
1971	28.1	17.1	24.1	13.4	2.7	29.6	9.6
1972	34.4	22.4	26.1	14.9	3.0	34.4	16.2
1973	41.8	21.5	28.5	17.0	3.3	39.7	15.4
1974	43.4	3.8	27.3	16.1	3.1	37.9	−4.5
1975	49.8	14.7	29.1	15.0	3.4	39.2	3.4
1976	59.1	18.7	31.1	15.9	3.6	43.5	11.0
1977	68.4	15.7	31.0	16.7	3.7	46.7	7.4
1978	77.9	13.9	31.7	17.0	3.7	49.4	5.8
1979	82.9	6.4	31.3	16.5	3.5	48.1	−2.6
1980	91.5	10.4	31.7	15.5	3.6	48.2	0.2
1981	94.8	3.6	30.1	14.0	3.3	46.1	−4.4
1982	88.2	−7.0	25.6	11.8	2.9	40.4	−12.4
1983	92.5	4.9	24.7	11.4	2.9	40.7	0.7
1984	97.6	5.5	23.7	11.5	2.7	41.3	1.5
1985e	106.0	8.6	23.7	11.2	2.8	43.1	4.4
1986e	102.6	−3.2	21.4	10.7	2.5	40.1	−7.0
1987e	100.4	−2.1	19.5	10.1	2.2	37.7	−6.0

e = estimated. (Advisory Commission on Intergovernmental Relations, *Significant Features of Fiscal Federalism,* 1985–1986 edition, p. 19.)

who are well removed from local policy pressures." This is because they are not as loyal to local interests as are elected officials.

Of course, there is not unanimity of opinion among policy professionals on all issues. Gormley (1987) found substantial agreement among state and federal administrators on water management issues, but less on air pollution and waste management issues. In regard to water management, Gormley concluded: "In short, on a wide variety of fundamental water policy questions, there are no significant differences between state and federal administrators" (pp. 289–290). But in air pollution policy, he found that there were a number of bitter disputes between administrators in Ohio and U.S. Environmental Protection Agency administrators. The most dramatic difference concerned whether the state should establish an annual automobile inspection and maintenance program in areas with severe air quality problems. Such differences did not exist in Wisconsin on air pollution, but in the area of waste management, Wisconsin officials were considerably more likely than federal regulators to believe that more landfills needed to be built.

On broad policy issues, such as the desirability of technological solutions and the relative reliability of particular technologies, there was considerable agreement between state and federal administrators (Gormley 1987, 296). Thus, while there may be disagreement between some states and federal administrators on specific policy problems, there was overall agreement about the means by which problems might be alleviated.

THE HISTORICAL DEVELOPMENT OF THE FEDERAL SYSTEM

In earlier periods of American history, the interaction between the federal and state governments was minimal; state and federal governments acted independently. *Dual federalism* characterized intergovernmental relations, although there is some evidence that when interaction did occur, it was cooperative rather than conflictual (Elazar 1984). Under a system of dual federalism, each level of government pursues its own separate functions without depending on the other. In the early days of the Republic, the only domestic program in which the federal government was involved was the postal service. Throughout much of the nineteenth century, because of suspicion of a strong central government that was embedded in the American political tradition, there was resistance to giving the federal government a greater role in domestic policy making.

The nation-centered model, in which the federal government dominates, has existed at various times. Alexander Hamilton was a proponent of this model and argued in favor of a national bank. Although he did not win this argument, the nation-centered model dominated for a time during the early years of the Republic. It became dominant again during the Civil War over the attempt of the southern states to secede, and during the 1930s as the federal government engaged in a number of efforts to pull the country out of the Great Depression. Obviously, states were not equipped to act together for the common good without leadership. Thus, the nation-centered model has tended to become dominant during times of crisis.

The state-centered model has been advocated primarily by conservatives and southern Democrats. The southern Democrats prefer states' rights because they oppose government interference in the area of civil rights of blacks; the conservatives have advocated states' rights because they oppose interference with business.

Dual federalism refers to a system in which each level of government is responsible for a separate area of policy and is completely autonomous over that policy area. This system requires that we be able to distinguish which governmental functions belong to each level, a task many scholars would say is not possible. Moreover, there is considerable evidence that such a system has never really operated except as constitutional doctrine of the U.S. Supreme Court (Elazar 1984; Elazar et al. 1969).

Although there has indeed been conflict and competition between the federal and state governments over the course of history, leading scholars of federalism (Grodzins 1963; Elazar 1984) believe that there always has been an intermingling of all levels of government. Called marble-cake federalism by political scientist Morton Grodzins, this system existed even in the nineteenth century in all areas of policy, from economic development to foreign policy.

Federal grants were made to the states from the earliest days of the Republic, but they were small, specific grants of land for the support of local education. These continued throughout the nineteenth century and in the latter part of that century they provided the foundation for land-grant universities in each of the states. For example, the 1862 Morrill Act made grants of land available to the states for them to create land-grant colleges. These were one-shot grants that did much to promote American higher education but did not greatly affect other aspects of state policy. The Hatch Act of 1887 was the first annual cash grant program. Among its purposes was the establishment of agricultural experiment stations. But still less than 1 percent of state and local revenues were provided by the federal government at the turn of the century.

The establishment of the federal income tax in 1917 changed all of this. The income tax provided the federal government with financial resources to give grants-in-aid to the states for such projects as highway construction and vocational education, which imposed planning and administrative requirements on the states for the first time. These were developmental programs that fell within the traditional sphere of local government activity; they contributed to the development of the local infrastructures that states and local governments needed for economic development. As Peterson, Rabe, and Wong point out (1986, 81).

> Because [these grants] merely augmented what state and local governments were already doing, the federal government minimized regulation, left the procedures for consulting citizens to local officials, accepted the fact that states would act as allies of local governments in the administrative process, and conducted few evaluations.

Such grants were naturally praised by state and local governments because they could be substituted for local revenues, thereby alleviating the need for state and local governments to finance these programs entirely out of their own, more limited, revenue sources. Through the income tax, the federal government had access to resources, while state and local governments had the needs and the means to implement the programs. Modern intergovernmental relations was born out of this interdependence.

Between 1933 and 1938 under the New Deal, Congress created sixteen grant-in-aid programs, most of which involved emergency programs aimed at alleviating hardships created by the Great Depression. By the late 1930s, the federal government was spending $1 billion annually on aid to state and local governments.

The Social Security Act of 1935 laid the foundation for a national social welfare system that remains largely intact today. The system has changed the nature of federalism by creating a link betwen the national and state governments that did not exist before. It enlarged the federal supervisory role and established the constitutionality of federal expenditures on policy matters that were beyond the immediate powers granted it in the Constitution (*U.S. v. Butler,* 1936).

Growth in the federal grant system slowed down during World War II. Growth remained slow until the 1960s. Then, the number and size of federal grants increased rapidly in numerous programs such as Medicare, Medicaid, Model Cities, and the Elementary and Secondary Education Act (ESEA) of 1965. In 1965 alone, 109 grant programs were enacted. By the end of 1966 there were 379 grant-in-aid programs for state and local governments.

In contrast to previous federal grants-in-aid that were primarily for developmental purposes, the 1960s witnessed a rash of grants for redistributive purposes. Developmental programs are intended to improve the economic position of a community in its competition with other areas. Redistributive programs are those that benefit low-income or needy groups. Federal aid to highways is a developmental grant; Medicaid is a redistributive grant. During the 1960s, redistributive programs designed to shore up individuals' incomes, such as Aid to Families with Dependent Children (AFDC), early childhood education, job training of the unemployed, and Medicaid, increased twice as fast as inflation. These continued during the 1970s; only revenue sharing and environmental grants distinguished the priorities of the 1970s.

The Beginning of Conflict in the Federal System

With the advent of redistributive grants (i.e., grants that redistribute income from the wealthy to the poor), conflict rather than cooperation began to characterize the federal system. For example, Model Cities and the War on Poverty programs, both of which were redistributive, set off conflicts between those who felt that the federal government should establish federal standards and goals for social welfare and civil rights and those who favored a decentralized approach to these policy areas.

The Johnson administration targeted grants to try to ensure that the agencies that received them would be forced to spend the money on the purposes it (the Johnson administration) wanted. It used project grants that allocated money on the basis of proposals submitted by agencies rather than automatically to all eligible recipients. In 1964, project grants accounted for one-quarter of grants spending, but they accounted for one-half by 1969 (Haider 1974, 55). The Economic Opportunity Act of 1964 attempted to bypass the established state-local welfare structure and link federal programs directly to the hard-core poor. This strategy generated a great deal of controversy and opposition. Chicago's Mayor Richard Daley refused to surrender control over local jobs and policy making. In a little more than a year's time, the Johnson administration backed away from this strategy.

By 1967, attempts were made to control the costs of welfare programs through the Work Incentive Program (WIN). This initiative required employable welfare recipients to enroll in job training programs. But by 1968, the employment policy was foundering in complexity. No less than 10,000 separate contracts had been issued by the Department of Labor to private businesses, nonprofit and community-based organizations, and state and local agencies (Robertson 1984, 21).

Controversy mounted, particularly among those who did not have the "grantsman's" skills to secure the federal monies. Elected officials at all levels felt that they were losing control of their governments (Haider 1974, 57–62).

These programs also raised questions about whether federal programs were working as intended. Early implementation studies of many Great Society programs (Head Start, compensatory education, Model Cities, job training) concluded that they had failed during implementation. One seminal study (Pressman and Wildavsky 1984) identified a confusing multiplicity of government and nongovernment agencies and decision points that made it almost impossible to achieve the "great expectations" conceived in Washington. Although subsequent studies (Schwartz 1983; Peterson, Rabe, and Wong 1986, 10) concluded that "many of the observed difficulties may have resulted more because the program was new than because it was federal," local government administrations often felt that they were awash in red tape. Thus, some changes in the system of federal grants had to be made.

The Switch to General Revenue Sharing

Categorical grants resulted in confusion as well as conflict. As a result, in 1974, the federal government required each state to establish a single state agency through which all federal grant money should be channeled. As a result of the conflict and confusion in the system, Richard Nixon received substantial support when he proposed revenue sharing as a new approach. Two kinds of revenue sharing were contained in Nixon's proposal: (1) general revenue sharing, which included no restrictions whatsoever in how and on what state and local governments could spend their funds; and (2) special revenue sharing, which targeted particular policy areas (e.g., education) with broad-purpose grants. Congress accepted the principle of revenue sharing in 1973 with the authorization of block grants such as the Comprehensive Employment and Training Act and the Community Development Block Grant in 1974.

Rather than decreasing during the 1970s under Presidents Nixon and Ford, federal aid grew as Congress developed a number of separate block grants. Grants were redirected to suburban, rural, and Sunbelt constituencies and away from cities. By 1975, the percentage of all federal grants for cities going to large cities had declined to 44 percent—down from 62 percent in 1968 (Palmer 1984, 36). The principal vehicle for this aid was revenue sharing, which gave states and localities broad discretion in how to spend the funds. State and local officials were naturally pleased with this shift in funding because these grants gave them a great deal of discretion in how the money was to be spent. But not all local officials were happy with block grants. Scarcely two years after Congress passed the 1974 Nixon Community Block Grant Program, some local leaders were calling it a waste of money. Representatives of the poor were especially critical. The Southern Regional Council said that local governments were permitted to deviate from the national responsibilities that the 1974 Act supposedly placed on them.

President Carter continued the emphasis on block grants, but it was not until 1978 that he introduced his domestic policy labeled the New Partnership. This policy channeled federal funds to more impoverished areas of cities. But, to the surprise of many observers, there were no new policy initiatives or requests for increased expenditures for federal aid by Carter. He argued in favor of more federal control over how and where local jurisdictions could spend their funds but, at the same time, his administration did not impose rigid guidelines or regulations on states. This hands-off approach was in keeping with his avowed disdain for the "Washington establishment," an opinion he had developed as governor of Georgia (Caputo 1984). The Carter period can be viewed as a transition from the earlier years of expansion in federal grants to the Reagan years of contraction. For example, in 1978, CETA spent $4.5 billion on public employment programs, funding 725,000 jobs. That marked the peak of the CETA program and its spending went down thereafter.

Reforming the federal system was one of Reagan's highest priorities when he came into office in 1980. According to Richard S. Williamson, Reagan's assistant for intergovernmental affairs (1982, 19), President Reagan had "a dream . . . to change how America is governed. . . . He is seeking a 'quiet revolution,' a new federalism which is a meaningful American partnership." In his 1980 inaugural address, Reagan set forth his plan for federalism:

> It is my intention to curb the size and influence of the federal establishment and to demand recognition of the distinction between the powers granted to the federal government and those reserved to the states or to the people. All of us need to be reminded that the federal government did not create the states; the states created the federal government. (Inaugural Address, Washington, D.C., 20 January 1981)

Reagan tried to make his dream a reality by creating nine new or substantially revised block grants in the Omnibus Budget Reconciliation Act of 1981 and by putting intergovernmental relations at the center of his agenda in 1982. The Reagan administration diminished the detail of federal prescriptions, reduced federal monitoring, consolidated grants, and reduced federal constraints. The price for this greater flexibility was a significant reduction in the amount of federal money going to the states. And when his goals regarding federalism conflicted with other highly held values, such as reducing the federal budget, deregulation, or advancing the conservative social agenda, federalism took a back seat. Thus, he cut block grants more than other forms of federal aid, proposed modifying and then terminating general revenue sharing. When states moved in to regulate business, he supported taking away regulatory power from the states.

In 1982, the Reagan administration tried to effect much more sweeping changes in the system when the president proposed swapping functions with the states. Under the proposal, the federal government would take over entire responsibility for Medicare and give welfare and forty other programs to the states along with some tax cuts to support them. State governments were cool toward the proposal, and although Reagan tried to strike a deal with the governors, "the philosophical gap proved to be too wide. To state and local officials, the President needed a bigger carrot than in good faith he felt he could offer" (Williamson 1983, 26). Reagan's proposal was rejected by Congress in 1983.

In a similar vein, Reagan's 1985 tax reform proposal to eliminate the federal income tax deduction for state and local tax payments, which is one of the largest federal subsidies for state and local governments, led some to question his commitment to federalism. However, the Reagan administration succeeded in reversing trends in federal aid that had begun in 1958 and redirected the cooperative model of federalism back into the dual federalism that had existed at the beginning of the century.

ADAPTATION AND INNOVATION IN PROGRAMS DURING IMPLEMENTATION

The stereotype of the federal system that is popular among those who oppose federal involvement in the economy depicts a system in which the federal government forces the states and local governments to achieve federal, not state or local, policy goals. In fact, this view is not correct. Even in regard to categorical grants, there has been more bargaining and negotiating than mandating (Ingram 1977; Salamon 1981). For example, the social services grant program of 1969 was adopted to combat poverty by supporting services to help the poor escape poverty. But grant recipients used the money for a wide variety of state services, many of which had no relationship to antipoverty programs (Nice 1987, 64). Rather than mandating states to do specific things in conformance with the program, the federal government typically bargained with recipient agencies. Bargaining has been increasingly prevalent since 1980 as third-party governments (i.e., private businesses) have become the main implementors of policy under contracts with the government.

This system of implementation, whereby local areas change programs, has been viewed in conflicting ways by implementation scholars. Some have viewed it as failed implementation while others have looked at it as necessary adaptation to local needs. We shall consider these views in more detail in the next section.

In developmental as opposed to redistributive grants, there has been almost no attempt by the federal government to control how the grant money is spent. For example, in the area of federal grants for impacted areas (i.e., areas where there is a substantial federal government presence such as a military base), money has been spent by the recipients however they wanted. One local administrator in the program noted: "It is a wonderful program. There is no direct tracking of the money; it can be used for anything; it blends right in with local dollars" (quoted in Peterson, Rabe, and Wong 1986, 83). The program has been administered by the U.S. Office of Education, but only a handful of federal administrators have been responsible for implementation. They are supposed to keep track of how the money is being spent in thousands of school districts. Needless to say, supervision cannot be very close with such a wide span of control.

Another major result of this system of implementation is that each recipient agency spends the money it receives for different purposes. This is what some scholars call adaptive implementation (Berman 1980). Political scientist Tim Conlan (1986, 36) notes:

> As the principal implementors of governmental programs, state and local governments have been firmly rooted in the realities of service delivery, aware of constraints on government's abilities, and reflective of legitimate variations in community preferences and values.

This widely varying use of federal dollars occurs in several different policy areas. For example, grants for vocational education and hospital construction—both of which are developmental grants—were used freely by recipients for the purposes they wanted. Peterson, Rabe, and Wong (1986, 84) state: "Using federal funds for vocational education became virtually indistinguishable from efforts to improve local education in general." Hospital construction aid was an ideal pork barrel project, says political scientist Frank Thompson (1981, 34, 38). It enjoyed a milieu free of major implementation barriers.

The same is true of the Community Development Program in which administrative simplicity and local control were emphasized. San Diego used the monies for high-rise development in the downtown area; the city of Milwaukee used it for maintaining owner-occupied housing and neighborhood improvements; Baltimore used it for the city's comprehensive downtown redevelopment plan (Peterson, Rabe, and Wong 1986). In all cases, the money was given to projects and groups who had supported the local political officials who were in power.

Even with the shift to redistributive grants in the 1960s, implementors continued to enjoy substantial latitude in program implementation. More regulations were adopted in redistributive grants than in developmental grants, but most of them required little more than token compliance. Moreover, as we said above, redistributive grants experienced more controversy. They were difficult to manage and found federal and state officials at cross-purposes. In programs such as compensatory education (which was aimed at giving educationally deprived children better schooling), rent subsidies and health maintenance programs, the federal government sought to reformulate the way social services were being delivered at the local level. They imposed numerous and complicated standards on local service providers who were being asked to take on responsibilities that were not part of their usual agendas.

Federal redistributive programs were based on lofty expectations for a better, more economically just America. Unfortunately, they engendered more conflict than cooperation among local, state, and federal governments. Compensatory education, health maintenance, and rent subsidies were meant to *supplement,* not *supplant* local efforts.

Little wonder, then, that the implementations of these programs were deemed to be failures rather than healthy adaptations to fit local needs. However, some scholars believe that to consider the implementation of these programs as failures is to pass judgment too soon and that, in fact, implementation proceeded in stages until a successful and cooperative relationship was achieved.

Peterson, Rabe, and Wong (1986) identify three historical stages of the redistributive grants. In the first, the programs were cast in vague language and local officials were recalcitrant. In the second stage, the federal government adopted more precise regulations and required evaluations of the programs. In the third stage, in the late 1970s, adjustments were made by local and federal participants. More professional cadres were recruited at the local level; local officials became more sensitive to federal expectations, and federal expectations became more realistic.

Compensatory education is a good example of this process. When it was introduced in 1965, the major educational policy interest groups that helped formulate it had high expectations, but the law was vague and there was little federal direction or accounting. Personnel in the Office of Education, which was in charge of implementing it, viewed themselves as educators rather than administrators. There were only 100 people as late as 1976 who had administrative responsibilities for supervising program operation of some 14,000 local school systems (McLaughlin 1975). No one really *knew* how to run a successful compensatory education program nor how to implement such a broad-reaching program (Williams 1980). But great variation in programs is a built-in characteristic of the federal system, says professor of public administration Jerome Murphy (1977, 60). With its dispersion of power and control, "the federal system not only permits but encourages the evasion and dilution of federal reform, making it nearly impossible for the federal administrator to improve program priorities; those not diluted by congressional intervention can be ignored during state and local implementation."

However, implementation of compensatory education improved during the second phase. New regulations were enacted to compel greater program unity. Local officials chafed under these, so there was an increase in conflict and confusion. Title I of ESEA was amended in 1968, 1970, 1974, and 1978. Each time there was an attempt to specify more clearly the congressional commitment to helping disadvantaged children. In addition, enforcement activities of the Office of Education became more rigorous.

Advocacy groups such as the National Association for the Advancement of Colored People (NAACP) supported the new changes, and lawsuits were brought in some cities such as Milwaukee, charging local officials with misuse of funds. By the late 1970s, poor, educationally deprived children were much more likely to be in the program than their better-off counterparts. Peterson, Rabe, and Wong (1986, 140) write: "Clearly, federal rules were shaping policy implementation at the local level by phase 2."

During the third phase, a new tolerance of local diversity and an appreciation of the limits of federal regulations developed. At the same time, local areas came to accept the need to direct the program toward poor, low-achieving students. Several states even supplemented the federal program with their own efforts. Hence, by the third phase, implementation of the program began to succeed. Peterson, Rabe, and Wong (p. 147) claim: "The one area of social life in which blacks have made clear, identifiable gains has been within the educational system. What is more, those gains have been greatest during the elementary years, the very years minorities attended the schools that were the focus of compensatory education programs."

Other programs besides compensatory education went through the three-stage process as well, including health maintenance and the Education of All Handicapped Children Act of 1975. Unfortunately, earlier implementation studies concluded that these programs have been unsuccessfully implemented but by the late 1980s, a number of scholars had raised questions about the accuracy of these implementation studies.

NATIONAL-STATE, NATIONAL-LOCAL AND INTERLOCAL RELATIONS

National-State Relations

President Reagan's New Federalism proposals were part of a long succession of efforts to curtail national involvement in domestic policy making. The first and second Hoover Commissions (1947–1949; 1953–1955), the Kestenbaum Commission on Intergovernmental Relations (1953–1955); and the Joint Federal-State Action Committee (1957–1959) all attempted to reduce national activities and separate national and state programs. In some cases it may seem logical to do this. There are some policies and programs that affect the entire society and would seem to be appropriately the purview of the federal government; national defense is a prime example. Some policies and programs seem to affect only one subdivision of society and thus may be logically a function of local governments. Playgrounds and senior citizen centers are good examples here. But as political scientist David Nice (1987, 97) notes, "Separating government activities into national, state, and local functions may be attractive for programs that have only national, only state, or only local effects, but few major policies meet that requirement." Even foreign policy is strongly influenced by state and local governments (Palumbo 1969). Thus, it has not been possible to make a neat, functional separation between the federal and state policy areas. This is largely because disputes over the powers of the federal and state governments usually are really disputes about the kinds of policies that should be followed. If a group opposes a policy that the federal government is following, it is likely to argue that the question is one over which the states should have preeminent power.

Civil rights has been an area of the most intense controversy in national-state relations. Southern states, in particular, have claimed that the question is one that should be under the control of states, and states did control civil rights policy from 1877 until the 1950s. "Jim Crow" laws were adopted by southern states that required segregation of the races in schools, public accommodations, transportation, and a host of other areas. These laws were given constitutional blessing by the U.S. Supreme Court in decisions such as *Plessey v. Ferguson* (1896). But in the 1940s the doctrine of separate but equal adopted in the Plessey case began to collapse. The 1954 Supreme Court decision in *Brown v. Board of Education* put an end to the constitutionality of the doctrine in education. And the Civil Rights Act of 1964 and Voting Rights Act of 1965 demonstrated that the federal government is indeed supreme in policy areas if there is sufficient public support for the policies it is proposing.

There has been controversy in other realms as well. For example, the Sagebrush Rebellion in the West has pitted western cattle ranchers and mining interests against the federal government and environmental groups. The battle here, again, is over the direction of policy, particularly in regard to the huge amount of land the federal government owns in the West. Environmental interests want to maintain federal control so as to keep the land in its protected condition. Western cattle ranchers and mining interests would like the land to be given to the states where they feel there is a more receptive ear to their interests.

Nevertheless, despite areas of conflict, there also has been considerable cooperation between the federal government and states. The federal government has provided technical assistance and grants to the states. The two levels have shared the operation of programs in areas such as parks and environmental protection, emergency assistance, use of flood control and recreational facilities, and in controlling the movement of stolen goods.

The U.S. Supreme Court has at times acted as arbiter of the system, but since the question involves politics and policy, the Court is heavily criticized whenever it becomes involved. The states throughout history have claimed a right to be the final judge of who should have power. But since they have often acted to deny citizens their rights, such as voting, the states' reputation to act as arbiters has been sullied. Moreover, the states have been criticized as not being adequately equipped to perform the arbiter role. They have been weak insofar as they lack competitive political parties; state legislators are part-timers who are paid low salaries and do not have adequate staff support; governors are only one of several elected executive officers (such as the attorney general and the secretary of state); the terms of governors are too short and they are paid low salaries; too many detailed policy provisions are contained in state constitutions, making it difficult to effect fundamental policy changes; and finally, state bureaucracies are lacking in essential professional expertise.

A number of these weaknesses have been corrected in recent years. For example, most states have merit systems and many state employees have been professionally trained in the large number of university programs designed expressly for them. A number of scholars now believe that the states are in excellent institutional shape today. For example, political scientist William Gormley (1987, 285) observes: "Governors are stronger, state legislatures are more professional, and state bureaucracies are better organized." Daniel Elazar (1984, 188) a leading scholar of American federalism says: "Institutional change in the states since 1960 has been substantial, principally directed to bringing state government into line with the managerial revolution." In addition, the public is much better represented in a number of areas.

Hence, the states are better equipped today to manage programs than they were in the past. But there still are major objections to giving them the role of arbiter in federal-state relations, or in giving them autonomy in many areas. The principal objection is that it would create considerable policy confusion as each state adopts different rules and regulations. For example, the state had the power to adopt rules and regulations in commerce before the U.S. Supreme Court began to take it away from them (in the Minnesota rate case of 1913 and the Shreveport decision in 1914). The volume and variety of state regulations posed a serious barrier for interstate commerce. In 1913, forty-two state legislatures passed some 230 railroad regulation laws affecting such areas as extra crews, hours of labor, grade crossings, signal blocks, and electric headlights. Many of the laws were contradictory and resulted in large expenses for the railroads. In 1914, the railroads claimed that they were forced to spend $28 million to meet the various requirements of state laws (Kolko 1986, 381). Little wonder, then, that the railroads asked for federal regulation. By 1916, the federal government gained the upper hand in this area.

There was a resurgence of state power in the middle and late 1980s, but the balance between federal and state power is likely to remain in a delicate balance with shifts in the direction of federal power alternating with shifts in the direction of state power (which is somewhat correlated with shifts in power from the Democrats to Republicans in national politics).

National-Local Relations

National-local relations have been a part of American government since the beginning of the Republic, but they never were very extensive until recent times. The Great Depression and increasing urbanization of the country are the main reasons for the growth in direct national-local relations. Prior to 1950, the states were reluctant to help cities solve the problems they began to confront, particularly those caused by the great migrations of blacks from the South to northern cities that began after World War II. State legislatures were dominated by rural interests. As a result, cities turned to the federal government for help and it responded by providing mortgage assistance, social security (which relieved local governments of the burden of providing for retired, disabled people), and financial assistance through loans and grants. Moreover, grants given to states often are implemented by local governments.

Programs conceived in Washington and implemented by local agencies do not always perform as expected (Pressman and Wildavsky 1984), but this is often because the priorities and incentives in each local area are different. As Howett (1986, 170) has observed, "The fundamental feature of policy making and management at the state and local level is its extraordinary diversity." Of course, federal programs have had a dramatic impact on local governments, creating agencies and then abolishing them (such as urban renewal), and the federal government has fostered citizen involvement in policy making, particularly among minorities. Thus, the federal government has been a major force in setting local policy agendas. Nevertheless, given the great diversity among localities and the difficulty of monitoring them, there is wide local discretion in most areas.

Title I of the ESEA of 1965 is a case in point. The federal government wanted it to be focused mostly on the educationally deprived, but local officials wanted to treat it as a system of national general aid to education. Local officials won, and even used the aid for purposes totally unrelated to the educationally deprived. The U.S. Office of Education did little to change this. The same is true of the Comprehensive Employment and Training Act. It was used to replace local revenues and support existing programs more than it was for helping chronically unemployed gain job skills.

A number of attempts have been made to improve coordination between the federal and state governments. The federal government has various tools with which it can try to convince local governments to respond. It can (1) determine eligibility requirements before an area can receive a grant (e.g., it must experience unemploy-ment above a certain level), (2) approve or disappove grant applications or specify the form and content of an application (e.g., planning requirements, review process), (3) issue regulations and guidelines, (4) institute financial controls (e.g., require approval to withdraw funds or threaten to withhold funds), and (5) provide technical assistance to help an agency meet requirements.

Through the use of these tools, the federal government *indirectly* tries to influ-ence how policies are administered by local areas. The administrative problem from the local perspective is more direct. It must deliver the services, such as providing housing or building public facilities. In doing so, it must balance conformance with federal requirements with the needs of the local jurisdiction. Thus, administration at the local level is part bureaucratic and part political. *Constituency building* is a large part of administration, both within government agencies and outside. In all cases, it is a balance between top-down and bottom-up management. No policy will ever suc-ceed through top-down management alone. And as long as bottom-up management exists, there will be wide diversity from place-to-place in the outcomes of policies.

Interlocal Relations

Interlocal relations in the United States are tremendously diverse. This is both a bless-ing and curse, depending upon your theoretical and ideological view. It is a problem from the perspective of classical, top-down public administrative theory. In this view, because of the diversity of local governments, there is not sufficient authority or power in these governments to tackle the problems that spill over the borders of exist-ing local governments. For example, air and water pollution do not confine them-selves to the legal boundaries of cities, counties, and states. No one government in contemporary metropolitan areas can ameliorate air or water pollution by itself. For example, Maricopa County, Arizona, in which the city of Phoenix is located, is large enough geographically to be able to help reduce air pollution in its boundaries. Phoe-nix has some of the worst air pollution in the country, but the city cannot solve the problem itself. Maricopa County, on the other hand, does not have the power or authority to adopt some of the solutions that would help reduce the amounts of car-bon monoxide, ozone, and particulates that pervade its air. The traditional public administration solution is to create a regional government, perhaps through city-county consolidation, that would be able to adopt and implement policies that might help reduce air and water pollution. However, this solution has been found to be politically unrealistic. For a variety of reasons, voters will not support consolidation. Instead, metropolitan area governmental cooperative bodies have been created. These generally are forums in which the various governments can get together in the hope of cooperatively finding some policies that will address the problems. These cooperative arrangements have not proven to be very effective.

From the perspective of public choice theory, on the other hand, the multiplic-ity of governments in metropolitan areas is not a problem because they act as a sort of market. According to public choice theory, the market is a better organizational structure for addressing problems because it is the best way to allocate resources and achieve efficiency. Problems will be handled even better, in this view, if some services are "privatized"—which means that private, profit-making agencies are allowed to provide services—or if the proper incentives are used. A public choice solution to air pollution would be to charge fees to those who pollute. The assumption is that they will have an incentive to reduce their pollution and the monies collected can be used to find better ways to reduce pollution. If industrial polluters are required to purchase permits for each given amount of pollution they produce, they will reduce their pollution when the cost rises so high as to eat away at their profits. A proposal such as this was proposed by the Bush administration in 1989. In this proposal industries that managed to cut their pollution would get a "credit" which they then could sell to another industry. The problem with this solution to air pollution in a place such as Los Angeles or Phoenix is that the principal air polluters are automobile drivers. Thus, a better solution would be to develop mass transportation facilities rather than freeways. But the latter is politically unrealistic.

A third view of interlocal relations is the class perspective: In this view, the multiplicity of local governments is desirable because it allows people to live in areas they prefer and can afford. The upper-middle class can live in their suburban enclaves while the poor live in the decaying cities. This is desirable, say those who hold this view, because in a democracy people ought to be able to live where they can afford to and want to live. If some cannot afford to do this, those who can should not be blamed nor forced to pay for those who cannot. Of course, the result is greater class and racial segregation, which is dysfunctional from a societal point of view even if the system is desirable from an individualistic perspective.

None of these three perspectives of interlocal relations is necessarily correct. Each tells us something different about interlocal relations.

THE FUTURE OF FEDERALISM

Criticisms of federalism that were made during the 1970s, particularly those pertaining to metropolitan areas and the implementation of federal programs at the local level, were based on the classical public administration view. This view sought neat, hierarchical solutions to metropolitan policy problems. However, the size and diversity of the nation are too great for programs mandated from Washington to work. What may be appropriate for Los Angeles is not necessarily appropriate for rural Iowa. The failures of top-down federalism provided the Reagan administration with justification for cutting back on federal aid to state and local governments. Even though federal aid was greatly reduced from 1980 to 1988, many programs continued to operate, although in reduced form. They survived because they had developed strong political constituencies and professional support.

Not all areas were cut equally. Caputo (1984, 195–196) reports that big cities were hit harder than small cities and found it more difficult to make up the difference. Thus, concludes Caputo (p. 197), "the Reagan policies have had a substantial impact in [large] cities and . . . the policies have led to substantial reductions in city services and increases in local taxes in many cases. Despite this, the dominant conclusion is that the Reagan policies have not led to the drastic reductions in services and increases in local taxes that many city officials feared."

The amount by which services were cut also depended on the policy area. Health care was the least altered because it had the greatest professionalization and constituency support. For example, Medicaid was cut each year from 1980 to 1988 and rules for eligibility benefits and payments were changed so that states could restrict expenditures and access to the program. But all this did was cut the rate of growth in expenditures rather than fundamentally alter it. Education was in the middle; some programs were virtually cut, such as federal aid for impacted areas and for vocational education. But compensatory education and aid for special education for handicapped children survived.

At the opposite extreme was housing, which was the least professionalized and had the least constituency support. Community development was cut severely and construction of new public housing was completely phased out. Tenants in low-income housing were required to contribute 30 percent of their income for rent. Reliance was placed on privatization as a way to solve housing problems. But research in Birmingham, Alabama, found that private, for-profit efforts to increase the supply of low- and moderate-income housing were not significant (Moore and Sink 1986, 220). However, the private, *nonprofit* sector made significant contributions to housing for the elderly. The researchers who conducted the study (Moore and Sink, 222) concluded that the Reagan administration "has threatened to impoverish government by delegating equal protection for adequate housing to levels of government not necessarily equipped to guarantee it."

Similar findings have been made in other policy areas. An analysis of state participation in water pollution policy (Wassenberg, 1986) found that states did not increase their own contributions after federal cuts were made in water quality funds (which were reduced by 42 percent between 1981 and 1983). Instead, they cut back on their programs. Water pollution policy was returned to the pre-1972 era in which state governments were the primary architects and enforcers of pollution standards. Under these conditions, a Gresham's law (Rowland 1982) took over environmental regulation: the amount of regulation in all states declined to the level of the states that were doing the least. This occurred because environmentally conscious states would be penalized by a loss of industry to states with looser regulatory standards. According to Wassenberg (1986), states lack the capacity and political will to carry out comprehensive pollution regulation.

The question of whether the states can handle problems in areas such as environmental pollution, disposal of hazardous wastes, civil rights, economic development, education, social welfare, and a number of other areas has yet to be answered. Some scholars believe that the grants strategy helped to boost the policy-making abilities of governors' offices, legislatures, and state agencies relative to national government officials. "State service delivery has increased steadily throughout the entire last quarter century. The federal role increase from 1913 to 1957, leveled off, and declined somewhat over the last twelve or thirteen years" (Stephens 1970).

There are advantages and disadvantages involved in having states control policy in these areas. Among the advantages, the federal system promotes diversity and adaptability. But as Wildavsky (1984, 7) observes, "The cost of adaptability has been a decline in accountability." Such a system, Kettl (1988, 86) adds, "makes it difficult to determine just who is responsible for a problem at hand or how it can be resolved.

Furthermore, it makes it impossible for anyone to tackle the problems of the system as a whole.'' Moreover, federal grants ''did virtually nothing to alter the financial disparities among the states. . . . Only one-seventh of the grant formulae by the 1970s explicitly included criteria that emphasized the redistribution of aid to needy areas'' (Robertson 1989, 13). The wealthiest states received the most grants per capita (Arnold 1979, 268).

Whether you believe that tackling the problems of the system as a whole is a good or bad idea depends on your political persuasion. Adherents of competitive individualism would say the system is good because it allows greater diversity and flexibility. Those who believe the government has an obligation to help the poor would be more negative in their judgment because, says Wildavsky (1984, 8), ''The more centralization of programs and the narrower their focus, the greater the likelihood that funds will be targeted toward those most in need.''

The American federal system is a mixture, combining elements of centralization and decentralization. This mix has been characterized as pluralism. We pay more for services in such a system. Wildavsky (1984, 10) says that under a centralized system, costs will be kept down by a central agency. Under a decentralized system that allows only private fees for services (such as in health), suppliers will be constrained by what the people can afford. But under a mixed system of ''private and public payments, with spending spigots at numerous levels of government—that is most expensive. Pluralism pays more.'' In addition, the grants strategy reduces the probability of success in implementing social policy because it multiplies net points by adding state and local governments and a host of other participants to each phase in the policy process. Political scientist David Robertson (1989, 25) concludes that ''absent national government intervention the American federal policy structure tends to produce domestic policy that is uneven, inadequate, and expensive.'' Other scholars agree. Political scientist Donald Kettl (1988, 54) notes: ''The very complexity of the system, built upon interwoven (and sometimes inconsistent) goals and aspirations, has made it even more difficult to manage programs well and to make them responsive to the needs of citizens.'' But whether the programs have been a success, says Kettl, is difficult to answer because success is a relative term, its definition depending on one's perspective. Since there are many groups involved, and since each has a different vision about what ought to be accomplished, judging success is a difficult business.

This Janus-like system has been a characteristic of the American system throughout history (Golembiewski 1984, 239). On the one hand, the managerial culture stresses achievement and performance, with unity, vigor and dispatch. But it also glories in separation of powers, federalism, and civil liberties. There has been a historical tension between principles such as *unity of command* and *individualism*. The tension has been built into the American constitutional system and cannot be taken out. The executive, under the Constitution, is to see that the laws are faithfully executed, but in implementing them, the executive makes policy, and this is perfectly legitimate under the principle of separation of powers (although we continue to battle over this, as witnessed by the Iran-Contra diversion of funds; see Chapter 10).

If the executive has been winning the battle over the separation of powers, so that bureaucrats actually run the country (Rosenbloom 1983), we might chalk up the victory to a flaw in the constitutional system for not endowing the other branches with enough power to offset that of the executive. There have been swings in power back and forth between the executive and the other branches throughout history and the same is true of the federal system. For such conflict to exist in the system is not all bad. As Gormley (1987, 298) notes, "If federal and state officials agreed on all issues at all times, they could learn very little from one another. One of the virtues of an intergovernmental system is that it generates creative tension and strong feedback, from which many benefits flow." Conflict has two sides. It can be dysfunctional as in the case of air pollution: The states are more willing than the federal government to sacrifice air quality to economic growth. But it also can be functional by allowing states to adopt policies most suited to their individual circumstances. Thus, the battle over whether the states or the federal government should be more powerful depends on who is advantaged and who is disadvantaged on the specific issue (Wildavsky 1984, 11). It is not always easy to predict who is the winner in these struggles. Conservatives who advocate states' rights sometimes discover that the struggle does not turn out as expected, particularly when Republicans lose in contests for state government. This is tantamount to winning the principle but losing the substance. And this is the advantage of the federal system: There is no final solution to policy problems—nor should there be—for politics is the lifeblood of democracy.

SUMMARY

Almost all governmental functions in the United States involve intergovernmental and private agencies. The American federal system includes thousands of different types of governmental agencies. The U.S. Constitution recognizes only two levels: the national and the state; all the rest are created through state government legislatures.

The complex web of governments has raised numerous questions about which governments should be responsible for what programs. The principal mechanism by which the federal government makes policy in the federal system is through grants-in-aid. The federal government tries to ensure that federal monies are spent on programs that are consistent with the objectives set in Washington. But the actual way the system evolves is more complex.

A major part of the way the system works is through policy professionals who are experts in particular policy areas. The emergence of these professionals is a fairly recent occurrence. The problem is that they do not always agree in all policy areas.

Throughout the nineteenth century there was relatively little interaction between the federal and state governments. There were few federal grants during this period. The major conflicts in this time were between a nation-centered model and a state-centered model. Although there has been ongoing conflict and competition between the federal and state governments, there also has been an intermingling of all levels of government.

Federal grants have been made to the states from the earliest days of the Republic, but not until the creation of the income tax in 1917 was there much growth. Most of the grants during this period were used to develop local infrastructures for economic development.

The next period of growth in the gi ant system occurred during the Great Depression when a number of new programs were created. This growth slowed during and after World War II, but picked up again in the 1960s. Grants originating in the latter time period were mostly redistributive in contrast to the earlier developmental grants, and they led to the beginning of conflict in the federal system. Model Cities and the War on Poverty were two of the most controversial programs.

Early implementation studies indicated that many of these programs were not working, findings that laid the groundwork for a switch to general revenue sharing. The attraction of revenue sharing was that it would give the states and localities greater freedom to decide how the federal money was to be spent.

Federal aid to the states increased during the 1970s under Presidents Nixon and Ford, leveled out under President Carter, and decreased greatly under President Reagan.

Reagan's stated intention was to curb the size and influence of the federal government, which he tried to do through block grants. However, the more extreme proposals of the Reagan administration to switch some responsibilities, particularly welfare, to the states were rejected by the states and by Congress.

Still with most grants, instead of engaging in conflict in which the federal government attempts to impose its will on the states, the states have been able to spend federal monies pretty much as they please, particularly developmental as opposed to redistributive grants. However, the states had considerable latitude even with redistributive grants; often this latitude meant that the grants did not actually help the poor as was intended.

Redistributive grants, such as compensatory education, went through three stages in which the implementation improved so that by the third stage it had begun to succeed.

The question of which level, federal or state, should have predominant influence in a particular policy area is a political one. If states had maintained control over civil rights policy, for example, there would not have been many advances in reducing discrimination, particularly in the South. There have been many improvements in the management capabilities of state governments in recent years so they are now better equipped to manage programs than in the past.

National-local relations grew after 1950 as cities turned to the federal government for help that state governments were not providing. But many of these programs have not been implemented as expected.

Interlocal relations in the United States are tremendously diverse. The many units of local government make it difficult to address problems that transcend local boundaries, such as air pollution, and there has not been much success in creating areawide governments to overcome this. From the perspective of public choice, the multiplicity of governments is not necessarily bad, and from a class perspective, some would argue that it is good.

Federal aid to states was cut significantly during the Reagan administration, but the states have not been able to take up the slack as was intended. The tension that has existed in the federal system throughout American history is likely to remain, and this is a part of American politics that is not likely to end.

CASE STUDY: A NATIONAL INDUSTRIAL POLICY

Introduction

The purpose of this case study is to highlight the policy and administrative problems inherent in a federal system in getting a new policy started. The case study involves issues about the role of the federal and state governments, regional conflicts, intergovernmental relations, the role of government in economic development, and the proper institutional arrangements for state and local industrial policy.

There are several roles that you can assume in this case study: that of a federal administrator who is charged with getting an industrial policy proposal accepted by various groups such as legislators, state, and local officials, labor unions, and businesses; a state-level administrator (economic development director) who has to decide whether to accept the federal proposal; a state administrator in charge of an existing industrial policy who has to decide whether to join the new federal program; or a state-elected official (governor) who has to decide whether your state should not participate in the federal program. In all these roles, you need to produce a proposal that you think will work. The kind of proposal you select will depend in part, of course, on which of the roles you are occupying.

The next section describes industrial policy, the experience that the federal government and two state governments have had with it, and the main strategies that might be taken along with the major issues that these strategies face.

What Is Industrial Policy?

The American economy in the 1980s produced good and bad news. On the good side, the economy experienced a long period of sustained growth following the recession of 1981–1982. On the bad side, the federal budget deficits, national debt, and trade deficits reached unprecedented heights. Particularly troublesome was the competition from foreign products that contributed to a rapid decline in the smokestack industries (manufacturing) and a shift to service industries. Since the latter did not pay the same wages as the older manufacturing jobs, workers without skills who had to take service jobs make substantially less money. Thus, real personal income failed to rise for most of the 1980s.

Some experts felt that the best way to meet the challenges of these economic changes was contained in "industrial policy." Industrial policy does not have a clear, single meaning. However, it has certain aspects that can be pointed out. First, let us cite two definitions from leading experts. Magaziner and Reich define it as the integration of "the full range of targeted government policies—procurement, research and development, trade, antitrust, tax credits, and subsidies—into a coherent strategy for encouraging the development of internationally competitive businesses" (Magaziner and Reich 1982, 343). Goldstein (1986, 262) defines it as a "coherent mix of specific policies whose targets are industrial sectors (or that affect industrial sector performance) and which is meant to achieve explicit objectives, such as increasing industrial competitiveness in world markets or raising the rate of productivity growth."

How would these broad and somewhat vague policies be implemented? There are three major facets to implementation: (1) gathering data and information about the economy with the purpose of trying to identify the sectors that are faltering and those that are rising; (2) establishing an economic cooperation council consisting of representatives of government, labor, and industry; and (3) creating an industrial development bank that would direct investment funds to certain industries or regions, use financial leverage to induce troubled industries to modernize, and lend money to new industries.

It is obvious that industrial policy is different from traditional economic development policy in several ways. The latter emphasizes recruitment of firms and development of small businesses. Recruiting firms usually involves competition among states so that there is not necessarily any overall growth for the country, even if there is in one state, because the firms that one state succeeds in attracting would have located in a different state. Industrial policy, on the other hand, aims at increasing the total economic growth of the country. Traditional economic development policies are usually uncoordinated with no explicit policy objectives, whereas industrial policy assumes that economic analysis and planning would guide policy.

A key element of industrial policy is the assumption that government has the analytic capability to determine which industries should be supported, who the winners and losers should be, and which losers should be saved. Decisions about these matters would be based on economic analysis rather than on politics. There are some economists who dispute that this can be done (Schultze 1983). Others see it in purely political terms. Ginsberg and Shefter (1985, 15) see it as

a political contract or treaty between organized labor and the new politics movement . . . that the federal government should take a greater hand in long-range economic planning and should, in particular, supervise what was said to be the inevitable transformation of the American industrial base from obsolescent smokestack industries to the high technology, energy efficient, and non-polluting industries that purportedly were the wave of the future.

Thus, industrial policy is as much a partisan political issue as it is an objective economic policy about how to cure American economic ills. Republicans and conservatives oppose it and Democrats support it.

The Fate of Industrial Policy Proposals at the National and State Levels

In the early 1980s, the Democrats in Congress saw industrial policy as the brightest star of what was a bleak political horizon. It was looked upon as a way of seizing the economic initiative from the Reagan administration. Among Democratic leaders in Congress, industrial policy came to be defined so broadly that it could be endorsed by almost anyone (Baker 1987, 111). Representatives from states with smokestack industries saw it as a way that government could play a role in saving their faltering economies; representatives from the Southwest felt that it held out the prospect of helping their high-tech industries.

But as the concept came to be defined in more specific terms, regional conflicts opened up. Southwestern representatives began to see it as a bailout operation for the smokestack states. Said one member: "The bank looks like a Northeastern thing; you know, save the smokestacks, stop the migration whether or not those industries could ever be made competitive" (Baker 1987, 117). The political appeal of the policy also was not too great. As one representative put it, "That's not a real grabber. Politically, its not one of the first things you write home about in your newsletter" (quoted in Baker, 116).

In addition, the public was suspicious about the government's controlling the economy, particularly through the Industrial Development Bank. The Reagan administration was in outright opposition to industrial policy, saying that it represented a species of state economic planning that was unacceptable. The major unions came out in support of industrial policy, which tipped some middle-of-the-roaders against it and spelled its end (Baker 1987). The proposal died in Congress in 1984.

Although the national debate quieted in 1984, many state and local governments went ahead on their own because they could not afford to wait for national action. Rhode Island developed the Greenhouse Compact in 1984 in an attempt to revitalize its sagging economy. The compact was administered by the State Strategic Development Commission, a body of nineteen members appointed by the governor. Its members reached agreement on a number of matters aimed at shoring up sunset industries and targeting certain high-tech industries for development: pharmaceuticals, robotics, and geriatrics, all industries in which Rhode Island had a competitive advantage.

The proposal was defeated in a 1984 referendum by a four-to-one margin. It was defeated because of perceived inequitable distribution of costs and benefits and the undemocratic way that decisions were to be made. The voters felt that the plan was meant for the big shots rather than the little guy. They also feared that their taxes would be increased. Conservatives opposed it on the basis that it involved too much government intervention in the economy. They argued also that the institutional arrangement represented by the commission allowed special interests to have their way. Finally, they argued that the commission was not capable of picking winners and losers and that the industries selected for government support would become dependent on government.

The conservatives won. Silver and Burton (1987, 287) conclude: "The general lessons from the Greenhouse Compact are that comprehensive economic development plans must be credible, legitimate, and fair." This means that democratic procedures must be used to select the members of the planning boards, and representatives of the community must be included.

Minnesota's experience points up yet another problem with industrial development policy. In Minnesota, an Iron Range Resources and Rehabilitation Board (IRRRB) operates an industrial policy for the Iron Range in northeastern Minnesota, a region of about 190,000 people. The region depends on iron ore, buts its unemployment level in 1983 reached 33 percent (Dewar 1986, 291). The IRRRB was established in 1941; amendments to the legislation in 1977 set up a Northeast Minnesota Economic Protection Fund to be used to rehabilitate and diversify industrial enterprises; 1984 amendments authorized expenditures from the fund. Forty-seven million dollars was amassed for the fund by 1982, and from 1982 to 1984, $26 million was spent. This money was targeted for tourism promotion, reduced dependence on iron ore, and promotion of industries to provide energy from indigenous resources.

In reaching its decisions, the IRRRB did not use economic analysis; it wanted immediate, visible projects that would pay political dividends (Dewar 1986, 292). But without economic analysis, the projects were hit or miss extrapolations from past economic policies, based mostly on unexamined assumptions. The board did not consider the opportunity costs of its choices, such as the jobs that would have been generated had the funds been spent for other projects. They relied on the judgment of private decision makers, such as bankers and bond underwriters, who were interested in immediate returns.

Institutional Arrangements

There are several different institutional arrangements possible for carrying out industrial policy. The most centralized and elitist is a tripartite board consisting of people appointed by business, government, and labor. It would be independent of government and restricted to a few, resource-holding representatives. The most decentralized type of arrangement would be informal arrangements among producers with autonomy from formal government oversight. A third arrangement would ensure that representatives from the community would play a significant role on the policy-making board.

The federal government could follow either a top-down or a bottom-up strategy in implementing industrial policy. In the top-down strategy, it could try to get intergovernmental cooperation by offering fiscal incentives to induce state and local participation. In the bottom-up strategy, the federal government could establish a partnership among business, labor, and government and let the states pursue their own policies. The question is whether an industrial policy could succeed without the active involvement of the states.

To get the states involved, the federal government could use grants and loans to help workers who lose their jobs because of plant closings of industries that are not supported. Such action might involve supplementing unemployment compensation, providing moving allowances, retraining, locating new jobs, and providing income maintenance. No doubt these would be expensive. In addition, grants would be needed to stimulate research and development and to provide risk capital for sunrise industries.

A bottom-up strategy would be far less costly for the federal government but, of course, more questionable as far as results were concerned. Bahl (1986, 316) concludes: "The upshot of the above discussion is that United States industrial policy must be formulated and carried out within a decentralized governmental system, where the impacts of state and local governments would be vital but where their resources would be limited and the financing of industrial policy would be only due to a number of competing claims on those resources."

Major Issues

The first issue that needs to be addressed in designing an industrial policy is how extensive government involvement should be. At the lowest level, government can engage in information gathering and consensus building. At the next level, it might create a separate agency charged with the responsibility of coordinating all existing federal agency programs that are related to industrial competitiveness. At the highest level is the creation of a development bank to make decisions about which sectors and firms should be helped and which left alone or restructured.

There is also a series of issues concerning how a tripartite council might be structured. Among these are the following: (1) How much tenure should the council participants have? (2) How much autonomy should the council have from elected political officials? (3) How much participation should elected officials have in the council's decisions? (4) What kind of rules should be used in making decisions (e.g., consensus, majority vote, rational calculation, bargaining)?

Discussion Questions

1. Could a national industrial policy, if one were adopted, work in the American federal system?
2. Would it be better for each state that wanted one to adopt its own industrial policy?
3. Who would be the winners and the losers in a national industrial policy?
4. How does industrial policy fit in with what has been traditionally called *economic development policy* in the United States?

References

Aaronson, David, C. Thomas Deines, and Michael Musheno. *Public Policy and Police Discretion: Processes of Decriminalization.* New York: Clark Boardman Co., 1984.

Aberbach, Joel D., Robert D. Putnam, and Bert A. Rockman. *Bureaucrats and Politicians in Western Democracies.* Cambridge, MA: Harvard University Press, 1981.

Ackoff, Russell L. *Scientific Method: Optimizing Applied Business Decisions.* New York: John Wiley and Sons, 1969.

Adams, Bruce. "The Limitations of Muddling Through: Does Anyone in Washington Really Think Anymore?" *Public Administration Review* 39, no. 6 (November/December 1979): 545–552.

Albritton, Robert, and Ellen Dran. "Balanced Budgets and State Surpluses: The Politics of Budgeting." *Public Administration Review* 47, no. 2 (March/April 1987): 142–152.

Alderfer, Clayton. *Existence, Relatedness, and Growth: Human Needs in Organizational Settings.* New York: Free Press, 1972.

Aldrich, Howard E. *Organizations and Environments.* Englewood Cliffs, NJ: Prentice-Hall, 1979.

Allison, Graham T. *Essence of Decision: Explaining the Cuban Missile Crisis.* Boston: Little, Brown and Co., 1971.

———. "Public and Private Management: Are They Fundamentally Alike in All Unimportant Respects?" In *Current Issues in Public Administration.* 2nd ed., edited by Fred S. Lane. New York: Penguin, 1982.

Altheide, David L., and John Johnson. *Bureaucratic Propaganda.* Boston: Allyn and Bacon, 1980.

Anderson, Jack. "How They Punish Heroes." *Parade Magazine,* 10 July 1988, 16–19.

Anton, Thomas J. "Intergovernmental Change in the United States: An Assessment of the Literature." In *Public Sector Performance: A Conceptual Turning Point,* edited by T. Miller. Baltimore: Johns Hopkins University Press, 1984.

Arendt, Hannah. *Eichmann in Jerusalem: A Report on the Banality of Evil.* Revised and enlarged edition. New York: Viking Press, 1976.

Argyris, Chris. "Some Unintended Consequences of Rigorous Research." *Psychological Bulletin* 70 (1968): 185–197.

――――. "Making the Undiscussable and Its Undiscussability Discussable." *Public Administration Review* 40 (1980): 205–213.

Arnold, R. Douglas. *Congress and the Bureaucracy: A Theory of Influence.* New Haven, CT: Yale University Press, 1979.

Associated Press. "FBI Chief 'Unaware' Legal Acts Probed." *Arizona Republic,* 24 February 1988, A14.

――――. "U.S. Judge Rules Drug Tests Violated Job Seekers' Rights." *New York Times,* 14 December 1989, 12.

Axelrod, Donald. *A Budget Quartet: Critical Policy and Management Issues.* New York: St. Martin's Press, 1989.

Axelrod, Robert. *The Evolution of Cooperation.* New York: Basic Books, 1986.

Bachrach, Peter, and Morton S. Baratz. "The Two Faces of Power." *American Political Science Review* 56 (1962): 947–952.

Bahl, Roy. "Industrial Policy and the States: How Will They Pay?" *Journal of the American Planning Association* 52 (1986): 310–319.

Bailey, Stephen K. "Ethics in the Public Service." In *Public Administration and Democracy,* edited by Roscoe Martin. Syracuse, NY: Syracuse University Press, 1965.

Baker, Ross K. "The Bittersweet Courtship of Congressional Democrats and Industrial Policy." *Economic Development Quarterly* 1 (1987): 111–124.

Banner, David K., Samuel Doctors, and Andrew Gordon. *The Politics of Social Program Evaluation.* Cambridge, MA: Ballinger, 1975.

Bardach, Eugene. *Implementation Game: What Happens after a Bill Becomes Law?* Cambridge, MA: MIT Press, 1977.

――――. "Implementing Industrial Policy." In *The Industrial Policy Debate,* edited by Chalmers Johnson. San Francisco: Institute for Contemporary Studies, 1984.

――――. "From Practitioner Knowledge to Scholarly Knowledge and Back Again." *Journal of Policy Analysis and Management* 7 (1987): 188–199.

Bardach, Eugene, and Robert A. Kagan. *Going by the Book: The Problem of Regulatory Unreasonableness.* Philadelphia: Temple University Press, 1982.

Barnett, H. C. "Political Environment and the Implementation of Social Regulation: The Case of Superfund Enforcement." Unpublished manuscript, July 1988.

Baron, James, Frank Dobbin, and P. Devereaux Jennings. "War and Peace: The Evolution of Modern Personnel Administration in U.S. Industry." *American Journal of Sociology* 92 (1986): 350–383.

Bass, Bernard M. *Leadership and Performance beyond Expectations.* New York: Free Press, 1985.

Baum, Lawrence. "Implementation of Judicial Decisions: An Organizational Analysis." *American Politics Quarterly* 4 (1976): 86–114.

Behn, Robert D. "A Curmudgeon's View of Public Administration: Routine Tasks, Performance, Innovation." *State and Local Government Review* 19 (Spring 1987).

Behn, Robert, and James Vaupel. *Quick Analysis for Busy Decision Makers.* New York: Basic Books, 1982.

Bell, Daniel, and Lester Thurow. *The Deficits: How Big? How Long? How Dangerous?* New York: Free Press, 1985.

Bellavita, Christopher. "Communicating Effectively about Performance is a Purposive Activity." In *Performance and Credibility: Developing Excellence in Public and Nonprofit Organizations,* edited by Joseph S. Wholey, Mark A. Abramson, and Christopher Bellavita, 235–244. Lexington, MA: Lexington Books, 1986.

Bem, Daryl J. "Cognitive Alteration of Feeling States: A Discussion." In *Thought and Feeling,* edited by H. London and R. E. Nisbett, 211–233. Chicago: Aldine, 1974.

Bender, Lewis G., and James A. Stener, eds. *Administering the New Federalism.* Boulder, CO: Westview Press, 1986.

Beniger, James R. *The Control Revolution: Technological and Economic Origins of the Information Society.* Cambridge, MA: Harvard, 1986.

Bennett, James T., and Thomas J. DiLorenzo. "Public Employee Unions, Privatization, and the New Federalism." *Government Union Review* 4 (Winter 1983a): 59–73.

———. *The Underground Government: The Off-Budget Public Sector.* Washington, DC: Cato Institute, 1983b.

Bennis, Warren. "Transformative Power and Leadership." In *Leadership and Organizational Culture: New Perspectives on Administrative Theory and Practice,* edited by Thomas J. Sergiovanni and John E. Corbally, 64–71. Chicago: University of Illinois Press, 1984.

Benveniste, Guy. *The Politics of Expertise.* San Francisco: Boyd and Fraser, 1972.

———. *Professionalizing the Organization: Reducing Bureaucracy to Enhance Effectiveness.* San Francisco: Jossey-Bass, 1987.

Berman, Paul. "The Study of Macro- and Micro-Implementation." *Public Policy* 26 (Spring 1978): 157–184.

———. "Thinking About Programmed and Adaptive Implementation: Matching Strategies to Situations." In *Why Policies Succeed or Fail,* edited by Helen Ingram and Dean Mann. Beverly Hills: Sage Publications, 1980.

Berry, Jeffrey M. *Feeding Hungry People: Rulemaking in the Food Stamp Program.* New Brunswick, NJ: Rutgers University Press, 1984.

Berube, Maurice, and Marilyn Gittel, eds. *Confrontation at Ocean-Hill Brownsville.* New York: Praeger, 1969.

Beyer, Janice M., Harrison Trice, and John Stevens. "Predicting How Federal Managers Perceive Criteria Used for Their Promotion." *Public Administration Review* 40 (January/February 1980): 55–66.

Bianchi, Carl. Untitled Speech. Kansas City, MO, National Academy of Public Administration, May 1988.

Bickman, Leonard. "The Functions of Program Theory." In *Using Program Theory in Evaluation,* edited by L. Bickman. San Francisco: Jossey-Bass, 1987.

Biggart, Nicole. "The Creative-Destructive Process of Organizational Change: The Case of the Post Office." *Administrative Science Quarterly* 22 (1977): 410–426.

Bingham, Richard, and Claire Felbinger. *Evaluation in Practice: A Methodological Approach.* New York: Longman, 1989.

Boffey, Philip M. "At Fulcrum of Conflict, Regulators of AIDS Drugs." *New York Times,* 19 August 1988, 23.

Bowers, Joseph L., and Charles J. Christenson. *Public Management: Text and Cases.* Homewood, IL: Richard D. Irwin, 1978.

Bowers, David G., and Stanley Seashore. "Predicting Organizational Effectiveness with a Four-Factor Theory of Leadership." *Administrative Science Quarterly* 11 (1966): 238–263.

Bozeman, Barry. *All Organizations Are Public: Bridging Public and Private Organizational Theories.* San Francisco: Jossey-Bass, 1987.

Bozeman, Barry, and Stuart Bretschneider, eds. "Public Management Information Systems," *Public Administration Review* 46 (Special Issue 1986): 473–602.

Bozeman, Barry, and David Landsbergen. "Truth and Credibility in Sincere Policy Analysis: Alternative Approaches to the Production of Policy-Relevant Knowledge." *Evaluation Review* 13 (August 1989): 355–379.

Branti v. Finkel. *445 US 507.*, 574–95. 1980.

Brassier, Ann. "Strategic Vision: A Practical Tool." *Bureaucrat* 14, no. 3 (1985): 23-26.

Broad, William J. " 'Smart' Machines Ready to Assume Many NASA Duties." *New York Times,* 6 March 1989, 1, 11.

Brown v. Board of Education of Topeka. *347 US 483.* 1954.

Bryson, John M. *Strategic Planning for Public and Non-Profit Organizations: A Guide to Strengthening and Sustaining Organizational Achievement.* San Francisco: Jossey-Bass, 1989.

Bureau of Labor Statistics. "Usual Weekly Earnings of Wage and Salary Workers: Third Quarter 1988." *News: United States Department of Labor* USDL 88-539 (28 October 1988).

Burke, John. "Policy Implementation and the Responsible Exercise of Discretion." In *Implementation and the Policymaking Process,* edited by Dennis Palumbo and Donald Calista. Westport, CT: Greenwood Press, 1989.

Burns, James MacGregor. *Leadership.* New York: Harper and Row, 1978.

Butler, Stuart. *Privatizing Federal Spending: A Strategy to Eliminate the Deficit.* New York: Universe Books, 1985.

Caiden, Naomi. "The New Rules of the Federal Budget Game." *Public Administration Review* 44 (March/April 1984): 109-118.

Calista, Donald J. "Linking Policy Intention and Policy Implementation." *Administration and Society* 18 (1986): 263-286.

———. "On the Orthodoxy and Tentativeness of Reform." In *Bureaucratic and Governmental Reform,* edited by Donald J. Calista, 3-19. Greenwood, CT: JAI Press, 1986.

Calsyn, T., L. Tornatsky, and S. Dittmar. "Incomplete Adoption of an Innovation: The Case of Goal Attainment Scaling." *Evaluation* 4 (1977): 127-133.

Cameron, Kim. "Measuring Organizational Effectiveness in Institutions of Higher Education." *Administrative Science Quarterly* 23 (1978): 604-632.

Cameron, Kim, and David Whetten. "Perceptions of Organizational Effectiveness over Organizational Life Cycles." *Administrative Science Quarterly* 26 (1981): 525-544.

Campbell, Donald T. "Reforms as Experiments." In *Readings in Evaluation Research,* edited by F. G. Caro. New York: Russell Sage Foundation, 1971.

———. "Assessing the Impact of Planned Social Change." *Evaluation and Program Planning* 2 (1979): 67-90.

———. "Guidelines for Monitoring the Scientific Competence of Preventive Intervention Research Centers." *Knowledge: Creation, Diffusion, Utilization.* 8 (1987): 389-430.

Campbell, Donald T., and Julian C. Stanley. *Experimental and Quasi-experimental Designs for Research.* Chicago: Rand McNally, 1966.

Campbell, John. "On the Nature of Organizational Effectiveness." In *New Perspectives on Organizational Effectiveness,* edited by Paul Goodman and Johannes Pennings, 13-55. San Francisco: Jossey-Bass, 1977.

Caplan, Nathan. "The Two-Communities Theory and Knowledge Utilization." *American Behavioral Scientist* 22 (1979): 459-470.

Caputo, David A. "Contemporary American Federalism: Implications for American Cities." In *The Costs of Federalism: In Honor Of James W. Fesler,* edited by Robert T. Golembiewski and Aaron Wildavsky, 187-200. New Brunswick, NJ: Transaction Books, 1984.

Carlisle, Norman V., and Doris McFerran. *Civil Service Careers for Girls.* New York: E. P. Dutton, 1941.

Caro, Francis G., ed. *Readings in Evaluation Research.* New York: Russell Sage Foundation, 1971.

Caro, Robert A. *The Power Broker: Robert Moses and the Fall of New York.* New York: Knopf, 1974.

Carpenter, B. "Superfund, Superflop." *U.S. News and World Report,* 6 February 1989, 47–49.

Carroll, James D. "Public Administration in the Third Century of the Constitution: Supply-Side Management, Privatization, or Public Investment." *Public Administration Review* 47 (January/February 1987): 106–115.

Chandler, Alfred. *Strategy and Structure.* Cambridge, MA: MIT Press, 1962.

Chelimsky, Eleanor. *Program Evaluation: Patterns and Directions.* Washington, DC: American Society for Public Administration, 1985.

Chen, Huey, and Peter Rossi. "Evaluating with Sense: The Theory-driven Approach." *Evaluation Review* 7 (1983): 283–302.

Cherniss, Cary. *Staff Burnout: Job Stress in Human Services.* Beverly Hills, CA: Sage Publications, 1980.

Child, John. "Organizational Structure, Environment, and Performance: The Role of Strategic Choice." *Sociology* 6 (1972): 1–22.

Chubb, John E. "Federalism and the Bias for Centralization." In *The New Direction in American Politics.* Washington, DC: Brookings Institution, 1985.

Cleveland, Harlan. "The Twilight of Hierarchy: Speculations on the Global Information Society." *Public Administration Review* 45 (January/February 1985): 185–195.

Cobb, Roger, and Charles Elder. *Participation in American Politics: The Dynamics of Agenda Building.* 2nd ed. Baltimore: Johns Hopkins University Press, 1983.

Cohen, Michael D., James G. March, and Johan P. Olsen. "A Garbage Can Model of Organizational Choice." *Administrative Science Quarterly* 17 (1972): 1–25.

Colby, Peter W. "Public Sector Productivity Improvement: A New Emphasis for Personnel Administration." In *Public Personnel Update,* edited by Michael Cohen and Robert Golembiewski. New York: Dekker, 1984.

Coleman, James. *Equality of Educational Opportunity.* Washington, DC: U.S. Government Printing Office, 1966.

Conger, Jay A., and Rabindra N. Kanungo, eds. *Charismatic Leadership: The Elusive Factor in Organizational Effectiveness.* San Francisco: Jossey-Bass, 1988.

Conlan, Timothy J. "Ambivalent Federalism: Intergovernmental Policy in the Reagan Administration." In *Administering the New Federalism,* edited by Lewis G. Bender and James A. Stener. Boulder, CO: Westview Press, 1986.

Connick v. Myers. *75 L Ed 2nd.,* 708–35. 1983.

Cook, Thomas. "Post Positivism Critical Multiplism." In *Social Science and Social Policy,* edited by R. Lance Shotland and Melvin M. Mark, 21–62. Beverly Hills, CA: Sage Publications, 1985.

Cook, Thomas, and Donald Campbell. *Quasi-Experimentation: Design and Analysis Issues for Field Settings.* Chicago: Rand McNally, 1979.

Cook, Thomas, and W. Shadish. "Program Evaluation: The Worldly Science." *Annual Review of Psychology* 37 (1986): 193–232.

Cronbach, Lee J., and Associates. *Toward Reform of Program Evaluation: Aims, Methods, and Institutional Arrangements.* San Francisco: Jossey-Bass, 1980.

Cushman, John H., Jr. "More Private Workers to Face Drug Tests." *New York Times,* 18 December 1989, 36.

Daicoff, Darwin W., and Robert H. Glass. *Who Pays Kansas Taxes? A Report to the Special Committee on Assessment and Taxation, Legislative Coordinating Council, State of Kansas.* Lawrence, KS: Institute for Economic and Business Research, November 1978.

Davis, Kenneth C. *Administrative Law Text.* 3rd ed. St. Paul, MN: West, 1972.

de Leon, Peter. "Policy Evaluation and Program Termination." *Policy Studies Review* 2 (May 1983): 631–648.

Dean, John. *Blind Ambition: The White House Years.* New York: Simon and Schuster, 1976.

Denhardt, Robert. *Theories of Public Organization.* Monterey, CA: Brooks/Cole, 1984.

DeParle, Jason. "Realizing the Rights of the Disabled." *New York Times,* 17 December 1989, E1, E5.

Dery, David. *Problem Definition in Policy Analysis.* Lawrence, KS: University of Kansas Press, 1984.

Dess, Gregory G., and Donald W. Beard. "Dimensions of Organizational Task Environment." *Administrative Science Quarterly* 29 (1984): 52–73.

Dewar, Margaret E. "Development Analysis Confronts Politics: Industrial Policy on Minnesota's Iron Range." *Journal of the American Planning Association* 52 (1986): 290–299.

Diesenhouse, Susan. "In Affirmative Action, a Question of Truth in Labeling." *New York Times,* 11 December 1988, 23.

Dodd, Lawrence C., and Richard L. Schott. *Congress and the Administrative State.* New York: John Wiley and Sons, 1979.

———. "The Rise of the Administrative State." In *Current Issues in Public Administration.* 2nd ed., edited by Frederick S. Lane. New York: St. Martin's Press, 1986.

Doig, Jameson W. " 'If I See a Murderous Fellow Sharpening a Knife Cleverly . . .': The Wilsonian Dichotomy and the Public Authority Tradition." *Public Administration Review* 43 (1983): 292–304.

Doig, Jameson W., and Erwin Hargrove, eds., *Leadership and Innovation: A Biographical Perspective on Entrepreneurs in Government.* Baltimore: Johns Hopkins University Press, 1987.

Dornbusch, Sanford M., and W. Richard Scott. *Evaluation and the Exercise of Authority.* San Francisco: Jossey-Bass, 1975.

Douglas, Jack D., and John M. Johnson, eds. *Official Deviance.* Philadelphia: J. B. Lippincott, 1977.

Downs, Anthony. *Inside Bureaucracy.* Boston: Little, Brown and Co., 1967.

Dror, Yehezkel. *Public Policymaking Reexamined.* New Brunswick, NJ: Transaction Press, 1983.

Drucker, Peter. *Innovation and Entrepreneurship.* New York: Harper and Row, 1985.

Dunn, William E. "The Two-Communities Metaphor and Models of Knowledge Use: An Exploratory Case Survey." *Knowledge: Creation, Diffusion, Utilization* 1 (1980): 515–536.

Durkheim, Emile. *Elementary Forms of Religious Life.* Translated by J. W. Swain. London: George Allen and Unwin, Ltd., 1915.

Eads, George C. "The Political Experience in Allocating Investment: Lessons from the U.S. and Elsewhere." In *Toward a New U.S. Industrial Policy,* edited by Michael Wachter and Susan Wachter. Philadelphia: University of Pennsylvania Press, 1981.

Eddy, William. *Public Organization Behavior and Development.* Cambridge, MA: Winthrop, 1981.

Edelman, Murray J. *The Symbolic Uses of Politics.* Urbana, IL: University of Illinois Press, 1964.

———. *Constructing the Political Spectacle.* Chicago: University of Chicago Press, 1988.

Edwards, George C. *Implementing Public Policy.* Washington, DC: Congressional Quarterly Press, 1980.

Eisner, Robert. *How Real Is the Federal Deficit?* New York: Free Press, 1986.

Elazar, Daniel. *American Federalism: A View from the States.* 3rd ed. New York: Harper and Row, 1984.

Elazar, Daniel, Bruce Carrol, E. Lester Levine, and Douglas St. Angelo, eds. *Cooperation and Conflict.* Itasca, IL: F. E. Peacock, 1969.

Elmore, Richard F. "Organizational Models of Social Program Implementation." *Public Policy* 26 (1978): 185–228.

———. "Backward-Mapping: Using Implementation Analysis to Structure Political Decisions." *Political Science Quarterly* 94 (Winter 1979): 601–616.

Etzioni, Amitai. "Mixed-Scanning: A Third Approach to Decision Making." *Public Administration Review* 27 (1967): 385–392.

Evans, Sara M., and Barbara J. Nelson. *Wage Justice: Comparable Worth and the Paradox of Technocratic Reform.* Chicago: University of Chicago Press, 1989.

Feinberg, Howard. "Public School Officials Out of Touch with Public." *Washington Post National Weekly Edition.* 8–14 February 1988.

Feldman, Martha, and James G. March. "Information in Organizations as Signal and Symbol." *Administrative Science Quarterly* 26 (1981): 171–186.

Feltner, Frank A. "American Charities." *American Journal of Sociology* 7 (1901).

Ferman, Barbara. "When Failure Is Success: Implementation and Madisonian Government." In *Implementation and the Policymaking Process,* edited by Dennis Palumbo and Donald Calista. Westport, CT: Greenwood Press, 1989.

Fesler, James W. *Public Administration.* Englewood Cliffs, NJ: Prentice-Hall, 1980.

Festinger, Leon. "A Theory of Social Comparison." *Human Relations* 7 (1954): 117–140.

Finer, Herman. "Administrative Responsibility in Democratic Government." *Public Administration Review* 1 (1941): 335–350.

Fischer, Frank. *Politics, Values, and Public Policy: The Problem of Methodology.* Boulder, CO: Westview Press, 1980.

———. *Technocracy and the Politics of Expertise.* Newbury Park, CA: Sage Publications, 1990.

Flyvbjerg, B. "Implementation and the Choice of Evaluation Methods." *Transportation Policy Decision-Making* 2 (1984): 291–314.

Fox, Charles. "Biases in Public Policy Implementation Evaluation." *Policy Studies Review* 7 (1987): 128–142.

———. "Implementation Research: Why and How to Transcend Positivist Methodologies." In *Implementation and the Policymaking Process,* edited by Dennis Palumbo and Donald Calista. Westport, CT: Greenwood Press, 1989.

Fox, Frederick V., and Barry M. Staw. "The Trapped Administrator: Effects of Job Insecurity and Policy Resistance upon Commitment to a Course of Action." *Administrative Science Quarterly* 24 (1979): 449–471.

Fredrickson, H. George, and David K. Hart. "The Public Service and the Patriotism of Benevolence." *Public Administration Review* 45 (1985): 547–553.

Fredrickson, James W., and Anthony L. Iaquinto. "Inertia and Creeping Rationality in Strategic Decision Processes." *Academy of Management Journal* 32 (1989): 516–542.

Freedman, Anne. "Doing Battle with the Patronage Army: Politics, Courts, and Personnel Administration in Chicago." *Public Administration Review* 48, no. 5 (September/October 1988): 847–859.

Freidson, Eliot. *The Professions and Their Prospects.* Beverly Hills: Sage, 1973.

Friedman, Thomas L. "Baker's World: If Politics Dictate the Secretary's Approach, Some Question the Course of Foreign Policy." *New York Times,* 21 September 1989, 1, 7.

Friedrich, Carl J. "Public Policy and the Nature of Administrative Responsibility." In *Public Policy,* edited by Carl J. Friedrich and Edward S. Mason, 3–24. Cambridge, MA: Harvard University Press, 1940.

Fritschler, A. Lee. *Smoking and Politics: Policymaking in the Federal Bureaucracy.* 3rd ed. Englewood Cliffs, NJ: Prentice-Hall, 1983.

Galbraith, Jay. *Designing Complex Organizations.* Reading, MA: Addison-Wesley, 1973.

Galbraith, John Kenneth. *The New Industrial State*. 2nd ed. New York: New American Library, 1971.

Gamson, William, and Norman Scotch. "Scapegoating in Baseball." *American Journal of Sociology* 70 (1964): 69–72.

Garfield, Eugene. "Science/Technology Policy, Part I: Will the Real Science Policy Please Stand Up?" *Current Contents* 20 (21 November 1988): 3–10.

Garson, Barbara. "Luddites in Lordstown." In *Life in Organizations: Workplaces as People Experience Them,* edited by Rosabeth M. Kanter and Barry A. Stein. New York: Basic Books, 1979.

Georgiou, Petro. "The Goal Paradigm and Notes toward a Counter Paradigm." *Administrative Science Quarterly* 18 (1973): 291–310.

Gervitz, D. *Business Plan for America: An Entrepreneur's Manifest*. New York: Putnam, 1984.

Ginsberg, Benjamin, and Martin Shefter. "A Critical Realignment? The New Politics, the Reconstituted Right, and the 1984 Election." In *The Elections of 1984,* edited by Michael Nelson. Washington, DC: Congressional Quarterly Press, 1985.

Gittell, Marilyn. *Participants and Participation*. New York: Praeger, 1967.

Goldstein, Harvey. "The State and Local Industrial Policy Question, Introduction." *Journal of the American Planning Association* 52 (1986): 262–265.

Golembiewski, Robert T. "Organizing Public Work, Roundtree: Toward a New Balance between Political Agendas and Management Perspectives." In *The Costs of Federalism: In Honor of James W. Fesler*, edited by Robert T. Golembiewski and Aaron Wildavsky. New Brunswick, NJ: Transaction Books, 1984.

Golembiewski, Robert T., and Michael White. *Cases in Public Management*. 4th ed. Boston: Houghton Mifflin, 1983.

Golembiewski, Robert T., and Aaron Wildavsky, eds. *The Costs of Federalism: In Honor of James W. Fesler,* Transaction Books. New Brunswick, NJ, 1984.

Goodnow, Frank J. *Politics and Administration*. Reprinted. New York: Russell and Russell, 1967 [1900].

Goodsell, Charles T. *The Case for Bureaucracy: A Public Administration Polemic*. 2nd ed. Chatham, NJ: Chatham House, 1985.

Gormley, William, Jr. "Intergovernmental Conflict on Environmental Policy: The Attitudinal Connection." *Western Political Quarterly* 40 (1987): 285–303.

Gosling, James L. "Wisconsin Item-Veto Lesion." *Public Administration Review* 46, no. 4 (July/August 1986): 292–301.

Gouldner, Alvin. *Patterns of Industrial Bureaucracy*. New York: Free Press, 1954.

Greenfield, S., A. Strickson, and R. Aubey, eds. *Entrepreneurship in Cultural Context*. Albuquerque: University of New Mexico Press, 1979.

Grodzins, Morton. "Centralization and Decentralization in the American Federal System." In *A Nation of States,* edited by Robert Goldwin. Chicago: Rand-McNally, 1963.

Gruber, Judith E. *Controlling Bureaucracies: Dilemmas in Democratic Governance*. Berkeley: University of California Press, 1987.

Guba, Egon, and Yvonna Lincoln. "The Countenances of Fourth-Generation Evaluations: Description, Judgment, and Negotiation." In *The Politics of Program Evaluation,* edited by Dennis Palumbo. Newbury Park, CA: Sage Publications, 1987.

———. *Fourth Generation Evaluation*. Newbury Park, CA: Sage Publications, 1989.

Gulick, Luther, and Lyndall Urwick, eds. *Papers on the Science of Administration*. New York: Institute of Public Administration, 1937.

Haider, Donald. *When Governments Came to Market: Governors, Mayors, and Intergovernmental Lobbying*. New York: Free Press, 1974.

Halberstam, David. *The Reckoning.* New York: William Morrow, 1986.

Hall, Richard. *Organizations: Structures, Processes, and Outcomes.* 4th ed. Englewood Cliffs, NJ: Prentice-Hall, 1987.

Hambrick, Donald C., and Richard A. D'Aveni. "Large Corporate Failures as Downward Spirals." *Administrative Science Quarterly* 33 (1989): 1–23.

Hamilton, Gary, and Nicole Biggart. "The Power of Obedience." *Administrative Science Quarterly* 29 (1985): 540–549.

Handler, Joel F. *The Conditions of Discretion: Autonomy, Community, Bureaucracy.* New York: Russell Sage Foundation, 1986.

Hannan, Michael T., and John H. Freeman. "The Population Ecology of Organizations." *American Journal of Sociology* 82 (1977): 929–964.

———. "Structural Inertia and Organizational Change." *American Sociological Review* 49 (1984): 149–164.

Hardin, Garrett. "The Tragedy of the Commons." *Science* 162 (1968): 1243–1248.

Hargrove, Erwin. *The Missing Link: The Study of the Implementation of Social Policy.* Washington, DC: Urban Institute, 1976.

Harris, L. *The Anguish of Change.* New York: Norton, 1973.

Harris, Richard. "A Scrap of Black Cloth." *New Yorker* 50, no. 17 and 18 (17, 24 June 1974).

Hayes, Thomas. "Savings Industries Costly Fraud." *New York Times,* 10 January 1989, D1, D5.

Hayford, Stephen L. "First Amendment Rights of Government Employees: A Primer for Public Officials." *Public Administration Review* 45, no. 1 (January/February 1985): 241–248.

Heclo, Hugh. *A Government of Strangers: Executive Politics in Washington.* Washington, DC: Brookings Institution, 1977.

———. "Issues Networks and the Executive Establishment." In *The New American Political System,* edited by A. King. Washington, DC: American Enterprise Institute, 1978.

Hedberg, B., P. C. Nystrom, and W. H. Starbuck. "Camping on Seesaws: Prescriptions for a Self-Designing Organization." *Administrative Science Quarterly* 21 (1976): 41–65.

Henriques, Diana B. *The Machinery of Greed: Public Authority Abuse and What to Do about It.* Lexington, MA: Lexington Books, 1986.

Henry, G. T., and W. Smiley. "Legislative Program Evaluation in the States: The Edge That Cuts." 15–17 April, Midwest Political Science Association Meetings, 1981.

Herzberg, Frederick. *Work and the Nature of Man.* Cleveland, OH: World Publishing Co., 1966.

Hicks, J. R. "The Valuation of the Social Income." *Economica* 7 (1940): 105–124.

Hilgartner, Stephen, and Charles L. Bosk. "The Rise and Fall of Social Problems: A Public Arenas Model." *American Journal of Sociology* 94 (July 1988): 53–78.

Hogwood, Brian, and B. Guy Peters. *Policy Dynamics.* New York: St. Martin's Press, 1983.

Howett, Arnold M. "Managing Federalism: An Overview." In *Current Issues in Public Administration,* edited by Frederick S. Lane. New York: St. Martin's Press, 1986.

Hummel, Ralph. *The Bureaucratic Experience.* 2nd ed. New York: St. Martin's Press, 1982.

Ingraham, Patricia W. "Politics and Administration: The Continuing Relevance of an Old Issue." In *Public Personnel Policy: The Politics of Civil Service,* edited by David H. Rosenbloom, 20–37. Port Washington, NY: Associated Faculty Press, 1985.

———. "Policy Implementation and the Public Service." In *The Revitalization of the Public Service,* edited by Robert Denhardt and E. T. Jennings, Jr. Columbia, MO: University of Missouri, 1987.

Ingraham, Patricia W., and Carolyn Ban, eds. *Legislating Bureaucratic Change: The Civil Service Reform Act of 1978.* Albany, NY: State University of New York, 1984.

Ingram, Helen. "Policy Implementation through Bargaining: The Case of Federal Grants-in-Aid." *Public Policy* 25 (1977): 499–526.

Institution of Program Evaluation. *Evaluation Activities of the Program Evaluation and Methodology Division.* Washington, DC: U.S. General Accounting Office, 1982.

Janis, Irving L. *Victims of Groupthink: A Psychological Study of Foreign Policy Decisions and Fiascoes.* Boston: Houghton Mifflin, 1972.

Janis, Irving L., and Leon Mann. *Decision Making: A Psychological Analysis of Conflict, Choice, and Commitment.* New York: Free Press, 1977.

Janowitz, Morris, D. Wright, and W. Delaney. *Public Administration and the Public: Perspectives toward Government in a Metropolitan Community.* Westport, CT: Greenwood Press, 1977.

Jelinck, Mariann, Linda Smricich, and Paul Hirsch, eds. "Organizational Culture." *Administrative Science Quarterly* 28 (1983): 331–495.

Johansen, Elaine. "Comparable Worth: The Character of a Controversy." *Public Administration Review* 45, no. 5 (September/October 1985): 631–635.

———. *Comparable Worth: The Myth and the Movement.* Boulder, CO: Westview Press, 1984.

Johnson, John, and David Altheide. *Bureaucratic Propaganda.* Boston: Allyn and Bacon, 1980.

Johnson, Julie. "Child Care Shortage Clouds Future of Welfare Program." *New York Times,* 12 December 1989, A1, A12.

Johnson, R. W., and R. E. O'Conner. "Intra-Agency Limitations on Policy Implementation: You Can't Always Get What You Want, but Sometimes You Get What You Need." *Administration and Society* 11 (1979): 193–215.

Johnston, Ronald J. *The Geography of Federal Spending in the United States of America.* New York: John Wiley and Sons, 1980.

Jones, John W., ed. *The Burnout Syndrome: Current Research, Theory and Intervention.* Park Ridge, IL: London House, 1981.

Jos, Philip H., Mark E. Tompkins, and Steven W. Hays. "In Praise of Difficult People; a Portrait of the Committed Whistle Blower." *Public Administration Review* 49 (November/December 1989): 552–651.

Kahn, Robert L. "Human Relations on the Shop Floor." In *Human Relations and Modern Management,* edited by E. M. Hugh-Jones, 43–74. Amsterdam, Holland: North-Holland Publishing Co., 1958.

Kaldor, N. "Welfare Propositions of Economics and Interpersonal Comparisons of Utility." *Economic Journal* 49 (1939): 549–552.

Kane, Edward J. *The S&L Insurance Mess: How Did It Happen?* Washington, DC: Urban Institute Press, 1989.

Kanter, Rosabeth M. "Power Failure in Management Circuits." *Harvard Business Review* 57 (1979): 65–75.

———. *The Change Masters: Innovation for Productivity in the American Corporation.* New York: Simon and Schuster, 1983.

Kanter, Rosabeth M., and Barry Stein, eds. *Life in Organizations: Workplaces as People Experience Them.* New York: Basic Books, 1979.

Katz, Daniel, and Robert L. Kahn. *The Social Psychology of Organizations.* 2nd ed. New York: John Wiley and Sons, 1978.

Kaufman, Herbert. *The Forest Ranger: A Study in Administrative Behavior.* Baltimore, MD: Johns Hopkins University Press, 1960.

———. *Politics and Policies in State and Local Government.* Englewood Cliffs, NJ: Prentice-Hall, 1963.

————. *Are Government Organizations Immortal?* Washington, DC: Brookings Institution, 1976.

————. *Red Tape: Its Origins, Uses and Abuses.* Washington, DC: Brookings Institution, 1977.

————. *The Administrative Behavior of Federal Bureau Chiefs.* Washington, DC: Brookings Institution, 1981.

————. *Time, Chance, and Organization: Natural Selection in a Perilous Environment.* Chatham, NJ: Chatham House, 1985.

Kearney, Richard C., and Chandan Sinha. "Professionalism and Bureaucratic Responsiveness: Conflict of Compatibility." *Public Administration Review* 48, no. 1 (January/February 1988): 571–579.

Keefe, William J., and Morris S. Ogul. *The American Legislative Process.* Englewood Cliffs, NJ: Prentice-Hall, 1969.

Kettl, Donald F. "The Maturing of American Federalism." In *The Costs of Federalism,* edited by Robert T. Golembiewski and Aaron Wildavsky. New Brunswick, NJ: Transaction Books, 1986.

————. *Government by Proxy: Managing Federal Programs.* Washington, DC: Congressional Quarterly Press, 1988.

————. "Expansion and Protection in Budgetary Process." *Public Administration Review* 49 (May/June 1989): 231–239.

Kidder, Tracy. *The Soul of the New Machine.* New York: Avon, 1981.

————. *Among Schoolchildren.* Boston: Houghton Mifflin Company, 1989.

Kilborn, Peter T. "Wage Gaps between Sexes Is Cut in Test, but at a Price." *New York Times,* 31 May 1990, A1, A12.

Kilmann, Ralph H. *Beyond the Quick Fix: Managing Five Tracks to Organizational Success.* San Francisco: Jossey-Bass, 1984.

Kimberly, John R. "Organizational Size and the Structuralist Perspective: A Review, Critique and Proposal." *Administrative Science Quarterly* 21 (1976): 577–597.

Kimberly, John R., and Robert H. Miles, eds. *The Organizational Life Cycle: Issues in the Creation, Transformation, and Decline of Organizations.* San Francisco: Jossey-Bass, 1981.

King, Paula J., and Nancy C. Roberts. "Policy Entrepreneurs: Catalysts for Policy Innovation." *Journal of State Government* 60 (1987): 172–178.

Kingdon, John W. *Agendas, Alternatives, and Public Policies.* Boston: Little, Brown, 1984.

Kipnis, David, and Stuart M. Schmidt. "Upward-Influence Styles: Relationship with Performance Evaluations, Salary, and Stress." *Administrative Science Quarterly* 33 (1988): 528–542.

Kirchoff, Bruce A. "Organizational Effectiveness Measurement and Policy Research." *Academy of Management Review* 2 (1977): 347–355.

Kirzner, J. *Perception, Opportunity, and Profit: Studies in the Theory of Entrepreneurship.* Chicago: University of Chicago Press, 1979.

Klingner, Donald E., and John Nalbandian. *Public Personnel Management: Contexts and Strategies.* 2nd ed. Englewood Cliffs, NJ: Prentice-Hall, 1985.

Knott, Jack H., and Gary J. Miller. *Reforming Bureaucracy: The Politics of Institutional Choice.* Englewood Cliffs, NJ: Prentice-Hall, 1986.

Kolko, Gabriel. "Railroads and Regulation, 1877–1916." In *State Politics and the New Federalism: Readings and Commentary,* edited by Marilyn Gittell. New York: Longman, 1986.

Kotler, Milton. *Neighborhood Government: The Local Foundations of Political Life.* Indianapolis, IN: Bobbs-Merrill, 1969.

Kraemer, Kenneth L., and John L. King. "Computers and the Constitution: A Helpful, Harmful, or Harmless Relationship." *Public Administration Review* 47, Special Edition (1987): 93–105.

Krislov, Samuel, and David H. Rosenbloom. *Representative Bureaucracy and the American Political System*. New York: Praeger, 1981.

Kurtz, Howard. "An FBI Probe Worthy of Hoover." *Washington Post National Weekly Edition* (8–14 February 1988): 32.

Kuttner, Robert. "The Fudge Factor: Too Many Cooks Spoil the Books." *New Republic* (19 June 1989): 22–24.

Langton, Stuart. "Public-Private Partnerships: Hope or Hoax." *American Civil Review,* May 1983.

Lawrence, Paul R., and Jay W. Lorsch. *Organization and Environment*. Cambridge, MA: Harvard University Press, 1967.

Le Grand, Julian, and Ray Robinson. *Privatisation and the Welfare State*. London: George Allen and Unwin, 1984.

Leonard, Herman B. *Checks Unbalanced: The Quiet Side of Public Spending*. New York: Basic Books, 1986.

Levin, Martin A. and Barbara Ferman. *The Political Hand: Policy Implementation and Youth Employment Programs*. New York: Pergamon Press, 1985.

Levine, Charles H. "Organizational Decline and Cutback Management." *Public Administration Review* 38 (1978): 316–324.

———. "The Federal Government in the Year 2000: Administrative Legacies of the Reagan Years." *Public Administration Review* 46, no. 3 (May/June 1986): 195–207.

Levine, James P., Michael Musheno, and Dennis Palumbo. *Criminal Justice in America: Law in Action*. New York: John Wiley and Sons, 1986.

Levitt, Barbara, and Clifford Nass. "The Lid on the Garbage Can: Institutional Constraints on Decision Making in the Technical Core of College-Text Publishers." *Administrative Science Quarterly* 34 (1989): 190–207.

Lewis, David, and Helen Wallace, eds. *Policies into Practice*. London: Heinemann, 1984.

Lewis, Eugene. *Public Entrepreneurship: Toward a Theory of Bureaucratic Political Power; the Organizational Lives of Hyman Rickover, J. Edgar Hoover, and Robert Moses*. Bloomington, IN: Indiana University Press, 1980.

Light, Paul C. "Social Security and the Politics of Assumptions." *Public Administration Review* 45, no. 3 (May/June 1985): 363–372.

Likert, Rensis. *New Patterns of Management*. New York: McGraw-Hill, 1961.

Lincoln, Yvonna, and Egon Guba. *Naturalistic Inquiry*. Beverly Hills: Sage Publications, 1985.

Lindblom, Charles E. "Still Muddling, Not Yet Through." *Public Administration Review* 39, no. 6 (Nov./Dec. 1979): 517–526.

Lindblom, Charles E., and David K. Cohen. *Usable Knowledge: Social Science and Social Problem Solving*. New Haven, CT: Yale University Press, 1979.

Linder, Stephen, and B. Guy Peters. "A Design Perspective on Policy Implementation: The Fallacies of Misplaced Prescription." *Policy Studies Review* 6 (February 1987): 459–476.

Lindsay, Alfred D. *The Modern Democratic State*. New York: Oxford University Press, 1962.

Lipsky, Michael. *Street-Level Bureaucracy: Dilemmas of the Individual in Public Services*. New York: Russell Sage Foundation, 1980.

Long, Norton. "The Local Community as an Ecology of Games." *American Journal of Sociology* 64 (1949): 251–261.

Love, Janice, and Peter Sederberg. "Euphony and Cacophony in Policy Implementation: SCF and the Somali Refugee Problems." *Policy Studies Review* 7 (1987): 155–174.

Lowi, Theodore. *The End of Liberalism: The Second Republic of the United States.* 2d ed. New York: Norton, 1979.

Lowi, Theodore, and Benjamin Ginsberg. *Poliscide.* New York: MacMillan, 1976.

Lowry, Ken. "Assessing the Implementation of Federal Coastal Policy." *Journal of the American Planning Association* 51 (Summer 1985): 288-298.

Lukes, Steven. *Power: A Radical View.* New York: Macmillan, 1974.

Lynn, Laurence E., Jr. *Designing Public Policy: A Casebook on the Role of Policy Analysis.* Santa Monica, CA: Goodyear, 1980.

———. *Managing the Public's Business: The Job of the Government Executive.* New York: Basic Books, 1981.

———. *Managing Public Policy.* Boston: Little, Brown, 1987.

Lynn, Naomi B., and Richard E. Vaden. "Bureaucratic Response to Civil Service Reform." *Public Administration Review* 39 (1979): 333-343.

Magaziner, Ira C., and Robert B. Reich. *Minding America's Business.* New York: Random House, 1982.

Majone, Giandomenico. *Evidence, Argument, and Persuasion in the Policy Process.* New Haven, CT: Yale University Press, 1989.

Majone, Giandomenico, and Aaron Wildavsky. "Implementation as Evolution." In *Implementation.* 2nd ed., edited by Jeffrey L. Pressman and Aaron Wildavsky. Berkeley, CA: University of California Press, 1984.

Malcolm, A. "Steps to Control Surrogate Births Stir Debate Anew." *New York Times,* 26 June 1988, 1, 11.

Manning, Peter K., and John Van Maanen, eds. *Policing: A View from the Street.* Santa Monica, CA: Goodyear Publishing Co., 1978.

March, James G. "Bounded Rationality, Ambiguity, and the Engineering of Choice." *Bell Journal of Economics* 9 (1978): 587-607.

———. "Footnotes to Organizational Change." *Administrative Science Quarterly* 26 (1981): 563-577.

———. "Theories of Choice and Making Decisions." *Society* 20 (November/December 1982): 32.

———. "How We Talk and How We Act: Administrative Theory and Administrative Life." In *Leadership and Organizational Culture: New Perspectives on Administrative Theory and Practice,* edited by Thomas J. Sergiovanni and John E. Corbally, 18-35. Chicago: University of Illinois Press, 1984.

March, James G., and Johan Olsen. "The New Institutionalism: Organizational Factors in Political Life." *American Political Science Review* 78 (1984): 734-749.

March, James G., and Herbert Simon. *Organizations.* New York: John Wiley and Sons, 1958.

March, Michael S. "Legislative Review at the Bureau of the Budget: The Shaping of Veterans Policies in the 1950s." In *Federal Public Policy: Personal Accounts of Ten Senior Civil Service Executives,* edited by Theodore W. Taylor. Mt. Airy, MD: Lamond Publications, 1984.

Marcus, Alfred. *Promise and Performance: Choosing and Implementing Environmental Policy.* Westport, CT: Greenwood Press, 1980.

Marmor, Theodore, and Phillip Fellman. "Policy Entrepreneurship in Government: An American Study." *Journal of Public Policy* 6, no. 3 (1986): 225-253.

Mashaw, Jerry L. *Bureaucratic Justice: Managing Social Security Disability Claims.* New Haven: Yale University Press, 1983.

Maslow, Abraham. *Motivation and Personality.* New York: Harper, 1954.

———. *The Farther Reaches of Human Nature.* New York: Viking, 1971.

Masuch, Michael, and Perry LaPotin. "Beyond Garbage Cans: An AI Model of Organizational Choice." *Administrative Science Quarterly* 34 (1989): 38–67.

Maynard-Moody, Steven. "Reconsidering Charity: Some Possible Negative Effects of Program Evaluation Research." *Administration and Society* 13 (February 1982): 379–403.

———. "The Fetal Research Dispute." In *Controversy: The Politics of Technical Decisions.* 2nd ed., edited by Dorothy Nelkin, 213–232. Beverly Hills, CA: Sage Publications, 1984.

———. "Beyond Implementation: Developing an Institutional Theory of Administrative Policy Making." *Public Administration Review* 49 (1989a): 137–144.

———. "Policy as Communication and the Naturalistic Study of the Use of Policy Research." *Knowledge: Creation, Diffusion, Utilization* 10 (1989b): 215–223.

Maynard-Moody, Steven, and Charles C. McClintock. "Square Pegs in Round Holes: Program Evaluation and Organizational Uncertainty." In *Evaluating and Optimizing Public Policy,* edited by Dennis Palumbo, Stephen Fawcett, and Paula Wright, 3–24. Lexington, MA: Lexington Books, 1981.

———. "Weeding an Old Garden: Toward a New Understanding of Organizational Goals." *Administration and Society* 19 (1987): 125–142.

Maynard-Moody, Steven, and John Nalbandian. "The Diversity of Kansas Local Government: Is It a Garden Choked by Weeds?" *Kansas Business Review* 11 (1988): 10–21.

Maynard-Moody, Steven, and Donald D. Stull. "The Symbolic Side of Policy Analysis: Interpreting Changes in a Health Department." In *Confronting Values in Policy Analysis: The Politics of Criteria,* edited by Frank Fischer and John Forester, 248–265. Newbury Park, CA: Sage Publications, 1987.

Maynard-Moody, Steven, Michael Musheno, and Dennnis Palumbo. "Street-Wise Social Policy: Resolving the Dilemma of Street-Level Influence and Successful Implementation." *Western Political Quarterly* 43 (forthcoming).

Maynard-Moody, Steven, Donald D. Stull, and Jerry Mitchell. "Reorganization as Status Drama: Building, Maintaining, and Displacing Dominant Subcultures." *Public Administration Review* 46 (1986): 301–310.

Mazmanian, Daniel, and Paul Sabatier. Implementation and Public Policy. Glenview, IL: Scott, Foresman, 1983.

McClelland, David C. *The Achieving Society.* Princeton, NJ: Van Nostrand, 1961.

McClintock, Charles C. "Administrators as Information Brokers: A Managerial Perspective on Naturalistic Evaluation." *Evaluation and Program Planning* 10 (1987): 315–323.

McGregor, Eugene B., Jr. "The Great Paradox of Democratic Citizenship and Public Personnel Administration." *Public Administration Review* 44, Special Issue (March 1984): 126–132.

———. "The Public Sector Human Resource Puzzle: Strategic Management of a Strategic Resource." *Public Administration Review* 48, no. 6 (1988): 941–950.

McKelvey, William. *Organizational Systematics: Taxonomy, Evolution, Classification.* Berkeley, CA: University of California Press, 1982.

McLaughlin, Milbry. *Evaluation and Reform: The Elementary and Secondary Education Act of 1965, Title I.* New York: Ballinger, 1975.

Meier, Kenneth J. *Politics and the Bureaucracy: Policymaking in the Fourth Branch of Government.* North Scituate, MA: Duxbury Press, 1979.

———. "Ode of Patronage: A Critical Analysis of Two Recent Supreme Court Decisions." *Public Administration Review* 41, no. 5 (1981): 558–563.

Meier, Kenneth J., and Lloyd Nigro. "Representative Bureaucracy and Political Preferences." *Public Administration Review* 36 (July/August 1976): 458–469.

Meindl, James R., Sanford B. Ehrlich, and Janel M. Dukerich. "The Romance of Leadership." *Administrative Science Quarterly* 30 (1985): 78–102.

Melman, Seymour. "The Peace Dividend: What to Do with the Cold War Money." *New York Times,* 17 December 1989, F3.

Meltsner, Arnold A., and Christopher Bellavita. *The Policy Organization.* Beverly Hills: Sage Publications, 1983.

Merton, Robert K. *Social Theory and Social Structure.* Rev. ed. New York: Free Press, 1957.

Meyer, Alan D. "Adapting to Environmental Jolts." *Administrative Science Quarterly* 27 (1982): 515–537.

Michels, Robert. *Political Parties: A Sociological Study of the Oligarchical Tendencies of Modern Democracy.* Glencoe, IL: Free Press, 1915.

Miles, Robert. *Coffin Nails and Corporate Strategies.* Englewood Cliffs, NJ: Prentice-Hall, 1982.

Miller, Arthur. *Death of a Salesman.* New York: Viking, 1949.

Milward, H. Brinton. "Policy Entrepreneurship and Bureaucratic Demand Creation." In *Why Policies Succeed or Fail,* edited by Helen Ingram and Dean Mann. Beverly Hills: Sage Publications, 1980.

Mintzberg, Henry. *The Nature of Managerial Work.* New York: Harper and Row, 1973.

———. *The Structuring of Organizations: A Synthesis of Research.* Englewood Cliffs, NJ: Prentice-Hall, 1979.

Mintzberg, Henry, and Alexandra McHugh. "Strategy Formation in an Adhocracy." *Administrative Science Quarterly* 30 (1985): 160–197.

Mitchell, Jerry. "Policy Community Politics: An Explanation for the Inconsistencies in Disability Policy." Ph.D. dissertation, University of Kansas, 1987.

Mohr, Lawrence B. *Explaining Organizational Behavior.* San Francisco: Jossey-Bass, 1982.

———. *Impact Analysis for Program Evaluation.* Chicago: Dorsey Press, 1988.

Moore, Charles H., and David U. Sink. "A Diminished Federal Role in Public Assisted Housing under Reagan." In *Administering the New Federalism,* edited by Lewis G. Bender and James A. Stener. Boulder, CO: Westview Press, 1986.

Moos, Rudolf H. *Evaluating Treatment Environments: A Social Ecology Approach.* New York: John Wiley and Sons, 1974.

Morgan, D. R., and R. E. England. "Evaluating Community Development Block Grant Program: Elite and Program Recipient Views." In *Policy Evaluation for Local Government,* edited by T. Busson and P. Coulter. New York: Greenwood Press, 1987.

Morgan, Gareth. *Images of Organization.* Beverly Hills, CA: Sage Publications, 1986.

Mosher, Frederick C. *Democracy and the Public Service.* 2nd ed. New York: Oxford University Press, 1982a.

———. "Public Administration." In *Current Issues in Public Administration.* 2nd ed., edited by Frederick S. Lane. New York: St. Martin's Press, 1982b.

Mullen, William F. *Presidential Power and Politics.* New York: St. Martin's Press, 1976.

Murphy, Jerome T. "Title I of ESEA: The Politics of Implementing Federal Education Reform." *Harvard Education Review* 41 (1977).

Musheno, Michael, James Levine, and Dennis Palumbo. "Television Surveillance and Crime Prevention: Evaluating an Attempt to Create Defensible Space in Public Housing." *Social Science Quarterly* 58 (1978): 647–656.

Musheno, Michael, Dennis Palumbo, Steven Maynard-Moody, and James P. Levine. "Community Corrections as an Orgaizational Innovation: What Works and Why." *Journal of Research in Crime and Delinquency* 26 (1989): 136–167.

Nachmias, David. "The Role of Evaluation in Public Policy." In *Evaluating and Optimizing Public Policy,* edited by Dennis Palumbo, Stephen Fawcett, and Paula Wright. Lexington, MA: Lexington Books, 1981.

Nachmias, David, and Claire Felbinger, "Utilization in the Policy Cycle: Directions for Research." *Policy Studies Review* 2 (1982): 300–308.

Nakamura, Robert T., and Frank Smallwood. *The Politics of Policy Implementation.* New York: St. Martin's Press, 1980.

Nalbandian, John. "The U.S. Supreme Court's 'Consensus' on Affirmative Action." *Public Administration Review* 49, no. 1 (Jan./Feb. 1989): 38–45.

Nalbandian, John, and Donald E. Klingner. "The Politics of Public Personnel Administration: Towards Theoretical Understanding." *Public Administration Review* 41 (1981): 541–549.

———. "Conflict and Values in Public Personnel Administration." *Public Administration Quarterly* 11, no. 1 (1987): 17–34.

Nalbandian, John, and Steven Maynard-Moody. "Risk Taking in Government: Taking Chances in the Public's Interest." In *Risk Taking by Public Managers,* edited by Roger L. Sperry, 13–30. Washington, DC: National Academy of Public Administration, September 1989.

Nathan, Richard P., Fred C. Doolittle, and associates. *The Consequences of Cuts: The Effects of the Reagan Domestic Program on State and Local Governments.* Lawrenceville, NJ: Princeton University Press, 1983.

National Commission on the Public Service. *Leadership for America: Rebuilding the Public Service.* Washington, DC: National Commission on the Public Service, 1989.

Neustadt, Richard E. "Foreword." In *Leadership and Innovation: A Biographical Perspective on Entrepreneurs in Government,* edited by Jameson Doig and Erwin Hargrove, i–ix. Baltimore: Johns Hopkins University Press, 1987.

Neustadt, Richard E., and Harvey Fineberg. *The Swine Flu Affair: Decision-Making on a Slippery Disease.* Washington, DC: U.S. Department of Health, Education, and Welfare, 1978.

Neustadt, Richard E., and Ernest R. May. *Thinking in Time: The Uses of History for Decision-Makers.* New York: Free Press, 1986.

Newman, Oscar. "The Repercussions of Dishonesty in Research Reporting." *Social Science Quarterly* 61 (1980).

Nice, David C. *Federalism: The Politics of Intergovernmental Relations.* New York: St. Martin's Press, 1987.

Nisbett, Richard E., and T. D. Wilson. "Telling More Than We Can Know: Verbal Reports on Mental Processes." *Psychological Review* 84 (1977): 231–259.

Nixon, Richard M. "Address to the Nation on Domestic Programs." In *Public Papers of the Presidents of the United States: Richard M. Nixon, 1969.* Washington, DC: U.S. Government Printing Office, 1969.

Office of Management and Budget. *Budget of the United States Government.* Washington, DC: U.S. Government Printing Office, 1988.

O'Toole, Laurence J. "The Public Administrator's Role in Setting the Policy Agenda." In *Handbook of Public Administration,* edited by James L. Perry, 225–236. San Francisco: Jossey-Bass, 1989.

O'Toole, Laurence J., and R. S. Montjoy. "Interorganizational Policy Implementation: A Theoretical Perspective." *Public Administration Review* 44 (1984): 491–504.

Ogul, M. *Congress Oversees the Bureaucracy: Studies in Legislative Supervision.* Pittsburgh: University of Pittsburgh Press, 1976.

Oleszek, Walter. *Congressional Procedures and the Policy Process.* 2nd ed. Washington, DC: Congressional Quarterly Press, 1984.

Orfield, Gary. "How to Make Desegregation Work: The Adaptation of Schools to Their Newly-Integrated Student Bodies." *Laws and Contemporary Problems* 39 (1975): 314–340.

Owen, v. City of Independence. *40CCH S. Ct. Bull.* 1980.

Palmer, Kenneth. "The Evolution of Grant Policies." In *The Changing Pattern of Fiscal Grants,* edited by Lawrence Brown, James Fossett, and Kenneth Palmer. Washington, DC: Brookings Institution, 1984.

Palumbo, Dennis, "The States and the Conduct of American Foreign Relations." In *Cooperation and Conflict.* Itasca, IL: F. E. Peacock, 1969.

———. "Politics and Evaluation." In *The Politics of Program Evaluation,* edited by Dennis Palumbo. Newbury Park, CA: Sage Publications, 1987.

———. *Public Policy in America: Government in Action.* San Diego, CA: Harcourt Brace Jovanovich, 1988.

Palumbo, Dennis, and Donald Calista, eds. "Implementation: What Have We Learned and Still Need to Know?" *Policy Studies Review* 7 (1987): 91–247.

Palumbo, Dennis, and Mike Harder, eds. *Implementing Public Policy.* Lexington, MA: D. C. Heath, 1981.

Palumbo, Dennis, and Kathy Hyer. "There Are as Many Ways to Implement Community Corrections as There Are Places in Which It Is Implemented." American Criminology Society, 1985.

Palumbo, Dennis, and James Maupin. "The Political Side of Privatization." *Journal of Management Science and Policy Analysis* 6 (Winter 1989): 24–41.

Palumbo, Dennis, and David Nachmias. "The Preconditions for Successful Evaluation: Is There an Ideal Paradigm?" In *Evaluation Studies Review Annual,* edited by Ross Coner, David Altman, and Christine Jackson, vol. 9. Beverly Hills, CA: Sage Publications, 1984.

Palumbo, Dennis, and Ann Marie Oliverio. "Implementing Theory and the Theory-Driven Approach to Validity." *Evaluation and Program Planning* 12 1989: 337–344.

Palumbo, Dennis, and Paula Wright. "Decision Making and Evaluation Research." In *Evaluating and Optimizing Public Policy,* edited by Dennis Palumbo, Fawcett Stephen, and Paula Wright, 25–34. Lexington, MA: Lexington Books, 1981.

Palumbo, Dennis, Steven Maynard-Moody, and Paula Wright. "Measuring Degrees of Successful Implementation: Achieving Policy versus Statutory Goals." *Evaluation Review* 8 (1984): 45–74.

Palumbo, Dennis, Michael Musheno, and Steven Maynard-Moody. "Public Sector Entrepreneurs: The Shakers and Doers of Program Innovation." In *Performance and Credibility: Developing Excellence in Public and Nonprofit Organizations,* edited by Joseph W. Wholey, Mark A. Abramson, and Christopher Bellavita, 69–82. Lexington, MA: Lexington Books, 1986.

Parmerlee, Marcia A., Janet P. Near, and Tamila C. Jessen. "Correlates of Whistle-Blowers' Perceptions of Organizational Retaliation." *Administrative Science Quarterly* 27 (1982): 17–34.

Parsons, Talcott, *Structure and Process in Modern Society.* New York: Free Press, 1960.

Patton, Michael Q. *Utilization-Focused Evaluation.* 2nd ed. Newbury Park, CA: Sage Publications, 1986.

———. "Evaluation's Political Inherency: Practical Implications for Design and Use." In *The Politics of Program Evaluation,* edited by Dennis Palumbo. Newbury Park, CA: Sage Publications, 1987.

Pearce, Jone L., and James L. Perry. "Federal Merit Pay: A Longitudinal Analysis." *Public Administration Review* 43 (1983): 315–325.

Perrow, Charles. "Demystifying Organizations." In *The Management of Human Services,* edited by R. Sari and Y. Hasenfeld. New York: Columbia University Press, 1978.

———. *Complex Organizations: A Critical Essay.* 2nd ed. Glenview, IL: Scott, Foresman, 1979.

Perry, James L., and Hal G. Rainey. "The Public-Private Distinction in Organization Theory: A Critique and Research Strategy." *Academy of Management Review* 13 (1988): 182–201.

Perry, James L., Beth Ann Petrakis, and Theodore K. Miller. "Federal Merit Pay, Round II; An Analysis of Performance Management and Recognition System." *Public Administration Review* 49, no. 1 (January/February 1989): 29–37.

Peters, B. Guy. *The Politics of Bureaucracy.* 3rd ed. New York: Longman, 1989.

Peters, Thomas, and Robert Waterman. *In Search of Excellence: Lessons from America's Best-Run Companies.* New York: Harper and Row, 1982.

Peterson, Paul, Barry Rabe, and Kenneth Wong. *When Federalism Works.* Washington, DC: Brookings Institution, 1986.

Pettigrew, Andrew. "On Studying Organizational Cultures." *Administrative Science Quarterly* 24 (1979): 570–581.

Pfeffer, Jeffrey, and Gerald R. Salancik. *The External Control of Organizations: A Resource Dependency Perspective.* New York: Harper and Row, 1978.

Pinkele, C. "Discretion Fits Democracy: An Advocate's Argument." In *Discretion, Justice, and Democracy: A Public Policy Perspective,* edited by C. Pinkele and W. Louthan. Ames: The Iowa State University Press, 1985.

Pitsvada, Bernard T., and Frank D. Draper. "Making Sense of the Federal Budget the Old Fashioned Way—Incrementally." *Public Administration Review* 44, no. 5 (September/October 1984): 401–407.

Piven, Frances F. "Militant Civil Servants in New York City." In *Politics/America,* edited by W. Burnham. New York: Van Nostrand Reinhold, 1973.

Piven, Frances F., and Richard A. Cloward. *Regulating the Poor.* New York: Vintage, 1971.

Plessey v. Ferguson. *163 US 537.* 1896.

Porter, Lyman W., Richard M. Steers, Richard T. Mowday, and Paul V. Boulian. "Organizational Commitment, Job Satisfaction and Turnover Among Psychiatric Technicians." *Journal of Applied Psychology* 59 (1974): 603–690.

Presidential Commission on the Space Shuttle *Challenger* Accident. *Report to the President.* Washington, DC, 6 June 1986.

Pressman, Jeffrey, and Aaron Wildavsky. *Implementation.* 3rd ed. Berkeley, CA: University of California Press, 1984.

Prottas, Jeffrey M. *People-Processing: The Street-Level Bureaucrat in Public Service Bureaucracies.* Lexington, MA: Lexington Press, 1979.

Quaintance, Marilyn K. "Moving toward Unbiased Selection." In *Public Personnel Update,* edited by Michael Cohen, and Robert T. Golembiewski, 73–112. New York: Marcel Dekker, 1984.

Quinn, Robert. *Beyond Rational Management: Mastering the Paradoxes and Competing Demands of High Performance.* San Francisco: Jossey-Bass, 1988.

Quinn, Robert, and John Rohrbaugh. "A Spatial Model of Effectiveness Criteria: Towards a Competing Values Approach to Organizational Analysis." *Management Science* 29 (1983): 363–377.

Rainey, Hal G. "Public Management: Recent Research on the Political Context and Managerial Roles, Structures, and Behaviors." *Journal of Management* 15 (1989): 229–250.

Rainey, Hal G., R. Backoff, and Charles Levine. "Comparing Public and Private Organizations." *Public Administration Review* 36 (1976): 233–246.

Randall, Donna M. "Commitment and the Organization: The Organization Man Revisited." *Academy of Management Review* 12 (1987): 460–471.

Rankin v. McPherson. *97 L Ed 2nd.,* 315–335. 1987.

Redford, Emmette S. *Democracy in the Administrative State.* New York: Oxford University Press, 1969.

Riley, Dennis D. *Controlling the Federal Bureaucracy.* Philadelphia: Temple University Press, 1987.

Ripley, Randall, and Grace A. Franklin. *Congress, the Bureaucracy, and Public Policy.* 3rd ed. Homewood, IL: Dorsey Press, 1984.

Robertson, David B. "Program Implementation versus Program Design: Which Accounts for Policy 'Failure?' " *Policy Studies Review* 3 (1984): 391–406.

———. "Planned Incapacity to Succeed: Policymaking Structure and Policy Failure." *Policy Studies Review* 8 (1989).

Roethlisberger, F. J., and William J. Dickson. *Management and the Worker.* Cambridge, MA: Harvard University Press, 1939.

Rogers, James M. *The Impact of Policy Analysis.* Pittsburgh: University of Pittsburgh Press, 1988.

Rohatyn, Felix G. "To Repair Our Nation." *New York Times,* 17 December 1989, E21.

Rohr, John, "Bureaucratic Morality in the United States." *International Political Science Review* 9 (1988): 167–179.

Romzek, Barbara S. "Personal Consequences of Employee Commitment." *Academy of Management Journal* 32 (1989): 649–661.

Roos, Leslie L., and Roger T. Hall. "Influence Diagrams and Organizational Power." *Administrative Science Quarterly* 25 (1980): 57–71.

Rosenbaum, David E. "From Guns to Butter: With Cutbacks Likely in Military Spending, Debate Will Center on Where Cash Will Go." *New York Times,* 14 December 1989, 1, 18.

Rosenbloom, David H. *Public Administration and Law.* New York: Marcel Dekker, 1983.

———. "Equal Employment Opportunity, Affirmative Action, and Public Personnel Management: Past Developments and Future Prospects." In *Public Personnel Update,* edited by Michael Cohen and Robert Golembiewski, 29–58. New York: Dekker, 1984.

———. *Public Administration: Understanding Management, Politics and Law in the Public Sector.* 2nd ed. New York: Random House, 1989.

Rosenbloom, David H., and Jay M. Shafritz. "Future Concerns of Public Sector Labor-Management Relations." In *Public Personnel Update,* edited by Michael Cohen and Robert Golembiewski, 215–232. New York: Dekker, 1984.

Rosenthal, Alan. *Legislative Performance in the States, Explorations of Committee Behavior.* New York: Free Press, 1974.

———. *Legislative Life: People, Process, and Performance in the States.* New York: Harper and Row, 1981.

Rosenthal, Alan, and Carl Van Horn. "The Impact of State Legislative Oversight: A Framework for Analysis." American Political Science Association Annual Meeting, 1982.

Rossi, Peter, and James Wright. "Social Science Research and the Politics of Gun Control." In *Social Science and Social Policy,* edited by R. Lance Shotland and Melvin M. Mark, 311–334. Beverly Hills: Sage Publications, 1985.

Rothschild-Whitt, Joyce. "The Collectivist Organization: An Alternative to Rational-Bureaucratic Models." *American Sociological Review* 44 (1979): 509–527.

Rourke, Francis. *Bureaucracy, Politics, and Public Policy.* 3rd ed. Boston: Little, Brown, 1984.

Rowland, C. K., and Roger Marz. "Gresham's Law: The Regulatory Analogy." *Policy Studies Review* 1 (February 1982): 572–580.

Roy, Donald F. " 'Banana Time': Job Satisfaction and Informal Interaction." In *Life in Organizations: Workplaces as People Experience Them,* edited by Rosabeth Kanter and Barry A. Stein, 192–205. New York: Basic Books, 1979.

Rubin, Irene S. *The Politics of Public Budgeting: Getting and Spending, Borrowing and Balancing.* Chatham, NJ: Chatham House Publishers, 1989.

Russakoff, D. "Protecting America and Itself: Battered and Wounded the CPSC Stills Tries to Do Its Job." *Washington Post National Weekly Edition,* 13–19 February 1989, 32.

Sabatier, Paul, and Daniel Mazmanian. "The Conditions of Effective Implementation: A Guide to Accomplishing Policy Objectives." *Policy Analysis,* Fall 1979, 481–504.

Salamon, Lester. "Rethinking Public Management: Third-Party Government and the Changing Forms of Government." *Public Policy* 29 (1981): 255–275.

———. *Beyond Privatization: The Tools of Government Action.* Lanhan, MD: Urban Institute Press, 1989.

Salancik, Gerald R. "Commitment and the Control of Organizational Behavior and Belief," In *New Directions in Organizational Behavior,* edited by Barry Staw and Gerald Salancik, 1–54. Chicago: St. Clair, 1977.

Savas, E. S. *Privatizing the Public Sector.* New York: Chatham House, 1982.

Savas, E. S., and Sigmund G. Ginsburg. "The Civil Service: A Meritless System?" *The Public Interest,* Summer 1973, 70–85.

Scalia, Antonin. "National Treasury Employees Union, et al., Petitioners v. William Von Raab, Commissioner, United States Customs Service." *Law Week* 57 (1989): 4344–4347.

Schattschneider, Elmer E. *The Semi-Sovereign People: A Realist's View of Democracy in America.* New York: Holt, Rinehart, and Winston, 1960.

Schein, Edgar H. *Organizational Psychology.* 3rd ed. Englewood Cliffs, NJ: Prentice-Hall, 1980.

———. *Organizational Culture and Leadership: A Dynamic View.* San Francisco: Jossey-Bass, 1985.

Scheirer, Mary Ann. "Program Theory and Implementation Theory: Implementation for Evaluators." In *In Using Program Theory in Evaluation,* edited by L. Bickman. San Francisco: Jossey-Bass, 1987.

Scheirer, Mary Ann, and J. Griffith. "Studying Implementation Empirically: Lessons and Dilemmas." In *Implementation and the Policymaking Process,* edited by Dennis Palumbo and Donald Calista. Westport, CT: Greenwood Press, 1989.

Schick, Allen. "Macro-Budgetary Adaptations to Fiscal Stress in Industrialized Democracies." *Public Administration Review* 46, no. 2 (March/April 1986): 124–235.

———. "Micro-Budgetary Adaptations to Fiscal Stress in Industrialized Democracies." *Public Administration Review* 48, no. 1 (January/February 1988): 523–533.

Schilit, Warren K., and Edwin A. Locke. "The Study of Upward Influence in Organizations." *Administrative Science Quarterly* 27 (1982): 304–316.

Schön, Donald A. *The Reflective Practitioner: How Professionals Think in Action.* New York: Basic Books, 1983.

Schultz, George. "The Abrasive Interface." *Harvard Business Review.* November–December 1979.

Schultze, Charles L. "Industrial Policy: A Dissent." *The Brookings Review* 2 (1983): 3–12.

Schumpeter, Joseph A. *Capitalism, Socialism and Democracy.* New York: Harper and Row, 1962.

Schwartz, Felice N. "Management Women and the New Facts of Life." *Harvard Business Review* 67 (January–February 1989): 65–76.

Schwartz, J. *America's Hidden Success: A Reassessment of Twenty Years of Public Policy.* New York: W. W. Norton, 1983.

Scott, Robert A. "The Factory as a Social Service Organization." *Social Problems* 15 (1967): 160–175.

Scott, W. Richard. "Effectiveness of Organizational Effectiveness Studies." In *New Perspectives on Organizational Effectiveness,* edited by Paul Goodman and Johannes Pennings, 63–95. San Francisco: Jossey-Bass, 1977.

————. *Organizations: Rational, Natural, and Open Systems.* Englewood Cliffs, NJ: Prentice-Hall, 1981.

Scott, William G., and David K. Hart. *Organizational America.* Boston: Houghton Mifflin, 1979.

Scriven, Michael. "Pros and Cons About Goal-Free Evaluation." *Evaluation Comment* 3 (1972): 1-4.

Seidman, Harold. *Politics, Position, and Power: The Dynamics of Federal Organization.* 2nd ed. New York: Oxford University Press, 1979.

Sharp, Elaine B., and David Elkins. "The Impact of Fiscal Limitation: A Tale of Seven Cities." *Public Administration Review* 47, no. 5 (September/October 1987): 385-393.

Sidlow, Edward I., and Beth M. Henschen. "Congressional Activity and Discretion in the Criminal Justice System." In *Discretion, Justice, and Democracy: A Public Policy Perspective,* edited by C. F. Pinkele and W. Louthan. Ames: Iowa State University Press, 1985.

Silver, Hilary, and Dudley Burton. "The Politics of State-Level Industrial Policy: Lessons from Rhode Island's Greenhouse Compact." *Journal of the American Institute of Planners* 52 (1986): 277-290.

Simon, Herbert. *Administrative Behavior.* New York: McMillan, 1946.

————. *Models of Man.* New York: John Wiley and Sons, 1957.

————. *The Sciences of the Artificial.* 2nd ed. Cambridge, MA: MIT Press, 1981.

Siu, Richard. "Chinese Baseball and Public Administration." In *Program Evaluation: Patterns and Directions,* edited by Eleanor Chelimsky. Washington, DC: American Society for Public Administration, 1985.

"Slothful Agency Told to Require Pension Contributions to Age 70." *Arizona Republic,* 27 February 1987, A16.

Sokolow, Alvin D., and Beth Walter Honadle. "How Rural Local Governments Budget: The Alternatives to Executive Preparation." *Public Administration Review* 44, no. 5 (September/October 1984): 373-384.

Stake, Robert. *Evaluating the Arts in Education: A Responsive Approach.* Columbus, OH: Merrill, 1975.

Staw, Barry M. "Leadership and Persistence." In *Leadership and Organizational Culture: New Perspective on Administrative Theory and Practice,* edited by Thomas J. Sergiovanni and John E. Corbally, 72-84. Chicago: University of Illinois Press, 1984.

Steelworkers v. Weber. *443 U.S. 193.* 1979.

Stein, Herbert. "Advice for a President: Tax the Rich, They Consume Too Much." *New York Times,* 23 October 1988, F2.

Stephens, G. Ross. *Statutory History of the U.S.: Income Security.* New York: McGraw-Hill, 1970.

Stevenson, William, Jone Pearce, and Lyman Porter. "The Concept of 'Coalition' in Organization Theory and Research." *Academy of Management Review* 10 (1985): 256-268.

Stillman, Richard J., II. *The American Bureaucracy.* Chicago: Nelson Hall, 1987.

Stinchcombe, Arthur L. "Organizations and Social Structure." In *Handbook of Organizations,* edited by James G. March, 153-193. Chicago: McGraw-Hill, 1965.

Stone, Charles. "The Implementation of Social Programs: Two Perspectives." *Journal of Social Issues* 36 (1980): 13-34.

Stouffer, Samuel A. *Studies in Social Psychology during World War II.* Princeton, NJ: Princeton University Press, 1949.

Stout, Russell. *Management or Control?: The Organizational Challenge.* Bloomington: Indiana University Press, 1980.

Straussman, Jeffrey D. "Courts and Public Purse Strings: Have Portraits of Budgeting Missed Something?" *Public Administration Review* 46, no. 4 (July/August 1986): 345-351.

Stull, Donald D., Steven Maynard-Moody, and Jerry Mitchell. "The Ritual of Reorganization in a Public Bureaucracy." *Qualitative Sociology* 11 (1988): 215–233.

Sundquist, James L. *The Decline and Resurgence of Congress.* Washington, DC: Brookings Institution, 1981.

"Superfund Fact Sheet." *EPA Journal,* 7 (1981).

Sylvia, Ronald D. *Critical Issues in Personnel Policy.* Pacific Grove, CA: Brooks/Cole, 1989.

Taylor, Theodore W. *Federal Public Policy: Personal Accounts of Ten Senior Civil Service Executives.* Mt. Airy, MD: Lomond Publications, 1984.

Thomas, Alan B. "Does Leadership Make a Difference to Organizational Performance." *Administrative Science Quarterly* 33 (1988): 388–400.

Thompson, Frank J. *Personnel Policy in the City.* Berkeley, CA: University of California Press, 1975.

———. *Health Care and the Bureaucracy: Politics and Implementation.* Cambridge, MA: MIT Press, 1981.

Thompson, Fred. "Why America's Military Base Structure Cannot Be Reduced." *Public Administration Review* 48 (1988): 557–564.

Thompson, James D. *Organizations in Action.* New York: McGraw-Hill, 1967.

Thurow, Lester C. *The Zero-Sum Society: Distribution and the Possibilities for Economic Change.* New York: Penguin, 1980.

Tobin, James. "The Future of Social Security: One Economist's Assessment." In *Project on the Federal Social Role.* Working paper #4. Washington, DC: National Conference on Social Welfare, 1985.

Toffler, Alvin. *Future Shock.* New York: Random House, 1970.

Tolbert, Pamela S., and Lynne G. Zucker. "Institutional Sources of Change in the Formal Structure of Organizations: The Diffusion of Civil Service Reform, 1880–1935." *Administrative Science Quarterly* 28 (1983): 22–39.

Tolchin, Martin, "U.S. Halts Loan Penalty for Welfare Recipients." *New York Times,* 11 December 1988, 37.

Tolchin, Susan. "The Political Uses of Evaluation Research: Cost-Benefit Analysis and the Cotton Dust Standard." In *The Politics of Program Evaluation,* edited by Dennis Palumbo. Newbury Park, CA: Sage Publications, 1987.

Tower, John, Edmund Muskie, and Brent Scowcroft. *The Tower Commission Report.* New York: Times Books, 1987.

Trice, Harrison, and Janice Beyer. "Studying Organizational Cultures Through Rites and Ceremonials." *Academy of Management Review* 9 (1984): 653–669.

Tullock, Gordon. *The Politics of Bureaucracy.* Washington, DC: Public Affairs Press, 1964.

United States v. Butler, *297 US 1.* 1936.

U.S. Congress. *The Iran-Contra Affair: With Supplemental, Minority, and Additional Views.* 100th Cong., 1st sess., Nov. 1987. H.R. 100–433. S. Rept. 100–126.

U.S. Department of Commerce, and Bureau of the Census. *Historical Statistics: Colonial Times to 1970.* Washington, DC: U.S. Government Printing Office, 1975.

U.S. House of Representatives, and Subcommittee on Manpower and Housing of the House Committee on Government Operations. *Hearings on CETA's Vulnerability to Fraud and Abuse.* Washington, DC: U.S. Government Printing Office, 1980.

University of California Regents v. Bakke. *438 U.S. 265.* 1978.

Valenti, Carl F., and Lydia D. Manchester. *Rethinking Local Services: Examining Alternative Delivery Approaches.* Washington, DC: International City Management Association, 1984.

Van de Ven, Andrew H. "The Three Rs of Administrative Behavior: Rational, Random, and Reasonable (And the Greatest of These is Reason)." In *Organization Theory and Public*

Policy, edited by Richard H. Hall and Robert E. Quinn, 37–54. Beverly Hills: Sage Publications, 1983.

Van Maanen, John. "Observations on the Making of Policemen." In *Policing: A View from the Street,* edited by Peter K. Manning, and John Van Maanen, 292–308. Santa Monica, CA: Goodyear Publishing Company, Inc., 1978.

Van Maanen, John, and Steven Barley. "Cultural Organization: Fragments of a Theory." MIT working paper #221–12H, Cambridge, MA, 1983.

Van Maanen, John, and Gideon Kunda. "'Real Feelings': Emotional Expression and Organizational Culture." *Research in Organizational Behavior* 11 (1989): 43–103.

Van Maanen, John, and Edgar H. Schein. "Toward a Theory of Organizational Socialization." In *Research in Organizational Behavior,* Vol. 1, edited by Barry Staw, 209–264. Greenwich, CT: JAI, 1979.

Van Meter, Donald S., and Carl Van Horn. "The Policy Implementation Process: A Conceptual Framework." *Administration and Society* 6 (February 1975): 445–488.

Van Riper, Paul P. *History of the United States Civil Service.* Evanston, IL: Row, Peterson, and Co., 1958.

Wallace, H. "Implementation Across National Boundaries." In *Politics into Practice,* edited by D. Lewis and H. Wallace. London: Heinemann, 1984.

Wamsley, Gary, and Meyer Zald. *The Political Economy of Public Organizations.* Bloomington, IN: Indiana University Press, 1973.

Warwick, Donald P. *A Theory of Public Bureaucracy: Politics, Personality, and Organization in the State Department.* Cambridge, MA: Harvard University Press, 1975.

Wassenberg, P. S. "State Responses to Reductions in Federal Funds: Section 106 of the Federal Water Pollution Control Acts Amendments of 1972." In *Administering the New Federalism,* edited by Lewis G. Bender, and James A. Stener. Boulder, CO: Westview Press, 1986.

Weatherley, Richard A. *Reforming Special Education: Policy Implementation from State Level to Street Level.* Cambridge, MA: MIT Press, 1979.

Weber, Max. "Bureaucracy." In *Max Weber: Essays in Sociology,* translated and edited by H. H. Gerth and C. W. Mills. New York: Oxford University Press, 1946.

Weick, Karl E. "Educational Organizations as Loosely Coupled Systems." *Administrative Science Quarterly* 21 (1976): 1–19.

———. "Re-Punctuating the Problem." In *New Perspectives on Organizational Effectiveness,* edited by Paul S. Goodman and Johannes M. Pennings, 193–225. San Francisco: Jossey-Bass, 1977.

———. *The Social Psychology of Organizing.* 2nd ed. Reading, MA: Addison-Wesley, 1979.

Weick, Karl E., and Larry D. Browning. "Argument and Narration in Organizational Communication." *Journal of Management* 12 (1986): 243–259.

Weimer, David L., and Aidan R. Vining. *Policy Analysis: Concepts and Practice.* Englewood Cliffs, NJ: Prentice-Hall, 1989.

Weiss, Carol H., ed. *Evaluating Action Programs: Readings in Social Action and Education.* Boston: Allyn and Bacon, 1972a.

———. *Evaluation Research.* Englewood Cliffs, NJ: Prentice-Hall, 1972b.

———. "Knowledge Creep and Decision Accretion." *Knowledge: Creation, Diffusion, Utilization* 1 (1980): 381–404.

———. "Measuring the Use of Evaluation." In *Utilizing Evaluation: Concepts and Measurement Technologies,* edited by Carol H. Weiss. Beverly Hills, CA: Sage Publications, 1981.

———. "Where Politics and Evaluation Research Meet." In *The Politics of Program Evaluation,* edited by Dennis Palumbo. Newbury Park, CA: Sage Publications, 1987.

Weiss, Carol H., and Michael J. Bucuvalas. *Social Science Research and Decision-Making.* New York: Columbia University Press, 1980.

Weiss, Janet A. "The Powers of Problem Definition: The Case of Government Paper Work." *Policy Sciences* 22 (1989): 97–121.

Weisskopf, M. "Superfund Abdication." *Washington Post National Weekly Edition,* 6–12 February 1989, 32.

Weissmann, Gerald. *The Woods Hole Cantata: Essays on Science and Society.* New York: Dodd, Mead, 1985.

Weizenbaum, Joseph. *Computer Power and Human Reason: From Judgment to Calculation.* San Francisco: W. H. Freeman, 1976.

Weschler, Barton, and Robert W. Backoff. "Policy Making and Administration in State Agencies: Strategic Management Approaches." *Public Administration Review* 46 (1986): 321–327.

White, Leonard. *Introduction to Public Administration.* New York: Macmillan, 1926.

Wholey, Joseph S. *Evaluation: Promise and Performance.* Washington, DC: Urban Institute, 1979.

Whyte, Glen. "Groupthink Reconsidered." *Academy of Management Review* 14 (1989): 40–56.

Whyte, William Foote. *The Organization Man.* Garden City, NY: Doubleday, 1956.

Wicklund, R. A., and J. W. Brehm. *Perspectives on Cognitive Dissonance.* Hillsdale, NJ: Erlbaum, 1976.

Wildavsky, Aaron. "The Self-Evaluating Organization." *Public Administration Review* 5 (September/October 1972): 509–520.

———. *Speaking Truth to Power.* Boston: Little, Brown, 1979.

———. "E Pluribus Unum: Plurity, Diversity, Variety, and Modesty." In *The Costs of Federalism: In Honor of James W. Fesler,* edited by Robert T. Golembiewsky and Aaron Wildavsky, 3–17. New Brunswick, NJ: Transaction Books, 1984.

———. *The New Politics of the Budgetary Process.* Glenview, IL: Scott, Foresman, 1988.

Wilkerson, Isabel. "Discordant Notes in Detroit: Music and Affirmative Action." *New York Times,* 5 March 1989, 1, 18.

Williams, H. "Foreword." In *Educating Policymakers for Evaluation,* edited by Franklin M. Zweig and Keith E. Martin. Beverly Hills, CA: Sage Publications, 1981.

Williams, Walter. *The Implementation Perspective: A Guide for Managing Social Service Delivery Systems.* Berkeley: University of California Press, 1980.

Williamson, Richard S. "The Self-Government Balancing Act: A View from the White House." *National Civic Review* 71 (1982).

———. "The 1982 New Federalism Negotiations." *Publius* 13 (1983).

Willner, Ann Ruth. *The Spellbinders: Charismatic Political Leadership.* New Haven, CT: Yale University Press, 1984.

Wilson, James Q. "The Bureaucracy Problem." *Public Interest 6 (1967): 3–9.*

———. "The Rise of the Bureaucratic State." In *Current Issues in Public Administration,* edited by F. S. Lane. 2nd ed. New York: St. Martin's Press, 1982.

Wilson, William J. *The Truly Disadvantaged: The Inner City, the Underclass and Public Policy.* Chicago: University of Chicago Press, 1987.

Wilson, Woodrow. "The Study of Administration." *Political Science Quarterly* 2 (June 1887): 197–222.

Winter, Soren. *Studying Implementation of Top-Down Policy from the Bottom-Up: Implementation of Danish Youth Employment Policy.* Denmark: Institute of Political Science, 1983.

Wood v. Strickland. *420 US 308.* 1975.

Worthen, Blaine R., and James R. Sanders. *Educational Evaluation: Alternative Approaches and Practical Guidelines.* New York: Longman, 1987.

Wright, Deil. *Understanding Intergovernmental Relations.* 2nd ed. Monterey, CA: Brooks/Cole, 1982.

Yanow, Dvora. "Toward a Policy Culture Approach to Implementation." *Policy Studies Review* 7 (1987): 103–115.

Yates, Douglas. *Bureaucratic Democracy: The Search for Democracy and Efficiency in American Government.* Cambridge, MA: Harvard University Press, 1982.

———. *The Politics of Management.* San Francisco: Jossey-Bass, 1985.

Yin, Robert K. *Changing Urban Bureaucracies: How New Practices Become Routinized.* Santa Monica, CA: Rand Corp., 1979.

Yuchtman, Ephraim, and Stanley Seashore, "A System Resource Approach to Organizational Effectiveness." *American Sociological Review* 32 (1967): 891–903.

Zelizer, Vivian A. "The Social Meaning of Money: 'Special Money' " *American Journal of Sociology* 95 (September 1989): 342–477.

Zimbardo, Philip. *The Cognitive Control of Motivation.* Glenview, IL: Scott, Foresman, 1969.

Zucker, Lynne G. "The Role of Institutionalization in Cultural Persistence." *Administrative Science Quarterly* 42 (1977): 726–743.

Index